THE LEVELLER MOVEMENT

To this Essay was awarded the
HERBERT BAXTER ADAMS PRIZE
IN EUROPEAN HISTORY
for 1915

The Leveller Movement

A STUDY IN THE HISTORY AND POLITICAL THEORY OF THE ENGLISH GREAT CIVIL WAR

BY

THEODORE CALVIN PEASE, Ph.D.
ASSOCIATE IN HISTORY, UNIVERSITY
OF ILLINOIS

GLOUCESTER, MASS.

PETER SMITH

1965

To

MY MOTHER

PREFACE

THE following essay was begun seven years ago as a study in Professor A. C. McLaughlin's history seminar at Chicago; the greater part of the material on which it is based was collected in the British Museum in 1911; and the completed essay was accepted as a doctoral dissertation at the University of Chicago in 1914.

Many persons and institutions have helped at one stage or another of the essay's progress. Professor McLaughlin suggested the subject and at every point in its development has been ready with needed advice or criticism. Professor Conyers Read of the University of Chicago has shown great interest in the study and has afforded me much help and encouragement. I have to thank the University of Chicago for permitting a resident fellowship to be partly used in foreign study; and the British Museum, the Bodleian, and the Newberry Library of Chicago for the privileges of their reading rooms. The Library of Congress and Harvard College Library have assisted me with the loan of certain rare pamphlets. Miss Addie F. Rowe has verified certain statements based on pamphlets in the Harvard College Library which the librarian did not feel free to lend. Messrs. B. F. Stevens and Brown of London have carefully rechecked very many statements, references, and quotations from pamphlets in the

Thomason Collection in the British Museum. Professor C. W. Alvord of the University of Illinois has read the essay in manuscript with a view to its literary form, and has offered valuable criticisms and suggestions. My brother has aided me greatly in improving the style and manner of presentation. Dr. H. Barrett Learned, chairman of the Publication Committee of the American Historical Association, has made himself responsible for the reading of the proof with copy and for the consistency of the printer's style in the volume; I have further to thank him for assistance in seeing the volume through the press. Miss Lucille M. Allen has assisted in the preparation of the index.

THEODORE C. PEASE.

Urbana, Illinois,
October 4, 1916.

CONTENTS

CHAPTER   PAGE

Introduction 1

I. The Doctrine of Parliamentary Sovereignty,
1640–1645 7

II. The Ecclesiastical Supremacy of Parliament
versus the Law of God, 1642–1646 50

III. The First Radical Criticism of Parliament..... 86

IV. 1646. The Radical Attack on Arbitrary Power.. 120

V. 1647. The Birth of the Leveller Party 156

VI. The First Agreement of the People 193

VII. The Organization of the Leveller Party: the
Appeal to Reason 229

VIII. November-March, 1648/49 258

IX. The Triumph of the Commonwealth 278

X. The Levellers' Case against the Commonwealth. 301

XI. The Climax of the Leveller Constitutional
Theories 326

XII. Conclusion 348

Bibliography 365

The Law is that which puts a difference betwixt Good and Evil, betwixt Just and Unjust; if you take away the Law, all things will fall into Confusion, every Man will become a Law to himself, which in the depraved condition of Human Nature, must needs produce many great Enormities; Lust will become a Law, and Envy will become a Law, Covetousness and Ambition will become Laws. JOHN PYM.

INTRODUCTION

THE establishment in England of a democratic government limited and bounded by law—that in a word was the vision pursued in the midst of the political strife and confusion of the Great Civil War by the men ordinarily called Levellers. To trace the evolution of this idea and of the corollaries to it that completed the Leveller platform, to show the political machinery devised by the Levellers to promote it, and in short to sketch the history of the Leveller movement as a whole is the purpose of this essay.

The political ideas of the Levellers at the outset were perceptibly molded by two different intellectual forces. The first of these originated in the series of controversies in the years 1640–43 through which the Long Parliament advanced from the doctrine of the supremacy of the law to the doctrine of parliamentary sovereignty. The second force came from the ecclesiastical dispute centering around the Westminster Assembly that gave form and spirit to the Independent idea of church government, originating in compact and limited by the supreme law of Christ. In the course of translating this idea into politics the Levellers in successive drafts of Agreements of the People developed the concept of a written constitution originating in a compact of the sovereign people and, therefore, superior to govern-

1

ment. Such ideas led them further still—almost
to the conclusion that the interpretation of their
constitution was of necessity a judicial function
belonging to the courts.

So defined, the Leveller movement has more than
antiquarian interest. The fact that such a thing
as the Leveller party existed, and professed constitutional ideas and methods similar to those
developed in American constitutional history is
more than an interesting coincidence. In truth
it reveals at a critical point in the development of
English political institutions a trend toward the
supremacy, not of government, nor of a branch
of government, but of law.

Historians, it is true, have assigned the idea
of the supremacy of law an important position
in the earlier stages of the Puritan Revolution.
They have quoted Coke's saying of 1628, "Sovereign Power is no Parliamentary word; . . . .
Magna Charta is such a Fellow that he will have
no Sovereign,"[1] and they have assigned due significance to the fact that in the Petition of Right
Parliament defined the ancient statutes of the
realm as a law paramount to the prerogative.
On the other hand they have recognized the fact
that the indirect consequence of 1640, 1660, and
1688 has been to make Parliament sovereign over
the law. "We have," wrote Professor Maitland,
"no irrepealable laws; all laws may be repealed
by the ordinary legislature, even the conditions
upon which the English and Scottish parliaments

[1] Quotation adapted.   John Rushworth, *Historical Collections*, I, 562.

agreed to merge themselves in the parliament of Great Britain."[2] In general, the meeting of the Long Parliament in 1640 is the point at which commentators center attention on the waxing idea of parliamentary supremacy, and ignore the waning idea of supremacy of law.

But while the dilemma of sovereign Parliament or absolute king is a statement of the constitutional issues of the Great Civil War sufficiently exact to put the war in its right historical perspective, the idea of supreme law did not disappear on November 3, 1640, as one might infer. The Long Parliament itself for a year maintained in its utterances that the law was sovereign; it was only as the interpreter of the law that it claimed sovereignty for itself in 1642. Moreover, from 1645 to 1653 Levellers preached to the nation the need for a sovereign law to bind the Parliament. The Levellers, therefore, as champions of supreme law, assume importance as exponents of the idea that was the necessary counterpart and opposite to the idea of absolute government.

This fact, the author thinks, has importance for both English and American constitutional history. We may not trace adequately the development of any political idea, if we ignore the opposition the idea encounters. As students of the English constitution, we can scarce hope to understand fully how a sovereign parliament came into being, until we understand also why men opposed it. Furthermore, we must remember that very

[2] Frederick W. Maitland, *Constitutional History of England*, p. 332.

much of the political theory of the American revolutionary and constitutional periods had its background in English thought. And while this last idea is by no means new, the fact that a subordinate party in the Great Rebellion assumed the doctrinal position of the American Whigs in the Revolution of 1775 has hardly been emphasized. The fact that in the seventeenth-century revolution men urged the establishment of a paramount law should certainly afford us a clearer perception of the eighteenth-century revolution that finally accomplished that same end.

Furthermore, the American Revolution left embedded in American constitutional theory the principles of John Locke. The idea that God created man free of subjection to government, the idea that the laws of nature protected the safety and happiness of individuals before government began, and continued after the formation of human society to protect the individual against the tyranny of his ruler; the idea that all just government originates in the consent of the governed; all these American political theories were stated by John Locke a year after the revolution of 1688. They had been stated by the Levellers forty years earlier in the revolution of 1640–1660.

The present treatment of this subject must necessarily concern itself almost exclusively with the events and theories of 1640–1660. Space will not permit of a comparative constitutional commentary. Similarly, attempts to trace back the Leveller ideas beyond the year 1640 are im-

possible in the scope of this essay. The origins
of such ideas, of course, lie centuries back in the
political thinking of England and Europe. It is
equally impossible to appraise the various factors
in the social and economic life of seventeenth-
century England, that, working through the minds
of the Levellers, influenced their ideas. All that
can be done is to note such obvious connections
between economic and social abuses and proposed
remedies as were actually present to the minds
of the Levellers themselves.

The material employed is in great measure
the controversial pamphlet literature of the time.
The dangers in its use are obvious. The need of
manuscript evidence to supplement it is great;
but such evidence is almost entirely lacking.
Living about London in close touch with one another, the Leveller leaders naturally communi-
cated by word of mouth rather than by letter.
A few scattered pieces of correspondence exist
here and there; but in such unexpected places as
to indicate the fact that the unearthing of any
considerable body of correspondence throwing new
light on the Levellers must be the result of accident rather than design.

For certain purposes this dearth of document
material is not serious. Controversial writings
are the best guide in the study of elaborated political ideas and theories. Even for the life of a
man or a political party, the pamphlet material,
written as it was by contemporaries with different

political viewpoints, becomes a valuable and self-correcting source of information.

The limitations of the material, however, are great. After one has recorded the obtainable facts of the Leveller movement, he feels he has told what we may know of it, rather than what we should like to know. In the following chapters John Lilburne is assigned a greater space than probably his comparative importance in his party would justify; but the surviving material naturally groups itself around his robust and active personality. We can only conjecture who devised the ideas, the manifestos, the machinery of the Leveller party; but we know that John Lilburne was the Leveller incarnate. In his doings and his martyrdoms for principle John Lilburne illustrated and popularized the ideas of the Levellers.

The method of treatment may appear unduly partial to the Levellers. In spirit the work is frankly an appreciation, although a prepossession in favor of the Levellers has not hindered the fair statement of any evidence to their discredit at all worthy of consideration. From the days of the Levellers themselves down to the present time hostile comments have been frequent. Impartial estimates of their part in the political struggle of the English Revolution may be found in modern historians. Here the attempt is to show what is best in the men and in their ideals; to indicate the contribution they made to the world's political ideas.

CHAPTER I

The Doctrine of Parliamentary Sovereignty, 1640–1645

I. THE DOCTRINAL EVOLUTION OF PARLIAMENTARY SOVEREIGNTY, 1640–1642

POLITICAL exigencies led the Long Parliament to propound during the first two years of its existence two conflicting theories of the English constitution. In 1640 Parliament met the king's claims to absolute power with the doctrine that the liberties of England were protected by fundamental law. In 1642, confronted with the necessity of waging war against the king, Parliament had to rid itself of the limitations that precedent had placed on its activity. It accomplished this end by claiming the right to interpret without appeal the fundamental laws of the kingdom. Soon all men could see that the right of interpretation as Parliament used it involved the right to make and set aside laws at pleasure. The power to interpret the constitution of the kingdom was the bridge that carried the Long Parliament from the doctrine of the supremacy of the law to the doctrine of the supremacy of Parliament.

But in 1640 the Parliament leaders were concerned with criticising the illegal acts of others, not with seeking legal justification for their own. In the expressed opinion of the leaders of the Long

Parliament the dangers confronting England arose from assumption of undue power by the king, the bishops, and the judges. The twelve common-law justices at Westminster in their answer to the king's question regarding the lawfulness of ship money had laid down the principle that the king, in case of a great and declared necessity, of the imminence of which he alone was judge, might require financial aid of his subjects without the intervention of a parliament. Subjected to such interpretation every law and liberty of the English people lay at the mercy of the king's whim. "Such Art," said a parliamentary pamphleteer, "hath been used to deny, traverse, avoid, or frustrate the true force, or meaning of all our Lawes and Charters, that if wee grant Ship-money upon these grounds, with Ship-money wee grant all besides."[1] One of the judges, Robert Berkeley, had expressed himself more bluntly than his fellows. On one occasion he had asserted that in certain cases judges on the bench were above an act of Parliament; on another he had announced "that there was a Rule of Law, and a Rule of Government, and that many things which might not be done by the Rule of Law, might be done by the Rule of Government."[2] The king himself, in a declaration published at the dissolution of the Short Parliament, had denounced

---

[1] *The Case of Shipmony briefly discoursed*, p. 2. Henry Parker. November 3, 1640. E. 204 (4). The numbers given here and hereafter are the British Museum pressmarks.

[2] John Rushworth, *Historical Collections*, II, 364, 323. (Cited hereafter as Rushworth.)

the Commons for censuring the government, "as
if kings were bound to give an account of their
regal actions, and of their manner of government,
to their subjects assembled in Parliament."³ The
representative assembly of the Church of England
had endorsed the doctrine of king and judges.
The bishops and delegates assembled in convocation after the dissolution of the Short Parliament
had promulgated a series of canons that based the
king's title on divine right, enjoined an extreme
form of passive obedience on his subjects, and pronounced that in consideration of the divine right
of their ruler they owed him tribute, subsidy, and
aid.   Nor had the churchmen failed to discover a
higher sanction than the statute law for their own
position in the state.   In one of the canons of 1640
they had prescribed to laymen an oath of fidelity
to the church government as it then stood.   Certain bishops, too, claimed that they held their bish-
oprics by divine right rather than by the law of
the land.⁴ Bishops, king, and judges, all alike
appeared to be setting themselves above the law
of the land.

However, the great mass of the members of the
Long Parliament who worked in concert during the
first months of 1641, acted on a far different theory

³ Cobbett, *Parliamentary History*, II, 578.
⁴ *Constitutions and Canons Ecclesiasticall.* 1640. E. 203 (2). The
oath mentioned above, the "Et Cetera Oath," had employed an et cetera
to sum up the church government which the taker of the oath swore to
maintain—"Archbishops, Bishops, Deanes, and Archdeacons, &c." To
the Puritans this was a delicious commentary on the divine origin
claimed for the episcopal hierarchy.

of the place of king, church, and courts in the English constitution. Their definitions of monarchy, of prerogative, of the function of Parliament, all pointed to one central theory—the supremacy of law.

In terming the English constitution a balanced monarchy, they implied the belief that the king, although supreme ruler of the nation, was bound by the law. They drew a distinction between what the king could do as a man and what he could do as a king; or, as Oliver St. John had put it in the argument on ship money, between the king's natural power and his legal power. They admitted that the law of England called the king the fountain of justice: they admitted that the law of England called itself the king's law. But they emphasized the fact that the king could lawfully dispense justice only through his courts and enact the law of England only through his High Court of Parliament. They admitted that the crown of England, in so far as it dispensed its benefits to the subject through constitutional institutions, was absolute; but, they said, it was absolute only because an act of the king not according to law was not an act of the crown.[5]

In so limiting the absolute authority of the king, they stripped the word prerogative of the sanctity with which judges, bishops, and king had sought to invest it. Prerogative, said the

---

[5] Rushworth, II, 485. St. John's statement is almost certainly typical of the average member's view. See also, *Mr. Speakers Speech in the Lords House of Parliament.* June 22, 1641. E. 198 (23).

men of 1640, was a special privilege pertaining
to the king for the defense of his subjects and the
support of his personal dignity;[6] but the extent
of the prerogative and the manner in which the
subject was bound to supply the king with money
for its support were strictly defined by the fundamental laws of the land, unalterable save by the
assent of king and people in Parliament.[7] In
1640 most Englishmen were ready to pronounce
the fundamental laws of England a special bounty
of divine Providence, so perfectly were those laws
contrived to the end of keeping the balance even
between the due liberty of the subject and the due
prerogative of the king.[8]

[6] "The Law of Nature best determines, that all Princes being publike
Ministers for the common good, that their authority ought to be of
sufficient latitude for that common good; and since Scripture is not
expresse concerning that latitude, as to all people, the same not being
to all alike necessary, the severall Lawes of severall Countries best
teach that certaine latitude." *A Discourse Concerning Puritans.* Henry
Parker. 1641. E. 204 (3) p. 47.

[7] Oliver St. John on ship money in 1637. Rushworth, II, 483–485.

[8] "by the true fundamentall constitutions of England, the beame
hangs even between the King and the Subject; the Kings power doth
not tread under foot the peoples liberty, nor the peoples liberty the
kings power." *The Case of Shipmony*, p. 7.

"Prerogative and liberty are both necessary to this kingdom; and,
like the sun and moon, give a lustre to this benighted nation, so long
as they walk at their equal distances; but when one of them shall venture into the other's orb, like those planets in conjunction, they then
cause a deeper eclipse. What shall be the compass then, by which
these two must steer? Why nothing but the same by which they are,
the law." *An Honourable . . . Speech spoken in . . . Parliament. By Mr. Smith*, Oct. 28, 1641, E. 199 (8). In *Harleian Miscellany*, V,11.

See also Sir John Holland's speech on grievances, Nov. 7, 1640.
Parliamentary History, II, 648; *The Speech Or Declaration Of The Lord
Faulkland*, Jan. 14, 1640/1, E. 196 (26).

Accordingly, the leaders of the Long Parliament in opposing the extensions of the prerogative based their arguments on the fundamental laws of the land. In Strafford's case, John Pym represented as treason the attempting to subvert the fundamental laws of the land; for since those laws determined at once the prerogative of the king and the liberty of the subject, an attempt to subvert them involved stripping the king of his legal right to his prerogative; and as the prerogative was designed for the king's protection, such subversion amounted to compassing his death. Said Pym in summing up against the Earl of Strafford:

There is in this Crime a Seminary of all Evils hurtful to a State; and if you consider the Reasons of it, it must needs be so: the Law is that which puts a difference betwixt Good and Evil, betwixt Just and Unjust; if you take away the Law, all things will fall into Confusion, every Man will become a Law to himself, which in the depraved condition of Human Nature, must needs produce many great Enormities; Lust will become a Law, and Envy will become a Law, Covetousness and Ambition will become Laws; and what Dictates, what decisions such Laws will produce, may easily be discerned in the late Government of Ireland . . . . It is the Law that doth entitle the King to the Allegiance and Service of his People; it entitles the People to the Protection and Justice of the King. It is God alone who subsists by himself, all other things subsist in a mutuall Dependence, and Relation.[9]

It was easier for Pym to assert the existence of these laws than to say where they were to be found. Certainly, Magna Charta, confirmed above thirty-

---

[9] Rushworth, VIII, 662.

three times by various kings of England and explained in the Petition of Right, contained some of them; other basic statutes did so too; but the application of the term, fundamental law, to the text of a statute or the text of several statutes was scarcely warranted by English traditional usage. As Professor McIlwain says: "If a constituent law ever existed in England it must be looked for mainly in the attitude of men toward the law, or, better, in the rules applied by judges in cases arising under the law. The fundamental law there may be contained in a document, or documents, as in the case of Magna Charta, but the validity of that law is not due to the form of the document or documents but rather to the character of the principles."[10] In seventeenth-century England "fundamental law" denoted a series of principles deducible from the common or statute law, or perhaps naturally inherent in the minds of all men.

Such principles of fundamental law would be of little avail unless given practical application by some body or person empowered to interpret them authoritatively and finally. The Long Parliament by virtue of being the king's highest court asserted its right to the office of interpreter. Its claim should teach us that the word "Parliament" means one thing to writers of the seventeenth century and another to writers of the twentieth.

[10] C. H. McIlwain, *The High Court of Parliament and its Supremacy*, p. 61.

Parliament is today the supreme legislature of the British Empire, but in the political thought of the seventeenth and of earlier centuries, Parliament was less and more than a legislature. Less, because many thinkers would have ascribed the power of legislation, the power of making new laws, to the king; although it was a power that he could exercise only in Parliament.[11] More, because Parliament, though its transcendent function was that of legislation as we understand the term today, was also the king's greatest council and the king's highest court. As the latter it had the duty of interpretation that of necessity belongs to any court—the duty of stating and interpreting a rule of law before applying it in the decision of a specific case. True, it is not easy to find the Long Parliament at work which we should today regard as judicial. But its contemporaries spoke of it as a court; and probably they considered such of its enactments as were declaratory of the older law as being decisions of a court rather than acts of a legislature.[12]

The august character of Parliament in its three functions of council, court, and legislature was traced to the fact that it represented the whole kingdom, and was the symbol of the perfect ac-

---

[11] St. John had taken this position in his argument of 1637 on ship money. *Supra*, p. 10. It is also expressed in *The Priviledges And Practice of Parliaments In England. Collected out of the Common Lawes of this Land*, 1640, E. 161 (1), p. 43. This view would hardly have gone unchallenged by 1642.

[12] See Note I on p. 43.

cord of king and people.[13] The wits of parliamentary orators and writers were exhausted in the search for quaint conceits to illustrate this relation: Parliaments were beds of reconciliation; as in the natural body the head and the members were one, so in the Parliament the kingdom and the king were knit into one body politic, and had but one will and one purpose.[14]

Having such exalted notions of the dignity of parliaments, the Long Parliament was sharp in its prosecution of those who in the era of personal government had infringed on parliamentary functions. This was true notably in the cases of Strafford and Laud, the men who in their practice had most notoriously departed from the rule of law to follow after the rule of government. Parliament found like offenders in the judges and in the clergy in convocation. The judges, it held, had abused to the advantage of the prerogative their function of declaring the law of the land, when

[13] The emphasis on the value of the mutual consent of king and people to laws as securing their justness is marked. "Now the great Buttresse or Foundation upon which the Lawes of England stand (if I be not mistaken) is upon the free consent of the King and subject in the composing and framing of them . . . And doth also prevent them [the people] most of all excuses or quarrells against the lawes, for since it doth in a sort make them all (for the considerable part in policy) as well parties and agents in the making of the yoke, as passive in the bearing of it, we are so much the more deprived of all plea and exception against it, untill it bee taken off, or abrogated by the like power and upon the same termes." Thomas Warmstry, *Pax Vobis*, Dec. 1641, E. 180 (24), pp. 24–28 *passim*.

[14] Sir Benjamin Rudyard, Apr. 18, 1640, *Parliamentary History*, II, 545.

in the case of ship money they had reversed a previous decision handed down by the High Court of Parliament in the Petition of Right.   Convocation had abused its power of declaring the law in matters of religion, when it had prescribed an oath to laymen, and had assumed to define the king's right to tax his subjects.   Both judges and clergy, therefore, stood convicted of having trespassed on the duties of the highest court of the land, the High Court of Parliament.[15]

The constitutional doctrine that Parliament was the final interpreter of the fundamental laws of the land contained, as has been indicated, the germ of the doctrine of parliamentary sovereignty; and the development of this latter doctrine divided the old constitutional party of the Long Parliament into the two parties that fought the civil war.   The development of the doctrine and the divergence of the parties are devious and difficult to trace.   Its first official appearance perhaps is the Grand Remonstrance passed November 22, 1641.   This is the first public utterance by the narrower party forming around Pym and Hampden that ignores the organic concept of Parliament—the concept that regarded the Parliament as the symbol of the unity of king and people. In ordering the Grand Remonstrance printed, the House of Commons bid against the king for the support of the nation.   Clear-headed Royalists saw what it meant and stormed for the right

[15] See Note I on p. 43.

of recording their protests against the measure. "When," said Sir Edward Dering, "I first heard of a Remonstrance, I presently imagined that like faithful Counsellors, we should hold up a Glass unto his Majesty: I thought to represent unto the King the wicked Counsels of pernicious Counsellors . . . . I did not dream that we should remonstrate downward, tell stories to the people, and talk of the King as of a third person."[16]

From this date the House of Commons began to emphasize its own importance in the state. Partly as a result of the attempt on the five members, statements of its privileges came to have a larger place in its utterances. Occasionally, as from Grimston's Guildhall speech[17], one gains the impression that the iniquity of the breach of privilege lay not so much in molesting the chosen servants of the nation, as in interfering with the privileges of a corporate body—privileges perhaps not wholly ancillary to the good of the kingdom outside St. Stephen's Chapel. Furthermore, the Lower House ventured to assume to itself the new-found augustness of the Parliament. The utterances of the House of Commons began to imply that in case of necessity it might lawfully act without the Lords. In a conference with the Lords, January 25, Pym insinuated that if the obstinacy of the Upper House prevented the Com-

---

[16] Nalson, *An Impartial Collection*, II, 668 (cited hereafter as Nalson). Dering's speech was on the first proposal to print, November 22. The printing was not carried till December 15.

[17] E. 200 (5).

mons from saving the kingdom with the Lords' concurrence, the Commons would save the kingdom without it.[18]

The Grand Remonstrance was the beginning of a paper war between the king and the Parliament that lasted well after the first shock of arms. At the very beginning, Parliament made long strides toward claiming supreme power. On the Militia Bill, by which for their own safety the Houses sought to get control of the militia organization of the kingdom, Parliament finally broke with the older policy, and the older theory of balanced power. March 15, the Houses declared that the Militia Ordinance was binding on the people, and that by the fundamental laws of the land it ought to be obeyed. In a resolution of March 16, they based their action on their right as supreme judicature of the kingdom to declare the law of the land. Briefly stated, their implied argument was that the law of the land in a time of great and evident danger was the law of *salus populi;* and that the Parliament as supreme judge of the laws of the land was judge also of the existence of such a law and of the necessity of invoking it.[19]

[18] *Parliamentary History*, II, 1060.

[19] *Commons Journal*, II, 479, 481. *Lords Journal*, IV, 648, 650. *An exact Collection of all Remonstrances, Declarations, Ordinances, . . . and other . . . passages between the Kings most Excellent Majesty and his High Court of Parliament*, Mar. 21, 1642/3, E. 241; E. 243 (cited as Husband), p. 114. The position stated in the last sentence of the above paragraph is the interpretation put by the declaration of May 19, on a phrase of the declaration of March 9. Husband, pp. 100, 197.

The position is clearly worked out in a Declaration of May 19, 1642, which is worth quoting at length. It states that the judgment of the Parliament on a point of law

is in the eye of the Law, the Kings Judgement in his highest Court; though the King in his person be neither present nor assenting thereunto . . . If his Majesty should refuse to joyn with us therein, [on the Militia Bill] the two Houses of Parliament being the supream Court and highest Councell of the Kingdome, were enabled by their own authority to provide for the repulsing of such imminent, and evident danger, not by any new Law of their own making, as hath been untruly suggested to his Majesty, but by the most ancient Law of this Kingdome, even that which is fundamentall and essentiall to the constitution and subsistance of it. . . . . this Law is as old as the Kingdome. That the Kingdome must not be without a meanes to preserve it selfe, which that it may be done without confusion, this Nation hath intrusted certaine hands with a Power to provide in an orderly and regular way, for the good and safetie of the whole, which power, by the Constitution of this Kingdome, is in his Majestie, and in his Parliament together; yet since the Prince being but one person, is more subject to accidents of nature and chance, whereby the Common-Wealth may be deprived of the fruit of that trust which was in part reposed in him, in cases of such necessity, that the Kingdome may not be inforced presently to returne to its first principles, and every man left to doe what is aright in his owne eyes, without either guide or rule, The wisedome of this State hath intrusted the Houses of Parliament with a power to supply what shall bee wanting on the part of the Prince, as is evident by the constant custome and practice thereof, in cases of nonage, naturall disability, and captivity, and the like reason doth and must hold for the exercise of the same power in such cases, where the Royall trust cannot be, or is not discharged, and that the Kingdome runs an evident and imminent danger thereby; which danger,

having been declared by the Lords and Commons in
Parliament; there needs not the authority of any person
or Court to affirme; nor is it in the power of any person
or Court to revoke that judgement.[20]

The assumption that when the king's actions
tended to the ruin of the kingdom his evil counsellors were responsible, was sanctioned by centuries of precedent. In view of the general distrust of the men like Lord Digby who had the
king's ear, what was more natural than to apply
the doctrine to Charles's refusal to assent to the
Militia Ordinance? In view of the fact that
Parliament was the king's supreme council, too,
it seemed only reasonable to infer that the king's
duty was to follow its advice, and during its sittings to pay no heed to counsel from any other
quarter. This doctrine had great possibilities.
If every regal act on the part of the king could be
supposed to be the result of counsel, and if he
were debarred from accepting other counsel than
that of Parliament, he became a mere automaton
to register its decrees.[21]

Indeed, the Houses found this a convenient line
of attack on the king's veto power, or "negative
voice." May 16, the Lords set a committee to
make research as to whether kings had ever denied
assent to public bills, save by withholding their

[20] Husband, pp. 197, 207–208 (arranged).

[21] A petition presented to the king after he had left Westminster
takes the position that the very essence of Parliament will be destroyed if its counsels are subject to reversal through the advice of private persons. *Parliamentary History*, II, 1350; see also Husband, p.
206.

consent for a time, by the tactful formula, "Le roi s'avisera." May 26, Parliament asked in another declaration why, if Parliament were judge between king and people on the question of what was law, it should not be judge likewise of the kingdom's need for a legal remedy for an abuse? In other words, if Parliament by passing a statute implied its belief that the people stood in need of the statute, the king had no right to express a contrary opinion by withholding his consent.[22]

Manifestly Parliament in the early months of 1642 was using its position of supreme interpreter to extract justification for its aggressions on the king's power out of the laws of the land and the law of *salus populi*. The indirection by which it thus claimed powers that were virtually sovereign characterized the forms under which it prepared to vindicate its claims by force. True, in its resolutions of May 20 it stated with directness the actual situation—that the king seduced by evil counsel was about to make war on his Parliament; that in so doing he was guilty of an act that was a breach of his trust and tended to the dissolution of the government. But with the actual approach of hostilities the Houses had recourse to the time-honored quibbles of raising armies for the king's defense, and for the rescue of his person. July 12 they voted: "That an Army shall be forthwith

---

[22] *Lords Journal*, V, 66; Husband, p. 269. An argument against the negative voice was developed also from the coronation oath wherein the king swore to assent to such good laws as the Commons should choose—*quas vulgus elegerit.*

raised for the safety of the kings person, defence of both Houses of Parliament, and of those who have obeyed their Orders and Commands, and preserving the True Religion, the Laws, Liberty and Peace of the Kingdom." Simple people were once more perplexed at an army on foot for the inconsistent purpose of making war on the king to secure the safety of his person.[23]

The Parliament, therefore, employed the older terminology of the constitution to cloak actions that in reality were defensible only as acts of a sovereign power. It employed its assumed power of interpretation in order to make the law of the kingdom something entirely different from that which it was on the face of statute and precedent. The forced constructions of the fundamental laws of the kingdom, however, answered the immediate purpose; they gave a show of legality to an assumption of power necessary to the safety of Parliament and its followers. And once the parliamentary leaders had provided for the pressing necessity of the moment, they probably did not look far into the future.

II.   PARLIAMENTARY SOVEREIGNTY AS BASED ON THE LAW OF NATURE

In the spring of 1642, arguments based on abstract principles of government began to supplement the constitutional technicalities that had filled the Parliament's official declarations. Un-

[23] Husband, pp. 259, 457.

doubtedly Parliament won valuable support by appealing to thinking men on general principles of political science. But the substitution of abstract reasoning for dogmatic legal assertions encouraged men to reason for themselves. In the end, many who did so arrived at conclusions that their earlier teachers would hardly have endorsed. The political philosophy used in 1642 by Parliament's partisans to defend its sovereignty is therefore important as a source of political ideas, if for no other reason.[24]

In May of 1642, relations between the king and the Parliament were passing beyond the stage where the recorded laws and precedents could by any interpretation be made conveniently to apply. The claim to supremacy being vital to Parliament's position, the Parliament's penmen had to delve back into the origins of government to justify that claim. Assertion that the Parliament possessed certain powers was not sufficient; demonstrations that in the nature of things it was expedient for Parliament to possess them were needed. Henry Parker's *Observations upon some of his Majesties late Answers and Expresses*, an original and brilliant attempt at a demonstration of this type, may be said to open a new era in the political controversies of the Great Civil War.[25]

The problem that Parker avowedly set himself was the inquiry into the "efficient and finall

---

[24] See Note II on p. 45.

[25] *Observations upon some of his Majesties late Answers and Expresses*, July 2, 1642, E. 153 (26).

causes" of both regal and parliamentary power.
Power and authority, he decided, were originally
inherent in the people, and were nothing else but
"that might and vigour which such or such a
societie of men containes in itselfe." The society
could transfer this inherent power to a ruler only
by a law "of common consent and agreement."
This law, when so transferring power, had God's
assent; "and so man is the free and voluntary
Author, the Law is the Instrument, and God is the
establisher of both." Hence it followed that "at
the founding of authorities, when the consent of
societies convayes rule into such and such hands,
it may ordaine what conditions, and prefix what
bounds it pleases, and that no dissolution ought
to be thereof, but by the same power by which it
had its constitution."[26]

As might be expected, Parker adopted a form
of the *salus populi* argument. The charter of
nature, he asserted, entitled "all Subjects of all
Countries whatsoever to safetie by its supreame
Law." The postulate that "the subject shall live
both safe and free" limited the prerogative of all
princes, no matter what the constitutions of the
nations they ruled. Thus the necessity of the
people's safety guided and defined the prince's
prerogative of calling and dismissing Parliaments,
and of assenting to their laws; of the measures
required to secure the safety of the nation, a Parliament was supreme judge.[27]

[26] *Observations*, pp. 1, 2.
[27] *Ibid.*, pp. 3, 4 ff.

Among the various checks imposed by the laws of specific nations, Parker instanced English parliamentary government as the highest stage yet attained in an evolution that had brought orderly government out of barbaric disorder and violence. At the dawn of government, the depravity of fallen and sinful man had silenced the dictates of the law that God had implanted in his breast; accordingly, the existence of an authority strong enough to "provide new orders, and to judge of old, and to execute according to justice," was necessary. Then, after the tyranny of magistrates intrusted with the execution of the laws had frustrated the benefit of this first remedy, the people had made trial of various expedients by which a law might be set above the magistrate and enforced. At times the people had risen in arms to redress their wrongs, but had achieved only confusion and bloodshed. Often in their ignorance they had only exchanged one tyranny for another.

till some way [Parker concluded] was invented to regulate the motions of the peoples moliminous body, I think arbitrary rule was most safe for the world, but now since most Countries have found out an Art and peaceable Order for publique Assemblies, whereby the people may assume its owne power to doe it self right without disturbance to it selfe, or injury to Princes, he is very unjust that will oppose this Art and order. That Princes may not be now beyond all limits and Lawes, nor yet left to be tryed upon those limits and Lawes, by any private parties, the whole community in its underived Majesty shall convene to doe juctice, and that this convention may not be without intelligence, certaine times and places and formes shall be appointed for its regliment, and that the vastnesse of its owne bulke may not breed confusion, by vertue of election and representation: a few shall act for many, the wise shall consent for the simple, the vertue of all shall redound to some, and the prudence of some shall redound to all.

To Parker, the kingdom was not the creator of the Parliament; rather the Parliament was the kingdom itself.[28]

The doctrine that there was or could be any difference of interest or opinion between Parliament and the people it represented was almost blasphemy to Parker. ". . . that great Priviledges," he said, "of all Priviledges, that unmoveable Basis of all honour and power, whereby the House of Commons claimes the entire rite of all the Gentry and Commonalty of England, has beene attempted to bee shaken & disturbed" from the fact that "the people upon causelesse defamation and unproved accusations have been so prone to withdraw themselves from their representations and yet there can be nothing under heaven, next to renouncing God, which can be more perfidious, and more pernitious in the people then this."[29]

Parker's doctrine, ably as it was stated, did not fit the actual conditions of 1642. He was aware that he was ascribing supreme and arbitrary power to the Parliament. His excuse for the ascription

[28] Pp. 10 ff. The author of *The Contra Replicant* (which Thomason ascribes to Parker also) calls the Houses the collective body of the realm, the equivalent of the councils that set up royalty and established its bounds in the first instance. January 31, 1642/3. E. 87 (5), p. 16.

[29] See Note III on p. 47.

was that "if the State intrusts this [power] to one man, or few, there may be danger in it; but the Parliament is neither one nor few, it is indeed the State it self." The facts were against this assertion. Were Parliament "the state it self," it must represent all the political ideas and aspirations of the individuals who made up the state; and with Royalists everywhere rallying to the king, Parliament's sayings and actions were but the sayings and actions of a party; at best, the sayings and actions of a government which a great part of the kingdom repudiated.

Parker did not consider that the actual situation militated against his theory. He never tempered his glorification of the nation's civil authority as an organic body by consideration for the rights or opinions of any of the individuals of whom the nation was composed. In ascribing absolute power to the English people assembled in Parliament, he turned his back on the old common law of England, with its blundering endeavors to secure certain rights to individual Englishmen. Parker's doctrine of parliamentary sovereignty was in the end to become the doctrine of the English constitution, but not till after it had met stubborn opposition from men who attempted to shelter the rights of the individual from possible encroachments of government—men who, as Parker was writing, were drawing their swords for the Parliament.[30]

---

[30] Parker is not perfectly consistent in his ascription of arbitrary power to the Parliament. In places he tries to assure the people that, since the people have elected the Parliament, the Houses cannot usurp

Parker's followers and successors stated in more extreme terms than Parker himself the practical consequences flowing from this doctrine of parliamentary absolutism. In one point they added to Parker's argument: they made fuller use of the theory first advanced in Parliament's own declarations, that the judgment of the Lords and Commons in Parliament bound all persons within the jurisdiction of the court of Parliament. Such a judgment, pamphleteers argued, was law, perhaps until the Houses recalled it, certainly until the end of the Parliament; and, thanks to the bill against the dissolution of the Parliament, that limit was under the Parliament's own control. They were prompt to disclaim any responsibility on the part of Parliament to judge according to any particular known laws. The author of *The Second Part of Vox Populi* declared that in the case of extreme necessity that confronted the Parliament, it could apply the law of necessity. It was, he wrote, the height of absurdity to talk

power without the assent of king and people. In a publication issued as late as August 26 (the *Observations* came out July 2), he limits the power of the two Houses to declare law to a necessity in which the king will not act with them. *The Observator Defended,* E. 114 (19), p. 2. In another publication (*A Political Catechism,* [May 20, 1643.] E. 104 (8).) he speaks of the two Houses as mediating between king and people, and of the whole Parliament as representing a union of aristocratic, monarchical, and democratic elements in the government (pp. 6, 10). In general, it may be said that he asserts formally that the people's grant of power to the king is irrevocable, and that the king has a real right to his powers; but his doctrine that in extreme cases Parliament may interpret those powers for the kingdom's welfare sweeps away all protection for the king's position.

of orders of Parliament being against the law. By what was the law established save by acts of Parliament? Any lawyer who presumed to sit in judgment on those acts might as well claim that his power to do so was of divine right. Surely England had not reached the Antipodes, where children corrected their fathers, that inferior courts should prescribe rules to the highest! As for past precedents of parliamentary procedure, the Long Parliament had all the rights enjoyed by its predecessors, of establishing new precedents suitable to the degeneracy of the time.[31]

These writers depicted the subordination of the people to the Parliament as well-nigh absolute. Some of them, it is true, limited the extreme power of Parliament to the existing emergency,[32] but all of them extended it to include rights over the estates of the subjects.[33] The people could not plead rights of property against the Parliament as they could against the king; for they somehow had endowed Parliament with rights which they had always withheld from him. Says the author of *A Disclaimer And Answer Of The Commons Of England:*

He knows nothing of the nature of Parliaments, that knows not that the House of Commons is absolutely intrusted with our persons and estates, and by our Lawes

[31] *The Kingdomes Case*, May 1, 1643, E. 100 (9), p. 9; *The Second Part of Vox Populi*, Oct. 31, 1642, E. 124 (34).

[32] *A Frivolous Paper, in Forme of a Petition*, Dec. 13, 1642, E. 130 (11).

[33] See also *The Vindication Of The Parliament And their Proceedings*, Oct. 15, 1642, E. 122 (19).

invested with a power to dispose of them as they shall
thinke meet, not onely by making new Lawes, but also
as they are a great Court above all our ordinary Courts,
to governe us, and determine of all things proper to the
power and jurisdiction thereof in all things tending to
the conservation of the Commonwealth and of our Religion, Laws and Liberties, and to be limited to be only
Proctors to speak for us is senselesse and ridiculous.[34]

The official utterances of Parliament adopted
but gradually such glosses by enthusiastic partisans
on its earlier declarations.   As late as November 2,
1642, a parliamentary declaration denied that
Parliament claimed the power to divest the king
of "his ancient unquestionable undoubted rights,"
but at the same time reaffirmed in even broader
terms its right to interpret in last resort the laws
of the land.   Men who were unskilled in the legal
casuistry of the time must have been puzzled to
know just what legal position and what relation
to the king Parliament claimed.[35]

To add to the difficulty, not all the men who
fought Parliament's paper battles interpreted the
compact theory as Parker and his followers had
done.   A few writers deduced from it not parliamentary absolutism, but rather a narrow doctrine
of popular sovereignty.   The divergence of the
two schools can be explained most easily by a
running summary of the manner in which two or
three typical authors stated the compact theory

[34] May 4, 1643, E. 100 (23), p. 2.   See also William Prynne, *The
Soveraigne Power of Parliaments and Kingdomes: Divided into Foure
Parts together with An Appendix*, 1643, pt. I, p. 34; *id.*, pt. IV, pp. 15,
26, 27.   *Infra*, p. 47.

[35] Husband, p. 705.   See Note III on p. 47.

and the rights that under it the Parliament enjoyed.

Henry Parker's theory, while already stated, may here be summed up briefly. The people for their preservation had set over themselves a ruler empowered to provide for their security according to the law. In case he were derelict to his duty, the kingdom could provide for its security in Parliament. If a certain *Discourse betweene A Resolved and a Doubtfull Englishman* be Parker's— and certainly it carries to a logical conclusion the reasoning of his signed works—he was inclined to handle the whole question of compact between king and people in an extremely off-hand way. To argue from the law of *salus populi*—we are here summing up the discourse between the two Englishmen—the remote predecessors of seventeenth-century Parliaments in setting up a king as chief magistrate, and supplying him (if they had done so) with a veto power, had acted for the safety of the people. Certainly they could not have intended that the form of government they had established should work the nation's ruin. Nor could the fact that they had constituted a certain form of government deprive their descendants of the right to alter anything in it that they found amiss. Accordingly, to Parker's mind, the Houses of Parliament whenever they thought it necessary were free to abrogate the ancestral compact with the king, and to abolish kingship.[36]

---

[36] The author of *A Disclaimer And Answer*, quoted above, has a suggestive paragraph on the origin of law in the kingdom. "In this

A second writer unwittingly illustrated the pit-
falls which lay hidden for parliamentary apologists
in the compact doctrine when he emphasized, not
the contrast and opposition of king and Parliament, but their co ordination.[37] A compact between king and people which sanctioned the co-
ordinate existence of the three estates of king,
Lords, and Commons was, he thought, of record in
the unchangeable and fundamental laws of the
land "consented to and contrived by the people
in its first constitution, and since in every severall
reigne confirmed both by mutuall oathes betweene
King and People" (p. 7). When the writer added
that the supreme power remained in the three
estates conjointly, he described the English constitution with more accuracy than was advan-
tageous to his argument. Accordingly he blundered

Kingdome the people originally agreed Lawes, such as they found by
experience to be good for them, which were therefore called the Customes of the Kingdome, Customary Law, Common Law, not imposed
upon them by Charters of Princes, or by Act of Parliament, but assumed
by them, . . . and are not written as Charter and Parliament
Lawes be; then they chose one from among them to be their King for
the defence of their Lawes, bodies and goods, and for these purposes
only they gave him power to governe them, and he cannot governe
them by any other power or rule; and for the preservation of the Lawes
against the Incroachments of the King . . . and for the making
of such new Laws as should be requisite" they ordained Parliaments
"and invested them with all power for the good of the Kingdome and
people" (p. 17). This is Parker's doctrine, only a little more plainly
put. There is a practically similar treatment of the law of England
in *The Subjects Liberty: Set Forth in the Royall and Politique Power of
England*, May 12, 1643, E. 101 (19), p. 6. *Infra*, p. 47.

[37] Charles Herle, *A Fuller Answer To A Treatise Written by Doctor
Ferne*, Dec. 29, 1642, E. 244 (27), pp. 3, 4, 7, 8–10, 25.

out of his difficulty into a self-contradiction: the "reason," he said, of the people, which had constituted the original form of the government, remained in the two Houses. Accordingly, they might provide for the public safety in time of danger, and declare the law in final resort. The fallacy is plainly apparent. If a contract between A and X intrusts powers over X to A, B, and C, it certainly does not follow that B and C may interpret the contract to the exclusion of both A and X.

The author's difficulty arose from the fact that he dared not ascribe active power of any sort to the people; therefore he could not say that X had hired A as his servant, or indeed distinguish X from B and C. Had he lodged the "reason" of the people elsewhere than in the two Houses, Royalists would have criticised his constitution as sure to end in an anarchical democracy. He protested bitterly against such an interpretation of the parliamentary position.

A 2d question begg'd is, that in case the King and Parliament should neither discharge their trusts, the people might rise and make resistance against both, a Position which no man I know maintaines, the Parliament is the peoples own consent, which once pass'd they cannot revoke, he still pursues his owne dreame [a polite reference to the Royalist, Dr. Ferne] of the people's reassuming power, whereas we acknowledge no power can be imployed but what is reserved, and the people have reserved no power in themselves from themselves in Parliament.

To a man with a fine sense of logic, the task of proving that thirty peers and three hundred members of the House of Commons rightfully exercised sovereign power without appeal was not an easy one.

Other pamphleteers attempted to defend the proceedings of the Long Parliament without claiming for it complete supremacy, or employing fallacies to deny the possibility of an appeal to the people. Philip Hunton, author of *A Treatise Of Monarchie*,[38] in general agreed with the writers above mentioned both in his doctrine of compact and in representing Parliament as the place in which the compact must be revised and interpreted. He agreed with them further that the two Houses in certain cases of necessity—such as invasion or the subversion of the fundamental laws—might assume the power of government without the consent of the king, provided their actions evidently tended to the preservation of king and kingdom. At this point, however, when he was confronted with the question as to who should judge whether or not the laws were subverted, he saw difficulties that the other authors mentioned above had glided over. "To demand which Estate may challenge this power of finall determination of Fundamentall controversies arising betwixt them is to demand which of them shall be absolute.[39] ... Whereas I

[38] *A Treatise Of Monarchie*, May 24, 1643, E. 103 (15), pp. 4, 17–18, 44, 66, 69–73.

[39] The omission is worth quoting in a note. "For I conceive that in the first part hereof, I have made it good that this finall utmost controversie arising betwixt the three Legislative Estates, can have no legal constituted Judge in a mixed government; for in such difference, he who affirmes that the people are bound to follow the Judgement of the King against that of the Parliament, destroyes the mixture into

take it to be an evident truth that in a mixed government no power is to be attributed to either Estate which directly or by necessary consequence destroys the liberty of the other." Hunton's belief that the king was an integral part of the state forbade him to identify the "reason" of the two Houses with the "reason" of the state. A judgment of Parliament lacking the king's presence and assent could not be called the king's judgment, because a similar judgment in his courts was so called; for in his courts the king was represented whether he were present in person or not; but in Parliament he could be present only in person. Hunton could offer no constitutional remedy to prevent a deadlock between king and Parliament. He could only suggest an appeal to arms; if each individual rallied to the side he thought just, the opinion of the majority of the people would in the end prevail.

Hunton was not the only apologist for Parliament who eschewed the extreme view of its supremacy. Thus, *Scripture And Reason Pleaded For Defensive Armes*,[40] a tract with official sanction, significantly condemned as unsound the analogy drawn by Royalist writers between resistance to the king by the people, and resistance to the head

---

absolutenesse: And he who afirmes that they are bound to cleave to the Judgement of the two Houses against that of the King, resolves the Monarchie into an Aristocracie or Democracie according as he places this finall Judgement." P. 69.

[40] *Scripture And Reason Pleaded For Defensive Armes . . . Published by divers . . . Divines.* Printed by command of the Commons Committee on Printing, Apr. 14, 1643, E. 247 (22), pp. 14, 38–53.

by the members; every man, it argued, was himself a reasoning being. Parker would have hesitated long before ascribing to individual subjects the capacity to arrive at valid conclusions in politics. More than this, *Scripture And Reason* ascribed to the body of the people the right to save the state in case the three estates in Parliament conspired to ruin it. If, it concluded, the three estates disagreed as to which one was guilty of practice ruinous to the state, only the body of the people could decide between them.

In the trace of Hunton and *Scripture And Reason* followed the most elaborate of the summaries of the parliamentary argument—Samuel Rutherford's *Lex Rex*. The essentials of Rutherford's position on the origin of government were not different from Parker's; but in discussing the compact between government and people, he lingered in his earlier pages over doctrines of social compact. He emphasized the fact that man was naturally free from subjection to magistracy. He admitted that the law of nature—a divine law—authorized government, and that man's power of ordaining government was, like his social propensities, a gift of God. But, Rutherford added, man was free to accept or reject this gift of God; the union of men in society was purely voluntary; and subjection to magistrates, unlike the subjection of children to parents, was not natural. Though men were born subject to the laws of their society, one generation of men was not bound by the political action of a preceding one; the right to change government was inalienable. Nevertheless, once a people had covenanted with a king, it was bound to obey him until he became tyrannical. Like Hunton, Rutherford saw the difficulty of finding an interpreter for the covenant between people and king. His conclusion was that the covenant gave a mutual coercive power to king and people—the one to enforce it on the other; accordingly, that the people might know when they were empowered to rise and resist the tyranny of the monarch, the interpretation of the covenant must be left to the law of nature which, so Rutherford said, was easily to be understood by all people. In supposing that the verdict of the people would be unanimous, and a plain application of self-evident laws, Rutherford was somewhat less practical than Hunton.[41]

As far as the actual political situation went, the doctrine of Hunton and Rutherford assigned little more political importance to the people than did the doctrine of Parker. Hunton, indeed, had merely recognized the fact that the individuals comprising the nation had taken the liberty of deciding between king and Parliament. In fact, the act against the dissolution of Parliament without its consent made impossible any expression of the popular will save a military one. Even a new election would have given the opportunity for political self-expression to one class only of the

[41] *Lex Rex: The Law and the Prince. A Dispute for the just Prerogative of King and People*, Oct. 7, 1644, E. 11 (5), pp. 1, 2, 10, 36 ff., 78, 81, 86, 91, 96–100, 213.

nation.   Constitutional forms by which the majority might declare its pleasure in orderly fashion
had yet to be devised; and if such forms had existed,
the nation lacked the political experience that
would have enabled it to use them.   Under the
circumstances Parker's doctrine that the Parliament was the nation articulate had much to com-
mend it.   Parliament might misrepresent the people's wishes; but neither precedent nor practice
could afford any other means by which the wishes
even of any considerable part of the kingdom might
be learned.

III.   ROYALIST CRITICISM OF THE PARLIAMENTARY POSITION

A student of the Leveller political theories is
concerned with the multitudes of Royalist pamphlets printed after 1642 only in so far as they
afford acute criticism of the parliamentary position.   Such criticism first appears in the state
papers drawn from the king by the controversies
that began with the Grand Remonstrance.   At
the moment when the Parliament abandoned the
exposition of the fundamental laws of the land for
the interpretation of the law of *salus populi*,
declarations and answers under the king's name
began to defend his prerogative by appeals to the
customs of the realm.   The king's answer to that
part of the Grand Remonstrance, or rather the
petition accompanying it, that related to the
taking away of the votes of the bishops in the
House of Lords, was "that their right is grounded

upon the fundamentall Law of the Kingdome, and constitution of Parliament."[42] The same phrase recurred again and again as the demands of Parliament rose higher. It was the king's answer to Parliament's demand for the power over the militia; to its demand regarding the appointment of governors of castles.[43] The declarations drawn for his use by Edward Hyde steadily protested against the Parliament's enlarged use of its law-declaring powers. Thus in the answer to the Declaration of May 5, Hyde made the king ask that Parliament state specifically the laws on which it based its militia ordinance, and tell where they were to be found.[44] If Parliament's marvellous secret now proved sufficient to divest the king of his rights, it might next be employed to take away the liberties of the subjects; for if the votes of the two Houses had such virtue in declaring new laws, they must be equally efficacious in repealing old ones.

The Royalists, however, were strongest in appealing to common sense against the inconsistencies of Parliament's theory and practice.[45] They subjected the Parliament's somewhat inconsistent claims to searching analysis. Royalists put aside the theory that Parliament could do no wrong because it was the kingdom incarnate. They

[42] Husband, p. 23.

[43] Feb. 28, 1641/2. Husband, p. 91; Answer to the petition of January 28, 1641/2, Husband, p. 60.

[44] Husband, p. 175. See also pp. 242, 250.

[45] Lack of space makes it necessary to ignore almost completely the Royalist theoretical argument.

pointed out that in fact the two Houses were some three hundred Englishmen who were exercising as real rights of government over the rest of their countrymen as ever the king had done. They insisted on regarding the Houses as *de facto* a governing body, and quite distinct from the body governed. From such assumptions the Royalists drew unpleasant practical conclusions. If the people might on occasion revoke the grant of power they had made to a king, why could they not revoke the grant of power they had made to their representatives?[46] In empowering the members of the House of Commons to act as their proxies, had the electors dreamed that they were empowering the members to do more than to sit and to act as Parliament men had acted time out of mind? Had the electors ever believed that they were yielding themselves up to the unrestrained wills and judgments of those whom they elected? If Parliament was the whole kingdom representatively, how did it come that non-freeholders and nine parts of the men of the kingdom were excluded from the choice of members? How had persons without votes conveyed any power to the members of the House of Commons? If the people had the right of self-preservation as against an act of the king that they judged destructive to themselves, why did they not enjoy the same right in respect to a parliamentary ordinance? The Houses were assuming to take measures for the nation's pres-

[46] *Animadversions Upon Those Notes Which The Late Observator hath published,* July 9, 1642, E. 107 (22), p. 12.

ervation that were not warranted by the recorded laws; was not this exactly the power claimed by the king in the case of ship money?[47]

The Royalists were assiduous in attempts to sow dissensions in the ranks of the enemy. In familiar conversational style, they told the plain people that they were being used as catspaws to gratify with riches and honor the avarice and ambition of nobles and commons.[48]   They insisted that

[47] *A View Of A Printed Book.*   Jan. 26, 1642/3, E. 245 (22), pp. 25 ff. There was really a marked resemblance between the position of the king in 1629–1640 and that of Parliament after 1642.   The following extract states the parallel clearly and in a style in which the Royalists excelled.   The title, *A Letter From A Grave Gentleman once a Member of this House of Commons, to his friend, remaining a Member of the same House in London,* gives the setting of the pamphlet.   May 19, 1643, E. 102 (13).

"How often have you told me, (when you have heard the Courtiers argue that without such a Power in the Crowne, no Parliament sitting, the Kingdome might be unavoydably destroyed) that with or without that Power We should be liable to mighty dangers but the wisdom of the Law had avoided those most that were likely to come oftenest; That now besides, the Question was not what was best to be Law, but what was Law; That Arguments from Convenience are good considerations in framing of Lawes or founding of States, but that the State being framed it was most ridiculous and dangerous to retyre from the Lawe to a disputable convenience or Necessity, and put our selves back again into the same Maze of Debates and Questions, which Lawes were framed to be rules to us to deliver us from."

[48] "I must plainly tell you," runs one of these, "there was never any civill War, wherein the good of the people was not most cryed up, and yet least intended.   For assure your selves, the Interests of discontented Nobles or Commons, that have gained a greater power in your affections, are not the same with you of lower ranke, and therefore they do but abuse you, and make you with hazard of your Estates, and lives, and souls, cut out way to their ends".   *An Answer To . . . Plain English,* Feb. 18, 1642/3, E. 89 (33), p. 8.

Still another cleverly sums up the logical weakness of the Parlia-

Parliament's course was leading the nation into democracy—using a word that ordinarily connoted what anarchy does today. Such attempts to arouse class feeling were probably not unfruitful. Undoubtedly the insinuations stuck in men's minds and in 1645 and 1646 induced the Levellers and their opponents the more readily to put the worst interpretation on each other's motives.

In fact the political thinking and political practice of 1640–1645 partly determined the course of the Leveller movement. Those years developed an irritating condition of affairs, and suggested a train of argument for attacking it. Parliament's members had assiduously lectured the kingdom on the existence of fundamental laws and the heinousness of endeavoring to abrogate or evade them. Then, by methods of indirection similar to those it had condemned, Parliament had extended its right of interpreting the fundamental laws till it had interpreted them into nullity. To justify Parliament's action, its supporters had stated a theory of parliamentary absolutism too unblushing for even Parliament to adopt in full. They had based their theory on the postulate that government derived its authority from its compact with

ment's actual position. "Seeing you are pleased to proceed thus farre, we beseech you make one ordinance more. That both Houses shall be a Corporation, to take Lands and goods to them and their Successors, and that they shall bee the onely Projectors of all the Lands and goods in the Kingdome, and when any of that Corporation dies, *toties quoties*, the survivor and none else shall choose a successor to perpetuity." *A Complaint To The House of Commons*, Jan. 2, 1642/3. E. 244 (31), p. 19.

the nation; and after their writings had familiarized men with abstract reasoning of the sort, other books by parliamentary writers had shown that the compact theory could not logically lead to the conclusion that the Houses were above the law. Rather it must lead to a democracy, however narrow and limited. The Royalists insisted that this conclusion was the only one possible. They stirred up class feeling in the parliamentary ranks; they undoubtedly began to teach men to distrust the arbitrary power assumed by Parliament. From 1642 to 1645 Englishmen were continually irritated by Parliament's absolutist claims and practice. At the same time, they were reminded that there were excellent arguments against an absolute Parliament—arguments based on the laws of nature and the fundamental laws of the land.

NOTES

I. The Juridical Function of Parliament

I have reserved to this note a few significant utterances by parliamentary leaders on the judicial power of Parliament. Instances in which Parliament is termed a court are frequent enough. "This great and high Court," said Sir Harbottle Grimston in his Guild hall speech, January 6, 1641/2, "is not only the powerfullest of all other Courts whatsoever . . . . ". E. 200 (5). Instances in which the typical function of Parliament is described in terms applicable to a court may occasionally be found also. "To remove therefore this uncertainty," wrote Henry Parker, "which is the mother of all injustice, confusion, and publike dissention, it is most requisite that this grand Councell and Treshault Court (of which none ought to thinke dishonourably) would take these *Ardua Regni*, these weighty and dangerous difficulties, into serious debate, and solemnly end that strife, which no other place of Judicature can so effectually extinguish." *The Case of Shipmony*, p. 2.

Pym's speech on the declaration of grievances, March 31, 1642, may be cited also: "That the house of commons considered that the law of God and the law of the land, was only fit for the representatives of the body of the kingdom to judge of; for if there must be idolatry against the law of God, it concerns them much to resist it, less they should incur the divine wrath; and nothing concerns them more than to see the laws of this kingdom executed: herein we may displease Man, we shall not God. For the Public Faith and League, it is less than that with God; we must respect the higher, and not the lower; no contract can oblige against the law of God, neither can any contract bind us against the law of this kingdom." *Parliamentary History*, II, 1163. The allusion is to the treaties with France, guaranteeing the queen liberty of worship.

It is very interesting to note that frequently parliamentary champions couple the offenses of bishops and judges as alike usurpations on the juridical power of the Parliament. Of the bishops, Nathaniel Fiennes said in a speech of December, 1640, on the canons of that year: "the framers of these Canons have assumed unto themselves a Parliamentary power, and that too in a very high degree, for they have taken upon them to define what is the power of the King, what the liberty of the Subjects, and what propriety he hath in his goods. If this bee not proper to a Parliament, I know not what is." He considered the convocation's action in prescribing an oath a usurpation of a parliamentary power higher even than the legislative; for this oath might bind individual Parliament members against altering a thing that Parliament had the right to alter. Fiennes's speech is in E. 196 (35). As to the judges, St. John in his argument before the Lords on ship money took the position that the judges in their opinion on ship money had reversed on the point of the king's power to overrule the known law a decision that Parliament had itself made in the Petition of Right; a lower court had had the presumption to reverse the decisions of a higher. Nalson, *An Impartial Collection*, I, 712. Other utterances on the action of the judges in the ship money case might be quoted. For instance, Harbottle Grimston said April 16, 1640, "and in the third year of His Majesties Reign that now is, we had more than a Confirmation of it [Magna Charta]; for we had an Act declaratory past; and then to put it out of all question and dispute for the future, His Majesty by his gracious Answer, *Soit Droit fait comme est desire*, invested it with the Title of *Petition of Right*. What expositions contrary to that Law of Right, have some men given to the undermining the liberty of the Subjects, with new invented subtil distinctions, and assuming to themselves a power, (I know not where they had it) out of Parliament to supersede, annihilate and make void the Laws of the Kingdom?" Nalson, I, 320. Waller in his speech on Justice Crawley's impeachment, July 6, 1641, said: "But this man, adding despaire to our misery, tells us from the Bench, that Ship-money was a Right so inhaerent in the Crowne, that it would not be in the power of an Act of Parlament to take it away. . . . so by this declaration of his he endevours to prevent the Iudgement of your Lordships too, and to confine the power of a Parlament, the onely place where this mischiefe might be redrest: . . . And because this man has had the boldnesse to put the power of Parlament in ballance with the opinion of the Iudges . . . " E. 198 (37), pp. 3–7. Lord Brooke ascribed to both judges and bishops a power of declaring law, but he distinguished it from the higher power in king and Parliament of making law. *A Discourse Opening The Nature Of That Episcopacie, Which Is Exercised In England,* Nov. 1641, E 177 (22), p. 29.

II. Parliamentary Applications of Political Theory before 1642

In the text of Chapter I it was necessary for the sake of brevity to omit any discussion of parliamentary arguments prior to July, 1642, that were based on political theory. However, before that year the parliamentary party had drawn arguments from principles of political science as well as from principles of constitutional law. One such principle was *salus populi suprema lex.* As early as September of 1640 Calybute Downing had hinted that Parliaments as well as kings might find useful the distinction between the rule of government and the rule of law. He reminded his hearers that as princes claimed not only *jura dominationis* but also *arcana dominationis,* so there were *arcana,* latitudes, allowed for the safety of the body of the state. The Commons ordered the sermon printed, though probably, if one may judge from the place in which Thomason bound it, not till the spring of 1641. *A Sermon preached to the Renowned Company of the Artillery,* E. 157 (4), pp. 29 ff.

To Strafford's avowed belief in the king's power to disregard the letter of the law for the sake of public safety in time of eminent danger, Pym retorted by assuring the Lords that the heinousness of Strafford's offense would best appear "if it be examined by that Law, to which he himself appealed, that Universal, that Supreme Law, *Salus Populi.*" "This," he continued, "is the Element of all Laws, out of which they are derived, the End of all Laws, to which they are designed, and in which they are perfected." Rushworth, VIII, 661. The author of *The Case of Shipmony* had agreed that *salus populi* was the "supreame of all humane laws, . . . for rather than a Nation shall perish, anything shall be held necessary, and legal by necessity." P. 7. Parliament itself gave the doctrine of *salus populi* official sanction when it justified the Militia Ordinance on the ground of its own right to interpret the law of England by the dictates of public safety.

The parliamentary party in the early days of the Parliament was the more cautious in supporting their position with arguments drawn from the law of God and the law of nature because both had been industriously used to support the unwarrantable extensions of prerogative power. Not only had the judges in the matter of ship money affirmed the right of the king, in the case of a great and declared necessity of which he was judge, to override the ordinary laws of the kingdom, but Banks in his argument on ship money had declared this right so inherent in the king that it was not derived to him from the people, but had been reserved to him when positive laws first began. "All Magistracy," he said, "is of nature, and Obedience and Subjection is of nature; and before any positive Laws were written, or any municipal Law, people were governed by the Law of Nature." The obnoxious canons of 1640 declared that "Tribute, and Custome, and Aide, and Subsidie, and all manner of necessary support and supply, be respectively due to Kings from their subjects by the Law of God, Nature, and Nations." Rushworth, II, 548; *Constitutions and Canons Ecclesiasticall.*

The parliamentary party, therefore, generally eschewed the doctrine that the law of nature was more than a very general principle governing the relations between people and prince. They relied on the more definite "laws of the land." "The Law of Nature," says Henry Parker in *A Discourse Concerning Puritans*, "best determines, that all Princes being publike Ministers for the common good, that their authority ought to be of sufficient latitude for that common good; and since Scripture is not expresse concerning that latitude, as to all people, the same not being to all alike necessary, the severall Lawes of severall Countries best teach that certaine latitude." P. 4. Parker regarded the book in which Samuel "wrote the manner" of Saul's kingdom as possibly the constitution of the Jewish monarchy; unfortunately it had not survived!

Fiennes voiced the Parliament's distrust of ecclesiastical applications of the law of nature. "But there was somewhat in it that these Divines aimed at, I suppose it was this. If Kings were of Divine Right, as the Office of a Pastour, in the Church, or founded in the prime Lawes of Nature, as the power of a Father in a Family; then it would certainly follow, that they should receave the fashion and manner of their government, onely from the Prescript of Gods Word, or of the Lawes of Nature, and consequently if there be no text neither of the Old nor New Testament, nor yet any Law of Nature, that Kings may not make Lawes without Parliaments, they may make Lawes without Parliaments, and if neither in the Scripture, nor in the Law of Nature, Kings be forbidden to lay taxes or any kind of impositions upon their people without consent in Parliament, they may doe it out of Parliament. . . . (Sir) if they bee due by the Law of God and of nature, they are due, though there bee no act of Parliament for them, nay (Sir) if they be due by such a right, a hundred acts of Parliaments cannot take them away, or make them undue." E. 196 (35). True, Fiennes later himself pronounces the "Et Cetera Oath" against the laws of nature.

Of course the parliamentary champions prior to 1642 did not rely solely on the fundamental laws as they stood revealed in common-law precedents. Some theory of the origin of government, which afforded a historical background for these precedents, must from the beginning have been in their minds. Only indistinct traces of it can be found. In 1641, St. John had spoken of the laws of the realm as "instituted at the first, and freely assented unto, and chosen by their Ancestors, for preservation of themselves, and us their discendants in our persons, lives, and estates." *The Speech or Declaration Of Mr. St. John*, E. 196 (1).

Pym in his speech against Strafford had held up as particularly heinous among his offenses his declaration that Ireland as a conquered nation was under absolute subjection; for, as England had been conquered, the same reasoning was applicable to it. If the various compacts between conqueror and conquered, by which the conqueror's might had been transformed into the king's lawful right were at the mercy of the king's whim, the subjects were not only deprived of their legal safeguards, but were also reinstated in their old right of resistance to the conqueror. Rushworth, VIII, 662.

III. Parker's Doctrines

The comparison of Parker's political philosophy when stated in terms of parliamentary absolutism with his doctrine of the supremacy of the civil power over the ecclesiastical will be instructive.

The True Grounds of Ecclesiasticall Regiment, published by him in November of 1641, is throughout a splendid glorification of the majesty and sufficiency of power—of the coercive might of civil government in contrast with ecclesiastical. Parker will allow no division of supreme power between church and state. Churchmen can show no grant of legislative power, either from God or from the assent of the body of the Church itself. Even God had not imposed his law upon his people through Moses without their consent. No churchman, says Parker, can anywhere find warrant for a power of coercion similar to that with which the members of a civil society have endowed their rulers. Above all, there can be no power in the Church to discipline civil rulers. The glory of the civil power is its origin in the consent of the people. Before the full majesty of the king, sitting in Parliament and therefore invested with that supreme power that the people had not granted even to the king himself alone, Parker stands in awe. Indeed he is almost pagan. He sweeps away all apostolic precedents with the remark that temporary expedients were necessary when the magistrates were not Christians; and he considers that if Caesar had aided the early Christian church, he would have effected more for the propagation of Christian doctrine than all the apostles, bishops, and evangelists! E. 176 (18), pp. 24, 36–38, 61, 72, 91, 92.

While on the subject of Parker we may notice a pamphlet, very possibly written by him, and designed to stir the Houses to a decided stand on their sovereignty. The title is *A Discourse betweene A Resolved and a Doubtfull Englishman*. Dec. 3, 1642, E. 128 (41). Apart from the matter, the sole evidence for Parker's authorship is that in format the tract is identical with some of his signed works.

The resolved Englishman in the course of the discourse vigorously disclaims any negative voice in the king as absurd and unbearable. The king was merely the highest magistrate, and the Parliament oversaw, disposed of, and displaced *all magistrates* (p. 2). Doubtful retorts that at any rate the Parliament calls itself the king's great council, and what are private men to do in such a case but to believe it and to obey the king if his commands and those of Parliament clash? "To my minde now," says Resolved, "I see some reasons inducing the Parliament to use such low expressions, and humble tearmes . . . . One reason may be the long disuse of the Parliamentary power, occasioned by a strong hand borne over them by the King, and most of his Predecessours . . . . so that now in our present age, men esteeme of the Parliamentary power, iust as Kings would have them . . . . Though no man can deny these things [the supremacy of Parliament] to be iust and reasonable, yet when they are spoken to the people, they grow angry, and are offended, and thinke it to be no lesse then treason; and therefore I conceive the Parliament ih their addresses unto the King have used such language as you have recited . . . . I have observed the Parliament have revealed their power but by degrees, and only upon necessity, that necessity might make the people know that that power was iust and reasonable." Doubtful, who appears to speak for the author, replies that when Parliament by sound reasons shall show it is the supreme power, and bound only to observe the supreme law of the people's safety and declare the position "not to be argued against by any condition of men whatsoever, upon the highest punishment. Then shall you see that I, and such as I am, will as readily comply with their commands, as you, or any the most Religious man in the Kingdome."

As a friendly criticism of Parliament's policy the *Discourse* is of great interest.

CHAPTER II

THE ECCLESIASTICAL SUPREMACY OF PARLIAMENT
VERSUS THE LAW OF GOD, 1642–1646

THE earlier constitutional position of the Long
Parliament was not the only source from
which the Levellers might have drawn a reverence
for paramount law. The Levellers generally were
Independents; and by 1645 the Independents were
the recognized advocates of the idea that there was
a supreme law in the ecclesiastical world, past the
power of Parliament to override. Independency,
as *par excellence* the ecclesiastical system of paramount law, gave both form and content to the
Leveller platform.

It is important, therefore, to understand exactly
what opinions on church government distinguished
the Independents from their contemporaries. The
ecclesiastical controversies surrounding the work
of the Westminster Assembly offer a mine of valuable material for this purpose. That Assembly, it
will be remembered, was called by Parliament in
1643 to substitute a new church government for
episcopacy. It drew up a Presbyterian model that
met strenuous opposition from the few Independent
members of the Assembly, finally passed the Parliament in such weakened form as to be disappointing
to the Presbyterians, and in the event never went
into effect. An analysis of the struggle over the
Assembly's proposals will reveal the distinctive

ideas of the Independents and, more important still, the political and constitutional conclusions and analogies to which they naturally led.

The exact distinction between Presbyterians and Independents in 1643 appeared in their definition of a church—their designation of the body which should judge, censure, and excommunicate professing Christians.[1] In theology the Presbyterians and the Independents of the Westminster Assembly and New England were alike orthodox Calvinists. They were alike in that each considered his ecclesiastical system ordained by Scripture and therefore of divine right; they differed only as to which system was *jure divino!* The Independents believed that the government of the church as above defined rested solely with the officers and members of the individual congregation—the unit in which Christians enjoyed the administration of the "ordinances" of preaching, the Lord's Supper, and baptism. The Presbyterians on the other hand considered the church for purposes of government to be an assembly of the elders and officers of the various congregations in a district or a nation.[2]

---

[1] The proposition over which there was the fiercest debate in the Westminster Assembly was, that a presbytery (the term is used both by Independents and Presbyterians in the sense of an assembly of elders) might be over several churches or congregations. It was debated February 2–March 13, 1643/4. John Lightfoot's notes of the assembly debates, in his *Works* (1823 ed.), XIII, 131 ff. (This is hereafter cited as "Lightfoot".)

[2] The Scotch commissioners who sat in the Assembly went so far as to admit that the elders of a particular congregation could transact business of that congregation. According to Robert Baillie, one of their

No other comprehensive distinction between the two polities can be made. For instance, without numerous qualifications, the statement that Presbyterianism was aristocracy and Independency democracy is inaccurate. At least it would not hold good for the five Holland ministers who championed Independency in the Assembly,[3] or for John Cotton and the New England divines who took part in the pamphlet controversies of the time. Robert Browne, the Separatist, it is true, had devised a church order that internally was a virtual

number, they later regretted this concession. Baillie, *Letters and Journals*, II, 182. (Cited hereafter as "Baillie".)

The Presbyterians and Independents were in substantial agreement in their enumeration of church officers. The Independent pastor and teacher found their counterpart in the preaching elders and doctors of the Westminster Directory. Independent and Presbyterian agreed in the designation of a lay elder or ruling elder to bear rule over the congregation in association with the elders who "labored in the word and doctrine." The Independents of the Assembly insisted that by Scripture the duties of teacher and pastor should be exercised by distinct persons. The Assembly rejected this proposition as far as it was based on divine right, but admitted the excellence of the distinction in practice. Baillie, II, 110. The Presbyterians themselves were divided on the point of the divine right of the ruling elder. Nye, one of the Independents, tried to base the office on grounds of human expediency. Lightfoot, pp. 60-69, 73. Shaw (I, 161) is scarcely right in saying the Independents opposed the institution of ruling elders *jure divino*.

[3] The five Holland ministers had been pastors of exiled English churches that had found refuge in Holland before the downfall of the Laudian system. There the ministers had worked out a congregational form of church government. They were Thomas Goodwin (to be distinguished from John Goodwin who was a radical Independent, suspected of Socinianism), Sidrach Simpson (to be distinguished from a certain "Symson the Antinomian" against whom the Commons later found it necessary to proceed for unlicensed preaching), Philip Nye, William Bridge, and Jeremiah Burroughs.

democracy. But in 1643 the Independents disclaimed the name of Separatists or Brownists, and
professed to steer a middle course between democracy and the supposed aristocracy of the Presbyterian system. Actually the Independents colored
with a tinge of democratic doctrine much undemocratic practice.[4]

In practice there could be but little difference in
the real power enjoyed by the membership of
Presbyterian and Independent congregations. The
Independents hedged about with restrictions the
right of the congregation to elect its officers.[5] True,
they taught that business should be transacted and
expulsions performed by the officers in the presence of the congregation; but actually they permitted the congregation only to assent to the decrees of its officers; or at most respectfully to reason with them and endeavor to convince them that
they did amiss.[6]   A New England congregation

[4] See Cotton's *Keyes of the Kingdom of Heaven*, p. 36 (reprint of 1852).
Cotton called the church government of New England mixed as having
monarchy in Christ's headship, aristocracy in the elders, and democracy
in the powers of the congregation. *The Way of the Churches Cleared*,
Feb. 9, 1647/8, E. 426 (8), p. 100.

[5] John Cotton in *The Way of the Churches Cleared* (p. 39), says that
a church has not power to choose whom it lists, but only whom Christ
has chosen. On such a point the pillars of the church are apt to have
a decided opinion!

[6] Cotton, in the *Keyes of the Kingdom of Heaven* (p. 52), says that the
elders may allow men to speak in the churches or put them to silence if
they speak amiss "and yet when the Elders themselves do lie under of-
fence, or under suspicion of it, the Brethren have liberty to require satisfaction, in a modest manner, concerning any public breach of rule."
See also *The Way of the Churches Cleared*, pp. 100, 102, and Thomas
Goodwin in Lightfoot, pp. 151–152.

exerted little more influence on the policy of the church than it would have done under a Presbyterian system.

Nor can it be said that Presbyterianism was synodical and Independency non-synodical. The Independents admitted the excellence of synods made up of the elderships of the various churches of a neighborhood; and these synods could and did advise individual churches on many points connected with their internal affairs, and that in an age when advice from an authority was in practice equivalent to a command. Synods could suggest expedients calculated to bring order to a distracted congregation, even to the expulsion of a member. And if the congregation refused to act on such "advice" the synod could recommend to other churches that they forbear communion with the offending church. The Independent synod could pronounce finally on matters of doctrine. It could not excommunicate or censure as a Presbyterian synod or assembly could, but it could recommend these measures to the congregations.[7] It could not perhaps denounce contumacious conduct to the magistrate for punishment; but in a land

---

[7] Baillie (II, 147) states that the Independents would admit a presbytery (here of course the word is applied to a synodical assembly) to be an ordinance of God, and capable of calling elders or ministers or any persons in its jurisdiction before it to examine and rebuke them for offenses in doctrine and life; and if need were, capable of turning them over to the civil magistrate. Cotton would not have gone so far. According to Baillie the Independents would even admit a synod's power of declaring doctrine.

like New England, where the magistrates were in sympathy with the established church order, synods met by permission of the civil authorities and acted in harmony with them.

If the Independents agreed, however, with the Presbyterians as to the lawfulness and expediency of synods, they dissented from the Presbyterian "subordination of assemblies." In a nationally organized Presbyterian church there was a succession of representative assemblies, the assembly of the classis above the session of the parish, the provincial synod above the assembly of the classis, and the national synod above all. Essential as such a subordination of assemblies was to the existence of a national church of Presbyterian type, it could not easily be deduced from the New Testament. The Presbyterians, therefore, were forced to defend it as agreeable to the light of reason.[8] The Independents condemned this hierarchy of assemblies as not only dangerous to the civil government, but also unwarranted by the

[8] The proposition of the Assembly regarding synods is here given in part. It illustrates the caution with which they handled this part of their system. "It is lawful, and agreeable to the Word of God, that there be a subordination of congregational, classical, provincial, and national assemblies; that so appeals may be made from the inferior to the superior, respectively. Proved from Matt. xviii, which holding forth the subordination of an offending Brother, to a particular church; it doth also, by a parity of reason, hold forth the subordination of the congregation, to superior assemblies. And it is agreeable to the light of nature . . . ." Benjamin Hanbury, *Historical Memorials relating to the Independents*, II, 496. For the answer of the Independents see pp. 497 ff. Herle, in the *Independency on Scripture of the Independency of Churches*, argues similarly. Summarized in Hanbury, II, 168.

complete and perfect law that Christ had laid down for his church.[9]

The Independents based their whole ecclesiastical procedure on the words of Matthew, xviii: 15–17, "Moreover if thy brother shall trespass against thee, go and tell him his fault between thee and him alone; if he shall hear thee thou hast gained thy brother. But if he will not hear thee, then take with thee one or two more that in the mouth of two or three witnesses every word may be established. And if he shall neglect to hear them, tell it unto the church; but if he neglect to hear the church, let him be unto thee as an heathen man and a publican." In these few lines, the Independents said, Christ had bequeathed his church a supreme law for its form and government; and they claimed that the congregational system was the necessary consequence of the dictates of that law.

Since Christ's law required that the congregation have a part in censures and excommunication, the Independents were necessarily forced into narrower church membership than the Presbyterians. The Presbyterian system admitted to membership

---

[9] *Certain briefe Observations and Antiquearies: on Master Prins Twelve Questions* [Oct. 4,] 1644, E. 10 (33), p. 2. The argument is most used by the more radical Independents. Lilburne claimed that Christ by his death had abolished the national church of the Jews, and had left his own rules in its place. *An Answer to Nine Arguments*, E. 25 (7), p. 37, Jan. 17, 1644/5—written five years previously. In *Rash Oaths unwarrantable*, June 25, 1647, E. 393 (39), p. 14, Lilburne argued that God the Father had appointed his Son sole lawgiver for the Church, and that Christ had not been remiss in this duty. Lilburne concluded that impositions by earthly lawgivers were therefore anti-Christian.

any person neither ignorant of essential Christian doctrine, nor of a scandalous mode of life. The two tests were appropriate for a national church— a church which admitted to its communion all adult members of a nation, save such as she held back for discipline or instruction. To such communicants, however, the Presbyterian Church could not commit the powers of excommunication, ecclesiastical censure, and ordination; these it reserved to the synods and representative assemblies of the eldership. On the other hand, since the Independent Church had to allow its members a share in the "keys," it could admit to membership only persons giving satisfactory proof of their spiritual regeneracy; they must be saints, as the term was, persons distinguished in the community as living the lives of regenerate Christians.[10]

Such a restriction of church membership made necessary a device by which the saints in a community could associate together in church fellowship. The device which the Independents adopted was covenant. An Independent church began with a covenant of the future members, one with another and all with Christ, to walk together as a church. Each new member admitted by elders and congregation renewed this covenant, thereby subjecting himself to the spiritual censures of his fellow members, administered in accord with Christ's law. The covenant of an Independent church was its basic law.[11]

[10] See Note I on p. 84.

[11] "In an Independent congregation, all the members by free and voluntary consent have submitted themselves to the regulation and

The internal life of an Independent church was felt to be regulated by a law past the church's power to change. The offices of the church had authority by divine right inherent in them and beyond the power of the people to diminish. The eldership or presbytery in an Independent church had power coördinate with that of the congregation. The congregation could no more cast out the presbytery, or any member of it without the assent of the others, than the presbytery itself could cast out of the church the whole congregation. Independent ecclesiastical polity was a balance of authorities regulated by a supreme law.[12]

order of the whole body, or, (which is the same) of the major part of it; and therefore this body having received a lawfull power in a lawfull way, for the reiglement of her respective members, may lawfully exercise it according to the tenor and true intent of the delegation of it." John Goodwin, *Innocency and Truth Triumphing together*, Jan. 8, 1644/5, E. 24 (8), p. 6.

"The form of such a visible church, I conceive to be the relation which by their mutual consent, is raised between them for spiritual ends; by which it is that they have power of jurisdiction, and may and ought to 'judge' those 'that are within': which jurisdiction no man can, lawfully, be subjected unto but by his own agreement. The superiority of jurisdiction, either in things spiritual or temporal,—if it be not natural, as the paternal,—must be voluntarily subjected unto, or it is usurped and tyrannical; therefore to raise this relation, which gives a power of judging, there must be a voluntary submission of themselves one to another testified by some act, whether you will call it a covenant, or consent, or agreement, between fit members for such ends." *The Saints Apology*, 1644, quoted in Hanbury, II, 231. See also Cotton, *Way of the Churches in New England*, Apr. 4, 1645, E. 276 (13), pp. 1–4.

[12] Nye and Goodwin in their introduction to Cotton's *Keys of the Kingdom of Heaven opened*, p. 5. "And whereas this corporation consisteth both of Elders and Brethren . . . . His scope is to demonstrate a distinct and severall share and interest of power, in matters of common concernement, vouchsafed to each of these, and dispersed away

Yet Independency did not, like Presbyterianism, imply the existence of a ministerial caste. Among Presbyterians, the preaching elders of a presbyterial assembly set a new preaching elder apart for his work by the imposition of hands. The Independents on the contrary assigned the work of ordination to the congregation over which a minister was to preside. More significantly, they insisted that ordination must not be general, but should be to a specific work in a specific place. John Cotton, noted in England as the ablest of Puritan divines, was ordained teacher of the Boston church in New England by imposition of the hands of John Wilson, the pastor, and of Nowell and Leverett, the ruling elders.[13]

[among?] both by charter from the Lord . . . . He giving unto the Elders or Presbytery a binding power of Rule and Authority proper and peculiar unto them; and unto the Brethren, distinct and apart, an interest of power and priviledge to concurre with them, and that such affairs should not be transacted, but with the joynt agreement of both, though out of a different right." See also Lightfoot, pp. 151, 152, Feb. 14, 30, 1643/4. Oct. 30, 31; *An Answer to W. R.*, July 27, 1644. E. 3 [18], p. 14.

Bridge in the Assembly treated it as a *reductio ad absurdum* of presbyterial excommunication that if, as the Presbyterians argued, the congregation for this act of authority were represented in the presbytery, all power must be in the people originally, and derived by them to the presbytery. The argument of course is weak, but the attitude is significant. Lightfoot, p. 160, Feb. 16, 1643/4.

[13] The third of the three points on which the Independents in the Assembly dissented was, "that a single congregation has not all and sole power of ordination." Baillie, II, 247. Goodwin argued that a minister might not ordain in another congregation, for ordination was a jurisdictional power. Lightfoot, p. 125. Independents in argument habitually linked the powers of ordination and excommunication as being of the same nature and belonging to the same body. *Ibid.*, p. 129; *Winthrop's Journal* (1908 ed.), I, 52, 110.

Erastian is a word usually balanced with Presbyterian and Independent in the ecclesiastical controversies of the Great Civil War; but it is not easy to frame an exact definition for it. The term was one of reproach, and applied to a set of men temporarily united to carry a point of policy rather than to a party with a definitely drawn platform to exemplify. At best Erastianism stands, not for a platform of ecclesiastical polity, but for a determination that Parliament should set up a church government without being harassed by claims that this or that must of divine right be included.

An analysis of the word will help a little. Thomas Erastus was a contemporary of Calvin who had questioned the right of church officers to excommunicate. As excommunication was the coercive weapon of the church, acceptance of Erastus's doctrine implied the further admission that the civil state alone had coercive authority in religious affairs. In the Westminster Assembly a few Hebraists like Selden, Lightfoot, and Coleman defended this doctrine with a theory of the relation of church and state in the Hebrew nation; namely, that the two resided in the same body, and were indistinguishable. Applied to English conditions, this would mean complete control of the church by the state.[14]

---

[14] In the above definition of Erastianism I have followed Canon Henson in his *English Religion in the Seventeenth Century*, pp. 125 ff. In the Assembly Lightfoot and Coleman argued that the Jewish elders were as much civil as ecclesiastical officers. Lightfoot, pp. 76, 77, Dec. 8, 11, 1643. Selden suggested that excommunication was a civil process. *Ibid.*, p. 106, Jan. 8, 1643/4.

Probably only a few scholars could follow Selden's reasoning; but in so far as his conclusion implied the supremacy of civil power over the church it was welcomed by men having no desire to submit their lives to the control and censure of the clerical elderships that the Assembly sought to establish. Many of the members of the Long Parliament had read law in the Inns of Court while men still remembered Coke's championship of the supremacy of the common law against the claim of the canon law to be its co-ordinate. The same motives that led such men in 1640 into a war on the courts dispensing the canon law, led them in 1645 to oppose the Presbyterian attempt to impose on England a religious code claiming a higher authority than the assent of Parliament.[15] Presbyterian Robert Baillie, a Scotch commissioner to the Assembly, grouped Hebraist and common lawyer under the elastic term Erastian.

After gauging the underlying principles of the three groups, it will be seen that while the theories of both the Presbyterians and the Independents conflicted with Erastianism, the theory of the Independents was diametrically opposed to it. Erastianism demanded freedom for Parliament to legislate as it saw fit in ecclesiastical matters; and the Independents would be more unflinching than the Presbyterians in declaring such legislation worthless where it ran counter to divine law, because the Independents were more uncompromising in their

[15] W. A. Shaw, *A History of the English Church during the Civil Wars*, I, 237.

insistence on the divine right of their system, and the nullity of all ecclesiastical impositions not directly warranted by Christ's word.

At times, indeed, the Presbyterians endeavored to support certain features of their system, such as the subordination of assemblies, by arguments based on the law of nature and the analogy of civil government. Their Scripture proofs of such points were framed cautiously. "It is lawful and agreeable to the word of God." "It is agreeable to the light of nature." Presbyterians seemed at times to argue that the Presbyterian system was a system deducible from Scripture; not the only system so to be deduced. The Independents on the other hand clung stubbornly to the last proposition, saying that Christ had not been so remiss as not to leave his church a complete and perfect law. The Independents were, therefore, the logical defenders of fundamental law in the ecclesiastical world against the Erastian doctrine of parliamentary legislative supremacy.

The Presbyterian hierarchy of assemblies of clergymen was, however, the bugbear of both Independents and Erastians, though for different reasons. Erastians feared it because it erected in the state a spiritual government as elaborately organized as the civil, with offices that might maintain a political party, and with authority to inflict spiritual censures that were also social—such as suspension from the sacrament. Erastian writers disagreed as to whether this system would prove a spiritual tyranny over the nobles and gentry, or

a spiritual anarchy.[16] The Independents, on the
contrary, opposed Presbyterianism because it imposed more on the conscience than Christ had set
there. Again they returned to the idea of a complete and perfect ecclesiastical constitution or
supreme law bequeathed by Christ to his church.

Naturally, therefore, the Independents at first
sought Erastian support by depicting in vivid
colors the danger to civil authority to be expected
from the hierarchy of semi-clerical assemblies.
Men like Nye argued that the Presbyterian system
erected a state within a state; a state that claimed
its order to be of divine right, and therefore independent of the civil magistrate, save when the
highest ecclesiastical assembly bade him draw the
civil sword to cut off heretics, or to punish the contumacious.[17] Independency, they said, had no

[16] *The Trojan Horse Of The Presbyteriall Government Unbowelled*,
Sept. 1, 1646, E. 353 (1), p. 14; Marchamont Nedham, *The Case of
the Kingdom Stated*, June 12, 1647, E. 392 (13), p. 3; *The Cry Of A Stone*,
p. 16.

[17] Nye stated the case for the Independents of the Assembly, February
21,1643/4. Lightfoot, p. 168. "If a power over a power, then there
is one over that and another over that; till you come to subdue all the
people unto an ecclesiastical government commensurate to the civil.

"3. The ordering of the church by Christ is such as may be without
jealousy and suspicion: now power over power in the church extends
itself equal with the civil; for it is inconvenient to nourish such a vast
body in a commonwealth. Now this is, 1. As great as the civil. 2. It
is spiritual. 3. It is so immediately upon the conscience.

"If it cannot stand well for a great commonwealth to have as great
a body grow within it, then is it not to be endured; but, *ergo*.

"1. Look abroad, and nothing troubles men more than to think
whether the presbytery shall be set up '*jure divino*'. 2. That if it
be, it will grow as big as the civil.

"2. Where two vast bodies are of equal amplitude, if they disagree
it is nought; if they agree, it will be worse, one will closely be working against another." See also Lightfoot, p. 130.

such elaborate organization to rival the civil power.
It did not call in the civil magistrate to enforce the
decrees of the church.   Since the magistrate had
the power of the "first table," it was his duty to
put down heresy on his own initiative; and he
might seek instruction from the churches as to
what was or was not heresy.   But the declaration
of non-communion launched by a church against
a contumacious member, or against a contumacious
church by other churches was the supreme discipline that the congregational system knew; therefore it needed no assistance from civil authorities.

This Independent tenet necessarily led to a complete denial of the magistrate's power to punish
religious offenses.   In Massachusetts Bay magistrates could exercise control over the churches
because every magistrate was necessarily a church
member.   But how would Independent churches
fare when civil magistrates, without seeking their
advice, imposed upon them innovations on Christ's
supreme laws?   Could a magistrate be trusted
with a power that would permit him to do so?
On this dilemma the Presbyterians thrust their
opponents.   If the Independents claimed that their
system was *jure divino*, how could they leave it at
the mercy of a civil magistrate unchecked by the
presence of a national church?[18]   Logically there
was but one escape for the Independents.

---

[18] *Some Observations and Annotations Upon the Apologeticall Narration*, Feb. 29, 1643/4, E. 34 (23), p. 47; *An Answer to a Libell Intituled,
A Coole Conference*, Apr. 16, 1644, E. 43 (4), *passim*.   Massachusetts,
as illustrating Independency triumphant, was repeatedly cast into the

However, Independents did not frankly accept the dilemma till 1644. Then Roger Williams, a certain unknown supposed to be Henry Robinson, and John Goodwin,[19] a London minister of suspected orthodoxy, stated almost at the same time the doctrine of liberty of conscience. As Goodwin's statement attracted more attention in England than the others, and was a link in a contemporary English controversy, we may examine it briefly. Goodwin flatly denied that the Independents could assign the civil magistrates any direc-

teeth of Independency militant in England. As typical, see W. R. (William Rathband) *A Briefe Narration of Some Church Courses Held in Opinion and Practice in the Churches lately erected in New England*, Mar. 9, 1643/4, E. 36 (11), pp. 21, 34, 35, 43. Its custom of requiring the assent of magistrates and of the elders of other churches to the erection of new churches was approved as being virtual presbytery; while its heresies and schisms were adduced as proof that that Presbyterianism needed further development. A doleful letter from a Mr. Thomas Parker in New England afforded excellent material. *The True Copy of a Letter; Written by Mr. Thomas Parker . . . . touching the Government practised in the Churches of New-England*, Dec. 17, 1643, E. 33 (22). It came out in print on February 19.

[19] *The Bloody Tenent of Persecution for cause of Conscience discussed*, July 15, 1644, E. 1 (2); *Liberty of Conscience; Or, The Sole meanes to obtaine Peace and Truth*. It came out March 24, 1643/4, E. 39 (1). For the question of authorship see *English Historical Review*, I, 144; IX, 715; *M. S. To A. S. With a Plea for Libertie of Conscience in a Church way*, May 3, 1644, E. 45 (3), pp. 32, 34, 40, 41, 43, 53, 54, 57. The authorship of this is sometimes denied to Goodwin, but the internal evidence argues that he wrote it; further, against his own denial of authorship (*Innocencies Triumph*, p. 4.), we have the ascription of it to him by Prynne, *A Fresh Discovery Of some Prodigious New Wandring-Blasing-Stars*, Dec. 16, 1645, p. 4, by Thomas Edwards (*Gangraena* II, 31), and by Baillie. Goodwin's denial, moreover, in view of the literary practice of the day, is not to be taken too seriously.

tive power over the church. Such powers Christ alone was fit to enjoy; and the magistrate who sought to force the consciences of men by temporal might usurped Christ's prerogative. The quelling of heresy and schism was no excuse; for to crush them God had appointed his Word and ministry, and not the hand of man. A magistrate who drew the temporal sword to cut off those whom he thought spiritual offenders might be ill-fated enough to learn too late that he had warred against God. Goodwin trenchantly criticised the Presbyterian delegation of power to the magistrate, terming it merely a power to force the kingdom to obey presbyters in all things. In a later pamphlet he suggested that the unregenerate freemen who had elected the members of the House of Commons could give them no authority over the church, made up as it was of saints. Thereby he came nearer yet to a doctrine of complete separation of church and state.[20]

To this end had attacks on the Presbyterian state church led the Independents. Attacking, with Erastian arguments, the expediency of Presbyterianism, they had come to a position still more dangerous from the Erastian viewpoint; for divine right in a system of ecclesiastical anarchy was even worse than divine right in a system of spiritual tyranny. The Independents after advocating such an anarchy *jure divino* had to defend the divine right principle against Erastian attacks.

[20] *Theomachia*, Oct. 7, 1644, E. 12 (1), p. 49.

Since 1641, Erastian theories of parliamentary legislative supremacy over the church had been developing rapidly. The first months of the Long Parliament's work had seen attacks by its partisans both on the powers assumed by the episcopal hierarchy, and on the claims of the bishops that their powers were determined by divine right. Lord Brooke and John Milton had argued that episcopacy was an institution, not of divine right, but of human origin merely, and of very questionable expediency. They had condemned the episcopal assumption of divine right as a trespass on the regal power of the king. The redoubtable Smectymnuus had told the culprit bishops that by claiming episcopacy to be a divine institution, and not merely one ordained by the laws of the land, they destroyed all legal foundation for the office. Milton had believed that if the bishops' claims were allowed, all manner of encroachments on the rightful powers of king and Parliament would follow. The king would be subject to excommunication; Moses's staff must bow before Aaron's rod.[21] Apart from these dire imaginary consequences of admitting a divine right in episcopacy, the Parliament, it will be remembered, had considered that it had at hand

---

[21] Brooke, *A Discourse Opening The Nature of That Episcopacie, Which is Exercised in England*; John Milton, *Of Reformation in England, The Second Book, Prose Works* (1834 ed.), pp. 16, 18; *An Answer to a Booke Entituled An Humble Remonstrance . . . . by Smectymnuus* (Stephen Marshall, Ed. Calamy, Thos. Young, Mathew Newcomen, William Spurstow), Feb. 1640/1, E. 161 (4), p. 66. See also *Certaine considerations*, Jan. 1641/2, E. 131 (17); *A Pack Of Puritans*, June, 1641, E. 208 (1), p. 46.

enough specific instances of the evil effect of ecclesiastical encroachments on the civil power—the canons, the "Et Cetera Oath," the abuses of the ecclesiastical courts. Henry Parker, in a pamphlet of 1641, had allowed but a narrow extent of legislative power to the church—a power of framing canons and ecclesiastical regulations that would take the force of law only from the assent of king and Parliament.[22]

Such a doctrine indicated the course that the reaction against the Laudian system was taking. Men saw the danger of allowing ecclesiastics to force on the kingdom a church government, doctrine, and ceremony to which all must conform; but they did not propose to avoid the danger by separating church and state; rather they assigned to the civil authority the power they refused to the ecclesiastical. If the church was to be reformed, it was the duty of the civil power to reform it according to the Word of God; the civil rulers might, perhaps must, obtain the pronouncement of divines as to what the law of God was; but they themselves were judges of the sufficiency of the clergy's proofs for the lawfulness of their recommendations, and they themselves must give those recommendations the force of law. The whole course of the transactions between the Parliament and the Westminster Assembly accorded with this theory. The civil authority had the right to frame legislation for the church, according to what it

[22] *The True Grounds of Ecclesiasticall Regiment*, pp. 81, 91-94.

believed was the command of the Scriptures interpreted in the light of reason.[23]

It was ominous that this principle was challenged as early as 1641. The House of Commons had on May 3 commanded the taking of a protestation to defend the "true reformed Protestant religion expressed in the doctrine of the church of England" against all popish innovations. Henry Burton, in *The Protestation Protested*, put a high interpretation on this oath and warned those who took it that they incurred a heavy obligation; for, while so many things of a popish flavor remained in the liturgy, discipline, government, and ceremonies of the Church of England, a man taking the Protesta-

[23]There was the possibility of bishops having a place in the House of Lords to resolve questions of religion. Of course the whole trend of Puritan thought at the time was in the direction of a church government founded on the Word of God, and no longer bound by the assumed power of the Church to decide on matter of indifference. Brooke thinks he has proved on philosophical grounds in his *Discourse* that nothing can be regarded as indifferent. Milton in his writings calls for a reformation of the Church according to Christ's commandments. *The Reason of Church Government, Works*, pp. 30, 46.

There is a pamphlet of Apr., 1642, E. 142 (19), *A Discreet And Judicious Discourse Betweene Wisedome And Pietie, Two worthy Members. Wherein is Declared the Power and Iurisdiction of Parliaments in their proceedings, and in the alteration of Church Government.* In it the question is asked: "But may a State Politique and Civill change the government of the Church, and establish a new forme of governement in the same, without advice of a Councell or Synod of Divines, that are grave and learned, elected and chosen out of every County of the Kingdome, and their consents to the change of government in the church?" The answer is, that while it cannot, it may choose the divines; and that no decision of such a synod is binding without assent of king and Parliament.

See also Thomas Fuller, *A Sermon of Reformation*, July 27, 1643, E. 36 (8).

tion might easily find himself conforming to that
which he had sworn to destroy. Burton's definition of popery was a broad one—anything imposed
on men's consciences in the way of rites, ceremonies,
or government that was not directly warranted by
God's Word. He anticipated a possible objection,
that the things in the Church of England to which
he took exception were established by acts of Parliament, with a startling doctrine: an act of Parliament directly contrary to God's Word was *ipso
facto* null, void, and of no effect.[24]

Of course such teaching was sure to call forth
protests. On July 10 the House of Commons committed the printer of the pamphlet, and a year
later one of the king's declarations cited the pamphlet as an example of the seditious writings that
Parliament permitted to circulate.[25] John Geree
replied to Burton in *Vindiciae Voti*, admitting
guardedly the validity of Burton's position, but
insisting that even if a law were contrary to the

---

[24] "For Popery (wee know) is Anti-christianisme. And Anti-christianisme is an opposition to Christ, so as this imposition upon the Conscience
is an opposing and overthrowing of Christs Kingly Office, who is the
sole King and Lord over the Soule and Conscience; an office incommu-
nicable to any Creature, or Power in Heaven or Earth. Whereupon
John saith, Who is a Lyar, but he that denyeth that Iesus is the Christ,
He is Antechrist. Now to deny Iesus to be the sole annointed King of
his Church, is to deny him to be the Christ. And he that sets up man
as Lord over the Conscience in prescribing and imposing what service
of God hee pleaseth of humane invention, denyeth Iesus to bee the
Christ, to wit, to be the sole King of his Church, who is the Sole Lawgiver to the Common-wealth of Israel, in his spirituall Kingdome." P.
6, E. 158 (14).

[25] Husband, p. 126. The king's answer to the petition presented to
him March 26. *Commons Journal*, II, 205, 269.

law of God it was not, politically speaking, void. Rather it was the duty of all to refuse to conform to it and to submit passively to whatever penalties followed. Both Geree and Bishop Hall declared in their answers that the civil authority must be the judge as to whether a thing were contrary to God's Word.[26]

A further answer to Burton was necessary from the point of view of men who hoped for the establishment of the Scotch Presbyterian church government. They could not reduce their whole ecclesiastical system to a single proposition based on the words of Christ, as the Independents based their proposition of government by the congregation on "Tell it unto the Church." The assertion that the imposition of any ecclesiastical form not warranted by Christ's words was null and void endangered their whole position. Accordingly, Thomas Edwards, a minister who later developed an unusual gift for the collection and arrangement of scandalous gossip, took up the cudgels against Burton. In arguing for the existence of a power in a synod to establish "rules for convenience," in addition to the outline of church government laid down in the gospels, Edwards almost adopted the bishops' old claim of authority to prescribe rules in "things of indifference."[27]

[26] E. 170 (8 & 9). The title of Hall's book is: *A Survay Of That Foolish, Seditious, Scandalous, Prophane Libell, The Protestation Protested,* 1641, E. 164 (8), p. 9.

[27] *Reasons against the Independant Government of Particular Congregations: As also against the Toleration of such Churches,* E. 167 (16), pp. 12, 18. It came out in August of 1641.

The issue between Erastian and Independent was joined again in 1644. William Prynne had sniffed the pamphlet battle between Presbyterian and Independent from afar; and he was soon in the thick of it. IIis first pamphlet was written in a lofty vein. He had no leisure to debate the unhappy differences on church government, but at the entreaty of some reverend friends, he had proposed Twelve Considerable Serious Questions which apparently he thought would convict the Independents of error and restore peace. Prynne never wrote a book that could not to advantage be condensed, and his comparatively short questions can be reduced to this proposition: Every nation must have the right to settle a form of church government in accord with its institutions, so long as the form is not repugnant to God's Word—for a complete church government is not to be deduced from Scripture. Therefore, if Parliament and the national synod set up such a government, all are bound to obey it. Defending the Presbyterian model by departing from its pretences to divine right cannot have been vcry pleasing to Presbyterians of the type of Adam Stewart and the Scotch commissioners; but for the moment they could scarcely disavow Prynne.[28] The Independ-

[28] Prynne's *Questions* appeared September 16, 1644. E. 257 (1). Thomas Edwards took him gently to task for his Erastian tendencies in *Gangraena*, part I, p. 146. But by the time *Gangraena* came out (Feb. 26, 1645/6), Prynne's Erastian position on suspension from the sacrament—*Foure serious Questions*, Aug. 23, 1645, E. 261 (8)—had called forth Presbyterian protests.

"The truth is," wrote Goodwin, "that Mr. Prynnes opinion concern-

ents, on the contrary, engaged warmly, and Prynne was soon in his element.

In a second pamphlet published ten days after his first,[29] Prynne developed the reasons why Independent practice was incompatible with his general proposition. Independency, he argued, really involved setting the church beyond the control of the state. In his opinion the church, outside of the things positively ordained in the Word, was so much a state affair that there was no difference between a freedom to gather Independent churches, and a freedom to set up republics or independent political states throughout the nation. In view of the control that Parliament and king had exercised over religion, Independency seemed to Prynne a legalization of anarchy.

Passing over Prynne's minor proposition to deny his major, John Goodwin, in a brief answer to the Twelve Questions,[30] took the ground that Independency was of divine right. It was, therefore, he urged, fitting that the state's law be subject to Christ's rather than Christ's to the state's. Would

ing an Ecclesiasticall spirituall Jurisdiction in the Civill Magistrate, which yet is his grand notion in all that he hath written upon the subject of Presbyterie, overthrows the main grounds and principall foundations upon which the Doctrine of Presbyterie is built by all her ablest and most skilfull workmen." *Calumny Arraign'd And Cast*, Jan. 31, 1644/5, E. 26 (18), p. 44.

[29] *Independency Examined, Vnmasked, Refuted*, E. 257 (3).

[30] *Certain briefe Observations and Antiquaeries: On Master Prins Twelve Questions About Church Government*, Oct. 4, 1644, E. 10 (33), p. 3. The Thomason catalogue assigns this to John Goodwin who answered an attack on it under his own name. The pamphlet is sometimes assigned to Henry Robinson.

Prynne really submit to any form of church government Parliament should set up—even episcopacy?
Prynne replied[31] that if Parliament should set up
a government contrary to God's Word, men should
passively submit or suffer.   For his own part, he
had attacked episcopacy in the days before 1640,
because bishops had claimed to be by divine right
and had "innovated" against acts of Parliament.
While Parliament might have nothing to do with
matters of doctrine, it assuredly had everything to
do with church government.   Prynne refused to be
driven from his ground by the application of a
reductio ad absurdum to his major premise.

Prynne based on the law of nature a further
argument for submission to a church government
ordained by Parliament.   The law of nature, he
said, taught men submission to a central government in civil affairs; the same law might by analogy
be presumed to dictate submission to a central
church government.   Both Goodwin and Robinson
who here entered the lists answered that, on the
contrary, to force a man's conscience was against
nature.   Prynne's analogy, they said, did not hold
for two reasons.   First, Christ was sole lawgiver
for his church.   Second, such actions as a man
might be justly commanded by a civil magistrate
to perform were performable solely by the outer
man.   But an act of worship or religious observance
must have the assent of the conscience before the
body could perform it; and no civil government

---

[31] *A Fvll Reply To certaine briefe Observations* . . . . *By William
Prynne,* Oct. 19, 1644, E. 257 (7), p. 7.

could lawfully enact that a man's conscience must assent to this or that.

Robinson continued Goodwin's attempts to demonstrate the absurdity of Prynne's general proposition. His arguments recall Burton's position of 1641. If parliaments and synods might justly be disobeyed when they enjoined popish observances, and the people were judge as to when they did so, why might not the Independents refuse obedience to things they considered popish? Was it not sinful for the people to submit their consciences to be burdened by a majority vote? Was it not ridiculous for men to submit in advance to any religion a parliament and synod might impose on them, without waiting to be convinced of its lawfulness? If Parliament by a majority vote had power to establish religion, was not the same power inherent in those who chose Parliament? Would it not be absurd to allow the unregenerate such power? Was it not much simpler to deny the power over religion to Parliament at the outset, than to palter with these cases of conscience?[32]

[32] *Certaine briefe Observations*, p. 7. *An Answer to Mr. William Prynn's Twelve Questions*, Nov. 1, 1644, E. 15 (5), p. 9. "The selfe same Law of Nature, God, and rectified reason which instructed and warranted all Nations to subject themselves unto some publique forme of Civill government, obliging all persons and societies of men alike, which they conceived most advantagious, doth not warrant us to doe the like in Church affaires; because whatsoever civill action the Civill Magistrate requires, may be performed by the outward man, or else be expiated by penalty without taint of conscience: But the Church government as it aimes at, and regards the Spirituall service and performance, Joh. 4.24, so the punishments must have a Spirituall effect, Mat. 18.18, and cannot be undergone, or worke upon a mans spirit unlesse he will himself, neither may he be willing thereunto, unlesse he apprehend them to be according to Christs Goverment and Institution."

Robinson, it will be seen, had here reopened the troublesome question as to the scope of Parliament's power, and the right by which Parliament might claim it.   If Parliament literally represented the people that chose the House of Commons, Burton's argument was irresistible.   It could have been met only by reverting to the earlier theory that the three estates of clergy, barons, and commons sat supreme in Parliament, enjoying certain powers by custom and precedent.   Since the clerical element had been expelled from Parliament, it was no longer possible to regard the estates of the realm as figuratively represented there.

Meanwhile Prynne and Goodwin came to the point where the advocate of parliamentary absolutism and the advocate of divine right were at an *impasse*.   Prynne argued that it was none of Goodwin's business as a divine to prescribe limits to the powers of Parliament; to speak mildly, it was presumption.   Goodwin sarcastically retorted with the suggestion that Prynne deign to mark off the domains he was willing to concede to Jesus Christ as sole ruler; Goodwin professed himself ready to abandon all the rest to Parliament.[33]

The question at issue in 1645 between Prynne, Goodwin, and Robinson was theoretical; but the struggle then impending between Parliament and Assembly translated the Erastian and divine right theories into practical politics.   The Presbyterians had overcome the Independents in the Assembly

[33] Prynne, *Trvth Trivmphing over Falshood, Antiquity Over Novelty,* Jan. 2, 1644/5, E. 259 (1), p. 109; *Innocency and Truth Triumphing together,* Jan. 8, 1644/5, E. 24 (8), p. 64.

by force of numbers; they had drawn up for presentation to Parliament a church polity distinctively Presbyterian.   The doctrine that this polity was of divine right was tacitly accepted by the Presbyterian majority, and quietly opposed by the few Erastian divines.   Not till the summer of 1645 did the latter show their hand.   July 30, Thomas Coleman of the Assembly preached the monthly fast-day sermon before the House of Commons and stated the Erastian position.   He urged the House to establish as little church government *jure divino* as possible.   He warned it to be careful how it allowed government to be based as *jure divino* on the authority of insufficient or uncertain texts. He bade it lay no more burden on the shoulders of ministers than Christ had laid on them, and he held up as a horrible example the usurped powers of the Pope!   Coleman professed he could not see how two coördinate governments exempt from superiority or inferiority could be in one state; he could find nothing of it in Scripture!   He laid down as the proper rule of division: "Give us doctrine, take you the government."[34]   Such a challenge from the Erastians, delivered in the face of the House of Commons and of reading London, the Presbyterians could not decline.   George Gillespie, one of the Scotch commissioners, undertook the task of refuting Coleman's argument in a sermon delivered under similar circumstances a month later.

[34] *Hopes Deferred and Dashed*, E. 294 (14), pp. 24–27.   There was a clever sally in it directed at the growth of lay preaching.   Coleman thought if it were not checked "the issue may be, that one may bind his sonne prentice to a Cobler, and at seven yeares he may goe out free a minister."   Gillespie's answer is in E. 298 (12), Aug. 27, 1645.

At the same time that the existence of a division in the Assembly other than that of Presbyterian and Independent was thus revealed, the Presbyterian majority was drifting into open hostilities with the House of Commons. The actual collision was caused by the Assembly's insistence on the divine authority for the powers it assigned to the presbytery. Without a coercive power in the eldership capable of searching and controlling the private lives of men, the Presbyterian discipline was worth very little. That power was supplied in the authority of the elders to suspend the ignorant and the scandalous from the Lord's Supper. The House of Commons was disposed to limit this power in the elderships, either by limiting them to a specific list of offenses, or else by allowing appeals from the discretionary power of the elders to parliamentary committees or to local boards of lay commissioners. So limited, according to Baillie, the power of the presbytery was merely nominal.[35] The decisive battle for the Presbyterian discipline had to be decided at this point.

That battle dragged on for a year, with platforms and declarations from the Assembly, petitions from the Presbyterians in London, and what not. Its results need only be summarized. In June of 1645, the Assembly first advanced its claim of divine right for the power to decide on the sins that should bar from the sacrament. In the next March, it made a similar demand under circum-

[35] Baillie, II, 307, 320, 325.

stances that aroused the wrath of the House, and
made the Erastians confident of success in pushing
matters to extremes. Under Erastian tutelage,
the Commons responded with a series of questions
to be answered by the divines; the questions took
up point after point of the Presbyterian system,
asking if each were of divine right, and demanding
Scripture proofs for the answers, with the names
of the divines accepting or rejecting each answer.
The Assembly never answered the questions. With
the authorization by Parliament of a limited Presbyterianism, with a standing committee at Westminster to judge finally of "unenumerated offenses," the fruitful period of the ecclesiastical
controversy was over. For the time Parliament
had vindicated its right to supreme legislative
power over the church.

The organization of presbyteries and assemblies
began. The work dragged, the extreme Presbyterians trusting that some future alteration in the
military or political situation would give them all
they had asked. In few parts of the kingdom was
more than a perfunctory Presbyterianism set up.
Years of political and ecclesiastical confusion,
followed by years of the rule of Saints and Iron-
sides who knew not Gillespie and Edwards, ended
at last in the restoration of episcopacy. The
Presbyterianism that Baillie had hoped to see
erected, the close, compact series of ecclesiastical
assemblies with power to inflict spiritual censure
on all men in the kingdom; the Presbyterianism
that Erastians had feared because by divine right

it made church equal with state, and that Independents had feared because it set more on men's consciences than Christ had set there, never took root in England. It was contrary to the spirit of English institutions, and it could have been set up only by a strong and stable government.

The ecclesiastical controversy of 1641–6 supplied political ideas to the Levellers. In the first place, it left them with a dread of government's forcing the nation to conform to a state church, whether Presbyterian or Erastian. If we are to understand the full significance of the Leveller movement, we must imagine the fear of the intolerant Presbyterian hierarchy as always present in the minds of Lilburne and his followers. To understand the Levellers we must understand also their opponent.

The Independent contributions to the Leveller party creed did not stop with the dread of Presbyterianism. There were positive as well as negative contributions. First, we may consider a possible Independent influence on the general attitude of the Levellers toward civil and ecclesiastical progress. Some Independents at least believed that their system, in spite of the elements of fixity that it contained, implied continual progress toward perfection. In Presbyterian writings, such as the letter of the London ministers of January 1, 1645/6, one can detect the idea that the Presbyterians sought a static reformation rather than a dynamic; a reformation that with the adoption of the Assembly's model would attain perfection. A directly opposite point of view appears in an Independent satire written against the letter. It assigns as an additional reason why the London ministers oppose Independency that, "the Independents will ever bee looking for further light, and go on still in Reformation, and would carry the people along with them to grow in grace and in the knowledge of Jesus Christ . . . . by which meanes things will never be setled perfectly while the Church is militant, therefore Independency is a mischiefe to the Church."[36]

One corollary of Independent thinking has already been considered so fully that in this summary it need only be mentioned. Once the Independents understood the full implications of their system of church government, they could not logically permit any close relation between church and state, unless the state was itself a theocracy. If, as they believed, the proper material for the building of a church was saints, they assuredly could not admit magistrates chosen by the unregenerate to a directive voice in the church. That might be permissible in a system like seventeenth-century Presbyterianism that regarded a church as a national institution; but it was to the last degree inconsistent with Independency. As the theocracy of Massachusetts Bay disappeared, the doctrine of John Goodwin and Roger Williams that the civil magistrate had noth-

[36] *A Letter Of The Ministers of the City of London, Presented . . . . to the . . . . Assembly of Divines . . . . Against Toleration,* E. 314 (8); *Certaine Additionale Reasons To those presented in A Letter By the Ministers of London to the Assembly of Divines.* Jan. 15, 1645/6, E. 316 (10), p. 6.

ing to do with the offenses of the first table gained
general acceptance in New England. In England
the doctrine of liberty of conscience had the support
after 1645 of most of the radical Independents;
it was a fundamental article in the creed of the
Levellers.

The strength of democratic ideas in seventeenth-
century Independency has already been estimated.
Here it is enough to repeat that, while the practice
of Independency was undemocratic, it could supply
extremely democratic theories. Quoting from Nye
and Goodwin's introduction to Cotton's *Keyes:*

It [the power of church government] hath now in these our
dayes been brought so neare unto the people, that they also
have begunne to plead & sue for a portion & legacy bequeathed
them in it. The Saints (in these knowing times) finding
that the Key of knowledge hath so farre opened their hearts,
that they see with their owne eyes into the substantialls of
Godlinesse, and that through the instruction and guidance
of their teachers, they are enabled to understand for themselves such other things as they are to joyn in the practice
of. They doe therefore further (many of them) begin more
then to suspect, that some share in the Key of power should
likewise appertain unto them.[37]

The Levellers also succeeded to the ideas that
distinguished Independency from Erastianism. The
Erastians ascribed to Parliament the supreme power
of legislation for the church on the same principle
that had already led them to ascribe to it a similar
power over the nation. The Independents were in
line with Parliament's earlier constitutional position when they insisted that there were certain

[37] P. 2. See Note II on p. 85.

fundamental laws in things ecclesiastical that no earthly legislator could abrogate. The Levellers simply transferred the principle to politics when they pronounced Parliament bound not only by the ecclesiastical law of Christ, but also by the law of the land, the law of God, and the law of reason.

To be more specific, the Independent system gave to politics a clear model of an ecclesiastical body limited and regulated by law. Independency assigned by divine right certain powers to the church officers; it assigned other powers no less by divine right to the church members. In either case these powers were limited and bounded by the supreme law—call it "constitution" if you will— that Christ had ordained his church. Each congregation enjoyed definite powers as being "indowed with a Charter to a body politique to Christ." The legislation of any inferior lawgiver could not interfere with the rights enjoyed by officers and people under this supreme law; for, in comparison with it, such legislation would be null and void. The first check imposed on the claims of Parliament by its own supporters was imposed by the radical Independent pamphleteers. Further, there is a significant analogy between the Leveller Agreements of the People—constitutions intended to be perpetual because, as their framers believed, they were based on rules of reason self-evident to all rational men—and the congregational church system, unchangeable because founded in the rules of God's Word.

Finally, the Independents in prescribing a method whereby their fundamental law might be made binding on men, had evolved a new doctrine of compact. At the same time that they had admitted that the law of nature commanded men's subjection to civil authority, they had fixed on covenant as the sole source of subjection to ecclesiastical authority. If the magistrate had no authority over offenses of the first table, and if the church had no such authority outside of its own membership, its disciplinary authority over that membership must be traced to the compact and covenant by which each member on entering into church fellowship submitted himself to such deserved ecclesiastical censures as by Christ's law his fellow members might deem it necessary to inflict on him. Once the Levellers transferred this theory to politics, the doctrine of the social compact took concrete form.

NOTES

I. Alleged Independent Exclusiveness

The restricted circle of membership peculiar to Independent churches sometimes gave a flavor of Phariseeism to their institutions. The Presbyterian champions, Bastwick and Edwards, twitted the Independents with the aristocratic exclusiveness of their churches. No doubt there was very much ground for such taunts. Lord Saye, who was an ardent Independent, was by no means a democrat. A chief objection with him to episcopacy seems to have been that it allowed men of low social standing to rise to a plane of political equality with the great nobles. *A Speech of Lord Viscount Saye and Seale*, E. 198 (16), in Hanbury, II, 132. Lilburne in later days habitually refers to him as "that Guilded fox". A more honorable motive for the restriction of membership is to be sought in the despair of pious ministers imbued with the deepest Calvinism at the stolid self-complacency of the average communicant in the English parish, content with negative goodness, and sure of a future reward so long as he partook of the sacraments of the Church of England. The following quotation is from Robert Coachman in *The Cry Of A Stone*, Feb. 1641/2, E. 137 (32). "Whereas contrariwise, when all manner of gracelesse men are fed with the seales and pledges of Gods favour, and invested into the full privilege and highest prerogative with the most godly in the Church, and that it is daily told him, there is the body and blood of Christ given for him, how presumptuous doe they grow? . . . . Tell them of wicked men and damnation, they'll send you to Rome, or Turkie, or India, amongst the Heathens or Papists, for why? they are Protestants, and have a sound Religion, and are borne, baptized, and brought up in a Christian common-wealth and Church, and eate the flesh, and drinke the blood of Christ, in whom they say, they trust to be saved, though they never imitate his examples, but notwithstanding all their presumption, they have not stroke one true stroke at sinne . . . ." (P. 15.) Coachman had the fairness unusual among Puritans to protest against attributing such conditions entirely to the sloth and negligence of the bishops, or to the corrupting influence of the ceremonies.

II. Alleged Democratic Doctrine in Williams and Cotton

Hermann Weingarten, *Die englische Revolutionskirche* (p. 290) would appear to assign a greater priority among democratic doctrines than they deserve to certain statements by John Cotton and Roger Williams on the sovereignty of the people in *The Bloody Tenent of Persecution* (1848 ed.) p. 212. Cotton had said: "First, the proper means whereby the civil power may and should attain its end, are only political. . . . First, the erecting and establishing what form of civil government may seem in wisdom most meet, according to general rules of the word, and state of the people." Williams's comment is that by this the original of civil power lies in the people "whom they must needs mean by the civil power distinct from the government set up." Accordingly, Williams concludes, the people may set up a government intrusted with what power they will. However, there is nothing in the passage to show that he actually means more than Parker did by a similar utterance. He uses it as a *reductio ad absurdum* for the power of the civil state over the church. His gloss on Cotton is unfair. Cotton was writing a "Model of Church and Civil Power" to be sent to the church at Salem. This, and the fact that he prefixed to his statement the postulate that every member of the commonwealth was also a member of the church, should make it clear that his application was narrowed to the freemen of the Massachusetts Bay colony.

CHAPTER III

IN the summer of 1645, a few of the lesser members of the Independent party began to criticise certain actions of the House of Commons as contrary to the fundamental law of the kingdom. One particular action in question was the imprisonment of Lieutenant Colonel John Lilburne for his refusal to answer the questions of a parliamentary committee till he was sure his answers might not be made the basis of legal proceedings against him. The man in question on this occasion, as in many other events of his life, registered by his action a concrete protest against an illegal or inequitable act of the government.

Because Lilburne continually exemplified in his actions the political principles of his party, it is difficult to disentangle the Leveller movement from the personality of the arch Leveller. Our estimate of the Leveller principles naturally varies with our estimate of the man. What we know of John Lilburne's life and character is told us partly by his friends, partly by his enemies, but mainly by himself. The comparative weight we attach to these sources of information will determine whether we regard Lilburne as a knave ready to feather his own nest in civil disorder, a blustering braggard, unable long to agree with any set of men, or a crusader for principles to which he clings through revolutions generally swayed by factional or personal considerations. To establish the proper weight to be assigned to each of these three views, a knowledge of his career before 1645 is necessary.

John Lilburne was the younger son of a Durham family whose lineage traced to the fifteenth, perhaps even to the fourteenth century. Lilburne, though he might forget his gentle birth in his ordinary intercourse with men, had it ever ready for use as a weapon. Thus, when he was on trial in 1653, he told Barkstead that it was fitter for him to sell thimbles and bodkins than to sit in judgment on a person so much his superior.[1] Like many other younger sons, Lilburne was apprenticed in London sometime between his thirteenth and fifteenth year, about 1630. His schooling had previously progressed far enough to give him a little Latin and Greek, and this education he supplemented in London by reading Fox's *Martyrs* and the Puritan divines.[2] Almost to the end of his career his information was confined to a few narrow fields. But the quickness with which he assimilated such learning as he needed from time to time, and the critical judgment he brought to bear on it should have put to shame many of his contemporaries whose reputation for wisdom depended on the amount of their information rather than on the originality of their thinking.

---

[1] *Calendar of the Clarendon Papers.* II, 245.

[2] *Innocency And Truth Justified*, Jan. 6, 1645/6, E. 314 (21), p. 8. He mentions as authors in whom he had read: Fox, Luther, Calvin, Beza, Cartwright, Perkins, Molin, Burton, and Rogers. *Legal Fundamentall Liberties*, June 8, 1649, E. 567 (1), p. 25. The second edition is cited here and hereafter.

From Lilburne's reading in divinity, as one would infer, he adopted Puritan doctrine. After 1637 he drifted into Separatism, and into a kind of religious mysticism that in his later life contrasted strangely with the lucid quality of his political beliefs. Meanwhile as a youth he associated himself with the little group of men who were in bitter opposition to the bishops and their works; thus he became acquainted with John Bastwick, then a prisoner in the Tower, and with a certain citizen named Thomas Wharton, at whose request Bastwick had written his *Letany* against the bishops. According to Bastwick, Lilburne asked for a copy of the *Letany* in order that he might print it and raise by its sale a stock in trade for himself; for such books brought a price proportionate to the danger of handling them.[3] Lilburne's after life showed he could consider his private interests when they did not conflict with what he thought his duty to the public; and on this occasion it is not unlikely that he believed he was justified in making his profit on books that would further God's work. Whatever his motive, he crossed over to the Low Countries to arrange for printing Puritan books, first coming to an understanding with Wharton who circulated such prohibited wares.

Lilburne, soon after his return, fell into the hands of the archbishop's *pursuivants*. His examination before the king's attorney, which took place January 14, 1637/8, revealed to Lilburne that a friend

[3] *A Ivst Defence of John Bastwick*, Aug. 30, 1645, E. 265 (2), pp. 10-15.

whom he had trusted had accused him[4] of printing
ten or twelve thousand books in Holland, and of
receiving money for them from Wharton.

With his examiner Lilburne took a defiant tone.
He showed a marked unwillingness to answer questions, and denied all knowledge of the charge; finally
he protested that it was unwarrantable by the law
of God and the law of the land to examine him
against himself on matters other than those he was
charged with, and not confront him with his accuser.
Ten or twelve days later Lilburne was brought
before the Court of Star Chamber, and here
Lilburne speedily found many things in the court's
routine to which he could not conscientiously conform. He refused to pay the clerk his fees; he refused to take the *ex officio* oath that was used to
examine men on the charges against them, for "he
wished to be better advised of the lawfulness of it."
Wharton's conduct, when he and Lilburne were
summoned before the court for sentence, showed
where Lilburne had learned to be scrupulous
about oaths. He thundered out that the oath
of churchwardenship, the oath of canonical obedience, and the oath *ex officio* were alike against the
law of the land.[5] No court could very well brook
such contempt of its orders; much less a seventeenth-
century court; least of all one of the august composition of the Star Chamber. Wharton and Lilburne were fined five hundred pounds each, and

---

[4] Edmund Chillenden. *The Christian Mans Triall*, Dec. 1641, E. 181
(9), pp. 1–4, 12.

[5] *Christian Mans Triall, passim.*

Lilburne was sentenced in addition to be whipped from the Fleet Prison to Westminster, and to stand in the pillory.

Lilburne always welcomed an opportunity to stand forth before the people as the champion or the martyr of a cause. On this occasion he met his sufferings under the Star Chamber's barbarous sentence with his spirit exulting that he was permitted to suffer in the Lord's cause. It seemed to the boy that the various incidents of his punishment —the sympathy of the bystanders, the regret of the executioner at doing his duty with the whip—all summoned him to testify by his sufferings to the "rottenness" of episcopacy. Therefore, as he stood in the pillory, his back smarting from five hundred lashes, he undertook to prove to the onlookers that the bishops were popish in origin and authority. Until the Lords of the Star Chamber sent word to the warden of the Fleet to gag his prisoner, Lilburne exhorted an audience whose sympathy he had apparently won for his cause.[6]

The Star Chamber savagely testified to its anger at this new defiance of its authority. At a meeting the same day it decreed that Lilburne should be laid with irons on hands and feet in the part of Fleet Prison where the basest prisoners were kept; no one must be allowed to visit him or to supply him with money. Accordingly, even his surgeon on the morning after the punishment was refused admission to him. The boy's friends were compelled to send him his food through the poor men of the

[6] Howell, *Complete Collection of State Trials*, III, 1326–1340.

prison who lived on public charity and, when that means was cut off by the authorities, through another prisoner in the room above Lilburne's. When he was sick to the point of death his servants and friends were often not allowed to dress his wounds. On one occasion, to save himself, as he thought, from being murdered outright, he had to hold his room as a fortress by force of arms.[7]

The authorities had no punishment that could quell his courage. In May he was again examined as to his conduct in the pillory. His examiners only drew from him such bold language that they begged him to hold his peace and save himself. He challenged the bishops to dispute with him before the king, engaging himself to show their calling to be of the devil—a challenge that loses some of its ludicrousness when we consider the situation of the challenger. The spirit of his warfare against the bishops was dangerously infectious; and even at this stage in his career he had begun to show a power of moving the masses by speech or writing. When the attempt on his life was made, he circulated among the apprentices at their Whitsuntide holiday in Moorfields an appeal for succor. This, so Lilburne said afterwards, caused a riot against Laud among the apprentices that nearly saved the hangman a labor in the end. The crusader still, Lilburne reiterated his enmity to the bishops even while he begged the apprentices to petition the lord mayor to remove him to a prison where his life would be safer. "I would scorne to flie, for I am

[7] *Ibid.*, III, 1341, 1342, 1351, 1352; *Historical Manuscripts Commission Reports*, IV, 33; *Innocency And Truth Justified*, p. 74.

resolved by the might and strength of my God, for the honour of my King and Country, and the good of future generations, to fight it out so long as I have a legge to stand on, and to waige professed warre so long as I have drop of blood in my bellie: with the domestick and home bred enemies of the King and State for I have a Souldiers heart within my innocent breast."[8]

November 3, 1640, the day of the meeting of the Long Parliament, marked a turn in Lilburne's fortunes. On that day he presented a petition to Parliament, and was at once granted his liberty to "follow his petition," as the phrase was. May 4, 1641, the Commons voted that his censure and imprisonment were illegal, and that reparation in the form of damages was due him; but the Lords delayed concurrent action until December 1, 1645.[9] Meanwhile Lilburne supported the parliamentary party in London. He probably advanced his pecuniary fortunes a little, and at some time before 1642 he married Elizabeth Duell. She identified herself with her husband's political ideals, and worked loyally beside him to realize them.

At the outbreak of war, Lilburne entered the Parliament's army in the spirit of many other ear-

---

[8] *Come out of her my people*, p. 27. (1640, Guildhall); *Innocency And Truth Justified*, p. 74; *The Prisoners Plea for a Habeas Corpus*, Apr. 4, 1648, E. 434 (19). I have assumed that the petition that Lilburne quotes in this book in 1648 is the one that was distributed in Moorfields. Lilburne dates that given above May 10, 1639. The contemporary petition (Dec., 1640) of Catherine Hadley, who describes herself as Lilburne's servant, and complains of being imprisoned on suspicion of having distributed the paper, dates it May 28. *Historical Manuscripts Commission Reports*, IV, 33.

[9] *State Trials*, III, 1342–1346, 1358. They revoked his fine.

nest men, who outstripped the legal technicalities
on which Parliament called them to arms, and enlisted for the war as for the supreme struggle against
the powers of evil.   In the literature of the Great
Civil War a book like John Goodwin's *Anti-Cavalierisme*[10] represents the spirit of such men.   The
Independent bade his hearers remember that as
Englishmen they stood in defense of their property
and political liberty against the godless cavaliers,
Satan's last hope.   "If you shall hold out this one
impression and onset which they are now making
upon you, and make good the ground you stand on
against them; you shall breake their cords in sunder,
and cast their bands from you for ever; you shall
make such an entaylement of this pretious inheri-
tance we speake of, your libertie, to your children,
and childrens children, that they shall never be able
to cut off.   If they be but now broken, they are not
like ever to make themselves whole againe: if you
will be perswaded to be men of wisedome once, you
may be men of comfort and peace ever after."   Nor
did Goodwin believe that the godly as martyrs
were to conquer by patience.   Martyrdom, he said,
he did not think that God would use much longer
to advance his kingdom.   Goodwin's book pre-
serves to us the early hopes and aspirations of the
men who later molded the temper of the New
Model, and later still, some of them, claimed their
liberties by the Agreement of the People.

Lilburne, it may be imagined, possessed a double
portion of the spirit of Goodwin.   As a boy, sick

[10] Oct. 21, 1642, E. 123 (25), pp. 38–39.

and in prison, he had dared to proclaim himself a
soldier against the Lord's enemies, the bishops,
when they sat in high places; as a man he would
not be wanting at Armageddon. Furthermore, the
same motive that had led him to stand against the
bishops and the Star-Chamber process in 1637, and
against the king in 1642, led him in the later years
of his short life to stand against the arbitrary power
of Parliament itself. Without understanding what
that motive was, one cannot do justice to his career.
Lilburne considered his life dedicated to a crusade
against wrong, injustice, lawlessness, and tyranny
wherever found. That fact once understood, his
seemingly tortuous and capricious political course
becomes straight and consistent.

The events of Lilburne's military career can be
briefly told. He enlisted in Lord Brooke's regiment
of foot, fought gallantly at Edgehill, and as the sen-
ior officer present commanded the regiment in its
desperate defense of Brentford, November 12, 1642.
That defense held back the king's army till the parliamentary train of artillery at Hammersmith could
be removed to safety; but Brooke's and Holles's
regiments, which made the defense unaided, were
cut to pieces and Lilburne was carried prisoner to
Oxford. There the Royalists, after trying unsuccessfully to gain him over, put him on trial for high
treason, and accorded him the treatment of a prisoner of war only as a result of Parliament's threat
of retaliation.[11]

[11] *A Letter Sent from Captaine Lilburne, To divers of his Friends*, Jan. 3,

After his exchange he refused a government place in order to continue his crusade for England's liberty. He held commissions, first as major of Colonel King's regiment, then as lieutenant colonel of the Earl of Manchester's dragoons. In Cromwell's disputes with Manchester, Lilburne sided with Cromwell, becoming one of Cromwell's witnesses against the earl in 1644. He quarreled with both Manchester and Colonel King, and preferred charges of treachery, cowardice, and embezzlement against King to a Parliament committee. He laid down his command early in 1645, refusing to take the Covenant as the New Model Ordinance prescribed.

This is the Lilburne of 1645. Already a careful observer of his life can distinguish his salient characteristics. He has a powerful intellect that will take nothing on credit, but persists, with a keenness that compensates for narrow information, in analyzing for itself any political situation. A moral courage seconds his intellect, impelling him ever to occupy the post of danger in the vindication of a new idea; at the same time self-esteem makes him conscious that the eyes of all men should be on him in his post of danger and duty. Withal, he has an instinctive insight into the thinking of the plain people that puts a force defying analysis into his long pamphlets, with their overgrown para-

1642/3, E. 84 (5); *Englands weeping spectacle*, June 29, 1648, E. 450 (7), p. 5; Chillenden, *The Inhumanity of the Kings Prison-Keeper*, Aug. 4, 1643, E. 63 (17), p. 10; *Innocency And Truth Justified*, p. 65; *Legal Fundamentall Liberties*, p. 27.

graphs and unwieldy sentences; he has an oratorical skill that by use of capitals or what not can make the most rambling paragraph climax with a crack like a whip-lash. A power of bitter invective couched in language as clean as that of the cleanest contemporary pamphleteer and an absolute freedom from a sense of humor complete his equipment for appeal to the masses.

For politics he is hampered by a credulity that makes him too trustful of seeming friends, and too ready to forgive repeated treacheries, if only they be interspersed with professions of penitence. A declared enemy he pursues relentlessly.[12] His high devotion to principle pardons no man's deviation from it in deference to passing exigencies. These traits are accompanied by a more than passive willingness to receive what is justly his due. But the dominating trait in his character, ignored both by contemporary and modern biographers, is the spirit of a crusader for the public good; and, as he endeavors to convince his critics, the attainment of the public good is the motive of his life.[13]

When John Lilburne took up his abode in London at the conclusion of his military career, his temper and pursuits drew him into active political life.

---

[12] For instance, he assisted his old betrayer Chillenden with money when both were prisoners at Oxford. He was several times deceived by Cromwell's professions of penitence. On the other hand, he pursued unsparingly his attacks on Colonel King.

[13] Many of his pamphlets are biographical, written with this end in view. The most noteworthy exposition by another is in *England's weeping spectacle*, June 29, 1648, E. 450 (7). Interesting also is *The Just Defence Of John Lilburne, Against Such as charge him with Turbulency of Spirit*, Aug. 23, 1653, E. 711 (10).

He had business of his own before Parliament and its committees. He had to secure a settlement of his accounts which, according to the military system of the age, included disbursements for his command. He hoped also to induce Parliament to complete the series of acts necessary to give him reparation and damages for his Star-Chamber sentence; further, he had his charges to press against his former commander, Colonel King. Moreover, he was already closely identified with the London Independent faction, out of which developed within a few months of his retirement from the army the more radical party that was the parent of the later Leveller organization.

The political distinction between Presbyterians and Independents, and the beginnings of an Independent party date from 1641. Soon after the Long Parliament had assembled, old school Puritans or Presbyterians began to be alarmed at the growth of Separatism. By August of 1641 Separatist meetings, and preachings by inspired tradesmen were common enough to call forth satires.[14] Meanwhile Independents of a more respectable type according to the world's estimate were trying, not unsuccessfully, to ingratiate themselves with Parliament. The Independent lords joined with thirty of the commons to write to New England asking that Cotton, Hooker, and Davenport might attend the Assembly of Divines.[15] Though the New Eng-

[14] Such are in E. 158 (1), E. 160 (23), both by John Taylor; E. 172 (11), *The Brothers of the Separation*; E. 180 (25), *The Discovery of a Swarme of Separatists*.

[15] *Winthrop's Journal*, II, 71.

land Independents did not appear, the Assembly contained men of their way of thinking. In the fall of 1643 the Assembly found in its midst certain men of unblemished orthodoxy who protested when it endeavored to put a check on the "gathering of churches," i.e. the forming of new congregations after the Independent model with members drawn from the old parish churches. Many such churches had been formed, notably by the five Holland ministers; they had grown up everywhere around prominent Independent preachers. December 22, 1643, when the Assembly finally issued a recommendation that no more of these churches should be gathered, the Independent members blocked a further proposal that the churches already gathered be disbanded.[16]

The undoubted respectability of the more aristocratic Independents protected a host of heretical opinions among the baser sort. In May, 1644, Baillie mournfully testified that Manchester's army was so full of Anabaptists, Antinomians, and Independents that he feared lest they corrupt the Scottish army on its arrival in England.[17]   June 7,

---

[16] Lightfoot, p. 92.   Edwards in 1646 enumerated seven Independent churches as having existed three years; apparently there were many more in 1646. *Gangraena*, II, 16.   Edwards meets the Independent attacks on the greed of the Presbyterian clergy by enumerating the rich plural lectureships held by Independents.   *Ibid.*, I, 71 ff.

[17] Baillie, II, 185.   When Lilburne joined King's regiment, by his own account he had done much to compose dissensions between King and the soldiers and townspeople of different religious persuasions—dissensions aroused by King's intolerance.   *The Iust Mans Iustification*, June 6, 1646, E. 340 (12), p .20; *Innocency And Truth Justified*, p. 42.   Bastwick's version was that Lilburne by his preaching of separation had caused

he attempted a dispassionate estimate of the relative strength of parties. He took comfort from the fact that the regular parish ministers of London with the exceptions of John Goodwin, Burton, and one "scrupling Paedobaptism" were sound Presbyterians. But he added the mournful fact that many of the lectureships were held by Independent ministers. Further, he thought he could see the leaven of Independency at work. Most of the Independents, he wrote, were lapsing into Antinomianism, Anabaptism, Socinianism and other heresies;[18] and "one Mr. Willams" had led off a part of the remainder into a new and extreme Independency.

Against heresy the House of Commons waged an intermittent warfare. In March it ordered prepared an ordinance against the dissemination of Antinomian and Anabaptist opinions. August 9 it voted that "one Williams his Books, intituled etc. concerning the Tolerating of all Sorts of Religion" were to be publicly burned. It set a committee at the task of considering means of checking the obnoxious sects.[19] November 15 the Commons ordered that no person who was not ordained in some reformed church should be allowed to preach—an ordinance aimed at the "mechanic" preachers who throve in both city and army.[20]

divisions all up and down Lincolnshire. *A Ivst Defence of John Bastwick*, p. 32. In either case the commentary on the religious divisions in Manchester's army is the same.

[18] Baillie, II, 191, 192.
[19] *Commons Journal*, III, 441, 585.
[20] *Ibid.*, III, 697.

Meanwhile the ecclesiastical controversy in the Assembly had found men to translate it into language understood by the people. "Sir Simon Synod," "Sir John Presbyter," the "Ordinance for Tithes"—all came in for a hard hammering in a series of tracts by "Reverend Young Sir Martin Marpriest son to old Martin the Metropolitan." One of them was printed "by Martin Claw-Clergie, Printer to the Reverend Assembly of Divines, and are to be sould at his Shop in Toleration Street, at the Signe of the Subjects Liberty, Right opposite to Persecuting Court."[21] Another tract of the series threatened the perquisites of the clergy. Why should the clergy, one-thousandth of the population of the kingdom, claim one-tenth of the kingdom's produce for their support? The Levite, it was true, had received the tenth by authority of the Old Testament, but the Levite had been bound to share it with the poor. If Paul had worked with his hands to sustain himself, why should not Presbyterian ministers do the like?[22] A third tract was a vigorous popularization of the attack on the proposed powers of the Presbyterian hierarchy. Was it to be set free to persecute the men who had served the Parliament so faithfully?[23]

[21] *The Arraignement of Mr. Persecution*, Richard Overton, Apr. 8, 1645, E. 276 (23). A trial scene in this pamphlet suggests a similar scene in John Bunyan's *Holy War* so forcibly as almost to bring one to the conclusion that Bunyan owed his inspiration to the tract.

[22] *The Ordinance for Tythes Dismounted*, Dec. 29, 1645, E. 313 (27). As early as June of 1644 refusals to pay tithes were causing the beneficed ministers of the Assembly much concern, as Lightfoot's notes show, Lightfoot, XIII, 281, 283.

[23] *Martin's Eccho*, June 27, 1645, E. 290 (2).

Lilburne threw himself into the thick of the fray. The line of argument that appealed to him as most telling was practical—that the Parliament in countenancing hostile proceedings against the Independents was harassing its truest friends. January 7, 1644/5, he wrote Prynne a letter in a style that was lofty when addressed to Prynne and abusive when directed at the Assembly. Complaining in this letter that the "Black coates" had closed the presses to Independent books, he challenged Prynne to debate with him the fundamental doctrines of Independency.[24] For printing this letter, and printing an explanation of it which he had given before a parliamentary committee, Lilburne was twice brought before the committee under arrest. All this he attributed to Prynne's malice.[25]

[24] Prynne neglected to answer the letter, saying later that he had been too busy to read it till three or four days after he received it. Meanwhile Lilburne printed it. Thomason dates it January 15, 1644/5, E. 24 (22). Prynne's account is in *The Lyar Confounded*, Oct. 15, E. 267 (1), pp. 3, 30.

[25] Prynne says that the committee dropped the matter in January out of compassion for Lilburne who had been lately run through the eye by a pike in Moorfields. *The Lyar Confounded*, p. 3. Lilburne's sight was probably seriously affected. A year later Edwards speaks of his face as still blemished from the accident (*Gangraena*, II, 104); and in 1647, Lilburne represented himself as forced to use spectacles, having but one good eye to see with. *The resolved mans Resolution*.

The committee summoned Lilburne on May 14 or 16. According to Prynne it allowed him to explain his letter of January in writing, but not to print what he wrote. According to Lilburne, he was told to print nothing till he had turned in his explanation in writing. *The Lyar Confounded*, p. 5; *Innocency And Truth Justified*, p. 9. Lilburne's printing his explanation at the press suspected of printing the Marpriest tracts caused the committee to summon him a third time. Thomason dates the printed explanation June 13, E. 288 (12). *The Lyar Confounded* is the authority for the other statements.

Presbyterian and Independent were ready to fly at each others' throats as the struggle with the king neared its crisis. The almost forgotten episode of the Windmill Tavern meeting illustrates the heights to which their mutual suspicion ran. Immediately after the loss of Leicester, two or three hundred citizens of London met at the Windmill Tavern and chose a committee of sixteen members to draw a petition to Parliament. Lilburne, though not the chairman of this committee, as Prynne stated, was a member of it; but Lilburne professed that he did not know at least a third of the other members, so far was the meeting from being a party affair. The committee, by his account, proposed to petition that the members of the Assemby be sent home to their respective parishes, to stir up the people to rise *en masse* against the Royalists. He added that this expedient had been suggested by an assembly divine to Major Salloway of the committee, and was eliminated from the petition at the committee's second meeting.[26] William Prynne, however, was convinced that Hugh Peters, the *bête noir* of the Presbyterians, had designed the Windmill Tavern meeting to secure the dissolution of the Assembly and the indefinite postponement of the Presbyterian model

[26] Prynne's account is in *A Fresh Discovery Of some Prodigious New Wandring-Blasing-Stars*, Dec. 16, 1645, E. 267 (3), p. 17. Lilburne's is in *Innocency And Truth Justified*, p. 4. See also *Commons Journal* for June 4, 1645. Edwards's account of the whole affair was that it had been proposed to petition not only for the dissolution of the Assembly, but also that certain Independent members of the Commons be set up as an extraordinary committee. *Gangraena*, I, 67.

of church government. The "device," according to Prynne, was dropped out of the petition by the common council of London when the petition was submitted to the council for presentation. To Prynne and Bastwick, Lilburne appeared to be the leader of a coterie of desperate Independents who plotted to elect their adherents to Parliament, dissolve the Assembly, overthrow the Presbyterians, and destroy the peerage and all ranks and orders in the state.[27]

Charges and counter charges of treasonable correspondence with Oxford marked the height to which party jealousy had arisen. Similar charges had clustered around the names of individual Parliament members since the beginning of the war; and now neither Presbyterians nor Independents

[27] *A Ivst Defence of John Bastwick*, pp. 29, 30. Lilburne commented on the accuracy of Prynne's account by stating that Peters was not present at the meeting. Hugh Peters was assiduously engaged in the summer of 1645 in securing the election of Independent members of Parliament as new writs were issued for one borough after another. The statement was made that he had admitted having two or three seats that he could bestow on whom he would. He was supposed also to be canvassing the relative strength of Presbyterians and Independents in the army. *Plain English: Or, The Sectaries Anatomized*, Aug. 17, 1646, E. 350 (11), pp. 3, 10. It was supposed for a time that Peters intended to bring in Lilburne and Walwyn as burgesses for a Cornwall constituency. *Gangraena*, II, 29. The electors of Southwark also considered choosing the two men. Lilburne wrote a letter against Bastwick this same summer to the electors of Rye, where Bastwick was seeking election. *Innocency And Truth Justified*, p. 8.

Peters's assiduity was a great vexation to the Presbyterians. Edwards gravely dismisses him with an account of a story he had told of flocks of pigeons that covered the sky in New England; they came from an island three miles wide by twenty long. What could one not expect of a man who told such tales? *Gangraena*, III, 127.

were above using them for party purposes. In
June of 1645, James Cranford, a zealous Presbyterian, got into trouble by accusing Crewe, Vane,
Pierrepont, and St. John of such dealings with the
enemy.[28]   In the same month Parliament investigated similar rumors touching Denzil Holles, notably an assertion by Lord Savile that Holles had
been in correspondence with Lord Digby. The
investigation brought to light the fact that Holles
had received a letter from Savile, written with
"white ink," while that gentleman had been an
ardent Royalist.   On July 19, the House by a division of ninety-five to fifty-five voted that this did
not amount to treasonable correspondence.[29]

Through this seemingly irrelevant incident, Lilburne's enemies brought him into collision with the
House of Commons.   July 18, he had brought a
witness to testify against Holles.   While at Westminster the next day, he met three friends who had
preferred to a committee of the Commons charges
of improper conduct by Speaker Lenthall.   The
three men retailed their charges to Lilburne, and
he brought Colonel Roe to hear also.   Colonel King
and John Bastwick at once laid an information
with the House of Commons to the effect that a
certain Captain Hawkins, after having talked with
Lilburne and Colonel Ireton, had come to the in-

---

[28] *Commons Journal*, IV, 212, July 19, 1645. He was assessed damages of £2,000 and committed to the Tower indefinitely. See *ibid.*, IV,
172, June 11, 1645; and Baillie, II, 277–280.

[29] *Commons Journal*, IV, 172, 212, 213. The test vote was taken on
putting the question.

formers and repeated the charges against the speaker. The House forthwith voted Lilburne and Hawkins to the custody of the sergeant.[30]

Bastwick later tried with small success to disprove Lilburne's accusation that the information was malicious. Bastwick said he had supposed that Hawkins had told his story to Lilburne more fully, and that Lilburne would be able to inform further; but Bastwick had worded his information unnaturally with the apparent purpose of bringing Lilburne in as principal instead of accessory. But while disclaiming any malicious intent, Bastwick unconsciously revealed what was perhaps the real motive for his persecution of Lilburne. In his *Ivst Defence*, he made no secret of his belief that the various persons concerned in the charges against Lenthall and Holles were members of a desperate Independent faction willing to attain its ends by the complete ruin of Presbyterianism and Parliament alike. Therefore, it is very likely that on July 19 he had scented a deep-laid plot in the various conferences among the Independents at Westminster, and had hastened to strike at the man who seemed to him the ringleader.[31]

On July 24, Lilburne was summoned before a

---

[30] *Innocency And Truth Justified*, p. 27; *The Copy of a Letter, From Lieutenant Colonell John Lilburne to a freind*, Aug. 9, 1645, E. 296 (5). There is a second edition, E. 302 (17). *A Ivst Defence of John Bastwick*, p. 7. Apparently Bastwick's and King's information also included an inquisition into Lenthall's doings by the Surrey and Salters Hall committees. *Commons Journal*, IV, 212, 213, 215.

[31] Besides the *Ivst Defence of John Bastwick*, see also *The Copy of a Letter*, p. 10.

committee of the House of Commons. When the
chairman asked him a question evidently based on
Bastwick's information, Lilburne refused to answer
until he was informed of the charges against him;
and he denounced as illegal the action of the House
in committing him without specifying the cause of
commitment. He was, therefore, recommitted. A
pamphlet in which he retailed the committee's proceedings and commented upon them came to the
attention of the House of Commons August 9. A
vote of the House empowered the committee to
remand Lilburne to prison, if on inquiry it found
him to be the author of the tract. On his refusal
to answer questions, the committee accordingly
sent him to Newgate. August 11, the House approved this step and ordered that Lilburne be tried
at the next quarter sessions.[32]

A petition in Lilburne's behalf signed by two or
three thousand persons was presented to the House
of Commons August 26. It asked that Lilburne
might be removed from Newgate, his case reheard,
and an allowance from his arrears assigned him
for his support in prison. The House thereupon
ordered two members to manage the charges against
the prisoner at the next general session, and assigned him a grant of one hundred pounds. It
returned answer to the petitioners that inasmuch

---

[32] *The Copy of a Letter*, p. 1. *Commons Journal*, IV, 235, 236, 237.
According to Lilburne, Prynne and Bastwick tried to injure him by putting out libels in his name, calling on the people to rise in his behalf;
these he disclaimed in a letter of August 21 to the lord mayor. *Innocency And Truth Justified*, pp. 28, 29, 34.

as Lilburne did not acknowledge the justice of the House's dealing with him, the House could not regard the petition as timely. In October a session of Newgate began. Lilburne appeared in court and, finding that no charges had been brought against him by the House, appealed to the lord mayor and recorder for his liberty; but they informed him that they could only apply to the House of Commons on his behalf. On the recorder's application the House discharged him October 14.[33]

Considerations of expediency can not have led Lilburne to refuse a reply to the questions of the committee. It is inconceivable that it could or would have dealt harshly with him had he answered its questions. In answering he could have said nothing that would have injured himself; and by keeping silence he could not have prevented the committee from discovering through other witnesses all that it could have learned from his answers. The only possible conclusion is that Lilburne had endured imprisonment rather than surrender what he considered to be a vital principle of personal liberty.[34]

His imprisonment made clearer the existence of a party looking to him for leadership. Hawkins and his other friends gathered round him. Bastwick sneeringly informs us that their watchword

[33] *Innocency And Truth Justified*, pp. 29 ff. *Commons Journal*, IV, 253, 254, 307.

[34] Edwards states that Lilburne's unlicensed pamphlets against the Parliament, which sold at a high price, were inspired by greed. *Gangraena*, I, 128. Why Lilburne should have risked the heavy sums due him from Parliament for such small stuff Edwards does not state.

was the privileges of the subject as secured by
Magna Charta and the Petition of Right.[35] Prynne
has his instructive sarcasm to add to Bastwick's;
it reveals Lilburne industriously engaged in a popular propaganda. "I am credibly informed," says
Prynne, "that this upstart monstrous Lawyer
since he was called to the Barre at Newgate where
he now practiseth, hath the Book of Statutes there
lying open before him, which he reads and interprets to all the poore ignorant people that visit
him, telling them, that he will in a few dayes make
them understand the Lawes and Statutes of the
Realm as exactly as any lawyer in the Kingdome."[36]

A pamphlet, probably by Lilburne,[37] affords
additional evidence that a more or less self-con-
scious radical Independent party existed; for *England's Birth-right Justified*, the pamphlet in question, is really a party declaration of faith, stating
the radicals' grounds for dissatisfaction with the
policy of the Long Parliament. The preamble
addressed to "All the Free-borne people of England" comes as the natural utterance of men who
had made *Anti-Cavalierisme* their text-book. It
recites that the Independent party, in spite of its

[35] *A Ivst Defence of John Bastwick*, p. 16.

[36] *The Lyar Confounded*, p. 22.

[37] E. 304 (17), Oct. 10, 1645. The author of *Regall Tyrannie discovered*, p. 3, says that the tract is not Lilburne's, as he is known to sign all
his work. If, as is sometimes supposed, *Regall Tyrannie* is Lilburne's,
the evidence would be against his authorship of *England's Birth-right*;
but as *Regall Tyrannie* is not signed, the rule would militate against Lilburne's authorship of that, and consequently against the authority of the
statement in it. The internal evidence points to Lilburne as the author.

struggle for English freedom, is now likely through the delinquency of those in power to lose all it had fought for,

. . . . and perceiving themselves now at last to be in a far worse condition, both in number and power (their Lives and Estates, yea and precious time also being so far spent) then they were at the first; and besides, like to loose all, and scarcely to have (or leave) so much as their Lives, Lawes, or Liberties for a prey.

And seeing by manifold examples of grievous experience, that neither Petitions can be easily accepted, justice truely administred, the Presses equally opened, the cryes of the poor heard, the teares of the oppressed considered, the sighes of the Prisoners regarded, the miseries of the widow and Fatherlesse pittyed, nor scarcely any that are in distresse relieved, but Lawes any way wrested, most of our freedoms restrained, Ordinances, Protestations, Oathes, and Covenants slighted, the hearts of all Estates, King, Parliament, Priest and People obdured, the wicked for the most part absolved, the just oftentimes condemned, and most of all in Authority perjured, not only by breaking that solemne Oath, which themselves did make, and compelling others to take, but neverthelesse, by persecuting those who make conscience to keep it, even because they will not break it. . . . .

To such a pass did Lilburne and his friends believe the Long Parliament's shortcomings had brought its party.[38]

The specific remedies proposed by the pamphlet are of as much interest as its party consciousness. Its wish that the law like the Bible were all in

[38] Lilburne's irritation at the failure of Parliament to recompense his services by granting him his arrears and Star-Chamber damages made all its actions seem to him unjust, selfish, and callous. He wrote repeatedly with heat of its neglect in allowing the widows and children of those who had served it to lack bread, while at the same time it gave its members allowances of three and four pounds a week and lucrative places. *The Copy of a Letter*, p. 16. When all possible excuses have been made for

English summarizes the meaning of the whole later Leveller movement. The pamphlet further suggests that the charters of London be put in English so that every citizen may know his own rights; in this connection it quotes with approval a petition of the City of London of April 15, 1645, asking that the citizens may have freedom to petition Parliament directly and not merely through the common council. *England's Birth-right* goes on to complain of the burden the excise lays on the poor; of the monopolies, notably that of the Merchant Adventurers on exported cloth;[39] of the censorship of the press,[40] and of the restriction to licensed preachers[41] of the right to preach.

The radical platform criticises the constitutional status as well as the policy of the Long Parliament. Annual elections should be held, so that the people may remove worthless members and replace them

them, the fact remains that members of the Long Parliament in the later years of the war were self-seeking, greedy, and corrupt. Charges of corruption were hurled at the members from all sides; the device of seventeenth-century finance of allowing public servants to make disbursements for the public service from their own pockets, and then reimbursing them in lump sums makes it well-nigh impossible at this day to say how far corruption extended. No financial expert could today clear up for us the accounts of the Long Parliament.

[39] Pp. 8, 22, 44. See Note on p. 118.

[40] The repression of unlicensed printing by the Stationers Company is too familiar to dwell on. Radical Independent tracts, such as the Martin Marpriest tracts and Lilburne's first three pamphlets of 1645, could not be printed under license and had to issue from hidden presses. January 17, 1644/5, the Stationers were taken to task by the House of Commons for remissness in allowing books like Lilburne's letter to Prynne to circulate.

[41] November 15, 1644, the House of Commons resolved that no person unordained in some recognized reformed church be allowed to preach.

with better ones. Members of Parliament should
be compelled to abandon their lucrative offices and
be paid for their services in Parliament; for it is
against justice that legislators hold judicial offices,
and thus execute the law as well as make it. It
may be alleged that certain members of the Long
Parliament such as Cromwell are performing notable service in military commands; but Cromwell's
design for a committee at which anyone oppressed
by a Parliament member could find redress,[42] shows
that he is capable of even more notable service in
his seat in the House of Commons. The radicals
differed from the dominating party in maintaining
that the victory against the king was to be won
not in the field, but in the public opinion of the
nation.

In its demand that the war be turned into a
democratic crusade against tyranny, *England's
Birth-right* reminds one of *Anti-Cavalierisme*. It
appeals to the people to rise as one man throughout the kingdom, force the king's remaining garri-
sons to surrender, and thus prevent the war from
dragging on for another year.[43]   Moreover, the rea-

---

[42] December 1, 1645, the House of Commons set up a committee to
deal with the cases of members who had accepted bribes; any person was
to have liberty to inform at it. *Journal*, IV, 362. The exemption of
members of Parliament and their servants from civil suits enabled them to
evade payment of their debts; the injustice of this rankled in the hearts
of many who had had dealings with them. The privilege was greatly
reduced in extent in 1648 and 1649.

[43] Pp. 38, 30, 31. The idea recalls the Windmill Tavern meeting.
The expedient had been proposed several times before—notably in 1643.
Commons Journal, III, 91, May 18, 1643. See also Lightfoot, p. 9,
Aug. 14, 1643.

son assigned against Parliament's permitting only licensed preaching is significant; licensed preachers are not the ones willing to go to the parts of the kingdom where they are most needed—where the people by ignorance were seduced to betray their liberties and take up arms for the king. By 1648 the idea that the sole strength of tyranny has been popular ignorance and can be overcome only by popular education, dominates the Leveller program. The friends of liberty must appeal to the reason that is innate in every man; that reason when rightly fostered will enable him to distinguish political good from political evil.

The most interesting feature for our purpose, however, both of *England's Birth-right* and of several contemporary pamphlets by Lilburne is the scattered sentences and fragmentary statements that contain the crude material of new constitutional and legal theories. These pamphlets mark successive stages in Lilburne's constitutional thinking. Thus in August of 1645 his ideas were incoherent and contradictory; but by October he had thought his way to a clear and consistent statement of the English constitution and of the nature of the security it afforded to the rights of individuals.

The title of the August pamphlet was *The Copy of a Letter*. It was rather incoherent in its legal doctrine, the noteworthy feature being Lilburne's novel use of Magna Charta and the Petition of Right in his argument against the committee's right to proceed against him. During the struggle with the king those documents had been cited often enough as safeguards to the Parliament and the nation against the king. The novelty in Lilburne's use of them was his emphasis on the fact that they safeguarded certain rights and privileges not merely to the nation, but to individual men as well. "By vertue of being a freeman," wrote Lilburne, "I conceive I have as true a right to all the priviledges that doe belong to a free-man, as the greatest man in England." He distinguished as pertinent to his own case the privileges assured in the thirty-ninth and fortieth articles of Magna Charta;[44] but he did not distinctly assert those privileges against the House of Commons. He drew a comparison between the actions for which Parliament abolished the Court of Star Chamber, and the doings of the Commons' committees in sitting with closed doors and questioning men under accusation. Yet even in these particulars he was willing to allow the Parliament itself reasonable latitude when it had treasons to search for, or other business of public concern requiring secrecy.[45]

England's Birth-right Justified contained a closer and more distinct statement of the powers of Parliament than any other of Lilburne's pamphlets of 1645.

[44] Lilburne quoted from the 9th H. III Ch. 1. "No freeman may be taken and imprisoned and disceased of his freehold, or his liberty, or his free Customes, or Out-lawed, or Banished, or any way destroyed; neither will we goe upon him, neither passe upon him but by the lawfull tryall of his equalls, or by the Law of the Land, justice and Right we will sell to none, we will denie to none, nor will deferre to none." P. 2.

[45] *Op. cit.*, p. 14.

It is confessed by all rationall men, that the Parliament hath a power to annull a Law, and to make a new Law, and to declare a Law, but knowne Laws in force & unrepealed by them, are a Rule (so long as they so remain) for all the Commons of England whereby to walk: and upon rationall grounds is conceived to be binding to the very Parliament themselves as well as others. And though by their legislative power, they have Authority to make new Laws, yet no free-man of England is to take notice (or can he) of what they intend till they declare it; neither can they, as is conceived, justly punish any man for walking closely to the knowne and declared Law, though it crosse some pretended priviledge of theirs, remaining onely in their own breasts.

The law of the land was men's authority for obedience to Parliament. If Parliament by its actions taught them to disregard that law, not only was its own authority at an end, but property and civilization itself were at the mercy of brute force. Nor could it be argued that all the people save members of Parliament were bound by the law. In such a case the people would have given the Parliament a power to harm and not to help them; and no law could give Parliament such a power. Since by the Parliament's own maxim the letter of all laws must be governed by their equity, it was impossible that any law could be so interpreted as to free Parliament from the law.

Lilburne deduced important consequences from the proposition that Parliament was bound to walk according to the law. First, Parliament in its executive actions must accept the guidance of the equity as well as the letter of the Star-Chamber act, and the Petition of Right. The equity of these laws condemned the late actions of parlia-

mentary committees; for *ex officio* examinations
violated the spirit of the Great Charter, the Petition
of Right, the Star-Chamber act, the Protestation,
the Covenant, and above all "the infallible Rules
of Gods own most sacred Word, which forbids
that any man should answer upon questions to
accuse, condemne and consequently kill and destroy
himself, or that any man should be condemned
before he be heard."[46]   To support his interpretation of the laws of England, Lilburne appealed to
the law of God.

His readiness to seek a higher justification for
the laws of England became more apparent in a
third pamphlet, *Innocency And Truth Justified*; in
1645 as in 1642 constitutional discussion led to
reflection on the principles of government.   Lilburne quoted Henry Parker's statements on the
origin of government in compact between the gov-
ernor and the governed, and on the people's right
of binding their government; but as Lilburne's
logic was not disturbed like Parker's by the idea
of the indivisibility of Parliament and nation, he
concluded that Parliament itself was bound by the
compact with the people in which its power had
originated.   Moreover, in support of his conclusion Lilburne appealed to the law of reason.   As
he conceived it, the law of reason existed by virtue
of a perceptive power innate in every man, taught
or untaught, enabling him to distinguish right and
wrong, good and evil.   The law of reason taught
every human being to know what was just and

[46] *England's Birth-right*, pp. 2, 3, 16, 48.

what was expedient for himself and his fellows. The Mosaic code, the law of God himself, was simply the most perfect of exemplifications of the law of reason. It necessarily followed that any human government could be just only in so far as its laws accorded with the principles of right reason and justice implanted in the hearts of all mankind.[47]

Three months before *Innocency And Truth Justified* appeared, an anonymous pamphlet entitled *Englands Lamentable Slaverie* had expounded far more radical doctrine.[48] After a few passing compliments in which the author assured Lilburne of his personal regard notwithstanding their differences of religion, he cited with approval Lilburne's stand for his constitutional rights against Parliament. For, while he was not the first to go to prison, rather than answer illegal questions of committees, the unknown assured him, he was the first to ground his refusal plainly on Magna Charta, or to draw the obvious and illuminating comparison with the Star-Chamber procedure. He must have known that such assertions would not meet the approval of Parliament men who considered their power absolute and unrestrained by Magna Charta or by any other law. "Others there are," the author continued, "(as good Wise and juditious

[47] *Innocency And Truth Justified*, pp. 11–13, 28, 38, 57–62. The discussion of the law of reason is drawn from the law dialogue of the Doctor and Student.

[48] Oct. 11, 1645, E. 304 (19). At a guess one would assign the pamphlet to William Walwyn. The view of Magna Charta expressed in it is the same as that in *Juries justified*, Dec. 2, 1650, E. 618 (9), p. 5. The author's analysis of his difference from Lilburne in religion, and his views of toleration are in a spirit characteristic of Walwyn. See p. 247.

men) who affirme, that a Parliamentary authority
is a power intrusted by the people (that chose
them) for their good, safetie and freedome, and
therefore that a Parliament cannot justlie doe any
thing to make the people lesse safe or lesse free
then they found them."

So far the unknown had merely approved Lilburne's reliance on Magna Charta. Now he made
a startling commentary of his own. "Magna
Charta (you must observe) is but a part of the
peoples rights and liberties, being no more but
what with much striving and fighting, was by the
blood of our ancestors wrestled out of the pawes
of those Kings, who by force had conquered the
Nation, changed the lawes and by strong hand
held them in bondage. . . . ." for, "though
Magna Charta be so little as lesse could not be
granted with any pretence of freedome", kings had
often with the unnatural assistance of Parliament
striven to make it less. For Parliament had often
in the past been amused with the making of trivial
statutes, and its members thereby diverted from
thought of their freedoms; and when waked out of
their stupor all they could do was to call loudly
for Magna Charta, "calling that mess of pottage
their birth right."[49]

Clearly here was an application of the doctrine
of natural right far beyond any that Lilburne had
so far imagined. He had taken his stand on Magna
Charta, considering it as an excellent epitome of
the people's liberties as set forth by the law of

[49] *Englands Lamentable Slaverie*, pp. 3, 4.

God and the law of reason.   Now he was told that
the people's liberties guaranteed by those two laws
were far wider than the narrow scope of the parch-
ment charter in the Tower.   But the author reas-
suringly told Lilburne that only so much the more
was he on solid ground when standing on Magna
Charta.   True, some things in it as, for example,
the constitution of the church, could be altered; it
was always in the Parliament's power to make the
people freer.   But on the popular rights guaranteed by Magna Charta, Parliament could not encroach.   There was in *Englands Lamentable Slaverie*
the promise of a radicalism far beyond Lilburne's.

Englands Lamentable Slaverie foreshadowed the
transformation through which Lilburne's ideas were
to pass in the next twelvemonth; but meanwhile
his thinking, if slower, had led him to important
results.   Formerly a loyal servant of the Long
Parliament, he had begun to criticise its policy.
In particular, he had criticised that policy as permitting intolerance and injustice to flourish in the
nation; more generally, he had demanded that
Parliament make its own actions accord with the
known law of the kingdom.   In criticising also the
policy by which the war had been carried on, he
had implied his own faith, and the faith of those
for whom he spoke, in the nation's capacity for a
measure of democratic government.

NOTE

The Monopoly of the Merchant Adventurers

In view of Lilburne's repeated attacks on the Merchant Adventurers'
monopoly and on Parliament for supporting it, a word of explanation is

needed. The House of Commons had in the early stages of the war been indebted to the Merchant Adventurers for loans. See *Journal* for Jan. 12, 1643/4, Feb. 23., etc., III, 364, 405. September 11, 1643, the House of Commons had confirmed their monopoly and their right to administer an oath such as should be approved by both Houses, and to imprison their members for certain offenses against the company. A proviso accompanied the confirmation expressly saving all rights depending on ancient charters or acts of Parliament. *Journal*, III, 237. The amended ordinance passed both Houses in October.

There is a very able discussion of the economic results of the Merchant Adventurers' cloth-exporting monopoly in *Innocency And Truth Justified*, pp. 48 ff., apparently based on a book called *A Discourse for free trade*. Lilburne maintained that the monopolists as a class had been supple to tyranny such as Strafford's. He quoted Pym's declaration that debasing the spirits of the king's subjects was more treasonable than debasing his coin; and argued that such was the effect of a monopoly. He objected to the Adventurers' power of imposing an oath of fidelity to their officers and statutes. He emphasized the saving clause in the parliamentary ordinance quoted above, showing that it could be used to root up the whole monopoly. If, as Parker had insisted, rulers were intrusted with power for the good of the ruled, what right had Parliament to make men slaves by a law, as they had done in the case of the Adventurers? Parliament's action afforded Lilburne one more text for his sermon that the law must be in accord with reason. A pamphlet of January 26, 1645/6, *A Plea for Free-Mens Liberties*, by one, Thomas Johnson, followed the same line of reasoning. E. 319 (1).

CHAPTER IV

1646. THE RADICAL ATTACK ON ARBITRARY POWER

I. THE ANTI-MONARCHICAL ELEMENT AMONG THE INDEPENDENTS IN 1646

IN 1646 Lilburne and his associates accomplished the task of fusing their scattered criticism of the Long Parliament into a new political philosophy. They asserted that all power not originating in the people's assent was arbitrary and tyrannical. Accordingly, they denied that the king and the House of Lords could justly claim any authority over the nation, and ascribed supreme power to the House of Commons as the representative of the people. In support of their assertions they advanced a theory of natural right based on the political writings of 1642–1644, but in content quite different from them, and in many respects a startling anticipation of Locke and Rousseau.

In part, the new constitutional position of the radicals represented merely the natural development of the Independent party. Lilburne could still consistently regard his political affiliations as Independent, partly because of his interest in the principle of liberty of conscience at stake in the ecclesiastical controversy until that controversy reached a temporary solution in July, but partly also because the winter and spring of 1646 had emphasized the fundamental differences of principle between Presbyterianism and Independency. While Presbyterians were becoming more conservative politically, Independents—at least a certain circle of them somewhat wider than Lilburne's following—were becoming more radical. Elated at the ill-success of the Presbyterians with the "recruited" House of Commons, they extolled the authority of the House, and no longer urged the limitations on its ecclesiastical powers that they had stated in 1644 and 1645. Already the radical Independents were writing of Presbyterianism and kingship as two forms of slavery.

The Presbyterians more and more defended the few surviving elements of the old political constitution; more and more they insisted on the establishment of church government according to the Word of God, not the Commons' idea of expediency. Their bitterness was pardonable. The rapid spread of strange, extravagant, or vicious religious doctrines, and uncouth or even immoral religious practices, proved to them the need for the sword of ecclesiastical discipline they had forged in the Assembly; and the Erastian House of Commons seemed ready to blunt it in their hands. The only satisfaction left private persons like Thomas Edwards was annoying the Independents by cataloguing the hundreds of religious and political vagaries the time afforded—not omitting the political teachings of Lilburne.[1] The corporation of

---

[1] In the three parts of *Gangraena*, Feb. 26, 1645/6, May 28, Dec. 28, 1646, E. 323 (2), E. 338 (12), E. 368 (5).

London could afford to speak more boldly than
Edwards.   On May 26 it presented humble remonstrances to each of the Houses of Parliament.   But
while the remonstrance to the Presbyterian House
of Lords was caressing in tone, that to the House
of Commons informed the House in so many words
that its conduct was leading the sectaries to hope
for a toleration not warranted by the Solemn
League and Covenant, and such as the supporters
of the remonstrance were pledged to oppose.

The Independents were ready with an answer.
On the day that the City Remonstrance was presented, Lilburne handed to members of Parliament
in Westminster Hall a tract entitled *A Word in
season*.   It warned Parliament against suffering
any intruder to interpret its obligations under the
Covenant lest, by so doing, it commit the great
treason of giving itself a master.   Addressing the
supporters of the remonstrance, the tract accused
them of presumption in venturing to speak for the
whole people of England; the remonstrators were
but a small part of the kingdom, and even if they
were the whole, it was not their place to speak as
they had done.   Parliament was absolutely free to
follow the dictates of its own understanding and
conscience, informed by the Word of God and the
principles of right reason, in choosing the course
that would most probably lead to the welfare and
safety of the people.[2]

[2] E. 1184 (3).   Thomason's copy is annotated: "Given about Westminster hall By Lilburne ye day ye cittie Remonstrance was presented
wch was 26 May."   The catalogue of the Thomason tracts assigns it to

Two pamphlets continued this line of reasoning. One of them, *The Interest of England Maintained*,[3] was prefaced by a disquisition on the power of Parliament, and the iniquity of anyone who sought to prescribe to it, with special application to the authors of the remonstrance. *The Interest of England Maintained* was plain spoken when it discussed the king's claims to consideration; it remarked that in the past the reigns of the best of kings had been tyrannical, and raised the question whether it was not best for the Parliament to use its military advantage over Charles in such a way as to secure in the most effectual manner possible the dawning freedom of the people from danger of him and his adherents. The words would permit of some extreme interpretations.

One, John Bellamy, undertook to uphold the Presbyterian side of the controversy. The second of the Independent tracts mentioned above, *A Moderate Reply To The Citie Remonstrance*,[4] had criticised the remonstrance for attributing only a share of the supreme power to the House of Commons; and the author of the *Interest of England Maintained*, by ascribing supremacy to the two Houses, had excluded the king from any share in it. Bellamy

---

"J. Sadler"; on what authority, I do not know. Its make-up is identical with that of two books of Walwyn's in reply to Edwards; Walwyn mentions it as his in *The Fountain Of Slaunder Discovered*, May 30, 1649, E. 557 (4), p. 7, and in *Walwyns Just Defence.*

The two remonstrances are in E. 338 (7), and E. 339 (1).

[3] June 8, 1646, E. 340 (5).

[4] June 12, 1646, E. 340 (20). Bellamy's book is *A Vindication Of The Humble Remonstrance*, July 6, E. 343 (2), pp. 15 ff.

cited these passages and added to them two or three from Lilburne's books, which attributed the supreme power to the Commons, and to the people a power to recall their representatives in Parliament. From this evidence Bellamy argued that the principles of the Independents would inevitably lead to the overthrow of the ancient constitution of king, Lords, and Commons.

July 24 a pamphleteer, answering Bellamy, avowed the doctrine of the supremacy[5] of the Commons in Parliament. "What meane you by fundamentall? you say the King Lords, and Commons are the three Estates, of which the fundamentall constitution of this Kingdome is made up, are there three fundamentals? I confesse I have not understood so much: I ever thought there had been but one, and that I took to be the Commons. . . . . First, because I ever thought, that the Commons made the King, and the King made the Lords, and so the Commons were the Prime foundation.

"Secondly, I ever took this for a truth likewise, that both the King and the Lords, were advanced for the benefit, quiet, and welfare of the Commons, and not the Commons made for them, and if I was deceived, the Common maxim of *salus populi suprema Lex* deceived me."

Bellamy had succeeded in fixing political doctrines on the Independents that, when carried to their logical result, would root up the authority of both king and Lords. Within a fortnight of the

---

[5] *The City-Remonstrance Remonstrated*, John Price, E. 345 (18), p. 23.

City Remonstrance, Lilburne had embarked on a contest with the Lords that led him to this very conclusion. With Presbyterianism temporarily checked, the little group of Independents surrounding Lilburne abandoned its agitation of purely ecclesiastical questions, and became absorbed in radical and far-reaching projects of constitutional change.

II. THE RADICAL ATTACK ON THE HOUSE OF LORDS

Lilburne's activity in prosecuting his impeachment of Colonel King earned him as an indirect consequence the hostility of the Lords. After his release from prison, in October of 1645, he continued to press his charges against King in the House of Commons.[6] In April of 1646 King, treating Lilburne's charges as slander, brought suit in common pleas for damages. Lilburne considered that a witness to a charge of high treason depending before the House of Commons was not bound

[6] He managed to advance a little the discharge of his old Star-Chamber sentence, securing also a vote from the Lords of £2,000 damages. With his arrears he made very little headway. At the committee to which he was referred for the settlement of his arrears and accounts he found his old adversary, Prynne, who required him to turn in a sworn statement of his claims. Lilburne demurred to this on the ground that he had lost many of his papers at the raising of the siege of Newark and accordingly could not produce a statement that he could swear to. Accordingly Prynne, after an examination of matters involved brought him in a debtor for £2,000 and, adding insult to injury, later held him up in a report to the Commons as an example of irregularity but, as nearly as can be judged from the *Journal*, without deigning to go into particulars. *Cf. Innocency And Truth Justified*, p. 68; *The resolved mans Resolution*, pp. 31 ff; *Commons Journal*, V, 62.

to answer for his testimony before any inferior court.[7] He instructed his lawyer to enter this defense; further, he wrote a letter to Justice Reeves of the court of Common Pleas protesting against the court's action in entertaining King's suit. The publication of this letter, under the title of *The Iust Mans Iustification*, embroiled the author with the House of Lords. In recounting his troubles with Colonel King he had alluded slightingly to the Earl of Manchester, saying that King's chaplains had persuaded Manchester's to throw a mist over their lord's eyes, that he might see no fault in Colonel King. Mild as this seems, it was too strong for the Lords who were extremely punctilious for the reverence due a member of their House. Their punctiliousness, indeed, had seemed to increase as in the course of the war their position in the state had grown more and more precarious. Several times as a result of their summary proceedings against commoners who had been guilty of breach of privilege of the peers, they had come into collision with the House of Commons.[8] Apparently not profiting by their past experience, the Lords on June 10 summoned Lilburne before them.

Lilburne acted on the principle that the Lords had no authority to summon or arraign commoners before them. He attended on the summons only from respect and civility to his social superiors, for

[7] *The Iust Mans Iustification*, pp. 2–3; *The Free-mans Freedome Vindicated*, June 22, 1646, E. 341 (12), pp. 1–2.

[8] See Note I on p. 153.

he considered that as the summons was illegal he
was not bound to obey it.   He urged the officer
who came for him to inform the House that such
must be his answer at their bar.   Before he was
summoned in, he begged one of the peers to bid the
Lords consider before they forced a contest on the
principle involved; for Lilburne, by his own account, would willingly have avoided a collision
with the Lords, could he have done so without
betraying the liberties of Englishmen.   In spite of
all his efforts, he was called in and asked if he knew
of the *Iust Mans Iustification*.   For reply he inquired if there were any formal charges laid against
him; and finding that he was held to the question
asked him, he handed in a protestation.   Naturally
the clerk would not receive it, and when Lilburne
withdrew, it was thrown after him.   He had to
wait in suspense for but a short time before a warrant came to commit him to Newgate for his contempt in handing in the protestation.   Lilburne
took up the gage of battle.   He at once drew up
a petition to the Commons asking protection, and
urging that they release him from his illegal imprisonment and assign him damages for it.   In his
protestation he had asserted that the Lords derived
their authority from prerogative, and not from any
trust committed to them by the Commons of England, "the originall and fountaine of power."   He
now addressed the House of Commons as "the
chosen and betrusted Commissioners of all the
Commons of England . . . .   unto whom all
the Commons of England have given so much of

their Power, as to inable you alone, to doe all
things whatsoever for their weale, safety, peace,
and prosperity, the end of all Government."⁹
Thus he read the Lords out of the government
altogether.

A few days later Lilburne published a book that
plunged him deeper into trouble. This was *The
Free-mans Freedome Vindicated*. In it he made a
few remarks on Manchester that were really worthy
the Lords' attention. Accordingly, on June 22 they
issued a writ to the keeper of Newgate commanding
that Lilburne be brought before them next day.
Lilburne refused to obey the order except under
force. When he was forbidden to talk to his friends
as he waited in the Painted Chamber, he fiercely
retorted that he would talk until the Lords, exceeding the cruelty he had found in the bishops, saw fit
to cut out his tongue, and sew up his mouth. Contumacious conduct was all that the Lords could have
expected of him. Nor were they disappointed.
By declining to kneel at their bar, he refused to
acknowledge their authority over him, and they
could only recommit him to Newgate.¹⁰
The Lords proceeded with his trial July 10.

⁹ *Lords Journal*, VIII, 368, 370; *The Free-mans Freedome Vindicated*,
pp. 3–6, 9.

¹⁰ *The Iust Man In Bonds*, June 29, 1646, E. 342 (2), pp. 3–4; *An
Anatomy of the Lords Tyranny and iniustice Exercised upon Lieu. Col.
Iohn Lilburne*, Nov. 13, 1646, E. 362 (6), p. 4; *Londons Liberty In
Chains*, pp. 24–26; *Lords Journal*, VIII, 388. In the second book mentioned he picks a number of technical flaws in the warrant recommitting
him; the Lords had no jurisdiction, the warrant was not under hand and
seal, no cause was specified in it, etc.

The first article of the charge against him covered the words of *The Iust Mans Iustification*. The remaining ones included the obnoxious parts of *The Free-mans Freedome*, and his conduct at the bar of the House.[11] When Lilburne was brought in to answer the charge July 11, he stopped his ears that he might not hear it read, saying that he appealed to the House of Commons and would stand to that resolution "as long as he had life". A second time he did the same thing. He was sent out to give him an opportunity for reflection; when he remained defiant, the House proceeded to judgment. It sentenced him to a fine of two thousand pounds and seven years' imprisonment, and pronounced him thenceforth incapable of public employment. Further, it ordered to be burned publicly the two pamphlets whose so-called seditious utterances had brought this fate upon him.[12]

Repeated petitions to the House of Commons at last induced it to consider Lilburne's case. It appointed a committee under the chairmanship of

[11] *Lords Journal*, VIII, 426–432. Lilburne argued that it was unjust to charge him with things that he had done in the heat of an unjust imprisonment, such as those of which the later articles accused him. *Anatomy of the Lords Tyranny*, p. 7.

[12] *Lords Journal*, VIII, 432. The warrant issued to carry Lilburne to the Tower contained a provision that his keeper should see to it that he published no more scandalous pamphlets. The keeper could devise no other way of doing this than by ordering that no one, not even Mrs. Lilburne, should speak to Lilburne save in his keeper's presence; if Mrs. Lilburne were allowed this privilege she must be imprisoned with him. This restraint the Lords ordered continued till the prisoner gave sufficient bail not to write any more scandalous books. The prohibition on visits from Mrs. Lilburne, however, was taken off September 16. *Ibid.*, pp. 435, 491. See Note II, p. 154.

Harry Marten to inquire into the Lords' proceedings. On October 27 and November 6 Lilburne
explained his case before this committee, and defended his position as to the Lords' lack of jurisdiction. November 9, he delivered his argument
to Marten in writing, and published it as *An
Anatomy of the Lords Tyranny*. Beyond acquaint-
ing the public with his case, however, his hearings
seemed to bring him no nearer to freedom.

Probably Lilburne's friends hoped to secure his
release only by arousing public opinion against the
House of Lords and the general shortcomings of
the government. Accordingly the radical pamphlets did not confine their attention to the wrong
done to Lilburne himself. Richard Overton represented him as a martyr who suffered because his
writings endangered corrupt interests—arbitrary
power, the presumption, arrogance, and intolerance of the clergy, the oppressive legal proceedings forced on the nation by the Norman conquest, the monopolies of trade.[13] Further, the
radical group linked Lilburne's case with those of
other men who could be represented as victims of
arbitrary authority.[14] Several such instances were
at hand. Early in 1645 John Musgrave had come
to London to push charges of treachery made by

[13] *An Alarum To the House of Lords*, July 31, 1646, E. 346 (8), pp. 7–8.
Overton was suspected of printing this book, and it is in his style.

[14] *A word to the Wise*, Jan. 26, 1645/6, E. 318 (5), contains advertise-
ments of *Innocency And Truth Justified*, and *England's Birth-right*. The
preface to the first-named book would suggest that some of Lilburne's
friends had taken up Musgrave's case. *An Alarum To the House of
Lords* mentions the books of Musgrave and Larner.

the men of Westmoreland and Cumberland against
Richard Barwis, member for Carlisle.   The House
of Commons, so Musgrave believed, first impeded
his efforts, and then imprisoned him.   In 1646
the House of Lords successively imprisoned William
Larner, his brother, and his servant for selling radical books.   The Lords imprisoned Richard Overton for printing such a book; for a similar offense
it soon after imprisoned his wife and his brother.
In all these latter cases, the prisoners pleaded the
rights of commoners against the Lords; and in
none of them did the House of Commons act with
more expedition than it showed in the case of
Lilburne.

Yet the radicals did not visit the same castiga-
tion on the House of Commons as on the House of
Lords.   To a dispassionate observer, the Lower
House would have appeared an accomplice with the
Lords in a series of high-handed attempts to suppress freedom of speech and of the press; attempts
each of which furnished the radical presses with
fresh ammunition.   But since the House of Commons was the center of the radicals' ideal constitution, they addressed it with respect, imploring
it to assume the position of sovereignty which
they assigned it.

III. THE RADICAL POLITICAL PHILOSOPHY IN 1646

In the course of 1646 there can be traced a distinct development in the radical program, both in
the reforms sought and in the political and constitutional basis on which they were posed.   The

simple demand that Parliament walk according to
the law was amplified, till out of it there evolved
a new constitution for England. The specific
measures proposed tended to be less destructive
and more constructive. Among them a few may
be singled out for especial consideration: reform of
the common law, decentralization of government,
and restoration to the citizens of London of a voice
in their city's affairs.

Traces of dissatisfaction with the law and its
administration may be found in pamphlets of 1645.
Lilburne had then wished that Parliament would
substitute for the cumbrous, expensive, and intricate common law a few rules that should be simple
and easily understood; would, he said, that the law,
like the Bible, were published in English! In general, however, he had been content to base his contest with the House of Commons on the law as
revealed in Magna Charta, though writers had not
been wanting to inform him that, when tried by the
natural rights of the people, Magna Charta itself
was but a mess of pottage.[15]

But Lilburne had himself developed a similar
antagonism to the common law in his *The Iust
Mans Iustification*, which he had written in June
of 1646 when confronted with a common law-suit
based on what he considered a vexatious technicality. The common law, according to *The Iust
Mans Iustification*, was a badge of slavery imposed
on the free people of England by the Norman conquest. In judgments like the ship-money judg-

[15] *Supra*, p. 117.

ment, that had destroyed the liberties of the people, had not the common-law judges professed to base their reasoning on the common law? The rules of the common law were locked in the breasts of the judges and could nowhere be found and read by the plain people. What little was to be met with in books was in Latin or Norman-French, languages which not one person in a thousand could understand; God, when he gave his law to Adam, had stated it plainly and had attached a fixed penalty. The iniquities of the common law were the work of William the Conqueror, who had deprived England of the laws of Edward the Confessor and had set up the common-law courts in opposition to the courts of the hundred and shire.[16] True, a few good laws could be found in Magna Charta and in the statutes, but too few to avail much. Magna Charta, though dearly purchased by Englishmen's blood in the past, and the best heritage that Englishmen possessed, in Lilburne's estimation fell far short of Edward the Confessor's

[16] The process by which this and similar notions of English legal history developed would be an interesting study. Lilburne quotes in support of the assertion chronicles like Speed, Daniel, and Martin. Lilburne himself, in spite of the narrowness of his reading, seemed to have an instinct that rejected the more absurd conceits of the legists and chroniclers. From one point of view the Levellers' proposed constitutional settlement may be studied as a more or less conscious and correct attempt to return to the Anglo-Saxon constitution of England. Lilburne, at least, seemed to sense correctly the broad outlines of that system. To show the mistakes into which men could fall with respect to Anglo-Saxon legal history, the author of *Vox Plebis*, a man of considerably wider reading than Lilburne, speaks of county courts in Alfred's 38 counties, formed after the model of the courts of King's Bench and Common Pleas (p. 19); Horn is his authority! See Note II, p. 154.

laws. He could only hope that Parliament would restore the essence of those laws by ordaining that all cases be tried in the counties and hundreds by elected juries, with appeal only to the Parliament.[17]

Lilburne's enthusiasm for the ancient courts of local jurisdiction leads naturally to the Levellers' desire for the restoration of local autonomy. In constitution, the England of the seventeenth century was more nearly a federation of counties than is ordinarily supposed. Local feeling in the counties died hard. Men's pride in their counties was comparable to the pride of a citizen of the United States in his state. Manchester and Cromwell originally appointed Colonel King commander in Lincolnshire because he was a Lincolnshire man;[18] unless the county were led by a native, they could not have hoped for concerted and hearty action in it. At the outbreak of the war, men of Yorkshire and of Cheshire attempted to negotiate a neutrality between Parliament men and Royalists in the two counties. Moreover, a tract condemning the Cheshire negotiation did not use the apparently obvious argument that, as Cheshire was an organic part of England, its inhabitants could not hold aloof from supporting either English king or English Parliament; instead, the tract complained of the terms on which the neutrality had been negotiated, and questioned whether the negotiators had been duly empowered by their county.[19] The

[17] See Note III on p. 155.
[18] *The Iust Mans Iustification*, p. 5.
[19] *Neutrality condemned by declaring the Reasons Why the Deputy-Lieutenants, intrusted by the Parliament for Cheshire, cannot agree to the*

Levellers probably felt the influence of this sentiment when they proposed to preserve and increase
local self-government. In 1646 Lilburne urged
that there be a re-apportionment of members of
the House of Commons among the counties according to the book of rates, and that the counties themselves be left each to district and apportion its
quota of members among its boroughs and hundreds. In later years even clearer evidences of the
decentralizing tendency can be detected.

The party that surrounded Lilburne in 1646
began, or rather continued, a crusade to make the

*Treaty of Pacification made by some of that County; At Bunbery, December
23, 1642,* Jan. 6, 1642/3, E. 244 (41). "For whom is it so agreed? themselves onely that subscribed? themselves with the rest of the Commissioners and Deputy Lieutenants? the Countrey? the neighbour Countries ready to imbrace an Association? or the Parliament? If for themselves, their conclusions are but personall and oblige no further: if for
themselves with the rest of the Commissioners and Deputy Liuetenants,
where and when was that authority deligated from all or any of those
absent to them that were present? or if so, by what power was it so
deligated? Instruments of all sorts, animate, as well as inanimate,
having either no motion, or to none effect, without the concurrence or
impulsion of their principall agent: if for the Country, where did they
authorize them, especially that part of it unconsulted withall? Or when
did the Country give either an expresse or implicite consent, that these
alone, either to that, or to any other purpose should be their body representative. If for the neighbour Counties, certainly without their
privity, and if no privity, no obligation: for who can imagine them so
stupid as to consent to that, which is utterly destructive to their de-
signes . . . . If for the Parliament, their Commission, or some
Order from thence, will shew it; but it is very probable that they had
thence, neither any such Commission nor Order." True, the pamphlet
condemns the agreement as against the decision of the Supreme Court of
Judicature on the Militia Ordinance; but the form of this statement is
suggestive in itself. Early in 1643, the counties of Cornwall and Devon
attempted to negotiate a peace between themselves.

city government of London democratic. On September 29, a citizen attempted to force himself into the meeting of aldermen and common council at which the lord mayor was to be chosen. Being forcibly excluded, he read to the assembled people a "Protestation". The city marshal thereupon carried the disturber before the court of mayor and aldermen, who examined him as to the authorship of the Protestation, but did not push the matter. On hearing of the incident, Lilburne bestirred himself, getting books and copies of records on the liberties of London. These he sent to a friend, who based on them a protest against the legality of the city government. The protest charged with usurpation aldermen and common councils past and present, in that they had excluded the "commonalty" of the city from rights guaranteed by the charters, and had themselves presumed to make laws and choose mayors and sheriffs. The protest traced to the long continuance of this abuse the rise of monopolies in the city, the ignoble surrender in the case of ship money; worst of all, the men of the city so long as they submitted to rulers they had not chosen were freemen in name only.[20]

[20] *Londons Liberty In Chains*, pp. 7, 8, 13, 21. The Protestation based the people's rights to choose their mayor on the analogy of the election of coroners by the freemen of the counties. For a later stage of the movement, see *Londons ancient Priviledges unvailed*, s. sh., Sept. 28, 1648, 669 f. 13 (23).

Two minor points on which distinct utterances by the radicals occur in this period are imprisonment for debt, and the sitting of members of Parliament as judges in inferior courts; in the latter case they urged that all advantages of an appeal to the Parliament were lost, and that the appellant was simply trying his case a second time before the man who had

Turning to the political philosophy expounded by the radicals in 1646, one notes in it important differences from the orthodox parliamentary argument of 1642–5. True, the one and the other can be reduced to propositions apparently similar in substance: no power is given by God to one man to rule over another man without that man's consent and agreement; all power of government therefore originates in agreement between the governors and the governed, perhaps agreement among the people before such things as governors exist. Accordingly arbitrary governments have no just authority because the law of nature, which is a preserver of man and not a destroyer, permits no man to give arbitrary rights over himself to another. All except the last of these propositions are deducible from Parker; the last at least from Rutherford or Hunton. The newer writings are distinguished from the older by their spirit; once that is sensed, their novelty is startling.

The first distinction between 1642 and 1646 to be noticed is the reliance of the radical authors of 1646 on the law of God and the law of reason. This distinction is one of emphasis. The idea is traceable in the earlier writers—the word "reason" itself is used by the writer who places the "reason" of the people in the House of Parliament.[21] But in

at first decided it adversely. *Liberty Vindicated against Slavery*, Aug. 21, 1646, E. 351 (2), p. 10; *Another Word To The Wise*, Feb. 20, 1645/6, E. 323 (6).

[21] *Supra*, p. 33; Coke, *Law Tracts*, 1764 ed., p. 224, *First Reading on Fines*: "for the Laws of *England* are *unwritten laws*, but divinely cast into the hearts of men, and built upon the irremovable rock of reason."

1646 the proposition that the law must be in accord
with reason is the major premise of the new political
logic. In *Regall Tyrannie discovered* there is an
elaborate attempt to demonstrate the essential
accord of the Mosaic law and the law of reason,
the author attempting to prove that each of the
Ten Commandments is reasonable and natural.[22]
Lilburne in *Londons Liberty In Chains* defined the
law of England as

the Perfection of Reason, consisting of Lawfull and Reasonable Customes, received and approved of by the people:
and of the old Constitutions, and modern Acts of Parliament, made by the Estates of the Kingdome. But such
only as are agreeable to the Law Eternall and Naturall, and
not contrary to the word of God: For whatsoever lawes,
usages, and customes, not thus qualified; are not the law
of the land; nor are to be observed and obeyed by the
people, being contrary to their Birth-rights and Freedomes,
which by the Law of God, and the great Charter of Priviledges, they ought not to be.[23]

The law of England is not law unless it is in accord
with certain axioms of right and justice, self-evident
to any rational man however mean his intellect.
These axioms, comprising the law of reason, are
higher even than the law of God, the Mosaic law,
because that law of God is itself tried and approved
by the law of reason.

Who in the last resort is judge of the consonance
of a statute or an act of government with the law
of reason? Here is a question that differentiates
still further the radical and the parliamentary

[22] *Op. cit.*, pp. 9 ff.
[23] *Londons Liberty In Chains*, p. 41.

writers. In 1646 a moderate Independent like John Cook, who in his *Vindication Of The Professors & Profession Of The Law* insisted that the law must be in accord with reason, still clung to the idea that the High Court of Parliament and not the people was final interpreter of reason.[24] Parker of course had been horrified at the idea of the "moliminous" mass of the people presuming to pass on the legality of Parliament's actions. Writers like Hunton who wrote of the three co-ordinate estates, only grudgingly allowed the people to decide by the sword when king and House disagreed.[25] But to Lilburne's friends it appeared self-evident that the right of judging finally in an orderly way as to the application of the law of reason belonged to the people.

A quotation from Lilburne, the tediousness of which must be excused by the fact that the author undertook to pack a whole philosophy into a single sentence, will reveal still other departures from the orthodox parliamentary position.[26]

God, the absolute Soveraign Lord and King, of all things in heaven and earth, the originall fountain, and cause of all causes, who is circumscribed, governed, and limited by no rules, but doth all things meerly and onely by his soveraign will, and unlimited good pleasure, who made the world, and all things therein, for his own glory, and who by his own will and pleasure, gave man (his meer creature) the sover-

---

[24] In every kingdom, he says, there must be a supreme tribunal to decide finally without appeal what the law is. *The Vindication Of The Professors & Profession Of The Law*, pp. 18, 87. Feb. 6, 1645/6, E. 320 (17).

[25] *Supra*, pp. 34 ff.

[26] *The Free-mans Freedome Vindicated*, pp. 11, 12.

aignty (under himselfe) over all the rest of his Creatures,
Gen. I, 26. 28. 29. and indued him with a rationall soule,
or understanding, and thereby created him after his own
image, Gen. I, 26, 27 and 9. 6. the first of which was Adam,
a male, or man, made out of the dust or clay, out of whose
side was taken a Rib, which by the soveraign and absolute
mighty creating power of God, was made a female, or Woman
cal'd Eve, which two are the earthly, originall fountain, as
begetters and bringers forth of all and every particular and
individuall man and woman, that ever breathed in the world
since, who are, and were by nature all equall and alike in
power, dignity, authority, and majesty, none of them having
(by nature) any authority dominion or magisteriall power,
one over or above another, neither have they, or can they
exercise any, but meerely by institution, or donation, that
is to say, by mutuall agreement or consent, given, derived,
or assumed, by mutuall consent and agreement, for the good
benefit and comfort each of other, and not for the mischiefe,
hurt, or damage of any, it being unnaturall, irrationall, sinfull, wicked, and unjust, for any man, or men whatsoever,
to part with so much of their power as shall enable any of
their Parliament men, Commissioners, Trustees, deputies,
Viceroys, ministers, Officers or servants, to destroy and undoe
them therewith; And unnaturall, irrationall, sinfull, wicked,
unjust, divelish, and tyranicall it is, for any man whatsoever, spirituall or temporall, Cleargy-man or Lay-man, to
appropriate and assume unto himselfe, a power, authority
and jurisdiction, to rule, govern, or raign over any sort of
men in the world, without their free consent, and whosoever doth it, whether Cleargy-man, or any other whatsoever,
doe thereby as much as in them lyes, endeavour to appropriate & assume unto themselves the Office and soveraignty
of God, (who alone doth, and is to rule by his will and
pleasure) and to be like their Creator, which was the sinne
of the Devils, who not being content with their first station,
but would be like God, for which sin they were thrown down
into hell, reserved in everlasting chaines, under darknes,
unto the judgement of the great day Iude ver. 6. And
Adams sin it was, which brought the curse upon him and
all his posterity, that he was not content with the station
and condition that God created him in, but did aspire unto
a better, and more excellent, (namely to be like his Creator)

which proved his ruin, yea, and indeed had been the everlasting ruin and destruction of him and all his, had not God
been the more mercifull unto him in the promised Messiah.
Gen Chap 3.

Here again the fundamental ideas—freedom of
man from natural subjection, origin of government
in compact, inalienable right—are all to be traced
to Rutherford. But they are figures of logic to
the writer of 1644, and vital facts to the writers of
1646. The form in which Lilburne states them is
significant. His emphasis of the doctrine that God
alone can be sovereign and rule absolutely of right,
reminds us of the Independent belief that Christ
alone as lawgiver for his church might impose
rules on the consciences of men. Lilburne is simply
transferring an ecclesiastical dogma to politics.

Furthermore, Lilburne's political philosophy is
framed for a practical purpose quite different from
Rutherford's. The purpose of Lilburne's reasoning is the protection of the rights of the individual
rather than the rights of the nation. Richard
Overton is even more emphatic than Lilburne as
to the rights of the individual. "To every Individuall," says Overton, "in nature, is given an
individuall property by nature, not to be invaded
or usurped by any: for every one as he is himselfe,
so he hath a selfe propriety, else could he not be
himselfe, and on this no second may presume to
deprive any of, without manifest violation and
affront to the very principles of nature, and of the
Rules of equity and justice between man and man;
mine and thine cannot be, except this be; no man

hath power over my rights and liberties, and I over no mans; I may be but an Individuall, enjoy my selfe, and my selfe propriety, and may write my selfe no more then my selfe. . . . ."[27]

This conception of the worth and importance of the individual influences the Leveller doctrine of compact. The Levellers indeed are the first of the thinkers of the Puritan Revolution who state clearly the theory of the social compact. Earlier definitions of compact were framed to demonstrate the sovereignty of a nation that had made a grudging dole of power to a monarchy it had created. The former authors who used this concept made of man's entrance into civil society a logical commonplace, fit only to introduce in a sentence or two the compact between people and king. It is left for the Levellers to use the doctrine of compact to emphasize the fact that the individual has certain rights pertaining to him as a man. This principle leads them to conclude that at the time when individual persons coalesced into a sovereign body politic, each person reserved certain rights which Nature and Nature's God taught him were inalienable—so vital to his safety that if he surrendered them he violated the instinct of self-preservation and committed murder on his own body. In 1647 a Presbyterian author undertakes to define the difference between the two theories of compact. The defenders of the Parliament against the king understood the law of nature to refer to the right enjoyed by heads of families in a patriarchal society

[27] *An Arrow Against All Tyrants*, Oct. 10, 1646, E. 356 (14), p. 3.

of establishing government over themselves and their households; but the postulate of the radical doctrine is far different, namely the breaking up of patriarchal authority and the setting up of every individual as a member of the sovereign people.[28]

Here also Independent influence appears. The Independent insisted that while subjection to civil government was natural to man, subjection to church government could lawfully arise only by the church covenant whereby the individual for certain purposes subjected himself to the government of church officers. The radicals now apply the doctrine to politics. The following definition of covenant from *Regall Tyrannie discovered* emphasizes the individual's free entrance into society by the way of the covenant, and his retention of certain natural rights as a result.

So in the same case among the Sons of Men, that live in mutuall society one amongst another in nature and reason, there is none above, or over another, against mutuall consent and agreement, and all the particulars or individuals knit and joyned together by mutuall consent and agreement, becomes a Soveraign Lord and King, and may create or set apart, for the execution of their Lawes (flowing from their will and mind founded upon the Law of God, ingraven in nature, and demonstrated by reason) Officers, which we call Magistrates, and limit them by what rules they judge convenient; always provided, they be consonant to the Law of God, Nature, and Reason; by the force of which, it is not lawfull for any man to subject himself, to be a slave.[29]

[28] *The Case Of The Army Soberly Discussed*, July 3, 1647, E. 396 (10), p. 6.

[29] *Regall Tyrannie discovered*, Jan. 6, 1646/7, E. 370 (12), p. 11. A saying of Lilburne shows how the law of nature was developing out of the Law of God. God, said Lilburne, had engraved on the mind of man

The radicals made important practical applications of these theories. Their doctrine of reserved and inalienable rights suggested an argument for liberty of conscience; for certainly the people in themselves had no power of coercion in religion to bestow on the Parliament. It was against nature for one man to give another the right of forcing him to worship God in any other way than that which his conscience bade him. Similarly, the radicals argued against the judicial power of the House of Lords. The people had never delegated to the House of Lords the power to judge them; therefore the House could have no inherent power of judging commoners.

If all just government originated in compact and agreement, how could the compact be enforced against the ruler? This question did not perplex the author of *Regall Tyrannie*. A contract broken by one of the contracting parties dissolved of itself. The whole course of Scripture was full of compacts between God and man that might serve as precedents. God had contracted with Adam; and when Adam broke the agreement, God inflicted the penalty; God had covenanted with the children of Israel; when they forsook his covenant he exacted the forfeiture.

The author brought his illustrations nearer home.

the golden rule; when with Cain men forgot that rule and became tyrannical and beastly, God had ordained "a perpetuall morall, unchangeable and everlasting Law" that whosoever violated the golden rule by oppressing or slaying his neighbor should himself die. Christ had enunciated the golden rule anew, thereby not destroying public order, but rather restoring it to its first perfection. *Londons Liberty In Chains*, p. 15.

The Norman kings had originally come in by conquest; but in 1087 William had been moved to have regard to his oath that he would maintain the laws of the Confessor. Stephen and John had come in by election. The royal power of Matilda had been broken because she would not maintain the Confessor's law. As for Magna Charta, "Whosoever readeth it (which every man may at large, at the beginning of the book of Statutes) shall find it an absolute Contract betwixt the Kings of England, and the People thereof, which at their Coronations ever since, they take an Oath inviolable to observe."[30] In the past, kings of England had ruled by compacts with their people, had broken their compacts, and had ceased to rule!

By the rules of abstract justice implied in these general propositions, the radicals had next to weigh the existing government of England, legally and nominally vested not only in the House of Commons, but also in the House of Lords and the king; actually vested in the peers as well as the representatives of the people. So weighed, it must have been found wanting. The author of *Regall Tyrannie* might, it is true, have disposed of the king's pretensions in the orthodox fashion. The king, he might have said, while ruling justly, was king by contract; for the rest, *Regall Tyrannie* went beyond previous books in its insistence that the king's violation of his contract was the end of his power and the beginning of his deposition. But similar reasoning could not have established on a basis of

[30] *Op. cit.*, pp. 10–26, *passim.*

equity the legislative power exercised by the Lords; clearly they had obtained it by grant of the king— and how could the king under contract principles have given them legislative power? Moreover, the author of *Regall Tyrannie* would have had to account for many things in the law courts and the common law that were tyrannical, and hence could not have originated in popular assent. All these puzzling problems found their answer in what we may call the "conquest theory"—that Englishmen in their government still wore the shameful badges of the Norman conquest.

In a sense, the "conquest theory" is the key to the attitude of the radicals toward the Great Civil War. The war was not to them the prosily and pedantically legal thing that the declarations of Parliament had depicted it to be. It was a crusade of Englishmen for the recovery of liberties which their fathers had held and lost. This spirit, as we have seen, was partly expressed by John Goodwin in *Anti-Cavalierisme;* but past all question it was still more prominent in the minds of men like Lilburne. In the year 1646 this sentiment found its best expression in *A Remonstrance Of Many Thousand Citizens . . . To their owne House of Commons.*[31]

The *Remonstrance* interpreted English history since the Norman conquest to prove that the nation had been held in bondage by the delinquencies of

---

[31] July 7, 1646, E. 343 (11). *The Ivst Man In Bonds,* June 29, 1646, E. 342 (2), p. 1, says of the Lords: "Sons of conquest they are and usurpation, not of choice and election, intruded upon us by power, not constituted by consent, not made by the people, from whom all power, place and office that is just in this kingdome ought only to arise."

kings and other "Officers of Trust" in the common-wealth. At first this bondage had been maintained by force, but latterly by infusing in the people false principles of kingship, parliaments, and free-dom; also by the corruption of the gentry, natu-rally the strongest prop of the people. The nation had borne with its bondage far longer than it should have done.

But in conclusion, longer they would not beare, and then ye [the House of Commons] were chosen to worke our deliver-ance, and to estate us in naturall and just libertie agreable to Reason and common Equitie, for whatever our fore-Fathers were; or what ever they did or suffered, or were enforced to yeeld unto; Wee are the men of the present Age, and ought to be absolutely Free from all kindes of Exorbi-tancies, Molestations or Arbitrary Power, and you Wee choose to free us . . . and Wee were full of Confi-dence, that yee also would have dealt impartially on our behalf, and made Us the most absolute People in the World.[32]

If it were admitted that the arbitrary power and injustice then existing was a yoke imposed by the Norman conquest and the usurpation of the king and his creatures the Lords, the question was how to release the commonwealth from its bond-age. This was the cause to which Lilburne con-sidered himself a martyr.[33] Overton had some idea of the real difficulty of what must necessarily come

[32] *Remonstrance*, pp. 4–5.

[33] He adds to the "proposition" on p. 144 the conclusion that next to revealing to men the knowledge of Christ, the best work a man can do is to "discover the privilege, that is, the Right, Due, and Propriety of all the Sons of Adam, as men: that so they may not live in beastlinesse, by devouring one another." It is also, says Lilburne, a man's duty to maintain such privileges against tyrants; and it was to this end that he engaged in battle with the Lords.

first—the awakening of the people to a sense of the oppressions they suffered and of their right to freedom; for, of course, in the *Remonstrance* the people of England spoke only figuratively to the Commons through the mouths of a few advanced thinkers. Overton in his *Defiance Against All Arbitrary Usurpations* bewailed the fact that usurpations had continued so long that the people were ignorant of their rights, and persecuted men who strove to establish them.

So that he whosoever he is, or shall be their Informer, must not look to conquer all where he may at first seem to prevail, yet that may not excuse his endeavours, which are the discharge of his duty; seeing the blessing comes in the use of the means, and it is impossible, that so great stupiditie should be either removed from this generation, or prevented in the next, except there be diligent, faithfull, continued, and powerfull endeavours used.[34]

In the spring and summer of 1646, two things appeared essential to the freeing of the people. First, the people must stick close to the House of Commons. Second, the House of Commons must itself recognize the duty intrusted to it by the people. The first essential had been emphasized by the radicals in the contest over the City Remonstrance.[35] The second is the theme of the *Remonstrance Of Many Thousand Citizens*.

This book is worth a very careful analysis. A seventeenth-century House of Commons could treat it only as a libel of the deepest dye. Yet through

---

[34] *A Defiance Against All Arbitrary Usurpations*, Sept. 9, E. 353 (17), pp. 2, 3.
[35] *Supra*, pp. 122–124.

all its violence of expression there runs an ideal of democracy that perhaps only the twentieth century can parallel. As a previous quotation would indicate, the *Remonstrance* professes the extreme democracy which teaches that the people need not on all occasions act through a duly constituted government. "For," runs another passage, "the effecting whereof [freedom from the yoke of conquest] we possessed you with the same Power that was in our selves, to have done the same: For Wee might justly have done it our selves without you, if Wee had thought it convenient."[36] In the year of grace 1916 this seems modern enough; but doctrine still more modern is to come.

Needless to say, the *Remonstrance* complains that the House of Commons has not done the bidding of its masters. Instead of quelling the king as a Norman tyrant it has used the doctrine of ministerial responsibility to cloak his misdeeds, "begging and intreating him in such submissive language . . . as if you were resolved to make us beleeve hee were a God".[37]

The House of Commons must completely reverse its policy. It must discard the forms under which it addressed the king with reverence and respect, and arouse the people to see the fruits of kingly tyranny only too apparent in the nation. It must declare its intention to have done forever with such tyranny; and in earnest of its intention must appropriate the king's revenue for the nation. The

[36] *Remonstrance*, p. 3.
[37] *Ibid.*, p. 5.

peers, surrendering their privileges and immunities, their pretended power of imprisoning commoners, and their "negative voices," must follow after the king. The Commons, being chosen by the people of the nation, have in themselves alone the power of making laws, of altering and of abolishing them; and they must no longer admit the form of the assent of king and Lords to legislation.

All this done, the House of Commons must still reform itself before it can free the people. In the first place, since its members were chosen according to the old law of England to sit in Parliament for but a year at most, they should not have continued their sitting so far beyond the period implied in their election. A system must be devised by which year after year a new Parliament or House of Commons may be elected in place of that of the preceding year; and for the future, the attempt of a local magnate to carry an election by influence must be made a serious offense. When it has accomplished this, the House of Commons of the Long Parliament may give place to a representative body fit to enjoy the whole government in practice as well as in right.

Meanwhile, the Commons will find many things in their own practice that call for reform. They must give up their highhandedness in ruling petitions to be breaches of privilege; they must surrender their immunities and become subject to the law of the land; they must lay aside their Star-Chamber methods of imprisonment and of *ex officio* examinations; they must abandon their designs of

compelling universal assent to a religious form.
How can they have the right of imposing such a
form unless each individual in the nation has transferred to them the power to force his conscience?
Also there are many things outside their own practice that claim their immediate attention: the "ex-
orbitances" in London's government; the monopolies of the great trading companies; the unworthi-
ness of the laws to serve a free people; the profession
of hired lawyers; imprisonment for debt; the wretch-
edness of the poor.

Above all the House of Commons must forget its
doubts and fears, and assume an attitude toward
its difficulties that will inspire the people to decisive action. In the past, to give a single instance, it had been faint-hearted in summoning
in the Scots instead of arming its own friends;
its faint-heartedness in that instance had involved
it in an attempt to enforce Presbyterianism on
men's consciences. If it had once shown a determination to make the people a free people, it might
have finished the war long since; as it is, the struggle
will drag on so long as Parliament lets the people
think that success means only exchanging bondage
to an irresponsible king for bondage to an irresponsible clique of Lords and Commons.

Forsake, and utterly renounce all craftie and subtill intentions; hide not your thoughts from Us, and give us encouragement to be open breasted unto you: Proclaime afore-
hand, what yee determine to doe, in establishing any thing
for continuance; and heare all things that can be spoken
with or against the same; and to that intent, set the imprisoned Presses at liberty, that all mens understandings may

be more conveniently informed, and convinced, as farre as is possible by the equity of your Proceedings.

Wee cannot but expect to be delivered from the Norman bondage, whereof wee now as well as our Predecessours, have felt the smart by these bloody warres; and from all unreasonable Lawes made ever since that unhappy conquest; as wee have encouragement, wee shall informe you further, and guide you, as we observe your doings.

The Worke yee must note is ours, and not your owne, though ye are to be partakers with us in the well or ill doing thereof.[38]

The spirit of the men who could write such a manifesto as this has hardly been assigned sufficient importance in the history of the Great Civil War. It is impossible to regard the men capable of conceiving of such democracy as mere fanatics; difficult to dismiss them as unprincipled self-seekers. Their ideas may with more truth be judged impracticable and useless for seventeenth-century England; yet Overton, at least, partly understood that such democracy could find its fruition only after an education of the people continued for generation after generation. It was useless to expect the seventeenth-century House of Commons to adopt the policy of the *Remonstrance*. The men who framed it were soon compelled to abandon the dream of a House of

[38] *Remonstrance*, p. 19. It may be interesting to compare this passage with Gardiner's estimate of the weakness of the Parliament's position in 1642: "The remedy for the evil lay not in the substitution of an irresponsible King for an irresponsible Parliament, but partly in the establishment of that responsible ministry which Pym had sketched out; partly, too, in securing that responsibility of Parliament to the nation, through perfect freedom of speech and writings . . . ." *History of England*, X, 216. By Gardiner's criterion the constitutional theories and ideas of the Levellers deserve a more important place in constitutional histories of the war than has ordinarily been accorded them.

Commons absolute because in accord with the national will. They were forced to seek other expedients to preserve the natural rights of the people. The *Remonstrance* represented but a step in the evolution of Leveller ideas; but, even so, two and a half centuries of democratic thinking have hardly brought us a finer ideal of the relation of government and people.[39]

The radicals based their democratic ideals on their faith in the dignity and worth of the individual. Appreciating the value of the individual man, they thought it inconceivable that he could be by right subject to any power arbitrary enough to enslave him; and to emphasize his dignity they pictured him as voluntarily placing himself under a government so limited that it might not harm him. On perceiving that this theory did not correspond to the facts, they summoned people and House of Commons to confide in each other and to coöperate as principal and agent in making all powers in England derive their authority from the assent of a nation composed of individuals—every man made in the image of God.

NOTES

I. The Lords' Jurisdiction over Commoners

Two years before Lilburne's collision with the Lords, two similar cases had arisen involving principles much like those in Lilburne's case.

Colonel King had been fined by the Lords in May of 1644, for alleged arbitrariness in his dealings with Lord Willoughby in Lincolnshire.

[39] Any attempt to determine the authorship of the *Remonstrance* must be a mere guess. The style, expression, and ideas suggest Overton's or possibly Marten's work; hardly Lilburne's or Walwyn's.

Prynne as King's attorney had made answer that the affair in question was then undergoing examination in the House of Commons; the House of Commons had decided that the Lords' action was a breach of the Commons' privileges, had called for a conference with the Lords on the subject, and finally ordered that King be discharged from imprisonment without payment of any fees; for he had given offense when the Lords called him in to hear his sentence read, and had been committed to the Fleet. *Lords Journal*, May 16, 30, June 3, 18, 1644, VI, 555, 573, 575, 595; *Commons Journal*, June 19, July 3, III, 534, 550.

In the same year the Lords had fined one, Captain Rous, one hundred pounds and had sought to make him kneel at their bar and confess the justice of the sentence. As a commoner he had thrown himself on the House of Commons, and had been committed to the Fleet; July 5, the House of Commons, on the ground that he was in attendance on the House as a witness, had ordered his discharge without fees. *Lords Journal*, June 1, June 18, 1644, VI, 574, 596; *Commons Journal*, July 5, III, 551.

The case of Clement Walker, who was fined by the House of Lords in 1643 for alleged reflections on Lord Saye, in connection with the prosecution of Nathaniel Fiennes, Saye's son, for cowardice in connection with the loss of Bristol is another case in point; but apparently the House of Commons took no action in his case.

II. Lilburne and His Jailers

Soon after his imprisonment in 1646, Lilburne was embroiled in disputes with his keepers over the heavy prison fees of the Tower, and over certain formalities that he considered designed to intimidate the friends who came to see him. His especial *bête noir* was John White. White was described somewhat leniently by the author of *Vox Plebis*, Nov. 19, 1646, E. 362 (20)—a man with far too keen a sense of humor to be Lilburne—as an old man who would be a good one, if only he would give over scribbling foolish books against the dissenting brethren and against men in affliction; but withal too slow to credit the extortions with which his under-jailers were justly charged. White had had a former passage of arms with Lilburne when the colonel was prisoner in Newgate. White, according to his own account, had visited Lilburne there out of charity, and had offered him some good advice (apparently on things in general); he felt much aggrieved that Lilburne had only threatened to throw him out for his pains. Considering what the probable tone of the advice was, the story is not unlikely. *Iohn White's Defence*, Sept. 15, 1646, E. 354 (4).

The author of *Vox Plebis* may possibly have been Harry Marten. It is written with a keen sense of humor; the descriptions of conditions in the Tower (where Marten had recently been imprisoned) suggest a first-hand acquaintance with the subject. The author quotes Reynard the Fox, a thing hardly apt to have fallen in the scope of the ordinary Leveller's reading. The temptation to ascribe anything showing an objective sense of humor to Marten is great. *Vox Plebis*, p. 53.

III.   A Lawyer's Summary of the Defects of Seventeenth-Century English Law

A comparatively impartial statement by a professed lawyer as to what the defects and injustices in English legal procedure really were may appropriately follow the Leveller demands. John Cook's *The Vindication Of The Professors & Profession Of The Law*, Feb. 6, 1645/6, E. 320 (17), is itself a protest against the tendency of some men of the time to regard all lawyers as rascals, but the book is moderately radical in its viewpoint. Cook would gladly have seen the whole law of England brought into accord with the Mosaic law—the law of God. His recommendations are various; for one thing, the raising of the limit of a suit *in forma pauperis*, since it is a grievous matter that a poor man cannot sue for twenty shillings without its costing him forty in fees. He objects to the abuse of technical flaws in indictments, wishes the abolition of imprisonment for debt, and of the abuses connected with the action for debt—an action used by pettifoggers as a convenient device for casting a man into prison. A man could be, and often was, imprisoned by one of these actions when the bringer of the action had no proof at all of any debt owed by the defendant. Cook wishes law proceedings to be in English; for he is ashamed to think that a country man should be served with a subpoena in Latin, when very likely he can find no one in five miles able to translate it to him—a badge of the Norman conquest this. Cook urges Parliament to provide courts for the more remote counties of the kingdom; he suggests that to prevent men from fraudulently incurring debts they can never hope to pay, the Parliament should establish in every county an office for the registry of deeds, leases, contracts, etc., so that for a small fee every man may know how land is encumbered; thus men will no longer be enabled to live beyond their estates, or to hold rich mortgages and feign poverty.

Further, he recommends that, to bring about the desirable accord between the law of England and the laws of God and reason, some grave, judicious man well versed in Scripture and in the common law should consider what changes would serve to bring the one into harmony with the other.

CHAPTER V

I. THE RADICALS QUARREL WITH THE HOUSE OF COMMONS

THE events of the spring and summer of 1647 molded the radical Independents into a political party. As early as April, the united support the radicals gave to a series of petitions to Parliament indicated their ability to work in concert. In August they formally severed connection with the Independent party, and became a political party with an entity and platform of its own. Its enemies soon bestowed on it the party name "Leveller."

The Leveller party was born amid political chaos. In June the New Model Army assumed an active part in politics; and for three months the Independents of the army and city were in close alliance with both Lilburne's friends and the king's against the Presbyterians. By the end of the summer this unnatural coalition had divided into three warring parties—Independents, Royalists, and Levellers. Meanwhile the Levellers, as a result of the reception accorded their petitions, had pronounced the House of Commons' power forfeited for misuse, and the chiefs of the New Model had invented ingenious excuses for professing obedience to a Parliament that they had coerced with the sword. Yet in the

156

midst of the confusion, Presbyterian, Independent, Royalist, and Leveller strove each according to his principles to bring about an orderly settlement of the kingdom; to escape from the confessedly extra-legal situation to one better warranted by recorded law or principles of reason.

The breaking of the old-time political alliances began when the radicals quarreled with the House of Commons. A disinterested observer might have predicted much earlier that the radicals would do so. The House hesitated to act decisively even on a point so plausible as Lilburne's denial of the Lords' jurisdiction over him, and let Lilburne languish in prison month after month, only taking notice of him when his writings became so outspoken as to provoke the censure of its committees.[1] As a result of the shifting of parties, the House in 1647 was even more hostile to radical ideas than it had been in 1646. Then it had been Independent in complexion only from distrust of the Scottish army and of the Presbyterianism advocated by the Assembly Once the one and the other had been disposed of, the balance of parties shifted, and the Presbyterian leaders, Holles and Stapleton, found no difficulty in mustering majorities for their measures. If the radicals had ever really believed that the House of Commons would assume the duties they had prescribed for it, its attitude of 1647 was sufficient to disillusion all save those who wilfully shut their eyes to conditions actually existing.

[1] In *The resolved mans Resolution*, Lilburne gives an account of such an inquiry into his writings.

By the spring of 1647 the radicals had resolved to force the House of Commons to choose between their program and their hostility. Perhaps under the guidance of William Walwyn,[2] they began the promotion of a petition that in its intended effect was a party manifesto designed to educate public opinion.[3] The petition disregarded the existence of the old constitutional forms by addressing the House of Commons as the supreme authority of the kingdom. It set off enthusiastic encomiums on the excellence of parliaments with denunciations of attempts to curb their activity. Because the Commons had tolerated such attempts, the petition continued, they had lost an opportunity of freeing the nation such as no previous Parliament had enjoyed; and the people, whose loyal assistance had given the Commons their opportunity, remained in bondage. The claims of the House of Lords to criminal jurisdiction over the commoners enslaved the nation. The monopolies of the Merchant Adventurers, imprisonment for debt, unjust and extortionate prison fees remained; men and women lived and brought up their children in beggary. Intolerance in religion still walked abroad to bar men because of their beliefs from serving Parliament.

The petition named the remedies that must be applied. The House of Commons must free itself from the "Negative Voice" of king and Lords, that unhindered it might complete the liberation of those

---

[2] *Infra*, Ch. VII, p. 252.

[3] *Gold tried in the fire, Or The burnt Petitions revived*, June 14, 1647, E. 392 (19). The petition is printed in full in E. 464 (19), Sept. 19, 1648.

whom it represented. It must revoke the fines
imposed without due process of law on commoners,
forbid examinations *ex officio*, and repeal all enactments forcing men against their consciences to take
oaths, protestations, or covenants. It must not
permit fallible magistrates to punish religious
opinions;[4] and so on for the other heads of the
preamble. In short, the petition stated in official
form the Leveller program so far as it had been
developed.

The Levellers were not suffered to proceed with
their petition in peace. March 15, while the work
of getting signatures was still going on, a copy of
the petition was brought into the House of Commons. The copy had been read at the Spittle on
Sunday the 14th, after a young man had endeavored
to "prove free will"! It had been signed by six
people at the meeting and about a hundred names
were on it already![5] Two days later the corporation of London petitioned the House of Lords for
the suppression of the Leveller petition.[6]

In self-justification, the supporters of the petition
presented to the committee having the matter in

[4] "5. That no Man, for preaching or publishing his Opinion in Religion in a peaceable Way, be punished or prosecuted as Heretical, by Judges
that are not infallible, but may be mistaken as well as other Men in their
Judgemente; lest, upon Pretence of suppressing Errors, Sects, and Schisms,
the most necessary Truths and sincere professors thereof may be suppressed, as upon the like Pretences it hath been in all Ages."

[5] *Commons Journal*, V, 112.

[6] According to the account of the petitioners, a copy of the petition
was carried to Recorder Glynn, who turned it over to a committee for the
suppression of unlicensed preaching. *Gold tried in the fire; Lords Journal*, IX, 83–85.

hand a certificate avowing the petition and asserting
that it was not a libel, but a *bona fide* petition
intended for presentation to the Parliament.   Nicholas Tew (or Tue) read this certificate to the crowd
waiting in the Court of Requests to avow the petition.   He did this in order that some who had not
previously heard the certificate might assent to it;
nevertheless the committee sent for him, and on his
refusal to answer questions, committed him.   The
House of Commons concurred in the committee's
action on the 19th, voting at the same time that
Major Tulidah be taken into custody as a delinquent.[7] According to Leveller accounts Tulidah
had been falsely accused of disorderly conduct before the committee by Holles, Stapleton, and Earle,
who had handled him roughly and had offered to
draw swords on the petitioners.

Undaunted by the ill fortune of their certificate,
the petitioners prepared a second petition.   In it
they demanded the release of their friends, the
silencing of the busybodies who had misrepresented
the first petition in Parliament, and lastly freedom
for themselves to promote that petition; for the
plea of military necessity that had cloaked Parliament's summary actions in former years could
hardly be pleaded in time of peace.   But the
House vouchsafed no answer to this second petition
for nearly six weeks, and then answered "The
House doth dislike this Petition;" later it committed

[7] *Commons Journal*, V, 118; *Gold tried in the fire*, p. 9.   The *Journal*
spells the name Tyllydah.

one, Browne, because of too great importunity, for an answer.[8]

While the House was apparently brooding over this oracular saying, the petitioners were busy with a petition still more outspoken. It argued that the people had commissioned the House of Commons to redress their grievances, and therefore enjoyed the right of presenting their grievances by petition. As for the reception the previous petitions had met, the House should consider the ill effects that would follow if the common council were allowed to prejudge petitions, and if the House committees were permitted to imprison without orders from the House. Accordingly, the petition continued, the House should hear the testimony against Holles, Stapleton, and Earle, free Tew (Tulidah had been bailed), and not judge of the "large petition" until the petitioners should present it. Perhaps in bravado the radicals gave this petition to Holles for presentation. The House voted it a high breach of privilege, and decreed that both it and the large petition should be burned by the hangman. In burning them, said Overton, the House virtually

[8] *Gold tried in the fire*, pp. 9, 6, 7. The answer was given May 4, *Commons Journal*, V, 162. Browne was committed May 20. He was reported to have said April 30: "That they had been waiting many Weeks for an Answer to their Petition; and now they see they shall have none, and take it for a flat Denial; therefore, now we are resolved to take another Way, or Course." Being asked his name he had said that the time might come when he would ask his questioner's name in another place. Having knelt at the bar of the House and denied his guilt, he was committed to Newgate. *Commons Journal*, V, 179. Gardiner seems incorrectly to ascribe these remarks to Tew in March. *Great Civil War*, III, 256.

burned the Great Charter of England, containing the liberties and freedoms of Englishmen, "for in those petitions were contained the chiefest heads of that Charter."[9]

The patience of the party that had supported the various petitions was almost exhausted. Some thought the time ripe to draw up a remonstrance to the kingdom, arraigning the members of Parliament as oath-breakers. Lilburne says that he recommended a petition to the effect that Parliament—since the petitions previously presented were such high breaches of privilege—would please to state its privileges, how it came by them, and what the subject might petition for.[10] Finally Lilburne's friends decided to attack the Presbyterian leaders of the House, instead of the House of Commons itself. One last petition described certain members as sowers of dissension between the Parliament and its supporters.[11] The House on June 2 accorded permission to present the petition, but voted, 128 to 112, to give no answer to it at the time. The petitioners then sent in word that they had heard of the vote, and discharged themselves from following their petition further for the present, "and will

[9] *Commons Journal*, V, 179, 180. The quotation is from *An Appeale From the degenerate Representative Body the Commons . . . . at Westminster*, July 17, 1647, E. 398 (28), p. 14.

[10] *Rash Oaths unwarrantable.* Lilburne's account of the petitions is in pp. 29–45.

[11] *Gold tried in the fire*, pp. 4, 12. The petition asked the appointment of a committee to inquire after persons in authority whose employment in places of public trust was either unsafe or contrary to parliamentary ordinances; further, it asked that the army's demands be granted, and those persons punished who sought to prejudice Parliament against it.

notwithstanding still seeke such just and equitable meanes for to ease the grievances of this poore distracted Kingdome, and comfortably put an end to the groanings of this miserable distressed nation."[12] As Gardiner remarks, it was the day on which Cornet Joyce was riding to Holmby.

The Levellers were at last convinced that the House of Commons would not play the rôle they had assigned to it. The House in expressing its disapprobation of the radical theories had arbitrarily violated what we now consider essential privileges connected with the right of petition. Yet there was some excuse for the heat of the House's displeasure with the March petition. As has been said, it was a manifesto rather than a petition; and even to tolerate passively its doctrine was to endorse a revolution whose completeness we can scarcely comprehend today. The Levellers had forced an open breach with the House of Commons when they proposed to present a petition embodying the doctrine of the *Remonstrance Of Many Thousand Citizens*.

II. THE NEW MODEL IN POLITICS; THE BREAK
BETWEEN LEVELLER AND INDEPENDENT

By the time the radicals had given over petitioning Parliament, the New Model Army had become a political factor, and its officers and men, in order to promote a program of political and social reforms, had discarded the ordinary relations of

[12] *Commons Journal*, V, 195; *Rash Oaths unwarrantable*, p. 47.

military discipline. Manifestly the army that
could do this was no ordinary army; indeed, a man
born in this generation is probably too far removed
from seventeenth-century England to understand
fully the spirit of the New Model Army or of the
men who composed it. The typical New Model
soldier was intellectually the child of an age of
transition. He reached after a system of political
ideas that anticipated the nineteenth century; the
fanatical and mystical shade of his Puritanism
represented the extreme of the sixteenth-century
reformation; yet withal his naïveness in applying
his theories, and his respectful deference to the
beliefs and judgments of his superiors in rank and
place were an abiding intellectual heritage from an
England still simple and catholic. In the twentieth
century the paradoxical complex of motives that
governed the political actions of the New Model
soldiery may be analyzed, but scarcely experienced.

All through 1646 the eyes of both Independents
and Presbyterians had been turned toward the
army either in hope or in fear. The small number of
sectaries—one in six, Edwards repeatedly assures
us—nevertheless disquieted him by their extreme
fanaticism; and the men whom Edwards called
fanatics ruled the spirit of the New Model. The
Independents regarded it as the sheet anchor of
their hopes. A picture with doggerel verse published in September of 1646 under the title of *The
Watchmans Warning-piece*[13] illustrates the popular
impression among the Independents. A man has

---

[13] The pamphlet is E. 354 (10).

carelessly laid aside his arms only to find the
Dragon of Popery, the Leopard of Prelacy, and the
Snake of Presbyterianism ready to attack a lamb.
"Shewing," as the subtitle runs, "that If our Ar-
mies lay down Arms before the Worke is at an end,
We may expect yet worser Harms, More pretious
lives and States to Spend." It concludes:

> But all the choycest Friends to Parliament,
> That joyn with one Unanimous Consent,
> A Blessing may expect on their Designes:
> Where wisdom guarded with an Army, shines.

To an age that believed in the immediate inter-
position of the hand of God in the affairs of men, it
seemed that Providence had marked that army for
great things, greater perhaps than any it had accomplished.[14]   Indeed the past achievements of the
New Model went far to justify such faith.   When
in 1645 it had taken the field there was no great
noble among its commanders to lend luster to it;
moreover, its leaders were men who with the exception of Skippon had never seen service in Germany,
and therefore in the eyes of professionals were but

---

[14]"It is an Army, I confesse, that hath had little worldly pomp or humane
glory to be seen upon it, and therefore hath been in the eye of the world,
even from its infancy, poore, meane, inconsiderable, contemptible: But
this hath been, and is the glory of it, that the Lord is their God, and that
there is the shout of a King amongst them.   Many of the members
thereof, especially those in the highest places of Command, being able
by an eye of Faith to behold him, who is the King of Saints, walking in
the midst of them, and continually furnishing them, even by his owne
Spirit, with wisdome, innocency, strength and courage sutable to their
present necessities." *A Just Apologie For An Abvsed Armie*, Jan. 29,
1646/7, E. 372 (22).

amateur soldiers.[15]   It was so contemptible to its
masked enemies among the Presbyterians, that
Baillie pronounced that they expected nothing good
from it; so contemptible to its avowed enemies
among the Cavaliers, that Charles, six days before
Naseby, could write that "my affaires were never
in so faire and hopefull a way."[16]   Yet the May of
1645 had seen the storm of Leicester by the king's
forces, and the May of 1646 had seen the king a
prisoner and the last Royalist fortresses holding
out only for honor.   The conclusion that God had
acknowledged the army was none too strong for
the facts.

For our present purpose it suffices that the army
was generally Independent in spirit, and through
the zeal of its unlicensed preachers a stumbling
block to the rigid Presbyterians.   In 1647, with
their faction in power, the Scots out of the kingdom,
and the king's forces put down, the Presbyterians
felt that they and the nation would be well rid of
this army and the heavy taxation its support en-
tailed.   In their impatience to attain their end
speedily they made insufficient provision for the
back pay of the regiments they proposed to disband.
In March the soldiers prepared a petition for fair
dealing on this and other matters of interest to the
army.   The House of Commons condemned the
petition, declaring that those who undertook to
promote it were public enemies.   In alarm at these

[15] So the above pamphlet, pp. 3, 4.   Fairfax, it is true, had seen a
siege or two as a boy.

[16] Baillie, II, 265; *The Kings Cabinet Opened*, 1645, E. 292 (27), p. 14.

and other proceedings of the government, the common soldiers in their various regiments chose "agitators" to watch over their interests. Sympathy with the men's demands soon led the subordinate officers to make common cause with them. Finally Cromwell and Fairfax, the general officers, did the same, Cromwell throwing in his lot with the soldiers simultaneously with the securing of the king's person on behalf of the army by Cornet Joyce.

On the 5th of June in a general rendezvous at Newmarket, the soldiers signed a "Solemn Engagement." They excused[17] their attitude of defiance by a recital of Parliament's ill usage of their petition, and its attempts to disband them piecemeal without satisfying their just demands. Such conduct, they argued, gave good ground for fear lest Parliament, after disbanding the New Model, take vengeance on those who had been forward in the soldiers' behalf. The engagers accordingly must refuse to disband or divide till terms providing for their safety in so doing were agreed to by a council consisting of the general officers and two soldiers and two officers from each regiment—the famous Council of the Army. Further, the engagers denied that their end was anarchy or license in religion, as had been alleged; but they avowed their intention of promoting without regard to parties "such an Establishment of common and equal Right and Freedom to the whole, as all might equally partake of . . . ." They assumed the right as impartial arbiters to bring the Great Civil War to an end.

[17] Rushworth, VI, 510–512.

A declaration of the army of June 14 set forth the political program promised in the Solemn Engagement. To make it plain once for all that the army's actions were something more than a mere mutiny of mercenary troops, the declaration asserted in words, often quoted thereafter, the army's right to a share in the political settlement of the kingdom, "especially considering, that we were not a meer mercinary Army, hired to serve any Arbitrary Power of a State, but called forth and conjured by the several Declarations of Parliament, to the defence of our own and the People's just Rights and Liberties." With this preface, the army proposed an elaborate scheme of reform which involved successive parliamentary elections, the restoration of the king on terms, and liberty of conscience.[18]

[18] Among the specific demands are the purging the House of Commons of delinquent or improperly elected members, and justice against certain members to be named thereafter, who have been guilty of practices against the Parliament. In the further stipulation that in future only those "acted . . . by a principle of Conscience and Religion in them" be elevated to high office is foreshadowed the rule of the Saints.

The declaration goes on to propose that the king be readmitted to power after the people's liberties have been vindicated. It urges the revoking of the arbitrary powers of county committees and deputy lieutenants as soon as they are no longer necessary. It urges an accounting of the moneys raised and spent in the course of the war, a general oblivion, and ease for tender consciences.

Commissary-General Henry Ireton, the author of the declaration, in developing his argument, seems almost consciously to attempt to steer away from the doctrines of Lilburne and Overton. The House of Commons is trusted only with the people's *interest* in the supreme power of the commonwealth; and in the strictures on the inconvenience of a perpetual Parliament, any reflection on the act against the dissolution of the Parliament or on the men who had secured it is especially disclaimed; whereas Lilburne had come to consider the assent to that act the most

The army, however, speedily discovered that it could enact its program only after it had imposed constraint on the civil power. June 16, the Council of the Army preferred charges against eleven Presbyterian leaders of the House of Commons. A march toward London on the 26th induced the House to give way, and at the same time to save its face by "allowing" the eleven to withdraw. But on the 26th of July the mob of the city invaded the Palace of Westminster, and forced the members to invite the king to London, and to repeal votes they had made a few days earlier against a "Solemn Engagement" circulated in the city for signatures. The invitation to the king would have given him the opportunity of negotiating terms of peace with the Houses on even terms, and probably would have resulted in a Royalist reaction.

The Independents took no chances. When Parliament reassembled on the morning of the 30th of July, it found that the speakers of the two Houses with eight peers and fifty-seven members of the

heinous of the breaches of trust of which the king had been guilty! *The resolved mans Resolution*, p. 22. True, the declaration pronounces for new writs for parliamentary elections, issuing as of course in accord with the provisions of the Triennial Act, and further suggests that there be a time fixed for the dissolution of each successive Parliament, so that the king may no longer dissolve Parliament at his pleasure. But when this has been done "we shall hereby, for our part, freely and chearfully commit our Stock or Share of Interest in this Kingdom, into this common Bottom of Parliaments. And though it may, for our Particulars, go ill with us in the Voyage, yet we shall thus hope, if Right be with us, to fare better." This whole theory of Parliament's proper constitutional position is extremely characteristic of Ireton.
The declaration is in Rushworth, VI, 564–570.

House of Commons had fled to the army. Relieved
of these members, Lords and Commons elected new
speakers, recalled the eleven, and made prepara-
tions to put the city in a state of defense. Defense
proved impossible, and on August 6 the army
marched into the city. The Lords who had sat
in the absence of their speaker absented themselves; but the Presbyterian majority in the Commons was still defiant. On the 9th of August, it
voted down a resolution to the effect that all that
had been done in the absence of the speakers was
null and void. When next day it rejected a resolution approving the action of the army, it forced the
officers to a plain demonstration of their military
strength and their resolution to use it. August 20th,
troops occupied Hyde Park; and the officers of the
army who were members of the House led a party of
soldiers to the door of the House and stationed
them there. To this show of force the Presbyterians yielded; they suffered the votes given under
the coercion of the London mob to be annulled.
Thenceforth they absented themselves in such numbers as to give the Independents control of the
House. Of the eleven members, seven had already
fled the country, and one was under arrest.[19]

For the moment the Independents were in control
of the political situation. They held the king's
person, and controlled the only effective army in
the kingdom. Thanks to judicious use of the New
Model, they had possession of the metropolis, and

[19] Throughout this section to this point I have followed Gardiner,
Great Civil War, III.

maintained narrow majorities in both Houses of
Parliament. A superficial observer might have
concluded that they had an excellent opportunity
of securing a permanent peace.

Yet at the very moment of their apparent triumph,
the army leaders must have known that the ground
on which they stood was unstable. They might
easily have foreseen the impossibility of reaching
a settlement satisfactory at once to king, Independents, and radicals. The army's alliance with the
king was hollow and uncertain. It depended for
its continuance on Charles's belief that the army
leaders would yield everything and exact nothing.
In the end, the failure of Cromwell and Ireton to
induce Charles to accept the terms they had embodied in the Heads of the Proposals led the radicals
of the city and the army to propose in the Agreement
of the People a constitutional settlement that
precluded any chance of the king's voluntary
coöperation.

Although this step marked the political severance
between the two factions in the Independent party,
a rift had appeared long before; in fact it had grown
too wide to be bridged a fortnight after the army
entered the city. When it began is hard to say.
Lilburne had long cherished a violent antipathy to
certain prominent Independents such as young Sir
Harry Vane and Oliver St. John. Some time early
in 1646 he had "unfolded" to Cromwell the base-
ness of these two "unworthy covetous earth-
worms."[20] Nor was this the only case of personal

---

[20] *Ionahs Cry out of the Whales belly*, July 26, 1647, E. 400 (5), p. 3.

jealousy. Many such would undoubtedly be revealed to us by a greater knowledge of the internal
politics of the London Independent congregations.
For instance, in February of 1647 Lilburne had
complained that members of John Goodwin's congregation had discouraged petitions from London,
Buckinghamshire, and Hertfordshire in behalf of the
victims of arbitrary power.[21] Walwyn tells us that
petitions of his authorship setting forth the ill
usage of the Independents throughout the kingdom
had twice been blocked by Independents. Yet, he
adds, in 1644 and 1645, the same men had cordially
accepted his political coöperation.[22] Apart from
any personal hostility to Lilburne, the Independents
had probably come to consider the Arch-Leveller's
forceful language and novel theories embarrassing.
However, they were sufficiently alarmed at the attitude of the Presbyterians to allow without protest
the framing of the "large petition" of March, 1647.
When the House of Commons had condemned it,
they drew closer to the radicals; thus Walwyn for a
time came again to be on friendly terms with John
Price and other members of the congregations.[23]

Until March of 1647 Lilburne himself was on
terms of intimacy with Cromwell. Cromwell had
shown him especial confidence in detailing him for

[21] *Ionahs Cry*, p. 5.   Lilburne names Sadler as directly responsible.

[22] *Walwyns Just Defence*, 1649, pp. 1, 2.   This book is not in the
British Museum, and I have seen it cited in no secondary work.   There
is a copy of it in the Newberry Library of Chicago.

[23] *Ionahs Cry*; *Walwyns Just Defence*.   Walwyn states he was inti-
mate with Cromwell also at this time (pp. 4–6).

service with Colonel King,[24] and after Lilburne had left the army, had given him a letter to assist him in pressing his claims before the House of Commons. Cromwell had carried his intimacy with Lilburne to the point of sharing one bed with him; and he had given so important an officer as Colonel Rich a thorough rating in the presence of Lilburne and Lilburne's wife.[25]

But in spite of his personal relations with Lilburne, Cromwell cannot have had any great sympathy with the doctrines that Lilburne and Overton had announced in the summer of 1646. March 25, 1647, Lilburne, "jealous over him with the height of Godly jealousy," wrote Cromwell a letter. He gratefully admitted that in the past Cromwell had been the mainstay of the poor people of God. But if he continued to do as he had done lately, and undermined such petitions as the army's, deliverance would arise to the oppressed from another place "than from you silken Independents, the broken reeds of Egypt in the House and Army." Should Cromwell continue his course, Lilburne promised to arraign him at the bar of God for delivering his friends into the tyrannical clutches of Holles and Stapleton "against whom we are sufficiently able to preserve our selves if it were not for hee O Cromwell."[26]

Cromwell sent some oral reply to the letter, but Lilburne pronounced it no more satisfactory than

---

[24] *Iust Mans Iustification*, p. 5.
[25] *The Copy of a letter*; *Ionahs Cry*, pp. 6 ff.
[26] *Ibid.*, p. 2. The letter was carried by Mrs. Lilburne.

anything else he had heard lately from Cromwell
and his overwise friends "that are not able to trust
God three halfe pence." It was in Cromwell's
nature to shrink from practical application in politics of the radical theories. Lilburne had soon
learned that what help he could obtain from the
army must come in spite of the higher officers. He
had been at work upon the private soldiers of the
army, and by his own account had had much to do
with putting them into a posture of resistance to the
Parliament.[27] The "gentlemen Independents" realized clearly enough the existence of this division
in their ranks. "Your trusty and good freind
Lilburne" ran a letter of information of July 8
written, Professor Firth thinks, by Scout Master
Watson, "is printing his [letter] against Rich and
the Abbott and me, and saith in so many words
(to Captaine White of the Tower) that he had
rather cutt Sir Harry Vane's throate than Hollis's.
It was in some bodys power to have quench'd this
fire (we speak not as to our own particulars) while

[27] "I applyed my selfe," he says, "vigorously unto the honest blades,
the private Soulders, I meane, of the Army. . . . And when by
much industry with much opposition from your selfe and others of your
fellow Grandees in the Army, I had been instrumentall with the expence
of a great deale of money, and with all the interest and industry I had
in the world; acted both night and day to settle the Souldiers in a compleat and just posture, by their faithfull agitators chosen out by common
consent from amongst themselves, as resolute, fit, and just instruments
to effect my Liberty, to give a checke to tyranny, and settle the peace
and justice of the Kingdome, not looking for any good at all from your-
selfe, and the rest of your fellow-great ones [who are selling the liberties
of England] . . . ." *Ionahs Cry*, p. 9. He tells a similar story
in a letter to Fairfax printed in *The Ivglers Discovered*, Oct. 1, 1647, E.
409 (22).

it was a spark, which perhaps in time may grow too great to be quenched."[28]

The chances for harmony between the army, the Parliament, and the radicals were not improved by the fact that the radical chief remained shut up in the Tower. Chafing under his detention in prison,[29] Lilburne taught his followers that the House of Commons had no legal authority so long as the members who had sat in the absence of the speakers remained unexpelled; therefore he refused to acknowledge this "linsey woolsey" House in any such way as petitioning the members directly for his liberty. This attitude would not, so he said, prevent him from accepting his freedom passively at their hands. At times his anger against them rose so high that he threatened to appeal to the

---

[28] *Clarke Papers*, I, 158.

[29] One incident may be noted to illustrate his irritation. In the spring, he thought that his failure to secure a hearing and a report on his case to the House of Commons was due to Marten's negligence. Lilburne could conceive of only one remedy; and he printed late in May an angry letter to Marten, *Rash Oaths unwarrantable*. Marten thought of replying in print; and Lilburne, having been convinced by Walwyn that Harry had really done his utmost, being as swift in his penitence as he had been in his anger, urged Marten to take this means of clearing himself. Like a chivalrous combatant of the pen, he offered to pay for the printing of Marten's retort. By the end of July when he made this offer, Marten seems to have thought better of rushing into print and merely returned Lilburne a good-humored, if somewhat patronizing, letter. Apparently Lilburne printed it along with one of his own in which he offered to stand good for Marten's printer's bill.

The beginning of a jocose pamphlet by Marten in reply is in the Loder Symonds Mss. Its title is "Rash censures uncharitable"! *Hist. Mss. Comm.* XIII, 400. The two letters printed by Lilburne are in *Two Letters: The One From Lievtenant Colonell Iohn Lilbourne To Colonel Henry Martin . . . With His Answer*, 8122 d 69.

army to cut them off; actually he made some such
appeal after September 14, saying he would see
what the hobnails and clouted shoes and the private
soldiers of the army would do for him and for themselves. He tried when in this mood to avoid ap-
pearing before a committee of the House that was
considering his case, pleading that he could not
conscientiously accept its authority.[30]

Lilburne and Overton also had misgivings of the
good faith of the officers. For Fairfax they had a
real esteem, but they heartily distrusted Cromwell
and Ireton and their adherents. Both of the radicals were quick to scent the officers' intention of
transacting business in the Council of War rather
than along with the "agitators" in the Council of
the Army; and they warned the soldiers to be on
their guard. Overton warned the men that there
was a plot afoot to rob the men of all voice in the
army's councils; for a declaration had issued from
Fairfax and the council of war instead of from
Fairfax and the officers and soldiers.[31] Lilburne
published his letters to Cromwell and Fairfax with
the avowed intention of putting the privates on

---

[30] *Two Letters Writ By Lievt Col. John Lilburne, Prerogative prisoner
in the Tower*, Sept. 22, 1647, E. 407 (41).

In *The Ivglers Discovered* he declared that had he done as the soldiers
wished—broken jail and come to them—he would have led them sword
in hand to cut off the tyrants at Westminster. Pp. 2, 3.

In spite of his scruples, he had a hearing before a committee, October
20; November 9 the House of Commons ordered that he be at liberty to
go abroad without a keeper, provided he return at night to the Tower.
Journal, V, 353.

[31] Overton's *Appeale*, p. 30.

their guard against the doubtful dealing of the "Grandees."

The radicals dated their formal break with the "gentlemen Independents" from about the 20th of August when Walwyn sought to persuade the officers to trust the guarding of the Tower to the city radicals rather than raise a new regiment for the purpose. Price and Lordell of Goodwin's congregation out-argued Walwyn. The radicals broke off relations, accusing the Independents of seeking to carry on a "New England design;" words fit to be pondered by one comparing parties in Old and New England in the days of the Great Civil War.[32]

The breach between the Levellers and the Grandees was of course welcome to the Royalist writers, who by September had turned against the army leaders. They gave the warmest encouragement to Lilburne's dread of Cromwell's ambition. Probably they thought that their policy was to foment by all means possible the attacks on Cromwell.[33] Down to the escape of the king from Hampton Court, Royalist journals such as *Mercurius Pragmaticus* and *Mercurius Elencticus* caressed Lilburne, the agents, and the Levellers. It is true they insin-

---

[32] *Walwyns Just Defence* (p. 1) puts the occurrence at the time when the army's headquarters were at Kingston. Rushworth (VII, 789) says that the question of a guard for the Tower had been considered for some days before the twenty-fourth; according to the same authority (p. 792) the headquarters were removed from Kingston to Putney August 28. The expression regarding the "New England design" is in Prince, *The Silken Independents Snare Broken*, June 20, 1649, E. 560 (24), p. 2. The same phrase is in *Two Letters*, E. 407 (41).

[33] Such attacks are in the second *Two Letters*; *The Ivglers Discovered*.

uated that Lilburne's fellow-prisoner, the Royalist judge, David Jenkins, had carefully trained him in resistance to the usurped authority of the Commons; but they gave the pupil full credit for his bold opposition to Cromwell. As late as October 26, they spread the report that Lilburne would soon declare for the king.[34]

The departure of the king from Hampton Court on the night of November 11 rid the Levellers of these would-be friends. Charles had named as one reason for his departure the fact that the Levellers had threatened to assassinate him. Under the circumstances the Royalist journals could only accept the statement for truth, and load Lilburne and his friends with the abuse which the sin of regicide merited.[35] The Levellers, clear of both the Independents and Royalists, could now develop their program unhampered.

[34] *Pragmaticus*, Oct. 19–26; *Elencticus*, Oct. 29–Nov. 5. The superficial resemblance of his political affiliations in the past to those of Marchamont Nedham might have suggested that his opposition to the governing powers would end like Nedham's; for Nedham had been a furious Parliament man and Independent until 1646. One of the ephemeral journals that endeavored to oppose *Pragmaticus—Mercurius Anti-Pragmaticus*—Oct. 12–19, declared that Nedham had assisted Lilburne in the composition of *The Ivglers Discovered*. This in itself is not very likely. Lilburne was also accused of being completely under the influence of the Royalists who fuddled him with drink, and then set him on to desperate designs against the state. *The additional Plea.*

[35] That there was any real plot among the Levellers to assassinate the king, as distinguished from bringing him to trial, is doubtful. See Note J p. 189.

III. POLITICAL THEORIES OF 1647

The party reversals and alliances of 1647 appear less arbitrary if studied in the light of the pamphlet controversy. In that controversy the different parties reveal their positions when they attempt to define the army's right to interfere in politics. The Royalists, when they hoped for the king's restoration at the hands of the army, stated that right as the right of good and loyal subjects to succor their king. The Levellers took an entirely different position. They were convinced that the failure of the House of Commons to fulfil the people's trust and free the nation had cancelled its power of attorney; therefore the kingdom was without government, and in a state of nature. Accordingly, every honest man was at liberty to promote the kingdom's welfare by what means seemed best to him; and if the army professed such an end, it had the right to pursue it. However, Ireton and the men who assisted him in drawing the army declarations were unwilling to adopt entirely either justification. They hesitated at such a restoration of the king as the Royalists demanded; and they minimized like cautious men the degree of the kingdom's reversion to a state of nature. Although their defenders pleaded the law of nature and necessity, the army leaders were eager to take shelter under the wing of parliamentary authority as soon as possible; and accordingly they shrank from admitting that the rightful authority of the constituted government was at an end.

As early as March the Levellers had pronounced the kingdom in a state of nature. Such utterances at dates corresponding with those of the burnt petitions create a suspicion that those petitions were intended to provoke Parliament to extreme repressive measures that would justify an appeal to the nation. On March 1, Lilburne and Overton in *The Out-cryes of oppressed Commons*,[36] threatened to make such an appeal in case the House continued to refuse them justice. They admitted that no legal form or warrant for appeal existed; it would destroy the constitution of the kingdom, and cast it back on the original law of nature. But the House of Commons by failing to do them justice according to the law of the land had itself rooted up the recorded rights and privileges of their fellow-commoners, and left England, void of just government, in a state of nature. Therefore the fundamental laws of the kingdom could be saved from destruction only by a recurrence to the law of nature and an appeal to the people.[37]

[36] E. 378 (13).

[37] *A Warning For all the Counties of England* is more specific. It charges the majority of the House of Commons with plotting to enslave the kingdom. One step in their design was to disband the army. A second involved weeding out the "faithful" members in the House by the imposition of oaths which they must in conscience refuse. The avowed program of this plot was the City Remonstrance. The "Warning" concludes by calling on the people to exact an accounting from their servants, and if it is not satisfactory, to recall power into their own hands. Mar. 24, 1646/7, E. 381 (13).

July 17, 1647, Overton really did issue an *"Appeale"* from the representatives of the people to the people themselves. Its logical content is not very different from that laid down in the *Out-cryes of oppressed Commons*. Overton sweeps aside the admitted lack of precedent for an

The breach between the House of Commons and the radicals which induced the latter to appeal to the people changed in a marked degree Lilburne's attitude toward the king. Lilburne no longer assailed the arbitrary power of the king and the Lords; neither did he exalt the power of the people's own trusted House of Commons. He was now compelled to admit that the salvation to which he had hoped the House had been leading the people during the past seven years was a vain dream. The House constituted an arbitrary and irresponsible government over the people, crushing them down by the law when the letter of the law was on its side, and overriding the law when it served as a bulwark of the people's freedom. Since the House's members could no longer sit in high seats above the law, and guide the people to freedom, they must be judged and condemned by the law; and the people must look elsewhere for deliverance. If the Houses attempted to take a stand on their legal position in the state to bar the people from marching to

appeal to the people with words taken from the Parliament declarations —reason is the fount of all just precedent. As reason gives being to all laws, they must all bend before reason. The principles of reason— that everything must defend its own existence, that necessity is a law above laws, that the equity of the law is superior to the letter—all warrant his appeal. A fourth principle of reason that he deduces tends still more to his end; namely, that trusted powers, if forfeited, fall into the hands of those who gave them; and that misuse of them automatically works such a forfeit. Declaring that he will no longer consider the traitors at Westminster a just House of Commons, he urges all the people of England to rise up with the army to cut them off. The people have it in their power to depute their natural power of self-preservation to any who rise up to do the work for them; but, says Overton, the army must beware of paltering with the people. Pp. 1–30.

freedom under new leaders, the Houses must remember that in 1642 they had justified the war against the king by the use of legal quibbles and arguments from *salus populi* that would far more easily apply to themselves. The king's power arose from the law, but the authority that Parliament had assumed could orginate only in the people's trust. Parliament could be supreme only by grace of the Commons' recognition that their power was derived from the people's trust, and designed for the people's welfare. When on such terms the Commons claimed supremacy, they empowered the people to revoke their trust if it was abused. The law of nature under which the members of the Houses had armed the people in 1642 would justify people and army in cutting them off in 1647.

Lilburne even considered that the king's past conduct compared favorably with that of the Houses. At least the king had never declared men traitors and rebels for petitioning him; and when all was said, his legal position was more plausible than that of Parliament. The army leaders in the declaration of June 14 had promised to effect the king's restoration after they had secured the people's liberties; and Lilburne, in urging Cromwell to keep a good understanding with the king, approved the avowed policy of the army.[38] Nor did he in this show himself inconsistent. He had in the past called the king a tyrant and murderer;

[38] In a letter of June 22. *Ionahs Cry*, pp. 6 ff. The rest of the paragraph preceding this is a paraphrase of parts of *Rash Oaths unwarrantable*.

but he was now convinced that the Houses were as bad. For the moment he thought it possible that the restoration of the people's liberties might come with the king. Lilburne had vehemently attacked kingship when the term was synonymous with arbitrary power; but he cared not what was the external form of the government of England, so long as that government was readily responsive to the people's wishes, and attentive to their rights and needs.

The Royalists in their printed utterances showed themselves willing to accept the army as the restorer of the kingship, either as the king's legal agent, or as the empowered representative of the people; a loyal people tired of the Parliament's six years' rebellion, although content to reap the fruits of Parliament's earlier efforts in behalf of their liberties. [9] The Independents, however, making a somewhat cautious application of radical arguments, did not accord the king quite such an important place in their program; to them his restoration was a means to an orderly settlement of the king-

[39] *The Riddles Unridled*, July 14, 1647, E. 398 (8); *A Letter Really written by a Moderate Cavallier to An Intelligent . . . Independent*, June 26, 1647, E. 394 (4).

Marchamont Nedham gave a cold-blooded analysis of the reasons that should induce the king to choose alliance with the Independents rather than the Presbyterians. His main reason was that the Presbyterian hierarchy was a dangerous enemy to monarchy, while the Independent system really involved a separation of church and state. *The Case of the Kingdom Stated, According to the Proper Interests of the severall parties Ingaged*, June 12, 1647, E. 392 (13). Of course divine-right tracts appeared side by side with more moderate Royalist writing. Jasper Mayne's *Ochlomachia*, E. 398 (19), came out July 15.

dom; not the only means, and in no wise the end itself. The Declaration of the Army enumerated necessary reforms in Parliament, engaged the army to submit freely to parliaments so reformed, and then suggested that after the king had assented to the proposed reforms he might be restored to his due rights so far as consistent with the freedom of the subject and with public security.[40]

The Independents were inclined to justify the army's defiance of Parliament and its constituted authority by assuming that the army acted as the agent, not of the king, but of the people. The people, they thought, were capable of deciding when acts of Parliament were likely to ruin them, and might lawfully plead the "law of necessity," the "necessity that knows no law," for opposing the Parliament; for the people had not yielded up their right to judge of necessity any more than a traveler who hired a guide parted with his right to use his own judgment in case the guide fell blind by the way.[41] To sum up in terms formerly employed by

[40] The same order is maintained in the Heads of the Proposals. *The Case Of The Armie* later claimed that this order had been departed from, and that the re-enthroning of the king with his veto before a settlement of the kingdom's liberties was secured might well enslave the nation. Oct. 19, 1647, E. 411 (9), p. 6.

[41] *The Army Harmelesse*, July 16, 1647, E. 398 (27). A point that the apologists for the army found hard to handle was the deduction that if Parliament must sequester eleven members on the demand of the army, it rested in the power of the army to expel the whole Parliament, and put an end to the liberties, even to the existence of parliaments. Here they were compelled to quibble. The army would not do such a thing; because one judge on a bench could be impeached or proceeded against by the others, it did not follow that the independence of the remaining judges was gone. *Reasons why the House of Commons ought . . . . to suspend the Members Charged by the Army*, July 1, 1647, E. 396 (1).

the radicals, the people were capable of deciding when the actions of their governors violated the law of reason, and the people could commission whom they would to execute their verdict.[42]

The theory that the people had employed the New Model Army to check the government in a passing emergency was quite different from Lilburne's theory that the kingdom was in a state of nature. The extreme to which he carried this doctrine alarmed the more moderate Independents. Speaking of the action of the army in taking the "Solemn Engagement" in June, he pronounced that the army by that action had resolved itself into a state of nature. Its members held their swords in their hands for their own preservation, and must thenceforth act by mutual agreement on principles of reason and safety arising from nature itself.[43] When in September the Council of the Army with a great flourish of trumpets had expelled a certain Major Francis White—a somewhat gloomy man and distinctly "otherwise minded"— for saying that there was no law in England but the sword, Lilburne cordially assented to the doctrine, professing that a righteous act performed by a troop of horse was as good law as he could now see in England.[44] The officers and those who repre-

[42] *A cleere and full Vindication Of the late Proceedings*, July 12, 1647, E. 397 (21).

[43] *Ionahs Cry*, p. 13.

[44] *Two Letters Writ By Lievt. Col. John Lilburne*, Sept. 22, 1647, E. 407 (41), p. 6. *The Copy of a Letter Sent to His Excellencie Sir Thomas Fairfax . . . . By Francis White, Maior of the Generalls Regiment of Foot*, Nov. 11, 1647, E. 413 (17).

sented their point of view realized the ill-effect on public opinion of the doctrine that the army was in a state of nature.[45]   They saw too that it abrogated the discipline of the army, and left on a very precarious footing the right of the officers to command.   Lilburne, on the other hand, was quite content to see military discipline at an end; for in such a case the power of the agitators would be as great as the power of the Grandees, and Lilburne trusted in the good intentions of the representatives of the common soldiers far more than in the good intentions of the officers.

The Presbyterians of course subjected the army's position to keen criticism.   It was easy to argue with truth that the army in reality had the support of but a small fraction of the people.   But the

---

[45] The authors of *The Case Of The Armie* protested against the recession of the army from the law of nature on which it had at first taken its stand.   Pp. 4, 5, 7.   In the middle of July the agitators desired a march on London to force the accomplishment of their ends; the officers, Cromwell especially, wished to delay, and trust to the efforts of their friends in Parliament for obtaining their demands.   The radical party in London sided with the agitators.   *Clarke Papers*, I, 205–209.   Ireton drew a sharp distinction between the condition of the army in July and that which it had occupied in June.   At the time of the "Engagement" "Wee were in all probability butt as ruin'd men, under noe acknowledgement nor own'd by noe body, by noe aucthoritie in the Kingdome."   Allen, one of the agitators, replied, attempting to show that even in July the army was not really "owned" by the Parliament.   *Ibid.*, pp. 199–201.   Cromwell and Fairfax moved the army on London only when the Parliament under the coercion of the city mob had already ceased to be a free Parliament.   After force had actually been used on the Parliament, Lilburne professed himself as unwilling to acknowledge it as a Parliament until the members of the Lords and Commons who had sat with the illegally elected speakers were purged out.

Presbyterians went farther.[46] They denied that there was any power in the people that could enable it to perform any act of government or employ extraordinary means for its own deliverance. The men of the army could judge only by right of the length of their swords; and as soon as a longer sword came, their judgment would be reversed. Above all, their proceedings would end in the establishment of a mobocracy. "Consider," said one author, "that if you let loose the bands of Government, and you that are Officers by your own example (and it may be further) teach the Souldiers to disobey the Parliament, that lesson will serve to teach them likewise how to resist their own Officers, and this you may take as a sure Rule, That a multitude will not long be servants to any designe, but within a while they will be Masters of it."[47]

The army leaders were far more uncomfortably conscious of the force of such criticisms than the Levellers. In fact the officers were eager to minimize the extent to which the kingdom or the army was resolved into a state of nature. They were aware of the contradictory nature of their position,

[46] There are many tracts that are mere wails of despair; for instance: *Works of Darkness Brought to Light,* July 23, 1647, E. 399 (36); *New Presbyterian Light springing out of Independent Darknes,* July 30, 1647, E. 400 (24); *Some Queries Propounded to the Common Councell,* July 30, 1647, E. 400 (26). There are satires in the same key. *The Totall and Finall Demands already made by, and to be expected from, the Agitators And Army,* July 21, 1647, E. 399 (9).

[47] *The Lawfulnes Of The Late Passages Of The Army,* June 28, 1647, E. 394 (12).

in claiming to act by authority of a Parliament
they had coerced by armed force. At best their
position was well-nigh revolutionary, disguise it as
they would. Of that the arguments of the army's
own pamphleteers were sufficient proof. The officers had reason to pay attention to those Presbyterians who warned them that the doctrine on
which they resisted the Parliament would allow the
private soldiers in their turn to mutiny against
their officers when they saw occasion. If in 1647
the Grandees disbelieved this, the future was to
afford them ample opportunity to quench in blood
mutinies kindled on the pretext of the "Solemn
Engagement." When they engaged against the
Parliament in 1647 for the sake of restoring the
people's liberties, they may not have foreseen the
possibility of a scene like that in Burford church-
yard on the 15th of May, 1649. But, unless they
were prepared to aver that their application of the
law of necessity was the only valid one, they must
at the end have admitted that the same law of
necessity justified the mutiny they abetted in 1647,
and the Leveller uprising of 1649. Almost to the
Restoration one succeeding government after another was driven to crush rebels whose aims it must
have admitted were just, and warranted by its own
engagements and pledges, even if inexpedient. The
curse was already on the track of the army officers
in 1647. The Levellers alone were to devise any
expedient that in the faintest degree offered a
possibility of escape from the vicious circle in which
Cromwell and his supporters were to be involved
deeper and deeper as the years went on.

The Levellers, frankly admitting in 1647 the revolutionary position of the kingdom, believed that a settlement in such a situation would restore a larger share of the nation's liberties than could otherwise be expected. In this belief for a time they had looked as opportunists to army, city Independents, and king for the security of the nation's rights. When they found none of these would serve, they were free to seek in the dissolution of all established authority a new method of making the people's liberties the supreme law of the kingdom.

NOTES

I. Alleged Leveller Assassination Plots in the Fall of 1647

Several pieces of contemporary evidence which have been treated by modern historians as more or less credible connect the Levellers with assassination plots against the king or against Cromwell in October and November, 1647. Perhaps the best known bit of evidence of this sort is the letter signed "E. R." which Charles I left behind him when he fled from Hampton Court. This letter is directed to the king and dated November 9. It states that the writer's brother had the night before been at a meeting where eight or nine agitators had discussed a design of making away with the king. These desperate men, says the informant, expected the support of the army preachers, Dell and Peters, because of the bitter language they had so often used against the king. Finally, the writer suggests his own house in "Broade Street" as a possible refuge for Charles.

The first and most important step toward deciding the authenticity of this letter is to determine as nearly as possible the source from which it originated. Dr. Gardiner (*Great Civil War*, IV, 15) suggested that the letter might have been written by Lieutenant-Colonel Henry Lilburne, and that John was his informant. A certain plausibility is given this conjecture by the fact that Henry Lilburne and Paul Hobson were later accused of spreading to the discredit of the agitators a story of their plot to assassinate the king. The tale went that John had told Henry of the designs of the agitators, and that Cromwell, on Henry's information, had written a letter to Colonel Whalley at Hampton Court that had scared the king away.   Lilburne, however, denied that he had told his brother anything of the sort; and though he and the men involved repeatedly protested against the circulation of the story, none of them, so far as I know, ever accused Henry of writing the "E. R." letter, though the letter had been published immediately after the king's flight.   *Innocency And the Blood of the slain Souldiers*, Aug. 9, 1649, E. 568 (12), p. 11; *The Prisoners Plea for a Habeas Corpus*, April 4, 1648, E. 434 (19).   There is hardly enough evidence to fasten the authorship of the letter on Henry Lilburne.

Further, if we assume that the letter was from Henry Lilburne we must suppose that he had reached a degree of intimacy with the king that would enable Charles to divine his identity from the cryptic signature "E. R."   The reference to the house in Broad street was probably misleading; for if Charles knew that the letter came from a friend and that the Broad street house was a genuine address, he would not have left behind him a clue by which the authorities might so easily hunt out one who had tried to do him service.   This leaves but one statement in the letter that is not either misleading or common gossip—that one regarding the presence of the writer's brother at a meeting of agitators. It is possible that some political confidant of the king had a brother on familiar terms with the agitators; it is as likely that Henry Lilburne was that confidant as that anyone else was.   But it is far easier to suppose that the statement regarding the writer's brother was a blind, and to reject as improbable the hypothesis that the letter was from a correspondent of the king, or was designed in good faith to furnish him genuine information.

The chances are that the letter was one of two things: a blind concocted by a Royalist close to the king, to afford a pretext for the king's flight; or a Presbyterian artifice to get the king away from the army. The latter hypothesis has some circumstantial evidence to support it.   At an earlier time the Scotch commissioners had first urged the king's coming to London, and then opposed it, with the design of getting him out of the quarters of the army and into their own hands.   This may have been another attempt of the same sort.   Berkeley's Narrative, Maseres, *Tracts*, I, 373–6.   In either case, the author's testimony as to the intentions of the Levellers is of little value.

Dr. Gardiner thinks worthy of mention (*Great Civil War*, IV, 21) a contemporary accusation that the Levellers conspired to kill Cromwell. The only authority for this is *Walwins Wiles*, p. 14.   The whole book is avowedly an attack on Walwyn; the story in question is told to injure him, but though a careless reader might believe he is accused of complicity, he really is not. The existence of the plot is vouched for on the authority of an anonymous witness who was told of it by a person concerned as a principal; Walwyn denied all knowledge of it. *Walwyns Just Defence.*

With this may be coupled a "plot" of the same sort unearthed by Godwin—one by Wildman and Lilburne to kill Cromwell in the late summer of 1647. Godwin's essential evidence is a statement from Holles's *Memoirs* that the radicals were in great wrath against Cromwell "and as appears by that business of Lilburn and Wildman, even resolve to take Cromwell out of the way, and murder him for an Apostate." Maseres, *Tracts*, I, 295. Manifestly Holles was speaking of something that was a matter of common report—past all doubt the accounts of the meeting at Wapping of January 16, 1647/8 that Lilburne and Wildman had attended. Undoubtedly the thing he referred to was their story that a certain member of the Commons (Harry Marten) had cherished a design of assassinating Cromwell for apostatizing to the king. It is difficult to be patient with Godwin when he turns this into a design by Lilburne and Wildman to murder Cromwell. As he lets the imputation color his account of the army councils of October and November, so that it becomes a narrative of the two guilty plotters' alliance with the high-minded republicans of the army, the vicious result of his mistake can easily be seen. Godwin, *Commonwealth*, II, 434.

II. LILBURNE'S ATTITUDE TOWARD THE COMMONS IN 1647

The only excuse for the violence of Lilburne's language against the Commons in 1647 is that over a year's illegal and expensive imprisonment had provoked it from a man whose spirit had been rasped, but not broken by illegality and injustice. In simple justice to him it should be said that he was importunate for a decision in his own case from a sense of the importance of the principle at stake, rather than from undue consideration of his own welfare. When he learned that the Army Council was considering the possibility of releasing him on bail, he begged that all thought of such a thing might be abandoned, as in a measure it would surrender the principle for which he had contended—that the jurisdiction of the Lords over commoners was illegal from top to bottom. If bail was the only device that occurred to the army, he begged to be left to his fate. "I walk not, nor act not from accidents," he wrote Fairfax, on another proposal of compromise, "but from principals, and being throughly perswaded in my own soule they are iust, righteous, and honest, I will by Gods goodnesse never depart from them though I perish in maintaining them;

. . . . and therefore I both must and will run the hazard of spending my heart blood, to root up and destroy their [the Lords] illegal and unjust usurpations . . . . and can never willingly without being a Trayter to my self and Country, consent in this to close, with them . . . ." *The Ivglers Discovered*, pp. 4, 9. To show his disinterestedness he offered to leave England until a permanent peace was made, if only the Commons would formally deny the Lords' right to jurisdiction in first resort over commoners, and either do Lilburne himself reasonable justice, or leave his case to the next Parliament. In a formal offer of this sort on October 6, he made his terms the nullifying of his sentence, £2,000 Star-Chamber damages, and £600 arrears. *The additional Plea of Lievt Col. Iohn Lilburne*, Nov. 1, 1647, E. 412 (11). But in spite of all his disinterestedness, his bias hindered his party from acquiescing in the army's dealing with the Parliament.

CHAPTER VI

THE FIRST AGREEMENT OF THE PEOPLE

I. .THE NEED FOR A STABLE CONSTITUTION

IN the fall of 1647 the radicals brought forth a new design for the realization of their political ideals. In the spring they had learned that the Long Parliament would not aid them in freeing the people; therefore they had pronounced the kingdom in a state of nature, and all lawful government at an end. Now a group of radicals in the army, acting under Leveller tutelage and following out the Leveller political ideas, planned that the people themselves secure their rights and end the civil war by establishing a government responsible to themselves and bound by paramount law from endangering their liberties.[1]

---

[1] *Infra*, p. 232, for the close relation between the civilian and army Levellers. At the beginning, an estimate of the book that has handled the theme of this chapter in most detail may be interesting. Dr. Walther Rothschild in *Der Gedanke der ʒeschriebenen Verfassung in der englischen Revolution* analyses minutely the development of the idea of the written constitution through the various propositions, proposals, and agreements. A criticism lies against his method in that he at once tries to prove too much and too little. He interprets every demand for the establishment of popular liberties or parliamentary privileges as implying a desire for a written constitution. Dr. Rothschild, however, does not take into account what is more probably implied in such demands—a sense of the binding force of custom and precedent, and a desire for its sanction to the new constitutional settlement. Again one returns to the words of Professor McIlwain quoted in an earlier chapter: "The validity of the law is not due to the form of the docu-

The idea of limiting government by law was in the air. A reëstablishment of the constitution in such form that it could not again be set aside by the rivalry of king and Parliament was probably the one thing that men of all parties desired. The army especially was concerned in seeing the results of the war embodied in a stable and enduring peace. By means that might easily be held seditious, it had achieved a political importance out of all proportion to its numbers; therefore it would be the first to suffer if the settlement it dictated were undone. Accordingly, self-interest suggested to the army the establishment of a peace that would curb the power of both Parliament and king; and with this end in view the radicals among the rank and file finally proposed something very close to a written constitution.

Under the circumstances it is surprising that the army leaders failed to devise any adequate security for the permanence of the constitutional settlement they sought to negotiate with the king. True, the changes proposed by Ireton's Heads of the Proposals[2] did not alter the ancient constitu-

ment, but rather to the character of the principles." The agreements and proposals that Dr. Rothschild catalogues of course are constitutional proposals and in writing, but only in a very narrow sense does this make them written constitutions. On the other hand, Dr. Rothschild hardly lays sufficient stress on the tendency to regard such proposals as statements of paramount law, although from 1647 to 1649 that tendency becomes more and more apparent.

[2] The Heads of the Proposals were probably drawn by Commissary-General Ireton with Lambert's assistance. A draft of them was in existence by July 17, and they were published August 2. *Clarke Papers*, I, xl–xli. See Note I, p. 226.

tional system in any of its essentials. The Heads
of the Proposals took the form of sketches for acts
of Parliament. If king, Lords, and Commons had
assented to these acts, the kingdom might have
passed from a state of war to a state of peace by
means of constitutional forms that were already
familiar and customary. One clause in the first
draft of the Proposals, making the king's veto
merely suspensive, might have presented difficulties; but in the finished document it was omitted.[3]
Once the king had assented to the acts of Parliament specified, he could have questioned the constitutionality of the settlement only by professing
that his assent had been extorted under duress.
On the other hand, the Lords and Commons of
the Long Parliament by passing the acts would
of their own accord have surrendered the illimi-
table powers they claimed over the nation to a
succession of parliaments, each limited by law to
eight months' duration.

Precisely because the Heads of the Proposals preserved the older forms, they lacked the element of
permanence. Being acts of Parliament, the provisions of the Heads of the Proposals could legally
be repealed by any future Parliament. Ireton's
solution pledged the nation to acquiescence in the
acts of absolute parliaments, limited only by eight
month leases of power and yearly elections; and
Ireton could offer no effective guarantee that even
these limitations might not be repealed. He him-

[3] *Putney Proiects. Or the Old Serpent In a new Forme*, John Lawmind
Wildman], Dec. 30, 1647, E. 421 (19), p. 14.

self would shrink from tampering with a constitutional settlement that professed to be permanent,
even though its abrogation were technically possible. The only safeguard for the Proposals would
be that so far his attitude was typically English.[4]

The point will be clearer if we contrast with the
Heads of the Proposals certain propositions published in *An Appeale* by Richard Overton:

Concerning Parliaments.

1. That for the future, the election and expulsion of
Parliament Members may be so setled in the Electors, that
none may be hindered, debard, or expulsed from serving his
Country under any colour or pretence whatsoever, as for
refusing the Covenant or other wise without order first,
assent or concurrence of their Countrey.

2. That for the better security of the interest and power
of the people, all titles by Prerogative, Priviledge, Pattent,
Succession, Peerage, Birth or otherwise to sit and act in
the Assembly of Parliament, contrary to, and without the
free choice and Election of the People, be utterly abrogated,
nuld and made voide, and that all such so sitting, may be
removed from sitting therein.

3. That the authority of Parliament may bee preserved
and secured for the future from the obstructions and preju-

---

[4] Ireton in debate put more emphasis on the constitutional side of
the Proposals than I have indicated. "Wee doe thinke that the settlement of peace is by having a settlement of itt in our hands; if ever
itt doe come to settle, itt must bee by setting downe some thinge that
may bee a rule to lay a foundation for the common rights and liberties
of the people, and for an established peace in the Nation." *Clarke
Papers*, I, 197, July 16, 1647.

The author of *A Plain, Short, And Probable Expedient* proposed as
a means of legally garnering the fruits of the war, that Parliament, in
accord with precedent in the case of the inability of the king to discharge his duties, appoint a regent who should proceed to frame a strin-
gent oath, and administer it to the king; this done, the king might safely
be restored. Nov. 4, 1647, E. 412 (28).

dice of a negative voyce in any person or persons whatsoever.[5]

Clearly new constitutional machinery must be
devised to put in effect such limitations of government. If the king's and Lords' negative voice were
taken away on the ground that it was and had
always been illegal, king and Lords could scarcely
be asked to give their consent to the act abolishing
their veto. Probably they would refuse assent; the
fact that their assent was asked would be a strange
commentary on the theory that their assent had
never of right been necessary. Moreover, Overton would surely demand further security for the
nation's freedom than limitations on future parliaments sanctioned merely by Long Parliament acts.

Stricter constitutional limitation upon government than the English people had known in generations was essential; and thought of this need and
of what might satisfy it had been running in men's
heads for months past. Thus pamphleteers were
demanding that the privileges of Parliament be
definitely stated, and assigned certain limits. However, even the Heads of the Proposals purported
to do this; the question was rather who should
determine and enforce the limitations. Very significant in this connection is one otherwise very
commonplace pamphlet—*The Lawyers Bane. Or,
The Lawes Reformation*.[6] It begins with the state-

[5] P. 32. See foot note 37, p. 180, *supra*.

[6] Aug. 13, 1647, E. 401 (36), p. 11. The note to the reader is signed
"Nicholsone". For the tendency mentioned above, see *The Lawyer
of Lincolnes-Inne Reformed* by Marchamont Nedham, July 1, 1647, E.
395 (4).

ment that since ignorance of the law excuses no one,
the laws should be short, few, and compendious,
"and withal so easy and plaine to be understood,
that if any man should plead ignorance of them,
it could be no other than wilfull & affected." The
writer proposes a thorough revision of the laws,
both common and statute; the sum of them in so
far as it accords with the "genius" of the people
is to be set down in short compass, and all other
law abrogated. In the light of this provision for
putting the laws of the kingdom into a form in
which they would be plain to all men, the constitutional conclusions of the piece acquire a new
interest.

since . . . . the Law is that which terminates and
bounds the rights and interests of all men, as well of the
King in his Prerogative, as of the people in their priviledges
and immunities, and seeing these are the two Poles, upon
which . . . . the Sphear of government moves, whose
influences, if they keep their equall and just distances, are
peace and happinesse; and on the contrary, if they interfere
and clash together, they produce certaine ruine and destruction to the Nation; and further considering that these two
. . . . having been the causes and originalls of all the
civill warres in this Nation, since the Norman-conquest (the
contestation between the White rose and the Red not
excepted: and therefore it were above all other things cordially to be wished and desired (the reformation of the Lawes,
as aforesaid scarcely excepted) that the limites and extents
of these two (viz. the Kings Prerogative and the peoples
priviledges) might be throughly and throughly examined
and enquired after, & being once certainly known and fo nd
out they might by the consent, and to the good and happinesse of all Parties, be boundered out to all posterities with
two Herculean pillars and a non plus ultra, in golden Capital
letters written on them, to the everlasting peace, quietnesse

and prosperity both of King and People, so far as humane prudence may extend) in this and all succeeding generations.

This cry for an end to constitutional innovation was characteristic of the time, for the seven years that had passed since 1640 had added to the nation's constitutional experience. Their events had taught men that the fundamental laws of the land could not resist interested and partial interpretation, because they were uncertain in content. *The Lawyers Bane* had suggested a written statement of the constitution, so plain as to be self-evident without interpretation. There was still the question of who should state the fundamental laws, and of how they might be invoked against government at need. The Levellers pressed on toward a solution of these questions, blindly at first, but with ever-increasing certainty as the years went by.

II. THE GENESIS AND NATURE OF THE FIRST AGREEMENT

The First Agreement of the People, the Leveller solution to the question of permanent peace, represents a strange medley of political ideas that are hard to understand, and harder yet to describe. The Agreement is, and it is not, a written constitution; yet it is the forerunner of agreements that answer every test that an American constitutionalist can apply. To be understood, the document must be studied as expounded by its authors; and their exposition in turn must be weighed with their view of the actual political situation of October, 1647.

The First Agreement of the People was the result of a growing consciousness among the rank and file that the army's situation was precarious in the extreme. By October the policy of Cromwell and Ireton had apparently broken down. The dullest observer would have dismissed as academic the question whether the Heads of the Proposals could ever be made the basis of a permanent constitution. The king would have none of the Heads of the Proposals or any other terms that Cromwell and Ireton could obtain for him from their supporters. Neither could the army depend permanently on the Parliament; for the slightest relaxation of military coercion would restore the Presbyterians to power. If the army could not soon obtain from some source a constitutional settlement of unquestioned validity, it might lose all it had won and at last fall victim to popular fury in a reaction that restored the king to power, unbound by conditions or bound only by those that he might disregard on plea of duress. Even if such a reaction merely restored the old constitution and the king's negative voice, the king with the support of a nation hostile to the army might repeal any ordinary act of indemnity that the army had obtained. Meanwhile the army was left by the government to find free quarter in private houses; and necessarily the best of armies in such a situation would be disorderly enough to provoke the hatred of its hosts.[7]

[7] A tract of 1649 urging the soldiers to win the affection of the people may afford an illustration. It exhorts them as follows: "be courteous and gentle towards all you meet, whether in the streets, or upon the

The attempt to secure by taxation sufficient funds to dispense with free quarter might render the army still more unpopular, not merely in the districts where it was quartered, but throughout the nation as well.

The growing distrust of Cromwell and Ireton in the army was unfounded; but it was natural. Only a later generation has possessed the evidence needed to explain their conduct on other motives than hypocrisy, deceit, and self-seeking. They had persisted in their overtures to the king, until a section of their party in the House split off under Rainsborough and Marten on republican principles.[8] Moreover, five regiments of horse, influenced by distrust both of their representatives in the Army Council and of their leaders, chose new agents who practically represented the Leveller point of

Roads; give them kind language & civil respects, without justling, or brushing or bustling for the way; a thing which some proud Officers have cherish'd too much in some rude persons: and at your Quarters exercise your selves in harmless refreshments, without noise or lavish expence and give the preeminence to the Master and Mistris of the Family, whether rich or poor." *The English Souldiers Standard To Repaire to*, Apr. 5, 1649, E. 550 (1), p. 10. See also *Vox Populi: Or The Svpplications and Proposalls of the Subjects of this miserable Kingdome: Languishing and almost expiring, under the heavy burden of Free Quarter*, Nov. 1, 1647, E. 412 (15).

[8] How closely Rainsborough was in touch with the Levellers at the time is uncertain. Marten was hand in glove with them. To draw a sharp line between the Leveller party and the republicans is impossible. There were many men with republican principles; but there was hardly a permanent republican party so definitely alined as the Leveller party. The Levellers can scarcely be defined as purely republican; and the two sets of men were finally divided by the question of accepting or rejecting the government of the Commonwealth. A man like Ludlow would have but little in common with the Levellers. Gardiner, *Great Civil War*, III, 366 ff.

view. The news sent out from headquarters, it is true, insinuated that the "new agents" had the support of but a small minority of the army; their actions, however, were confident and decided.[9]

In a statement presented to Fairfax on October 15, the agents registered their disapproval of the political course hitherto pursued by the army leaders. Nothing, the agents complained, had been done toward redressing the grievances that had first driven the army into revolt. Parliament's vote against the army's petition remained unrepealed, a standing disgrace to the army. Parliament vouchsafed no consideration to the political reforms that the soldiers had demanded as Englishmen. Parliament itself was still defiled by the presence of corrupt and delinquent members; no date had been set for its dissolution. In the nation such old abuses as tithes and arbitrary committees still flourished. In the army itself there was bad faith; the provision of the Solemn Engagement that pledged the army neither to divide nor disband till full satisfaction was obtained had been technically violated. Moreover, the Grandees of the Army Council insidiously urged the soldiers to be content with demanding redress of their grievances as soldiers, and to abandon the political reforms which they had pledged themselves to secure as Englishmen. Inducing the soldiers to

---

[9] *Clarke Papers*, I, xlvii. The choice of agents took place in the first part of October. By November eleven other regiments had chosen agents. *Papers From The Armie Concerning His Excellency and the Generall Councell, their dislike of the Papers from the new Agents*, Oct. 23, 1647, E. 411 (19).

cheat the nation of the natural right and freedom they had promised, it was bad enough in itself; but the result was likely to be even worse. The king, with his right of veto, seemed likely to return to power before the people's freedoms were sufficiently secured. Thus the pledges made to the people by the Declaration of the Army would all be broken and discredited. Small wonder, the agents concluded, if the nation's affection toward the army had cooled; for, if the nation could hope for nothing but tyranny, why should it prefer a hundred tyrants to one?[10]

Perhaps *The Case Of The Armie* exaggerated the army's unpopularity. It may have been far lighter, far more a passing mood than the agents for the five regiments supposed. But the blindest man in the army must have seen some degree of danger. Formerly there had appeared to be two ways of averting it. First, the army might have restored the king on terms that would have given it genuine security, and at the same time would have pacified the people with the reforms proposed in the Heads of the Proposals. Second, the army might have united with the Parliament, the only other legal or *quasi* legal authority in the kingdom, and have forced the king to terms by its aid. The first expedient had been tried and had failed because the king would not frankly meet the army halfway on the Heads of the Proposals; there was ever in his mind the possibility of a diplomatic game with

[10] *The Case Of The Armie Truly stated*, Oct. 19, 1647, E. 411 (9). See Note II, p. 227.

the English or Scotch Presbyterians in which the
Covenant, the establishment of an intolerant Presbyterianism, the militia, and the negative voice
would be the counters.   The second expedient—accord with the majority of the House of Commons—
was impossible for any length of time; first, because the hold of the army's friends on the House
could not be permanently relied on; second, because
the army had repeatedly denounced long sessions
of parliaments and, as public opinion then stood,
it would be a matter of years at least before the
army leaders could venture on a new election.

Under these circumstances could the common
soldier of the army, conscious of the hatred of
fathers whose children were stinted in their scanty
subsistence by the free quarter on which he lived,
discover a third way out of the difficulty?   It was
plain to him that the hearts of the people were not
with the army.   Yet surely the people still desired
the liberties for which the soldiers had engaged in
the Parliament's quarrel with the king.   Perchance
the people's hearts had turned away from the army,
because the army had neglected the people's liberties.   If, then, the soldiery were able to devise
an ample form of guaranty for the people's liberties,
would not the people's hearts return to the army?
A political catch-phrase of the time seemed to suggest such a guaranty.   For the past six months
politicians and pamphleteers had enumerated the
various "interests" of the kingdom and discussed
the possibility that some happy combination of
interests might give lasting peace.   The soldiers

had heard of the "king's interest," "the House of Commons interest," "the City interest," "the Presbyterian interest," "the Scots' interest," "the army interest." Lilburne had repeatedly complained that in the "army interest" the common soldier had too small a voice. Further, Lilburne had taught that England was in a state of nature, and the legal authority of constituted government at an end. This doctrine would sanction the employment of a novel method to bring about a combination between the soldiers' interest and the people's interest. If these two interests could once come to an agreement on a program, might they not be able to bring the war to a happy end by establishing the freedom that both soldiers and people seemed to crave? This idea in the minds of simple men, unaccustomed to sophisticated views of politics, produced the name and the original idea of the Agreement of the People.

Numerous proofs can be advanced to show that this was the idea in the minds of the agents who framed the Agreement of the People. First, in *The Case Of The Armie* the people were commiserated on finding in turn king, Parliament, and army to be all broken reeds. ". . . we wish therefore that the bowells of compassion in the whole armie might yearne towards their distressed brethren, and that they might with one consent say each to other, come let us joyne together speedily to demand present redresse for the peoples grievances, and securitie for all their and our own rights and freedomes as Soldiers and Commoners" (p. 13). *A*

Cal To All The Souldiers Of The Armie, October 29, urged the soldiery to seek the support of the people, "joyne and be one with them in heart and hand, with all possible speede in some substantiall and firme Agreement, for just freedom and common right, that this nation may no longer flote upon such wavering, uncertain and sandy foundations of Government, which have been one of the greatest causes both of all your, & our predecessors miseries." Most significant of all, *A Letter sent from several Agitators of the Army To their Respective Regiments,* November 12, said: "we were constrained to propound the foundations of freedome to be forthwith established by a mutual agreement between the people and you. . . . ."[11]

---

[11] The two last pamphlets cited above are E. 412 (10) and E. 414 (8). Additional instances might be multiplied. *An Alarum To The Headquarters,* Nov. 4, 1647, E. 413 (10), p. 4, thus addresses the cabinet council: "Doe but you your duty, remove all oppressions, ease the Country, down with all monopolies, and tyrannous oppressions; draw up a Declaration fully to the People, and Remonstrate that this ye will doe for them, this yee will have, this yee have fought for, this you will maintaine, live and dye, for resolvedly: wee'le warrant you hobnailes and clouted shooes will give you harty thankes and help and assist you: You need not feare them, ease them of their oppressions, pitty their cries, redresse their grievances, and the work is done for them; for what say people, doe something or nothing; and if yee will not do it, tell the people so, if yee be faint-hearted . . . . if it be so, give way, let others come in, whose firme resolutions will stand, to engage for common right and freedome, for liberty and for justice unto bloud, doe not therefore hinder others . . . . but suffer us to free our selves, and the whole commonalty of the Kingdome . . . ."

The address to "the Free born People of England" that accompanied the Agreement of the People contains this passage: "Its grief and vexation of heart to us, to receive your meat or moneyes, whilest you have no advantage, nor yet the foundations of your peace and freedome

In short, the Agreement of the People was a device to "avoid both the danger of returning into a slavish condition and the chargeable remedy of another war," by means of an accord between soldiers and people. The principle on which this coalition was to act was partially suggested in the *Remonstrance Of Many Thousand Citizens* — popular control of government. Like the *Remonstrance*, the Agreement called for a succession of annual parliaments composed solely of the people's representatives, and elected in orderly course by the people. But the experience of the year that had elapsed since the *Remonstrance* had convinced the Levellers that this by itself was not enough. A higher power than Parliament must prescribe parliamentary elections, meetings, and adjournments, and must also limit the legislative power of Parliament in the interest of the people's safety. The Agreement of the People was the agency by which the nation was to accomplish these ends.

The Agreement of the People avowed as its immediate purpose the protection of the nation against being disappointed in future of "frequent national meetings in council." To this end representation must be equally apportioned according to the population of the kingdom. The Long Parlia-

surely layed: & therefore upon most serious considerations that your principall right [is concerned in their efficient representation in Parliament] . . . . wee desire you would consider, that as these things wherein we offer to agree with you, are the fruites & ends of the Victories which God hath given us . . . . and when you and we shall be joyned together therein, [in the Agreement] we shall readily joyn with you to petition the Parliament . . . ."

ment must dissolve on the last day of September
of 1648; the people in March of each alternate year
must as of course choose themselves a new Parliament to sit until the last day of September following. As for the power of this Representative it
was to be

. . . . inferior only to theirs who choose them, and
doth extend, without the consent or concurrence of any other
person or persons, to the erecting and abolishing of offices
and courts, to the appointing, removing and calling to
account magistrates and officers of all degrees, to the making war and peace, to the treating with foreign States, and,
generally, to whatsoever is not expressly or impliedly reserved by the represented to themselves:

Which are as followeth.

1. That matters of religion and the ways of God's worship
are not at all entrusted by us to any human power, because
therein we cannot remit or exceed a tittle of what our consciences dictate to be the mind of God without wilful sin:
nevertheless the public way of instructing the nation (so it
be not compulsive) is referred to their discretion.

2. That the matter of impresting and constraining any of
us to serve in the wars is against our freedom; and therefore
we do not allow it in our Representatives; the rather, because
money (the sinews of war), being always at their disposal,
they can never want numbers of men apt enough to engage
in any just cause.

3. That after the dissolution of this present Parliament,
no person be at any time questioned for anything said or
done in reference to the late public differences, otherwise
than in execution of the judgments of the present Representatives or House of Commons.

4. That in all laws made or to be made every person may
be bound alike, and that no tenure, estate, charter, degree,
birth, or place do confer any exemption from the ordinary
course of legal proceedings whereunto others are subjected.

5. That as the laws ought to be equal, so they must be

good, and not evidently destructive to the safety and well-being of the people.

These things we declare to be our native rights, and therefore are agreed and resolved to maintain them with our utmost possibilities against all opposition whatsoever; being compelled thereunto not only by the examples of our ancestors, whose blood was often spent in vain for the recovery of their freedoms, suffering themselves through fraudulent accommodations to be still deluded of the fruit of their victories, but also by our own woeful experience, who, having long expected and dearly earned the establishment of these certain rules of government, are yet made to depend for the settlement of our peace and freedom upon him that intended our bondage and brought a cruel war upon us.[12]

This document inevitably tempts comparison with American written constitutions. In drawing such a comparison we must proceed with caution. We may not assume that similar phraseology proves similar content; because to our own age one constitutional idea appears the inevitable consequence of another, we may not assume that it so appeared to seventeenth-century England. If we do otherwise, we shall fall into ludicrous mistakes. Professor Maitland has warned us that if we introduce the idea of the *persona ficta* into the heads of too early a generation of medieval lawyers, we shall blunder as badly as if we armed Hengist and Horsa with machine guns or pictured the Venerable Bede correcting proofs for the press. Accordingly, with this seventeenth-century "constitution," we may let its advocates tell us in their own words what they thought it; and with this we must be content, however meager or contradictory our results appear.

[12] The Agreement can most easily be consulted in Gardiner, *Constitutional Documents*, p. 333.

Beginning with the obvious, we may be sure that the Agreement was designed as a paramount law to limit Parliament. Thus it enumerated certain legislative powers as withheld by the people from Parliament. True, this "bill of rights" was the only part of the instrument specifically declared unalterable by Parliament; yet we are not assuming too much when we suppose that the Agreement's avowed aim, biennial parliamentary elections, was also intended to be unalterable. Thus the provisions regarding the "negative voice" would have enforced themselves; for if one set of representatives had admitted a "negative voice" in king or Lords, the people might have chosen more faithful servants at the next election. Therefore the more important clauses of the Agreement recited a law unalterable by Parliament.

The next question that naturally arises is of the manner of interpreting the paramount law defined by the Agreement. In practice, this power would have rested with the people. The Agreement directed them to proceed to new elections at stated times, without waiting for writ or warrant to legalize their work. Thus the people might have enunciated their interpretation; by exacting pledges of the representatives elected, they might also have enforced it.

When we seek after the method by which the nation was to indorse and adopt the Agreement we are on less sure ground. A certain soldier who goes in the report of the army-council debates by the name of "Bedfordshire Man" spoke of acting

for the people's good by petitioning or otherwise
"wherby the fundamentalls for a well-ordered Governement for the people's Rights may bee established."[13] Cromwell at one turn of debate advanced the supposition that the supporters of the
Agreement intended to put it into effect by getting
"hands to itt;"[14] a remark of Rainsborough's may
possibly be taken as an indication that numbers of
civilians had already subscribed the paper. Certainly it had been circulated for signatures in the
army.[15] While the framers of the Agreement regarded their constitution as an emanation from
the people at large, they had no clear concept of
the manner in which the people were to approve
or disapprove it.

Cromwell at once fastened on this weakness and
repeatedly recurred to it in the army-council debate. He urged the difficulty of getting the people
to accept the Agreement's provisions at all; and
he insisted that it be referred for approval to Parliament as the duly constituted authority of the
nation.[16] Otherwise, he said, the army ignored
the power that had created it, and thereby disavowed its own legal status. Evidently he would
not willingly have seen the Agreement established
by revolution. The Agreement's defenders could
not reply to him by specifying a procedure through
which the nation might formally adopt its new

---

[13] *Clarke Papers*, I, 252.
[14] *Ibid.*, p. 237.
[15] *Ibid.*, pp. 291–293.
[16] *Ibid.*, pp. 237, 369.

constitution. Therefore Cromwell and Ireton persisted in ignoring the Agreement's theoretical claims to consideration as a potential constitution for the English nation; instead, they treated it as the creed of a minority party.

In several respects the Agreement of the People represented to its proposers something narrower than a national constitution. It was not a complete description of government; it specifically declared that the power of constituting such governors and courts as the people required rested with the Parliament. Parliament, limited only by the few restrictions contained in the Agreement, was to write the real constitution of the kingdom in statute law.[17]

Moreover, the provision that the Long Parliament should not adjourn for a full year is significant. Apparently those who drew up the Agreement thought there was a better chance of securing desirable legislation from the Long Parliament than from the "people's representatives." Seen in this light the Agreement appears merely a device for protecting certain parts of the work of the Long Parliament, and especially its work of oblivion, from the destroying hand of some later Parliament which might wish to mete out vengeance to either Independent or New Model soldier. John Wildman, a young barrister who defended the Agreement in the Army Council, said of it:

[17] To be specific, the question of the retention of the king and Lords as constitutional figureheads might well be one that in this connection might engage the attention of the people's representatives.

this paper doth lay downe the foundations of freedome for all manner of people. Itt doth lay the foundations of souldiers [freedom], wheras they found a great uncertainty in the proposalls: that they should goe to the Kinge for an act of indempnity, and thus the Kinge might command his Judges to hange them uppe for what they did in the warres; because the present Constitution being left as itt was, nothing was law butt what the Kinge sign'd, and nott any ordnance of Parliament. And considering this, they thought itt should bee by an Agreement with the people, wherby a rule betweene the Parliament and the people might bee sett, that soe they might bee destroyed neither by the Kinge's Prerogative, nor Parliament's priviledges. . . . . They thought there must bee a necessity of a rule betweene the Parliament and the people, soe that the Parliament should know what they were intrusted to, and what they were nott; and that there might bee no doubt of the Parliament's power to lay foundations for future quarrells. The Parliament shall nott meddle with a souldier after indempnity. Itt is agreed amongst the people, wheras betweene a Parliament and Kinge—if the Kinge were nott under restraint—should make an Act of Indempnity—wheras another Parliament cannott alter this.[18]

Furthermore, we are not sure that the Agreement was intended to bind persons who did not assent to it. Cromwell suggested that every county in the kingdom might assume the liberty to establish its own agreement. Further, the trend of an army-council debate of November 2 seems to imply that the peers thenceforth, though deprived of a negative voice, should be bound only by legislation to

---

[18] *Clarke Papers*, I, 354. Clarke's notes are confused here, but the meaning is apparent enough. King and Parliament can alter an ordinary act of indemnity, but not an Agreement of the People.

John Wildman was a young man with some legal training and considerable natural aptitude as a debater. As a civilian spokesman for the agents in the Council of the Army he was in 1647 just entering on a career of political agitation that was to extend over well-nigh half a century.

which they themselves had given their assent.[19] Men were not quite sure how far one may be bound by a law to which one has not assented either immediately or by a representative.

Moreover, a few of the radicals who took part in the army debates regarded the Agreement as a bestowal of certain immunities or liberties—using the terms in their older sense—on certain favored individuals. Since the Agreement implied the right of each individual to the liberty of choosing the men who were to make the laws that should govern him, it was possible to reason that this liberty should belong only to men whose actions had proved their desire for it—perhaps only to men who had put forth efforts to obtain it. One of the soldiers who presented the Agreement of the People to the Council of the Army said: "I thinke itt will bee strange that wee that are souldiers cannott have them [for] our selves, if nott for the whole Kingedome . . . ."[20] Later Agreements specifically confined their benefits to those who had given them formal assent. In the amended Agreement of the People that was debated October 30 in committee, a clause provided that the House of Commons then in session determine the proper extension of the franchise; the clause suggested an extension to include those who had served in the war and had contributed to the Parliament's support.[21]

The foregoing discussion should have proved the

[19] *Clarke Papers*, I, 405.
[20] *Ibid.*, p. 236.
[21] *Ibid.*, p. 366.

complexity of the idea that the Agreement of the People connoted to its framers. We must admit that to them the Agreement implied a measure of special privilege. We must also admit that both in its provisions and its essence, the document was the product of the soldiers' desire to provide for their own safety by coming to terms with the people. But in spite of all this, the central idea of the Agreement was the people's control of their government by a paramount law originating in themselves.

III. THE ARMY-COUNCIL DEBATES OF NOVEMBER, 1647

When the friends of the Agreement argued for it as an embodiment of the nation's liberties, their opponents challenged them to demonstrate two points: the nation's right to these liberties, and its right also to take measures to secure them. In general the radicals demanded them as belonging to the people by natural right, and demonstrated the people's right to take them by the fact that a five years' war had been carried on avowedly for their recovery. The Leveller agents were prone to dogmatize on the subject of their natural rights. They refused to let their opponents cite chronicles in rebuttal, because chronicles had in all ages been written in the interest of those who had kept England in bondage.[22] They saw yawning behind them the Norman conquest, not as Ireton saw it,

---

[22] *Clarke Papers*, I, 318; Wildman.

a struggle between Harold and William as to which
one was of right king of the English,[23] but an
abstract Norman conquest that had swallowed up
the nation and its liberties; a Norman conquest
not passed away six centuries before, but a Norman
conquest out of which they themselves had climbed
in the past few years, setting their feet at Marston
Moor and Naseby. Were they to fall back into
the abyss, or were they to be permitted to establish their footing and that of all Englishmen on
their natural rights? They were very tender of
this conception of the Norman conquest, deduced
partly from their belief in the natural rights of
man and partly from their own evil experience of
oppression in earlier days.[24]

The tenacity with which they insisted on these
natural rights and on a settlement that would secure
them excited the wonder of Cromwell. All governments were, he said, but as dross and dung in
comparison with Christ, "and why wee shall soe
farre contest for temporall thinges, that if wee cannott have this freedome wee will venture life and
livelihood for itt. When every man shall come to
this condition I thinke the State will come to
desolation."[25]

Here, to digress for a moment, was precisely the
difference between Cromwell and the Saints on the

[23] *Clarke Papers*, I, 401.

[24] *Ibid.*, pp. 316 ff. A further example is afforded by Cowling, p. 368;
but he believed that there had been vassalage in England before the
Conquest.

[25] *Ibid.*, p. 370, Nov. 1, 1647.

one hand, and the Levellers on the other.   Men like Goffe, and to a lesser extent Cromwell, were always awaiting a divine command.   They sought it in extraordinary ways; from special providences, from words that a comrade spoke professing to have them from God's spirit.   Cromwell, less inclined than others to have faith in guidance of the latter sort, always reserved to himself the right to judge by the effect made on his own spirit by words spoken as from God, and rather sought the directing hand of God in material happenings and the turn of political events.[26]   Seeking divine guidance in politics in this simple fashion was a thing completely foreign to men like Lilburne, Overton, Walwyn, and Wildman.   Their aims were frankly secular, for they were convinced that the one thing needful was a just political settlement.   They felt that the spiritual freedom that Cromwell craved could follow only in the train of a political freedom secured by law.   Naturally, therefore, they governed their political conduct by their political philosophy.   Like other men they could see in outward happenings evidence of divine approval of their work; but for guidance they ever looked to their principles and not to passing events.   When contrasted in this respect with Cromwell and the Saints they are strangely modern.   In debate in the Council of the Army, Wildman dismissed announcements by mystics of the will of God in much the same way that a pious man in political council might today.   They would best follow God's will,

[26] See the *Clarke Papers*, I, 367–375, Nov. 1, 1647.

he said, if they considered what things had justice and mercy in them, and set about doing them. "If itt please this honourable Councill to consider what is justice and what is mercy, and what is good, and I cannott butt conclude that that is of God. Otherwise I cannott thinke that any one doth speake from God when hee sayes what hee speakes is of God."[27]

Dismissing for the time the mental distinction between Saints and Levellers, it may be well to recall the proposition stated at the head of this section; a logical demonstration of the Agreement as an attempt on the part of the people to recover their natural rights lost in the Norman conquest demanded the establishment of two premises—first, that the natural rights of the people had ever existed, or had been such as the Levellers thought them, and, second, that the people had the right to recover their lost rights by altering the political constitution of the kingdom.

Commissary-General Ireton led the debate on the Agreement of the People in the Army Council (October 28–November 8), traversing with great acuteness and great bitterness the two positions named above. He put the Levellers on the defensive almost immediately; and the debate thereafter centered around his own constitutional theories. The argument began with a question from Ireton as to whether the Agreement implied manhood suffrage. He was answered that the supporters of the Agreement demanded the franchise on grounds

[27] *Clarke Papers*, I, 384, Nov. 1, 1647.

of natural right. It was against nature for a man to be bound by laws which he had not had a voice in choosing; against nature that his God-given reason be denied the opportunity to preserve him from danger by guiding him through his representatives in his choice of laws. Thereupon Ireton developed his theory of the English constitution, namely, that it was intended to secure property. To that end it had limited the suffrage to those who had a fixed stake in the kingdom. Once extend this franchise to all men on the ground that by nature they had a right to it, as necessary to their liberties, and all property was gone; for it could be argued on the same ground that by nature any man had a right to any property that he needed for his support.[28] When the supporters of the Agreement inquired bitterly after the rights for which the common soldier without property rights had adventured his life,[29] Ireton coolly answered that the common soldier had done it that he might live, not under a tyrannical and capricious ruler, but under a government controlled by those with a property stake in the kingdom, and by the fixed and certain laws that their representatives would provide.[30]

The radicals, feeling instinctively that political democracy does not imply communism, stumbled after the fallacy that they knew must lie hidden in Ireton's argument. Rainsborough urged first that the law of God, "Thou shalt not steal," protected

---

[28] *Clarke Papers*, I, 299–308, 311.
[29] *Ibid.*, pp. 323 (Sexby), 325 (Rainsborough).
[30] *Ibid.*, pp. 326–327.

property. Ireton replied that the law of God laid down only a general principle; the law of the land defined what property consisted in, and was the actual safeguard. For that matter, he said, how did the law of God support property more immediately than it supported the vested right of a few men to the exclusive choice of members of Parliament?[31]

The Levellers fared better in attacking on the practical side Ireton's theory as to the inevitable union of property and political power. Rainsborough saw that in practice Ireton's system made the franchise a sort of property. "As for estates, and those kinde of thinges, and other thinges that belonge to men," he said, "itt will bee granted that they are propertie; butt I deny that that [the franchise] is a propertie to a Lord, to a Gentleman, to any man more then another in the Kingdome of England." Pettus, one of the agents, laid his finger on the weak point of Ireton's insistence that a constitutional change must imply the alteration of property institutions. It would be very dangerous, he said, if arguments of this sort were to coerce men into keeping one form of government to all eternity.[32]

The essential conservatism of Ireton becomes apparent in other of his opinions. He had in common with Selden the lawyer-like notion that the whole existing structure of society was built upon compacts between man and man sanctioning all social, economic, and political relations. To his

[31] *Clarke Papers*, I, 309–310.
[32] *Ibid.*, pp. 311, 336.

mind, the power of the English nation to reconstruct itself on principles of natural right was limited by the implied governmental contracts which the English nation through its forefathers had made with Lords and king. If Lords and king could show a legal warrant for their negative voices, the nation must not disregard it. The whole political and social structure depended on the keeping of contracts—these implied contracts with king and Lords as well as the more specific contracts relating to property. To show that a given contract was unjust and noxious made as little difference in one class as in the other. "What right hath any man to any thinge if you lay nott that principle, that wee are to keepe covenant? If you will resort onely to the law of Nature, by the law of Nature you have noe more right to this land or any thinge else then I have." To appeal in one case to natural rights and natural law against recorded law was sufficient to overthrow the whole structure of society.[33] Like the Levellers, Ireton desired the supremacy of law. The Levellers, however, desired it as an expedient whereby the people might bind their government by rules of justice. To Ireton, it was valuable as securing the permanence of the existing social order, and depended for its

---

[33] *Ibid.*, pp. 263, 322, 336. It is true Ireton admitted that there were certain arguments against the king's veto of a kind he could approve. He was surprised that Parliament had never cited as a precedent the article against Richard II that (so Ireton said) accused him of failing to assent to the good laws his subjects had proposed to him. *Ibid.*, p. 402. As for natural law, Ireton regarded it as safeguarding men's persons, but not their property.

stability on the control of the government by the classes interested in the perpetuation of that order.

Ireton's political theories, while abreast of the liberal thought of his own day, were all in all more conservative than those of Hunton or Parker. From the democratic viewpoint of today, Ireton seems almost naïvely antiquated. He serenely advocated class government. He calmly framed arguments that would condemn a nation to hold forever to a constitution it had outgrown rather than disturb in any particular the established order. He could not see that the right of men to a voice in their government was not bound up with the overthrow of property, or that the struggle to reach abstract justice in the constitution of the government need not imply the introduction of communism. His thinking was distinctly of the past as the thinking of the Levellers was the thinking of the future.

Ireton had the best of the army-council debates as a conservative usually has the best of a logical combat with a radical. His ideas had the maturity given them by generations of close thinking, and were therefore exactly stated and linked into orderly sequence. The radicals of the army were groping on the verge of new ideas that were as yet less logical than intuitive. Universal franchise and democratic government seemed innately just to them; therefore they declared that these rights antedated government itself. Ireton easily nonplussed the radicals by suggesting that if some of the conditions that preceded society were to be renewed, disorder and absence of property might return also. The Levellers had not sufficiently visualized their state of nature to be able to give a clear answer.

Yet undoubtedly they had at their command a logical reply if they could have formulated it. As it was, they told Ireton that democratic government had originally been established in a state of nature for the purpose of protecting property. Overton had previously based the sanctity of property on the rights of the individual. In the present case he might have argued that the right to the peaceable enjoyment of one's possessions, like self-government and liberty of conscience, was guaranteed by the law of nature and inalienable. Thus a return to one ordinance of the law of nature— perfect political equality—would be the reverse of destroying property.[34]

The arguments and theories of the Levellers were fragmentary and vague because their ideas were new. The uncertainty of their thinking appears in their vague idea of a state of nature and of natural rights. It appears also in their explanations of the Agreement of the People. Its framers were not sure whether they were drawing up an *entente* between the rank and file of the army and the rank and file of the nation, or whether they were devising a scheme by which the people might control their government by law. But in the future course of events, the second idea prevailed and expanded; accordingly the Levellers have an important place in the history of constitutional thought.

[34] *Clarke Papers*, I, 312–313 (Pettus); 330, 338–339 (Clarke).

IV. THE OUTCOME OF THE FIRST AGREEMENT

The remainder of the story of the First Agreement of the People is soon told.   In the debates in the Council of the Army, October 29–November 8, the Levellers seemed to have their own way; they carried the proposition for the universal franchise on which Ireton had centered his opposition.   November 5, they secured a call for a rendezvous of the whole army, probably intending to secure the assent of the whole rank and file to the Agreement. Cromwell, alarmed by the danger to discipline, and shocked by the bitterness toward the king's person which passing events tended to increase in the Army Council, made a supreme effort November 8.   He branded the proposal for the universal franchise as anarchy, and carried a vote dismissing officers and agitators alike to their regiments.   The rendezvous for the army was held on three different days, beginning with the fifteenth.   When it came to the test, the Levellers could not hold the soldiery in line for the Agreement.   In vain they issued a letter, November 12, urging the men to beware of the army chiefs and their fair offers of pay and arrears.   The Agreement was too fine spun, no doubt, for the soldiers' understanding; and when Fairfax proposed in its place a new engagement by which they were to agree to obey his orders under the understanding that he would urge Parliament to dissolve speedily and to adopt measures that would for the future make the Commons more truly representative, the men accepted it eagerly.   At the first rendezvous, two regiments appeared on the field at Corkbush, contrary to orders; the men of one had the Agreement of the People with the additional words "Englands Freedoms Soldiers Rights" stuck in their hats; but a few threatening words from Cromwell availed against the attempt of officers who sympathized with the Levellers to make the men stand firm. Of these officers, Ayres and Bray were arrested; Arnold, a private in Colonel Robert Lilburne's regiment, was shot for his part in the mutiny; and discipline was restored in the army.

John Lilburne, who at the time was allowed to be much at large from the Tower, had come out of London as far as Ware to await news of what passed at the rendezvous; but hearing of the discomfiture of the Levellers, he returned as he had come. A somewhat fanciful account with which *Mercurius Pragmaticus* dismissed the event is worth quoting for its exquisitely good-natured malice if for no other reason.[35]

London Agents appeared to the Army at the Rendezvous, and scar'd them heyon [beyond] their Orders; These Agents were no other but Agent Overton, Agent Lilburne, and the very same Agents that conspir'd the death of the King: The agreement of the people of the Spittle-Congregation was sent thither for the Souldiers to weare in their hatts, a pritty device to distinguish the Righteous from the Wicked; but

[35] *Mercurius Pragmaticus*, Nov. 16–22. See also *A Full Relation Of The Proceedings at the Rendezvous of that Brigade of the Army that was held in Corkbush field*, Nov. 16, 1647, E. 414 (13); *A Remonstrance From His Excellency . . . . Concerning The late discontent*, Nov. 16, 1647, E. 414 (14).

the intention was for another end; brother Box and Brother Overton knowes well enough to what end to divide the Sheepe from the Goates . . . . John Lilburne was to be Crown'd King of Ware; and then by those papers he might know his Subjects from King Toms; this was the Sea coale of the businesse: but wise John staying at Ware (bigge with expectation of the successe) had news brought him, That three of his people were condemned by a Counsell of Warre to bee hang'd, and one shot to death, and Englands Freedome, and Souldiers Rights knockt off of their Cox combes: John hearing of this, cry'd out Treason, Treason, give me my Horse, which was no sooner brought him, but he mounted his Palfrey, and rid like any Beggar a Horseback, till he came to his Court at Bedlam, where with a heavy heart, he told Queen Besse, That the Whore of Babbylon was in the Headquarters, and that Sir Thomas was a Tyrant and a Traytor to the people; and so went to bed supperlesse with a heavy heart.

NOTES

I. THE HEADS OF PROPOSALS AND THE RADICAL PLATFORM.

The specific reforms outlined in the Heads of Proposals may be briefly contrasted with Overton's suggested reforms in *An Appeale*. The Proposals stipulated biennial parliamentary elections, limited to eight months the duration of each Parliament, and forbade a royal dissolution before four months of the session had passed. Of course the Heads dealt with the militia, the appointment of the great dignitaries of the kingdom, etc., as every treaty *agendum* since 1642 had done. Further, they vindicated the right of commoners to be tried by commoners. There was to be a reapportionment of seats on the basis of rates paid by the various counties. Members were to have liberty to "enter dissents," and hence power to record their votes on crucial matters, in a way that had hitherto been impossible in the House of Commons. In the counties men might indirectly choose justices of the peace and sheriffs. The Heads of Proposals further demanded the abolition of all *ex officio* oaths and proceedings; relief from imprisonment for debt in the case of debtors who surrendered their estates; law reform—though mentioned in vague terms—a remedy for the "unequal troublesome and contentious way" of maintaining ministers by tithes; removal of monopolies; the taking off of the excise on necessaries; vindication of the right of petition; repeal of all orders forcing the taking of the Covenant—an impo-

sition that Lilburne had protested against in *Rash Oaths unwarrantable*
(pp. 8 ff.); repeal of acts forcing the use of the Book of Common Prayer;
"An Act to be passed to take away all coercive Power, Authority, and
Jurisdiction of Bishops and all other Ecclesiastical Officers whatsoever,
extending to Civil Penalties upon any; and to repeal all Laws whereby
the Civil Magistracy hath been or is bound upon any Ecclesiastical
Censure to proceed (ex officio) unto any Civil Penalties against any
Persons so censured."

Overton's proposals concerning Parliament have been already quoted
above (p. 196). Further, according to his scheme every county was to
have liberty to inquire as to its customs by commissioners of its own
choice, and to bring to trial its members in Parliament on any impeach-
ments laid against them for betrayal of trust. Should a member be
convicted, a new one was to be chosen. All courts not warranted by the
old just law of the land were to be abolished. No new ones were to be
imposed on the people contrary to the law of the land by either the
king or the Parliament. There were to be courts in every hundred
competent to deal with all civil and criminal cases. Such officers as by
the ancient laws of the kingdom should be chosen by the people, were
so to be chosen. The jails were to be thoroughly reformed. Prisoners
were to be lodged at the expense of the state. All laws were to be in
English; *ex officio* oaths, and statutes compelling men to attend the reading of the Prayer Book were to be abrogated. In all things all men were
to be equal before the law. Imprisonment for debt was to be abolished;
theft was no longer to be punishable by death. The limitations that the
monopolies imposed on trade were to be summarily ended. Tithes
were to be abolished; ancient grants for free schools were to be restored,
and schools were to be erected at the public expense in the counties
destitute of them, "that few or none of the free men of England may
for the future be ignorant of reading and writing." Glebe lands were
to be converted to the use of the infirm and the old, and of widows and
orphans; old inclosed commons were to be laid open.

II. Debate in the Council of the Army on the Agreement of the People.

Sexby's speech at the opening of the debate in the Council of the Army
on the Agreement of the People probably represents the spirit that
prompted the framing of the Agreement. "The Kingdomes cause requires
expedition, and truly our miseries with [those of] our fellow souldiers cry
out for present helpe. I thinke, att this time, this is your businesse, and
I thinke itt is in all your hearts to releive the one and satisfie the other.

You resolv'd if any thinge [reasonable] should bee propounded to you, you would joyne and goe alonge with us.

"The cause of our misery [is] uppon two thinges. We sought to satisfie all men, and itt was well; butt in going [about] to doe itt wee have dissatisfied all men. We have labour'd to please a Kinge, and I thinke, except wee goe about to cutt all our throates, wee shall nott please him; and wee have gone to support an house which will prove rotten studds, I meane the Parliament which consists of a Company of rotten Members." *Clarke Papers*, I, 227.

Cowling said: "I shall onely offer this, the necessity of expedition if the people shall consider the necessities that they and we are in. Wee live now uppon free-quarter, and wee have that against our wills. . . . . I have seene this paper, and uppon second reading of itt I sett my hand to itt, that wee may nott lie as drones to devoure their families . . . ." *Clarke Papers*, I, 293.

Sir Hardresse Waller said in the same debate: "This paper sayes, that this Parliament is to continue a yeare, butt will the great burthen of the people be ever satisfied with papers [whilst] you eate and feede uppon them? I shall be glad, that [if] there bee nott any present danger, you will thinke of some way to ease the burthen that wee may take a course [to do it]; and when wee have satisfied the people that wee doe really intend the good of the Kingdome [they will believe us]—Otherwise if the four Evangelists were heere and lay free quarter uppon them, they will not believe you." *Clarke Papers*, I, 345. Although Waller was skeptical of the Agreement's power to reconcile to the army a nation estranged by free quarter, he realized the need of such a reconciliation.

The Case Of The Armie contained the usual proposals for the social betterment of the kingdom; they included immediate removal of all such excises as bore on the poor, and the speedy abolition of excises; faithful auditing of accounts throughout the kingdom; removal of monopolies; relief of prisoners for debt; repeal of the statutes for reading common prayer, and of the ordinance against conventicles; abolition of tithes and of the oath of supremacy; vindication of the freedom of Englishmen from *ex officio* oaths; law reform and the establishment of county and hundred courts; restoration of embezzled almshouses; as well as a new proposal that the freemen of London should be empowered to demand an accounting from the corporation, and from the halls of the city companies. Pp. 16–19.

CHAPTER VII

THE ORGANIZATION OF THE LEVELLER PARTY: THE APPEAL TO REASON

I. THE DEVELOPMENT OF THE LEVELLER PARTY ORGANIZATION

THE events of November 15 only checked for the moment the development of the Leveller party. Within two months a chance event revealed the existence of a democratic party organization, used in a supreme effort to establish Leveller principles by means of an appeal to the reason of the nation. This movement failed because its democratic character enabled the authorities to detect it before it was well begun. But the means they employed to suppress it brought Lilburne to devise a new constitutional check on Parliament—the doctrine of the separation of the powers of government.

In November the Levellers took no overt part in politics except for a few protests against the conduct of the army leaders. November 23, five men addressed a petition to the House of Commons, naming it the "Supreme Authority," and asking for justice on the officers for their offense in imprisoning the soldiers concerned in the Agreement and executing Arnold. This only procured the commitment of the five, and supplied the news basis for an "extra" whose scarehead promised a "Bloody Independent Plot . . . . to Murder the King,

Divide the Army, Levell the Nobility and Gentry, Abolish the Protestant Religion."[1]

Lilburne contributed his share to the protests against the arbitrary conduct of the army chiefs. He published petitions from William Thompson, John Crosseman, and John Ingram, in which they protested against being held and judged by martial law in time of peace. For, so Thompson argued, as the House of Commons had no right to take away a man's life arbitrarily in time of peace, it could delegate no such power to Sir Thomas Fairfax. Very likely Lilburne himself was the author of Thompson's petition at least, for he uses its line of reasoning elsewhere.

He further developed an elaborate argument against the power of officers of the New Model to punish their men by courts martial. The military authority of the officers, he said, had ended when the army took the Solemn Engagement; thenceforth officers and men continued in arms for no other purpose than securing the rights of the kingdom, and lived under a new form of government set over the army by an Agreement. The fact that the Council of the Army, the visible form of this government, was contrary to all rules of military discipline proved that military discipline in the ordinary usage was at an end.[2] The argument seems valid.

---

[1] *Commons Journal*, V, 367. The petition is in 669, f. 11 (98). The scarehead is in E. 419 (2). The five men concerned were Prince, Chidley, Larner, Taylor, and Ives.

[2] The book mentioned in the paragraph above is *The peoples Prerogative and Priviledges, asserted and vindicated*, Feb. 14, 1647/8, E. 427 (4), pp. 42–55.

William Thompson was a soldier of Whalley's regiment, who in August

The officers of the army were indeed acting in a double rôle when they undertook, now to determine the policy of the army in council with representatives of the enlisted men, now to retain the men in strict military obedience. In this as in many things their only excuse was the iron law of necessity.

The persecution of the army Levellers ended at Windsor, December 21–23, in a general peacemaking and oblivion among the officers. The differences between Leveller and Grandee were washed away in a flood of prayers and tears. The men from the agents' faction imprisoned by the army were set at liberty and forgiven.[3] Lilburne looked with suspicion on these proceedings; mystic as he was he was always skeptical of too great intrusions of religious enthusiasm into politics. Accordingly he served notice on the Grandees that unless thenceforth they showed themselves seriously intent on

of 1647 had got into a brawl in an inn in Colebrook and had made a charge of theft against the inn-keeper that he later admitted was incorrect. He was cashiered September 14, 1647, by sentence of a council of war, but was allowed to remain with his troop after sentence had been pronounced. His attempt to stir up the men of another regiment for the Agreement of the People led to his arrest a second time. On this occasion he was given leave to go to London on urgent private business. There he again betook himself to agitation and in February was taken under arrest once more by Cromwell's own orders. So far the accounts of Thompson and the authorities agree. As Thompson claimed, he was now carried before a council of war and sentenced to death for refusing to admit its authority. By his own admissions Thompson was a desperate man of bad habits; but his arrest under martial law after being cashiered was undoubtedly dangerous to civil liberty. *A True and Impartial Relation . . . . concerning the proceedings of several Councels of War*, Mar. 20, 1647/8, E. 432 (23); *A Vindication Of Lieut. Gen. Cromwell, And Com. Gen. Ireton*, Mar. 7, 1647/8, E. 431 (7).

³ *Clarke Papers*, I, lvii.

securing the just liberties of Englishmen, they might still count on his opposition.[4]

The prisoners did not take all the attention of the Levellers. During the autumn of 1647 we can begin to trace in the city of London and in the surrounding counties the existence of a definite political organization that we may call the Leveller party. Simultaneously with the October army councils, certain men whom the speech of the day termed "London Agents" were taking counsel together in the city. Wildman was undoubtedly the intermediary between these men and the agents of the army; moreover, if we may believe *Mercurius Pragmaticus*, Lilburne controlled the army agents. In fact, meetings of army agents at which Lilburne and Overton were present were held during November at the Mouth in Aldersgate, and at the Windmill in Coleman Street.[5] The meetings soon were called to the attention of Parliament; and on November 20 Lords and Commons completed the organization of a joint committee to inquire into the doings of the "London Agents." That same week letters from Nottinghamshire advised Parliament that the people there were being stirred up to

---

[4] *The peoples Prerogative*, pp. 55–58.

Sir John Berkeley's narrative would lead one to infer that Cromwell's penitence for Corkbush Field dated back to November at least. Maseres, *Tracts*, I, 385. See Note I on p. 254.

[5] *Pragmaticus*, Sept. 28–Oct. 6; Nov. 9–16, 17–24. An attempt in the House of Commons to incriminate Marten as attending the meetings of this organization and being responsible for its actions, led him to the defiant retort that if the agents stood at that very moment at the House door, he presently would go out and advise with them. *Elencticus*, Nov. 12–19; *Perfect Weekly Account*, Nov. 10–17.

subscribe the Agreement, and to send their subscriptions up to the Saracen's Head tavern in London. In December, Rutlandshire ministers complained that a certain Anabaptist preacher lately
come into that part of the country was securing
signatures to the Agreement of the People.[6]

Late in 1647 the Levellers temporarily abandoned the Agreement of the People and the assumption that Parliament had no legal authority,
and busied themselves with a new petition. It urged
the House of Commons to free itself from the ham-
pering veto of king and Lords, and establish the
people's freedom. The petition carried the usual
list of specific reforms, omitting mention of any
that might tend to divide rather than unite the
nation. Thus, in the hope of promoting a general
agreement among the people, it did not touch tithes
or other "contentious" subjects.[7]

The framers of the petition devised a careful
organization to promote it. They appointed ten
or twelve commissioners whose duty it was to advance the petition by agents throughout the kingdom. These commissioners met three days of the

---

[6] *Commons Journal*, V, 363–365; *Lords Journal*, IX, 529 (Nov. 17),
571 (Dec. 11).

[7] Wildman, *Truths triumph, Or Treachery anatomized*, Feb. 1, 1647/8,
E. 520 (33), p. 4. The Leveller leaders found difficulty in persuading
some of their followers that petitioning Parliament again was worth the
trouble. *A Declaration Of some Proceedings*, Feb. 14, 1647/8, E. 427 (6).
This pamphlet contains the petition in question. Lilburne said a year
later that he had hoped for a hundred thousand signatures. *An Impeachment Of High Treason Against Oliver Cromwell*, Aug. 10, 1649, E. 568 (20),
p. 22. Thirty thousand petitions were to be printed. *A Declaration
Of some Proceedings*, p. 17.

week in London, and other three in Southwark and elsewhere to consult with their friends regarding the promotion of the petition. The funds necessary for expenses were raised by voluntary contributions ranging from two pence to half a crown a week.

The Leveller leaders consciously attempted to build up local party organization throughout the kingdom. In the several wards of London and in the out-parishes, they formed committees of interested persons, to appoint fit men to read the petition and solicit subscriptions at set meetings. To the out-lying counties into which the propaganda was to be spread, notably Kent, Buckingham, Oxford, Cambridge, Rutland, and Hertford, Lilburne suggested a similar method—meetings to choose proper men for carrying on the business in every town.[8]

The Leveller party maintained an organization of this type for at least two years. In November of 1648, a meeting of Leveller agents in the city of London chose certain men to represent the party in council with the army leaders.[9] An organization something like that described above was employed to promote the petition of September 11, 1648. Repeatedly in the course of 1649 the Levellers in various parts of the kingdom were urged to send up representatives to discuss with the London Levellers policies for putting into effect a later Agreement of the People.[10] Leveller meetings were probably

----

[8] *A Declaration Of some Proceedings*, pp. 13, 17; letters from Lilburne and Wildman quoted in the book. See Note II, p. 254.

[9] *Infra*, p. 263.

[10] For instance, in *An Impeachment Of High Treason*, p. 7.

continued till the fall of 1649; and we find them mentioned in the winter of 1652.[11] Finally, from May of 1648 to September of 1649, a news-sheet, the *Moderate*, inculcated Leveller principles and gave news with a Leveller bias, so that it may fairly be called a Leveller party organ.[12] The Leveller party was consciously an organized political party during the events of 1648 and 1649.

But to return to the petition of the fall of 1647. Its supporters approached their work in a spirit that distinguished the later Leveller movement. At the time when the petition was framed, they said, a new war seemed to be imminent; but had seven years of a war ostensibly waged for liberty left any legacy of peace? Could not the new civil war, even then foreshadowed in the disillusionment and discontent of the kingdom, be averted by setting all men to seek out and to inquire of each other after the chief principles of the freedom for which the old war had avowedly been waged? Surely, if once men could reach an understanding on these principles, no man could be so depraved as to seek to bring on a new war by failing to support them; and the path of peace would lie open to England.[13]

This may be dismissed as day dreaming; but it was splendid day dreaming. To meet the people fairly, trying by reason to convince them of the excellence of the Leveller ideals instead of seeking

---

[11] *The French Intelligencer*, Jan. 13–21, 1651/2. *Infra*, n. 12, p. 332.

[12] June 22–29, 1648 to Sept. 25, 1649.

[13] Paraphrased from a letter of Lilburne and Wildman quoted in *A Declaration Of some Proceedings*.

to accustom them to ideals righteous enough in themselves, but maintained only by the sword of the New Model—here in a word was the difference between the Cromwellian policy and the Leveller policy. Looking back, it is not difficult to see that the Cromwellian settlement must ever have been a settlement by the sword. It could never have risen higher than its source. To undertake to convince the people of England of the justice and excellence of a settlement that had been maintained over them by the army was to undertake the impossible. On the other hand, the chances were heavily against the success of a propaganda so advanced as that of the Levellers; nevertheless their scheme had the innate soundness of any democratic political movement; the degree of its success would have measured the political capacity of the English people of its generation. At the least, the Leveller methods would have afforded England opportunity for a democratic expression of her real political beliefs, even though if expressed they probably would have proved to be Royalist.

Tried by the abiding value of the political philosophies involved, the Leveller idea also had an advantage over the Cromwellian idea. The Levellers had discovered that the sound foundation of the nation's government was to be sought by convincing the people of the excellence of certain political principles; for the attainment of their ends, they relied on persuasion and argument, man to man; they entrusted their propaganda to a party locally organized on a democratic basis; and all these things were valuable contributions to the world's stock of political ideas and political experience.

The seventeenth century could not allow men to proceed with such a scheme in peace. January 19, Lilburne and Wildman were summoned before the House of Commons on an information laid with the Lords the day before by one, George Masterson, who undertook to report the proceedings at a meeting in Wapping at which Lilburne and Wildman had been present. The sum of his testimony was that there had been words spoken against the Lords, and that the leaders of the meeting expected a serious riot against the Commons, should the House fail to receive the petition favorably.[14] The Houses listened to Masterson's accusation; above all they must have regarded as dangerous the very existence of the Leveller organization. In spite of Lilburne's and Wildman's bold answers to Masterson's charges, the House of Commons committed them to prison and

---

[14] A George Masterson, clerk, was a witness against the regicides in 1660. The Levellers denounced the informer as a turncoat, saying that he had been Prelatist, Presbyterian, and Independent by turns. The tone of his own writings is not such as to discredit this estimate of him.

According to Lilburne, the intention of the meeting was to induce the people who attended it to cling to the House of Commons as being the best and most legal authority left in the kingdom, and accordingly to promote the petition to the House. *An Impeachment Of High Treason*, pp 10 ff.

Masterson's accusation was verbal, and he was not sworn. *A Speech . . . . in the . . . . House of Commons. By Sir Iohn Maynard*, Aug. 11, 1648, E. 458 (2), p. 6. Lilburne in answering the charges expressly stated he was not bound in any way to pay attention to a verbal charge. *A Whip for the present House of Lords*, Mar. 6, 1647/8. E. 431 (1), p. 9.

referred them to the King's Bench for trial;[15] but months of imprisonment apparently brought them no nearer a legal arraignment.

John Lilburne's political and constitutional theories always originated in concrete situations. He lacked the imagination or the inclination to produce an abstract theory or a complete system of political thought. But let him be the victim of a governmental procedure that seemed unjust in itself, and he at once evolved a constitutional theory to meet it; this theory he might alter or reverse when confronted with a different situation.

His actions on this occasion afford a fair example of his intellectual habits.[16] In pamphlets setting forth his demand on King's Bench for a writ of *habeas corpus*, he arrived at a doctrine of the separation of the powers of government. He perceived

[15] *Commons Journal*, V, 436–438. The two men refused to go to prison until a legal warrant was drawn for their commitment; with the backing of a hundred of their friends they made their refusal good and were respited until next morning. Then they presented themselves at Westminster; Lilburne, when the warrant was served on them, claimed that it was still illegal because the charge was stated in general terms. In his own words he "fell of preaching law and iustice out of Sir Edward Cookes institutes, (then in my hands) and the Parliaments own declaration to the Souldiers that guarded the House;" his exhortations were so efficacious that the guard refused to arrest him. However a new one was called, and Lilburne was not given time to convert it. He resisted arrest; a riot resulted, but of course an unsuccessful one; and after running danger of his life he was carried off to the Tower. *A Whip for the present House of Lords*, pp. 23 ff. The account in this is corroborated in *Heads of Chief Passages in Parliament*, Jan. 19–26.

[16] He had answered the questions put to him by the House of Commons with a salvo that, as the charge against him was not in writing, he was not legally bound to recognize it. *A Whip for the present House of Lords*, p. 9. Wildman made a similar plea. *Truths triumph*, p. 3.

that if the House of Commons in time of peace was able to commit him after an informal hearing and to bar him from a legal trial, the House of Commons could destroy any man it saw fit. To Lilburne a situation such as this was intolerable, and he cast about for some constitutional principle that would meet the difficulty. He found his principle in the theory that lawmakers such as the members of the House of Commons should not also be law executors.[17] While the House of Lords might enjoy the jurisdiction of an appellate court, to Lilburne's mind the House of Commons had no legal warrant for exercising the functions of a court of original resort, or indeed any functions of a court. Assuredly neither one of the Houses had the right to imprison a principal in a case brought before them in first instance; for their doing so would deprive the man they had imprisoned of the advantage of an appeal to the Lords as a court of last resort.

Admitting all this, the question remained as to how such arbitrary actions of the House of Commons might be forestalled. Lilburne himself had on former occasions repeatedly declared that House the supreme power of the English nation; but he had always implied that Parliament was supreme only when it walked in accord with the fundamental laws of the kingdom. To check it when it passed those bounds, a student of Sir Edward Coke would

---

[17] The doctrine appears in *A Defiance to Tyrants*, a plea that Lilburne had published December 2 against the proceedings of a parliamentary committee engaged in prosecuting the "London Agents." It appears in pp. 67 ff. of *The peoples Prerogative*.

naturally turn to the common-law courts of the realm; for, since Parliament was supreme only when its actions accorded with the law, it could be checked when it transgressed by the application in any common-law court of a common-law remedy, such as a *habeas corpus*. True, Lilburne in 1646 had denounced both Westminster courts and Westminster law as fruits of Norman tyranny. But he now appealed, not to the intricate quibbles of the common law in civil cases, but to the few fundamental principles of personal liberty that it guaranteed; and he turned with relief from his "unsworn judges" of the House of Commons to men who had at least taken an oath to judge justly and according to law.

In several letters written to the judges during the spring of 1648 Lilburne pressed his claims to a writ of *habeas corpus*. When he found that for fear of the House of Commons no lawyer dared move for the writ, he announced his intention of stirring up the honest men of London to petition the King's Bench for it. Finally he himself petitioned the judges to let him move for a writ for himself and argue his claim to it in court on the ground of the illegality of his commitment.[18] He obtained opportunity to do so on May 8. His argument was on the line indicated above. First, he said, his commitment was illegal because it was in general terms. Second, it was illegal because the Commons had no right of judgment over any man; judgment being by the law left in the hands of a sworn judge

[18] *The Prisoners Plea for a Habeas Corpus; The Prisoners mournfull cry*, May 9, 1648, E. 441 (17).

and jury acting on a true bill found by good and lawful men. Third, if the House of Commons departed in its actions from the just scope of its powers as defined by the law of the land and the writ of summons, the contract between the members and those who chose them, a court like King's Bench could apply a legal remedy. When, Lilburne concluded, the Commons departed from the just exercise of powers entrusted to them, they must certainly cease in any sense to be a court. It was the duty of the courts of England such as King's Bench to decide all cases coming before them according to the known law, without regard to the question whether in so doing they went counter to the decision of a superior court or the illegal action of a legislative body that usurped the functions of such a court.[19]

Here was a new development in the constitutional thinking of the Levellers. It indicated that they had outgrown the simple first Agreement of the People and the petition of January, 1647/8, both of which had indicated as the function of the Commons the declaration of the bounds of the authority of every officer and court. They no longer designed that Parliament should be a supreme constituent body free of all restraint from lesser authorities and subject to reversal only by the people. Advancing a step further with their doctrine that the Parliament must be subject to law, they suggested the possibility of an inferior court's sitting to review actions of the High Court of Parliament

[19] *The Lawes Funerall*, May 15, 1648, E. 442 (13).

manifestly contrary to the law of England. The doctrine of Lilburne left Parliament supreme as a legislature, but erected beside it a judiciary bound by the known law, but nevertheless capable of checking the legislature if it passed the bounds of that law.

II. WILLIAM WALWYN

The Leveller appeal to reason suggests to the student of contemporary controversy the writings of one of the most baffling personalities of the Great Civil War—William Walwyn. We have to judge him not so much by his own acts, as by the sentiment he inspired in other men; and the accounts of friend and enemy are so contradictory that at times it scarcely seems possible that both can apply to the same person. He could inspire men like Lilburne with warm and loyal friendship and admiration; but certain men of fine character like William Kiffen regarded him with such animosity, dread, and abhorrence that they could not speak of him temperately. His own writings when sympathetically studied afford some insight into his character and aims. But they were written in self-defense, and therefore guardedly; and we leave them wondering if the real Walwyn was not a different person from what either friend or foe imagined him. Moreover, after all the evidence is in, we feel that it is impossible to estimate Walwyn's real influence. A recital of the political events of his day would not need to mention his name; why, then, did the enemies of the Levellers attack him so bitterly? What was the cause of his influence with the Levellers and how extensive was it? These questions we can answer only by conjectures; Walwyn, the man, remains in great measure inscrutable to us; but at least we can be sure of one thing, that Walwyn, whatever else he was, was not commonplace.

In 1649, William Kiffen with several Independents of high reputation published a lengthy arraignment of Walwyn.[20] It depicted him as the evil genius of the Levellers; it was Walwyn who drew petitions for them and suggested to them their complaints against the government. Thus he set one faction of the godly at variance with the other in order to frustrate the establishment of England's liberties that both really desired; thus he hoped to achieve the end that he had had in view since the beginning, the ruin of the parliamentary party.

The method of this Machiavelli, Kiffen asserted, was to seduce men one by one in private conversation. With men of ability he began by suggesting doubts of the good faith of Parliament; he slightingly compared the parliamentary government of England with the constitutions of other states. By subtle questions as to the ground of his hearers' religious faith, he led them to doubt the authority of the Scriptures. By ribald and jesting remarks

[20] *Walwins Wiles; Or The Manifestors Manifested*, May 10, 1649, E. 554 (24). It is an account signed by William Kiffen, David Lordell, John Price, Richard Arnald, Edmund Rosier, Henry Foster, Henry Burnet. According to Walwyn, the materials for it had been collected some years earlier, when first he had fallen out with the London Independents. *Walwyns Just Defence*, p. 3.

with a show of wit on religious questions he gradually profaned the things that the mind had before held holiest. Finally, he turned his victims' thoughts from the ideal of religious reform avowed by Parliament and fixed them on purely secular policies and reasonings. With persons of weaker minds or lower station he had another method of approach. He blamed the Parliament for the neglect of its best and truest friends, and assured his hearers that those in authority sought not the public good so much as their own aggrandizement. To the lowly he expressed his opinion that men should be preferred in public office in proportion to their ability, whether they were nobles or cobblers; to desperate men of strong heads but small understanding he proposed communism. He embodied in petitions increasingly violent his tirades against the abuses of the government, such as violations of the Self-Denying Ordinance, exaction of tithes, and heavy taxation, till finally he inflamed his hearers to the point of plunging into bloodshed and accomplishing their own ruin.

Such a portrait anyone will reject as unsatisfactory; the lines may be in the main correct, but they are so combined as to make the face a mere caricature. The known facts of Walwyn's life can be quickly told. He was born about 1600 and was a member of the Merchant Adventurers; he was married and was the father of twenty children.[21]

---

[21] In 1646 he was about 45 years of age. *A Whisper In The Eare of Mr. Thomas Edwards*, Mar. 13, 1645/6, E. 328 (2), p. 3; *The Charity of Church-Men* by Dr. Henry Brook, May 28, 1649, E. 556 (20), pp. 5, 10, 11.

His conscience did not compel him to withdraw from the parish churches when Presbyterianism was preached in them; but as early as 1643 his personal beliefs were nearly Antinomian.[22]   When the Long Parliament met, he and others first set about reforming their parish of St. James, Garlic Hill. Next they secured the election of officers of the right temper in their ward; and finally Walwyn urged the common council that it petition Parliament to confirm certain maxims of government These maxims, according to Walwyn, defined the relation of the Parliament and king so exactly that, if the Parliament had adopted them at the outset, they would have reclaimed many men whose ignorance seduced them into fighting for the king's arbitrary power.[23]   Although Walwyn was, as we have seen, nominally Presbyterian, he crossed swords with Edwards on behalf of the Independents, issuing a series of pamphlets parallel with *Gangraena*.[24]   He allied himself with the radical Independent faction, and was present at the Windmill Tavern meeting.

When the split between Independents and Levellers occurred he followed the Levellers. His personality had been one of the causes of the breach.   He was personally obnoxious to Independents like John and Richard Price and John Good-

---

[22] *Walwyns Just Defence*, p. 8.

[23] *A Whisper In The Eare*, p. 4.

[24] *A Whisper In The Eare of Mr. Thomas Edwards*, Mar. 13, 1645/6, E. 328 (2); *A Word More To Mr. Thomas Edwards*, Mar. 19, 1645/6, E. 328 (20); *A Prediction Of Mr. Edwards His Conversion, and Recantation*, Aug. 11, 1646, E. 1184 (5).

win; and in 1646 they began, by his account, to collect and retail scandalous stories and reports concerning him, being encouraged to persevere by his own temperamental unwillingness to reply in print.[25] Although he had little to do with the Levellers after January of 1649, he was nevertheless one of the four men who were arrested in March and charged with the authorship of the second part of *Englands New-Chaines Discovered.*[26] He was released after the trial and acquittal of Lilburne that same year. Beyond the fact that he wrote in 1650 a defense of trial by jury, we know nothing further of his life.[27]

Let us now turn to the interpretation given us by Walwyn and his friends. We can keep in mind two touches from the hostile portrait—the man's tireless reasoning with his acquaintances, and the excuse he was made to give for trying by questions the religious faith of men, "to understand how men are setled in their faith, and to help them therein."[28] Walwyn had a supreme faith in the power of reason. "All the war I have made," he said, "hath been to get victory on the understandings of men."[29] Even to the climax of the Levellers' propaganda in 1649, he had faith that their ideal settlement could be secured if only they set about convincing men of its

[25] *Walwyns Just Defence*, pp. 3–4.

[26] *The Picture Of The Councel of State*, Apr. 11, 1649, E. 550 (14), p. 2. A second edition of *Englands New-Chaines* is avowed by Lilburne, Overton, and Prince—mention of Walwyn being omitted.

[27] *Juries justified*, Dec. 2, 1650, E. 618 (9).

[28] *Walwins Wiles*, p. 5.

[29] *A Whisper In The Eare*, p. 3.

excellence by argument. Nothing, he said, was so certain to secure peace and harmony, whether in nations or families, "as the giving, and hearing, and debating of reason."[30]

If this quiet, middle-aged neighbor, thinking his conscience imposed on him the duty of seeking the good of all men, went quietly from man to man reasoning in this fashion, one can understand the alarm he caused Presbyterian, Independent, and Anabaptist alike. A man who steered his course in life by reason alone![31] A man on whose spirit the peace of the Antinomian had fallen so that religion no longer seemed bound up with ecclesiastical platforms and establishments, but merely a motive to send individual men about seeking to do good to their fellows! Small blame to Kiffen and Price if they shuddered more at the probable result of such teaching than at the "licentious provoking daringness" of Lilburne, or the "notorious profanness" of Overton![32]

Walwyn's style of discourse afforded enemies a ready means of attacking him. If, like Socrates, he touched the fundamentals of men's beliefs by his questionings, his questions could be used to prove

---

[30] *The Fountain Of Slaunder Discovered*, pp. 15, 18.

[31] "Admit then my Conscience have been necessitated to break through all kinds of Superstition, as finding no peace, but distraction and instability therein, and have found out true uncorrupt Religion, and placed my joy and contentment therein; admit I find it so briefe and plaine, as to be understood in a very short time, by the meanest capacity, so sweet and delectable as cannot but be embraced, so certain as cannot be doubted, so powerfull to dissolve man into love, and to set me on work to do the will of him that loved me. . . . ." *Ibid.*, p. 6.

[32] *Walwins Wiles*, p. 2.

his own impiety. If with the intention of making his hearers try all things by reason, only to hold fast to what was good, he followed out a chain of reasoning to a logical conclusion that seemed the paradox of current beliefs and customs, his conclusions might be attributed to him as his real opinion.[33] Probably at times he displayed an irreverent appreciation of the unconscious humor in the religious phraseology of his day; and he soon had to complain that his enemies caught up his remarks, second, third, or tenth hand, distorted them, and turned them against him. His backwardness in refuting his opponents at the first encouraged them in this style of attack. When finally he and his friends undertook to reply, they found that the charges against him were based on undated and garbled conversations, so that it was impossible to refute every one specifically. Walwyn himself undertook to reply to his critics by revealing the true purpose of his communion with men and manner of life; thus he hoped to explain the reason for the enmity displayed against him.[34]

[33] For instance, take the reasoning on communism attributed to him. "*That it was a sad and miserable thing that it should so continue, and that it would never be well untill all things were common*; and it being replyed, *will that be ever?*   Answered, *we must endeavour it:*   It being said, That this would destroy all Government; Answered, That then *there would be lesse need of Government, for then there would be no theeves, no covetous persons, no deceiving and abusing of one another . . . .*" *Walwins Wiles*, p. 13.   See Note III on p. 255.

[34] *The Fountain Of Slaunder Discovered; Walwyns Just Defence; The Charity of Church-Men.*   This last book is signed "R. B." and is attributed to Dr. Robert Brook by Lilburne. *Legal Fundamentall Liberties*, p. 25.

The charges against him can be divided into the following groups. First may be put such extravagant and unlikely statements as did not appear in print, but circulated the streets—as that he was a Jesuit, was incontinent, believed in polygamy, was a drunkard, painted his face for effeminate reasons.[35]

Second, there was a body of blasphemous sayings attributed to him, such as a remark that there was more wit in Lucian than in the Bible, such as jestingly telling a woman that in not visiting his wife she sinned the sin against the Holy Ghost, such as persuading the same woman to commit suicide. These Walwyn and his friends denied or explained one by one so far as they were able.[36]

Third, various radical religious views were imputed to him, such as denial of the authority of the Scriptures, disbelief in eternal punishment, belief that good works were the only real worship; even atheism. The first and last charges Walwyn denied categorically, referring to one of his earlier books for a statement of his views; a friend guardedly denied for him the second also. At the best, however, Walwyn's theology was unconventional.[37]

The charges that he taught "levelling" or communism he repeatedly denied; stating as his creed on such subjects the Burnt Petition of March, 1647,

[35] *The Charity of Church-Men*, p. 10; *The Fountain Of Slaunder Discovered*, p. 7; *Walwyns Just Defence*, p. 13.

[36] These are found in *Walwins Wiles*, pp. 7, 9. All mentioned above are explained away in the three books mentioned in note 35.

[37] *The Fountain Of Slaunder Discovered*, p. 6; *The Charity of Church-Men, passim*. The book to which he refers, *A Still & Soft Voice*, is not in the British Museum.

the Manifestation, and the later Agreement of 1649. He once admitted his hope that a proper settlement of the government would make it possible to rearrange England's economic system, so that every man willing to work might live in comfort. "Every man," he said in stating his religious creed, "ought to be protected in the use of that wherein he doth not actually hurt another," and possibly he would have assented to the transference of the principle to economics.[38]

On every point Walwyn's political doctrine traced back to his faith in the efficacy of an appeal to man's reason. On this ground he defended the doctrine of toleration against Edwards, taking up for particular attention Edwards's sarcasms on preaching cobblers. If learned men were unable to agree as to the meaning of many passages of Scripture, common men who were bound alike with the learned by the divine command to try all things must have a right to judge for themselves on points of doctrine; if they judged badly after having sought earnestly for knowledge, could their weakness of understanding be attributed to them for a crime?[39]

If it be correct to ascribe *Englands Lamentable Slaverie*[40] to Walwyn's authorship, he had by 1645 come to regard as the bulwark of English liberty not Magna Charta itself so much as the eternal rules of equity and justice which it had imperfectly exem-

---

[38] *Walwyns Just Defence*, pp. 23, 24, 30; *The Fountain Of Slaunder Discovered*, p. 7.
[39] See Note IV, p. 256.
[40] *Supra*, p. 116.

plified. Those rules of course were rules whose
fixation and interpretation lay only within the reason of man. It is true that in *A Word in season*,
published at a time when it was to the interest of
the Independents to encourage Parliament to a
decided stand against Presbyterianism, he had
seemed to argue for parliamentary absolutism; but
although he had 'nsisted on the power of Parliament
to decide finally on questions of church government,
he had qualified this assertion with the proviso
that its judgment must be according to the laws of
God and the rules of equity and reason. Under the
circumstances it could scarcely have been politic
to suggest that the common people of England had
a right to judge as to whether the parliamentary
ecclesiastical establishment accorded with equity,
reason and the law of God.[41]

One finally asks what was the influence of Walwyn
on the Leveller movement. That we shall probably never know with certainty. According to Dr.

[41] *A Word in season* is sometimes attributed to Sadler, a member of
Goodwin's congregation. The edition in the British Museum corre-
sponds in make-up with that of Walwyn's pamphlets against Edwards.
Walwyn claims the authorship of it (*Walwyns Just Defence*, p. 31), and
adds that Goodwin's congregation had spent 50s toward 10,000 copies
of it.

Walwyn's political ideal was probably Switzerland. The organization of the little republic, keeping up no army though by nature far
more exposed to attack than England, but relying on the discipline of
its militia to secure the respect of foreign powers; punishing sternly
any corruption in its officers and accounting in them as the worst of
offenses the exceeding of their lawful authority, made a deep impression
on his imagination. He hoped for a settlement of England on similar
lines in politics. *The Fountain Of Slaunder Discovered*, p. 15.

Brook, Walwyn had rescued most of the people's
liberties "out of a heap of contrary Doctrines, and
Politick concealments   .   .   .   .   He hath studied
the Peoples Freedoms so radically, and hath brought
to light Principles so supportive thereof, and so essentiall thereunto, that no other Designe but their
good, can with any pretence be fixt upon him."[42]
A modern critic applies to him the epithets, maun-
dering, half-educated, of small ability.[43]   But to the
minds of Kiffen, Price, and their friends, Walwyn
was the director of the whole Leveller movement,
and Lilburne his mere puppet.   To Walwyn they
ascribed the device of circulating Leveller manifestos under the form of petitions; to Walwyn they
ascribed the authorship of the petitions themselves.
There is good reason for assigning to him at least
a share in the composition of that of March, 1647.[44]
Other evidence attests his importance in that year.
A cipher key apparently for use by the Levellers and
Republicans at some time in 1647, after the entrance
of the army into politics, has cipher symbols for the
names of Wildman, Marten, Overton, and Walwyn
among the Levellers.   The omission of Lilburne is
perhaps due to his comparative inactivity in the
Tower, perhaps to his comparative unimportance
in the movement at the moment.[45]   The little ex-
tant evidence of Walwyn's activity inclines one to

[42] *The Charity of Church-Men*, p. 11.
[43] David Masson, *Life of Milton*, IV, 45.
[44] *Walwins Wiles*, p. 18; *The Fountain Of Slaunder Discovered*, p. 7.
[45] Loder Symonds Mss., *Hist. Mss. Comm.*, *15th Rep.*, App., Pt. iv, p.
401.   These contain some of the papers of Henry Marten.

the opinion that his part in the Leveller movement is easier underestimated than overestimated.

One wonders if he first suggested the idea that the soldiery of the army combine with the people to promote their common interest by an Agreement of the People. It is impossible to trace the men who wrote the first Agreement, though what evidence we have points to its origin among the soldiers themselves. Yet the obscurity of its origin is what one would expect in something begun by Walwyn.

At all events, in the Leveller policy delineated in this chapter it is impossible to see anything else but Walwyn's influence. The conscious resolution to frame an excellent constitutional settlement and then trust to its conquering men's reason by the very appearance of goodness and justice in it, is typical of Walwyn as of no other man of the time. The appeal to the men of England to reason with one another like brothers, to inquire one of another what the liberties they had fought for really were— this is all the simple transference of Walwyn's method of proselyting to the whole kingdom. The Levellers have been accused of impracticability and building of air castles simply because their attempt to appeal to the reason of the people, and their faith in the ability of reason to overcome all things have been ignored. They have been pictured as narrow fanatics who sought to force upon the kingdom, to quote Carlyle, a doctrinaire "Sieyès-Bentham constitution." But in their propaganda the Agreement of the People was not in itself an end, but merely a device that promised to secure the establishment of certain rules of justice and liberty. The Leveller movement was a crusade for the establishment of those rules—rules believed to be so consonant to reason that the nation, if it would but listen to friendly argument, could not help but be captured by them.

NOTES

I. The Prophecy of John Saltmarsh

Perhaps the penitence of the army leaders for Corkbush Field was caused in part by the dying prophecy of John Saltmarsh. Saltmarsh had been a chaplain with the army, but generally had kept free of politics. On December 4, he left his home and set out for the army, telling his wife he had received in a trance directions to announce what the Lord had revealed to him. Prophesying to some of his friends on his journey his approaching death, he arrived in the camp; he warned an agitator to leave the army lest he perish with it in the wrath of God; he told the Council that God had forsaken them because they had imprisoned their faithful brethren and had sought to destroy the people of God. With speeches of the same sort to Cromwell, Fairfax, and others as individuals, he left the army forever; he died on the eleventh of December. Such a thing would have its effect on the men who made up the New Model, even on men like Cromwell. It is significant of the real rationalism of the Levellers that they never attempted to utilize this incident as a divine judgment on their opponents. *Wonderful Predictions Declared In a Message, as from the Lord, To . . . Sr Thomas Fairfax and the Councell of His Army*, Dec. 29, 1647, E. 421 (16). Strange as this account is, I can see no reason for doubting its authenticity. The pamphlet has a convincing air of truth, and so far as I know its statements were never questioned. Cf. *Clarke Papers*, II, 247, 249; *Englands Friend Raised from the Grave*, July 31, 1649, E. 566 (13).

II. A Hostile Description of the Leveller Organization

An organization such as Masterson's information unearthed in January is described in an anonymous pamphlet, *The Case of The King Stated* (E. 416 [5]), which Thomason dates November 18. The fact that the author uses *Pragmaticus's* motto, "Nemo me impune lacessit," as well as the style suggests Nedham as a possible candidate for the honor of authorship. The author accuses the agents of the army of seeking to dissolve the Parliament, and in a new one "of their own framing" to sentence the king to death. "Nor," he proceeds, "doe they sleep in this cursed businesse, but have Agents of their own in all Quarters of the Army, the Countries abroad, and the City of London, to draw in Persons to subscribe to the aforesaid damned particulars [apparently the *Case Of The Armie*]. And it hath been my good hap to light upon a Copy of Instructions agreed upon by the Agents of the City of London, and the Army, to the respective Counties, Cities, and Parishes, whereunto severall Papers of those particulars were directed by the chiefe Conspirators, for the more orderly carrying on, and the more speedy effecting and bringing in the subscriptions. The Instructions are these:

"First, that the Papers be delivered to such faithfull persons, as will be vigilant, and active in prosecution of them.

"Secondly, That they be desired to meet at places which they shall judge most convenient, to take the Subscriptions of the City or place where they reside.

"Thirdly, That there be appointed one, or more Agents, as they shall judge meet, to bring in the Subscriptions as soone as possibly they can, to the Saracen's Head in Friday-street in London, where there will be Agents to receive them, or the Master of the House (let that fellow be taken notice of) will direct them where they shall be received.

"Fourthly, that one or more active faithfull man be appointed for each County, City, or Place, as aforesaid, to act and transact such things as may conduce to the good of the work in hand."

III. WALWYN AND COMMUNISM

As Mr. Gooch in his *English Democratic Ideas*, p. 211, has connected Walwyn with communism, the evidence for believing him a professed communist may be considered for a moment. The sole piece of unequivocal testimony is the passage quoted above from *Walwins Wiles*—a book written almost with the avowed intent of making Walwyn despicable in all ways possible. Charge after charge in the book is refuted by Walwyn and his friends. The communistic reasoning quoted above on p. 248, like most of the book's charges, has no one's name to evidence it. It is possible to interpret it as proving only that Walwyn could see the force in certain arguments for communism; this does not prove that he advocated it, any more than it does in the case of one-half the educated men of today. Both Walwyn and Brook stated that Walwyn was in favor of communism no further than was implied in the Manifestation, the Agreement of the People of the spring of 1649, and the petition of March,

1647. The Manifestation expressly stated that communism would be impossible till every man consented to it. The Levellers were scarcely so simple as to think this principle would make its way readily to universal acceptance with men of property. It is hard to see why Walwyn cannot be left with his own denial of his belief in community of property. At the time *Walwins Wiles* was published, the opponents of the political Levellers were deliberately striving to make them responsible for the communistic beliefs and practices of the little group of Diggers.

IV. WALWYN AND LIBERTY OF CONSCIENCE

Walwyn has usually been set down among the chief supporters of liberty of conscience in his day. Brook stated that Walwyn had had a hand in the earliest of the books written in behalf of liberty of conscience; and this passage has been interpreted as referring to Henry Robinson's *Liberty of Conscience*. It has occurred to me, however, that Brook's remark may refer to an earlier work, and one, if I am right, far more characteristic of Walwyn. In 1641 a small book, *The Humble Petition Of The Brownists*, was obscurely printed and amid the polemics of the day passed completely unnoticed. Of secondary writers referring to it, Dr. Wallace St. John in a doctoral dissertation, *The Contest for Religious Liberty in England* (University of Chicago Divinity School, 1900, p. 56), is deceived by the title into thinking it was actually addressed to the Parliament. In common with R. Barclay in his *Religious Societies of the Commonwealth* (p. 476), and H. A. Glass in his *Barbone Parliament* (p. 21), he assumes from the title that it is a Separatist piece. The likelihood of Separatists referring to themselves as Brownists is not great, however—the term was too generally used as a reproach. Gardiner thinks the piece a caricature (*History of England*, X, 35); and probably at first sight that is the most plausible explanation.

Disregarding for the moment any possible satirical tendencies in the book, it appears as a daring exposition of the principle of liberty of conscience. It meets unflinchingly the question of tolerating the papist, even the Adamite and the Separatist. "There is no man," it states, "that professeth a Religion, but is in conscience perswaded that to be the best wherein to save his soule, & can give no doubt some reason, yea, and alleage some authority out of the word of God for it, which is an argument that not his will, but his Judgement is convinced, and therefore holds it unreasonable to be forced to follow other mens Judgements and not his owne in a matter of so great importance. . . . . If the Puritans will not use the Service Booke, Corner Cap, Surplesse or Altar, nor bow at the name of Jesus, their pure hearts esteeming it

Idolatrie, Let them alone, they are great readers of Gods booke, and if they bee in errour, they will sooner finde it, having liberty of conscience, then being oppressed with the Tyranny of the High Commission Court or other kindes of persecutions which disquiet their consciences and troubles their patience. . . . . Let the Adamites Preach in vaults & caves as naked as their nailes, and starve themselves with cold, they thinke themselves as innocent as Adam and Eve were in their nakednesse before their fall, let them therefore alone till some innocent Eve bee so curious as to eate forbidden fruit, and then they will all make themselves aprons of figge leaves perceiving their nakednesse." The excuse for quoting this passage must be that it offers strong evidence regarding the authorship of the piece. If my analysis of Walwyn be correct, he was just the man to put truths of this sort in a way that to one not in tune with his spirit might seem the merest ribaldry.

The consideration that militates against regarding the petition as a satire on the sects is that the satire, if satire it be, was far too delicate for the popular consumption of the age; seventeenth-century political satire went plainly labeled. Further, there is nothing in the piece to indicate at first hand what religious belief its author was supporting. An Anglican satirizing the sects would not have included apologies for the Arminian; Hyde had the skill to forge the book, but would scarcely have made it politically so pointless. Admitting the petition to be serious in intent, the internal evidence all points to its composition by a man mentally nearer like Walwyn than any other writer of the day.

A comparison of the plan of the piece, which handles the Brownists, Socinians, Arminians, Papists, and Familists, in the same manner as the Puritans and Adamites, with a passage in *A Prediction Of Mr. Edwards His Conversion, and Recantation,* affords additional evidence. "You shal then see him a man composed of all those opinions he hath so much reviled! an Independent: so far as to allow every man to be fully perswaded in his owne mind, and to molest no man for worshiping God according to his conscience.

"A Brownist; so far, as to separate from all those that preach for filthy lucre; An Anabaptist: so far, at least, as to be rebaptized in a floud of his owne true repentent teares: A seeker; in seeking occasion, how to doe good unto all men, without respect of persons or opinions; he will be wholly incorporate into the Family of love, of true Christian love, that covereth a multitude of evils . . . . "

If the surmise be correct that Walwyn was the author of this plea, so daring that it could admit the worst practical effects that might result occasionally from the broad application of its principle, he assuredly deserves a high seat among the men who fought the battle of liberty of conscience.

CHAPTER VIII

NOVEMBER–MARCH, 1648/49

I. THE LAST ALLIANCE OF LEVELLER AND INDEPENDENT

IN the crucial six months of English history beginning with November, 1648, the alinement of parties in a measure was determined by the fact that Levellers and army Independents agreed on their destructive, but not on their constructive program. In November the Grandees were prepared to exemplify the theory of national sovereignty by doing away with king and Lords; and thus far they had a right to expect Leveller support. But, although they seemed ready for a time to exemplify their theory further in an Agreement of the People, they speedily dismissed the project when they no longer needed the Levellers, and established the Commonwealth government on very different lines. The Levellers, after sitting in sullen silence for three months after the king's execution, renounced and defied the Commonwealth that the officers had set up, and recurred to their own political project, the Agreement of the People.

The turn of political events in 1648 again brought the Levellers to the side of the army Independents. Forgetting the ill-usage they had suffered in the army councils and the rendezvous of November, 1647, the Levellers adhered to the Independents and rejected the overtures of the Presbyterians, who were more or less openly alined with the Royalists. The Presbyterians indeed by August had become assiduous in their attentions to Lilburne. On August 1 the House of Commons under Presbyterian tutelage removed the restraint it had put him under in January, and referred to a special committee the task of satisfying his Star-Chamber damages and settling his arrears. Next day the Lords revoked their former sentence against him.[1] But Lilburne, not to be won over by his old enemies, wrote Cromwell a letter pledging him the support of the Levellers. As Cromwell received it at the height of the rebellion of 1648 when he hardly knew friend from foe, Lilburne's avowed support must have been welcome.[2]

Moreover, the army officers were inclined to favor the decisive measures advocated by the Levellers rather than the cautious policy of the city Independents. Thus the Levellers on September 11th presented a petition to the Commons that addressed them as the supreme authority and urged them to forbear treating with the king; and, although the city Independents held aloof from the petition, Cromwell, by Lilburne's account, heartily approved it.[3]

---

[1] *Commons Journal*, V, 657, 658; *Lords Journal*, X, 406; *A Speech Spoken in the Honourable House of Commons. By Sir Iohn Maynard*, Aug. 11, 1648, E. 458 (2).

[2] *Legal Fundamentall Liberties*, pp. 32 ff.

[3] The petition protested against the Commons recognizing the negative of king or Lords; it rehearsed the usual Leveller reforms. It was mainly intended as a protest against a treaty with the king. *Mercurius*

Yet the fundamental differences in policy between Grandees and Levellers appeared as soon as conferences began. Each side regarded the other with suspicion and planned to use its ally to further its own ends. Thus when the leaders of the two factions conferred at the Nags Head Tavern in November, the city Independents, again in unity with their brethren of the army, insisted on breaking up the Parliament and doing justice on the king immediately. The Levellers refused to trust the army with the execution of this policy until the army had assured them of its good faith by setting up an Agreement of the People and a new Parliament. Meanwhile, as Lilburne admitted, the Levellers proposed to make sure of fair dealing from the army by holding both king and Parliament as political countersets to it, to be played against it if occasion should arise.[4]

The Independents, finding that hot words would not melt the determination of the Levellers, submitted the question at issue to a second conference between four men of each party. The Levellers gained their point in this conference. The joint committee agreed on the following resolutions,[5] whose phraseology, it will be seen, resembles in a startling degree the stock phrases that denote the

Pragmaticus, Sept. 12–19, asserted Henry Marten was the author; *Pragmaticus* further stated that the Levellers claimed 40,000 signatures to it. *Legal Fundamentall Liberties*, p. 33.

[4] *Legal Fundamentall Liberties*, p. 33.

[5] *Ibid.*, p. 34. John Price and Walwyn were dropped because of Price's refusal to have any dealings with Walwyn.

powers and functions of an American constitutional convention.

That some persons be chosen by the Army to represent the whole Body; and that the well-affected in every County (if it may be) chuse some persons to represent them: And those to meet at the Head-Quarters.

That those persons ought not to exercise any Legislative power, but onely to draw up the foundations of a just Government, and to propound them to the well-affected people in every County to be agreed to: Which Agreement ought to be above Law; and therefore the bounds, limits, and extent of the peoples Legislative Deputies in Parliament, contained in the Agreement to be drawn up into a formall contract, to be mutually signed by the well-affected people and their said Deputies upon the dayes of their Election respec- tively . . . . [6]

Ireton, to whom as the representative of the officers this scheme was submitted, could hardly be expected to approve it. Within a day or two of the time it was presented to him, he had secured the adoption by the council of the army of a remonstrance of his penning. This army platform demanded the bringing of the king to justice, and proposed an Agreement of the People that put only

[6] *Legal Fundamentall Liberties*, p. 34.

A similar proposition appears in *The Humble Representation of the Desires of* . . . *the Regiment of Horse, for the County of Northumberland*, Dec. 5, 1648, E. 475 (13). Each regiment and each county are to choose two or more representatives "joyntly to sit consult and act in the behalf of themselves, the people, and Army; and that the removal of our oppressions, and obtainment of our Freedom, acording to the premises above-said, be the only work of their Agitation." The power of the deputies extends for but two months, when the people and regiments are to choose anew. These bi-monthly elections are to continue till the task is done. Among other things this petition demands the abolition of servile tenures originating with the Norman conquest.

such limitations on the recurring "representatives" as would serve to keep power in their own hands, secure regularly recurring elections and prevent interference with the act of indemnity.[7] Ireton knew too well that the Levellers would never accept such an Agreement of the People; he knew also that it could not pass the constitutional convention that they proposed without a renewal of the bitter debates of 1647.[8]

However, the Levellers were the only group of men who had in the past maintained so radical a position as that of Ireton's remonstrance; and it therefore was important that they be conciliated.   Colonel

[7] E. 473 (11). *The Remonstrance* is dated Nov. 16, and was presented to Parliament Nov. 20. The Agreement it contained limited the franchise to persons who had accepted the Agreement and to those who for a term of years had not warred against the Parliament.

The doctrine of the sovereignty of the people, employed by Ireton in the Remonstrance, was no such new discovery as one might imagine from Gardiner (*Great Civil War*, IV, 235). I cannot find Gardiner's authority for the statement that the Agreement in the last paragraphs of the Remonstrance was added by a committee of Levellers and Independents. There is not a word to that effect in the pages of *Legal Fundamentall Liberties* he quotes as authority. Also, I cannot see the force of his criticism of the Agreement as inconsistent with the doctrine of the sovereignty of the people (Gardiner, IV, 239). Surely their relation was means and end.

[8] The idea of an Agreement had been revived by army agents in April of 1648. They had petitioned for the establishment of a biennial "representative" and further "that there be a known and certain rule between the people and their representatives that are chosen and intrusted with that supreame power of making Lawes." The paper added several limitations on the power of representatives, and then proposed that the rule between people and representative be sealed in a contract between them on days of election. *The Armies Petition*, May 3, 1648, E. 438 (1). The same idea elaborated appears in a *New Engagement, or Manifesto*, Aug. 3, 1648, 669 f., 12 (97).

Harrison undertook the task. He frankly admitted to Lilburne that the usage the Levellers had had from the army in the past justified them in demanding for the future proofs of good faith expressed in deeds rather than words. But Harrison also frankly explained the difficulties of the officers. It was essential that they advance on London and begin proceedings against the king at once. They could not wait while a constitutional convention, such as the Levellers demanded, was called and set to deliberation.[9]

When so dealt with, Lilburne was always amenable to reason. On this occasion he admitted the force of Harrison's arguments. He suggested that the absolute power of framing an Agreement be deputed to a committee consisting of four officers, four city Independents, four Independent members of Parliament, and four Levellers; he would be willing, he said, to see four Presbyterians also on the committee. His only stipulation was that the document produced by the committee be accepted as final, and submitted to the people without amendment; and this stipulation he understood the officers to accept.[9]

The committee duly assembled. Henry Marten was the only representative of the Independent members of the Commons who attended; Lilburne, Walwyn, Wildman, and Maximilian Petty represented the Levellers, being chosen at a meeting of agents from London and its environs; Ireton of

[9] *Legal Fundamentall Liberties*, pp. 34 ff.

course was one of the army representatives. In the meetings of the committee long and hot debates were caused by the narrow measure of religious toleration that Ireton thought desirable, and his insistence that Parliament be left the power of inflicting penalties for offenses not defined as such by the law. At last these points were adjusted, and the completed document was referred to the council of war.

When the council of war began to debate and to amend the committee's draft Agreement, the Levellers considered that the officers had broken faith. Lilburne and his friends withdrew from the council in anger. They published the Agreement as framed by the committee; and in presenting it to the people of the nation, reaffirmed their faith in the power of things reasonable in themselves to convince men. With the publication of the Agreement, the alliance between Leveller, Grandee, and Independent was at an end.[10]

Probably the Levellers were justified in their complaint that the officers, in sanctioning the amendment of the Agreement, broke their bargain. At the same time it must be admitted that the attitude of Ireton was much more conciliatory than in the debates of 1647. He laid aside his arrogance, and labored earnestly for the adoption of an Agreement that would have some chance of being accepted by the nation. He included in the Agreement a clause fixing the time at which the Rump should dissolve,

[10] *Legal Fundamentall Liberties*, p. 40. The Agreement published is in E. 476 (26).

hoping that this might tempt the people to accept the Agreement.[11] Moreover, in an effort to attain the same end he seems to have sacrificed his own opinions. Thus he acquiesced in the Agreement's setting outside the reach of the new "representative" certain specific powers such as the power of impressment, although he himself retained the opinion that the ideal constitution was a Parliament restrained only from the right to perpetuate itself.[12]

In urging the council to adopt the Agreement in the form he desired, Ireton had to contend with the vague feeling of unrest, uncertainty, and indecision that made many officers hesitate to take a decisive step. In the days between Pride's Purge and the king's execution, when no man could tell whether events would lead to the king's restoration, arraignment, or deposition, the fanatics of the army were inclined to wait for a direct manifestation of God's will. An army chaplain of note, William Sedgwick, in a series of tracts visited partial condemnation on all parties, but absolute condemnation on none, not even the king's. The whole nation, he announced, under the woes that God had inflicted on it must humbly bewail its sins and sit still to await divine guidance. Under these circumstances it seemed to Sedgwick carnal presumption for any set of men to seek a carnal remedy like an Agreement of the Peo-

[11] *Clarke Papers*, II, 170–171.

[12] ". . . . lett us make such a distribution of the publique trust in such hands as shall give everyone an equall share, an equall interest and possibility, and lett us submitt ourselves to these future Representatives, and if wee bee nott satisfied in one Representative itt may bee satisfied in the next." *Clarke Papers*, II, 82. See also pp. 176–177.

ple for the woes with which God had afflicted the
kingdom.[13] To hotter fanatics who felt that the
great day of the Lord was at hand, it seemed impious for mere men to do anything but wait on
the Lord's will. Some distrusted the Agreement as
the imposition on men's consciences of a new Covenant. Others regarded it as burdening men with a
new government. Still others thought it an impious
temptation of Providence as putting into the hands
of carnal men the power that divine dispensations
had put into the hands of God's Saints.[14]

Ireton did his best to answer these objections.
He told one objector that the Agreement was not

---

[13] *Justice upon the Armie Remonstrance. Or A rebuke of that evill spirit
that leads them in their Counsels and Actions*, Dec. 11, 1648, E. 475 (34);
A second view of the Army Remonstrance, Or Justice done to the Armie,
Dec. 23, 1648, E. 477 (20); *The Leaves of the Tree Of Life: For the healing
of The Nations*, Aug. 25, 1648, E. 460 (40). In this last pamphlet he
arraigns the Levellers.

"Thy errors are these, Thou canst not bear the Kingdomes suffering
under the hand of God, nor thy owne; but in a carnall love of this
worldly state, seekest to uphold it against the justice of God; and so
fallest into the same evill of thy Fathers self-love and preservation, in
enmity to the Lord. To save thy self, that the overflowing scourge
may not come nigh thee; thou makest a Covenant with hell, and an
Agreement with death; the Agreement of the People, who are turned by
the Divine justice into a hel and death.

"Thou art ignorant of that wisdome of God, that only can save the
nation; and having gathered some scraps of earthly knowledge from
others, thy proud heart is lifted up, and thou conceivest highly of thy
self, as if thou art able to save the kingdome: and so presumest upon
that which thou art not called unto." Pp. 45, 46.

[14] *Clarke Papers*, II, 175, 176–177, 178, 183. Erbury, who thought
the Agreement set up a new government, argued that what the country
needed was not a constitutional settlement, but a committee of twelve
or twenty-four to redress abuses forthwith according to God's Word.
His attitude reminds one of a certain type of modern social reformer.

the setting up of a new power, but rather a limiting and restraining of powers already established. Harrison assisted Ireton in answering the objection that the Agreement divested the Saints of power God had entrusted to them. The future Fifth Monarchy man confessed that in his belief the nation would not accept the Agreement. The fact that the Saints had proffered it would prove that they had not selfishly clutched at the power that God had put into their hands; but they might rest assured that God would retain the power where he had placed it.[15] In the attitude of the army council can be found sufficient reason why the Agreement of the People, once it was referred to the Rump, was not again heard of.

In conclusion we may note any new developments in the political thought of the Levellers or of Ireton. First, the Agreement itself may be briefly sketched. As it came from the committee, it provided for the dissolution of the Rump and the election every two years of a Representative of 300 members by householder suffrage.[16] In the intervals between the sittings of these biennial Representatives a Council of State was to be entrusted with power. The Agreement stated the powers of the Representative; they extended to establishing courts and public offices, making and repealing laws, and in general to all matters not expressly reserved from them. The reservations were as follows. The Representa-

---

[15] *Clarke Papers*, II, 176–177, 183.

[16] For the first six months, only those who had signed the Agreement could vote; afterward, all householders not Royalists could do so.

tive, while it could set up a form of public worship, had not authority over individuals in matters of religion. It could not impress for military service, appoint its members to lucrative public office, call any one to account for his past activity in the war, enact or continue any law or privilege that did not apply equally to all men, interfere with the execution of the laws, or punish in the absence of a known and declared law. Above all the Representative had no power to alter the Agreement that created it.

The army council made important changes in this Agreement. It struck out the clause forbidding compulsion in matters of religion, providing instead for toleration to all but papists and prelatists. It also dropped the provision for the abolition of all special privileges: it added a postscript distinguishing certain parts of the Agreement as fundamental and certain others as prescribed merely for convenience. As the wording of the instrument forbade taking away "any foundations of common right freedom and safety in the Agreement," the council of war by its amendments left the Representative free to alter the things that were merely "convenient."[17]

The reasons for several amendments to the Agreement are to be sought in the contrast between the political theories of the Levellers and of Ireton. Ireton's belief that Parliament's power should be limited only by the term for which the people elected it, induced him to press for the removal of clauses

[17] The Agreement as amended is most conveniently studied in Gardiner, *Constitutional Documents*, p. 359.

denying it specific powers. The chief restraint on its power that he removed was that prohibiting interference with freedom of worship. He urged this alteration on the ground that in the Jewish nation the civil magistrate had had jurisdiction over offenses of the first table. The argument, it will be seen, was purely Erastian.[18]

It points to another article of Ireton's political faith. Personally he believed that the business of an Agreement was not to determine the extent of the magistrate's power; for by nature and divine right certain powers pertained to magistrates under any form of government. Rather he thought the Agreement should serve to indicate the hands in which this power should rest. Such a view of the instrument's function was different from that of John Goodwin, who was present at the conference, and declared that the question was of what powers the sovereign people saw fit to trust to their magistrates.[19] However, Ireton himself recognized the fact that in form the Agreement was a designation of the powers that were or were not allowed the rulers by the people.

This of course represented the idea of the Levellers. The Agreement marked a distinct advance in their political thought. They were no longer uncertain, as they had been in 1647, of the nature of the constitutional device they proposed. They regarded

---

[18] *Clarke Papers*, II, 79–81, 101, 112.

[19] *Ibid.*, pp. 117, 118. He stated, however, that the people, having no coercive power in religion themselves, could not grant such a power to their magistrates.

it as a solemn act of the people, not only designating
the persons to rule, but designating also the powers
that the rulers were to enjoy. More important
than this, they were now ready with an answer to
one question that puzzled them in 1647. The
Agreement would have authority, first, because it
originated in a body of men chosen by the people to
establish a frame of government and to do nothing
else; second, because the people by signing the
frame of government gave a visible sign of their
assent to it.

However, it must be admitted that one provision
of their Agreement indicated that the Levellers
shrank from the full application of their broader
theories. They expressly limited to the "well-
affected"—to the Parliament party or a fraction of
it—the right of choosing members of a constituent
convention, assenting to the adoption of an Agreement, or voting for representatives under it. The
Levellers still retained their faith in the power of
reason to conquer; but no doubt they felt safer in
putting the Agreement into operation before trusting to the naked power of reason.

II. THE LEVELLERS DEFY THE COMMONWEALTH

The Levellers, bitterly though they might resent
the bad faith of the officers, could only protest. The
joint committee had amused them during the weeks
when they might have overset the policy of the army
leaders. After Pride's Purge their scheme of playing off king or Parliament against the army was no

longer possible. By publishing their draft of the
Agreement of the People the Levellers might protest
to the world of the duplicity practised against them,
but after they had made this protest they could
only await passively the outcome of the army's
policy. In October and November their party was,
comparatively speaking, closely knit by the prospect
of success. In December it disappeared as an active political factor.

Some of the Leveller leaders, perceiving the
wreck of their political program, hastened to obtain
what they could for themselves. Wildman and
Sexby were thought by their old associates to have
got their price from the Grandees. Lilburne himself, by playing on the fears of the officers while
they still felt none too secure, obtained the revenues
of certain sequestered Durham estates in part com-
pensation of his claims against the government.
Toward the end of December he set out for Durham
to secure his newly acquired property, and did not
return till after the execution of the king. He
frankly admitted the means by which he had secured
settlement of his claims, saying that he had resolved
to secure what was due him before the officers were
so firm in the saddle that he must be their slave to
obtain justice.[20]

He was, however, deeply disgusted with the political situation. He had refused office under the new
government on the ground that he could not by
accepting office acquiesce in a perpetual Parliament.

[20] *Legal Fundamentall Liberties*, pp. 46, 69; *A Preparative To An Hue
And Cry after Sir Arthur Haslerig*, Sept. 13, 1649, E. 573 (16), pp. 18–35.

Moreover, he felt that since the king was gone the other "corrupt interests" of the kingdom—the clergy with their tithes, the lawyers with their fees, the corporation men with their monopolies of trade—were all sheltering with the Rump. The Rump itself, he thought, would last till the officers were ready to set up one of their number as king, when the shadow of republican forms would vanish away.[21]

The activity of the High Court of Justice was sufficient to stir up to action Lilburne's smoldering discontent with the government. The erecting of a special court to try three or four men and the arraigning of men without juries on capital charges were alike contrary to the best ideals and theories of English law. So also was the court's procedure in trying the Duke of Hamilton, the Earl of Holland and Lord Capel on charges for which they had already been sentenced.[22] The belief that personal liberty was in danger induced Lilburne to rally the Leveller party for a new struggle with the Grandees.

Lilburne had stated his objections to the court in declining a seat in it when it sat to try the king. He had refused to countenance what he regarded as an illegal fashion of trying a guilty man. He and his friends had been among the first to advocate stripping the king of the immunities that his station gave him; but they would be the last to deprive any man born on English ground of the rights of an Englishman. Let the king be indicted in King's

---

[21] *Legal Fundamentall Liberties*, pp. 46 ff., 68.
[22] *Op. cit.*, p. 70 (mispaged).

Bench under the general law of England assigning death as the penalty for murder. Thus treating the king of England as amenable to the law in an ordinary court like the meanest subject, would do more to root up belief in regal irresponsibility than would tacitly admitting that kings must be tried in an extraordinary way. Yet even so he condoned the action of the court in Charles's case because of the king's haughty assertion that he was accountable only to God. When, however, the High Court of Justice arraigned Hamilton, Holland, and Capel, three men who admitted their accountability to the law of England, Lilburne took alarm in good earnest; for he considered that injustice against any of them became a precedent to "destroy me, or the most righteous man in England, if the swaying faction pleased." [23]

At the moment he bestirred himself in the defense of the three peers. Lord Capel's gallant bearing, his cool pleading of the law and his demand for a jury completely won Lilburne's heart. He urged the prisoners to plead the lack of jurisdiction of the court and the Rump, and was bitterly disappointed when they submitted to stand trial. After they had taken this step he would not act as counsel for them, but he still stood ready to offer assistance with papers, books, or testimony. [24]

By the time the High Court of Justice had completed its work, Lilburne had renewed his former political activity. The first moves of his party can-

[23] *Legal Fundamentall Liberties*, pp. 46–47, 70.
[24] See Note on p. 276.

not certainly be told. Probably they included an attempt to stir up the soldiery to demand the readmission of agitators into the council of the army. As a result, in a council of war held February 22, the officers resolved on methods of checking petitions from the soldiers. They even proposed to ask Parliament for an ordinance making civilians who tampered with the soldiery amenable to the penalties of martial law.[25]

Lilburne at once retorted to the council's demands by petitioning the Rump to throw off the domination of the army and become a rightful representative of England by doing the works of one. As means to this end he suggested the immediate enforcement of the Self-Denying Ordinance, the abolition of the Council of State and the High Court of Justice, and the promotion of a real Agreement of the People. This was the substance of *Englands New-Chaines Discovered* presented by Lilburne to the Rump on February 26.[25]

Mercurius Pragmaticus was probably right in his surmise that the ruling powers would have allowed Lilburne short shrift, had it not been for Leveller activity in Hertfordshire. In close accord with Marten, the Levellers were again at work. In the market place of St. Albans soldiers read papers and petitions which came from Lilburne's pen. In Hampshire and Berkshire, Levellers stirred up the people to refuse payment of excise. In London sol-

---

[25] *Englands New-Chaines Discovered*, E. 545 (27). An officer was reported to have said that a court martial could hang twenty—either civilians or soldiers, apparently—ere a magistrate one.

diers petitioned against the limitation that the council of war had set on their right of petition, and were promptly cashiered.[26]

March 24 the Levellers published *The second Part Of Englands New-Chaines Discovered.* It was a review of political events of 1647/48, drawing the moral that the Junto by its duplicity had frustrated all hopes of a peaceful settlement. It accused the Junto of discriminating against officers like White, Rainsborough, and Reynolds who were known to sympathize with the Levellers. It interpreted the Grandees' restriction of the press and their grasping for martial power over citizens as designed to pave their way to a military despotism. In conclusion, it assigned as the most probable remedy the restoration of representative government, in the army by the reëstablishment of the council of the army, and in the nation by the carrying into effect of the Agreement of the People.[27]

The Levellers probably proposed to attain their end by forcing Parliament either to act justly or else to use such means for silencing them as would

[26] *Mercurius Pragmaticus*, Mar. 6–13, 13–20; *Certain Occurrences*, Mar. 9–16; *The Hunting of the Foxes from New-Market and Triploe Heaths*, Mar. 21, 1649, E 548 (7).

Berks in the previous summer had been the scene of some escapades of Harry Marten, who had raised a regiment and horsed it by raids on private stables. Harry had ordered juries as the "supreame Authority and Majesty of England" to remain covered before judges, forbidden the yielding of homage at Courts Baron, and done various other unprecedented things. *Pragmaticus*, Aug. 15–22, 29, 1648; *Commons Journal*, V, 673, 676. May 1-8, 1649, *Pragmaticus* hinted that Marten was drifting from the Levellers to the Grandees.

[27] E. 548 (16).

strip it of all defense before the people.[28]   Certainly
the Junto acted promptly on the Levellers' provocation.   March 28 heavy guards of soldiers arrested Lilburne, Walwyn, Overton, and Prince, and
marched them with all military caution to the
Council of State at Derby House.   There the
prisoners refused to incriminate themselves by
answering questions.   Lilburne denied that the
Rump by its members could legally exercise judicial powers in the High Court of Justice.   Through
the keyhole of an ante-chamber door, he heard
Cromwell punctuating by thumps of his fist his conviction that the Council had no way to deal with
"these men" but to break them in pieces.   A
motion to bail them was overruled by one vote,
and the four were committed to the Tower.[29]   The
Levellers, finding that the Independents would not
adopt their program, had turned to their old political methods to overthrow the Commonwealth
government; and the Junto had lifted the gauntlet
that the Levellers had thrown down.

NOTE

LILBURNE AND LORD CAPEL

Lilburne's account of his proffer of assistance to the men arraigned
before the High Court of Justice has especial interest in that it affords
the opportunity of checking the reliability of Lilburne's numerous auto-
biographical statements.   At first blush, even in a generally reliable
source, a commoner's narrative of his intimacies with peers might be
regarded with suspicion.   One would be inclined to presume that what
actually happened was that the commoner had pressed his company
and counsel on the peer and perhaps had been mildly rebuffed.   Accord-

[28] *Strength out of Weaknesse*, Oct. 19, 1649, E. 575 (18), p. 5.
[29] *The Picture Of The Councel of State*, pp. 7, 8, 12, 14, 15, 18.

ingly, an independent confirmation of such an account adds very much to the confidence we can place in statements on similar authority. Such a confirmation is offered by the following from the Beaufort Mss. (*Hist. Mss. Comm., 12th Report*, App., Pt. IX, p. 33.):

"Advice for L. C.

"To insist upon your banishment and to make that argument valid, mention Seyres case declared in Cook's Hist. in his 3rd booke the 104 cap. 230 P. Then desire that Col. John Lilborne may have leave to declare the proceedings in his tryall at Oxford. If this prove not sufficient then desire the judgment of the Parliament may be had as to this point of the law, and for the obtaining of this their shall be a petition readie drawne to be delivered to the Parliament." Apparently this originated with some one who rejected Lilburne's advice to plead to the jurisdiction of the Rump, yet deemed his testimony and support of value.

Lilburne mentions such an incident in the case of Holland, probably confusing the men for the moment. He told Capel that he should be ashamed either as a king's man, a peer, or a freeman of England to acknowledge the Rump. *Legal Fundamentall Liberties*, p. 73.

CHAPTER IX

The Triumph of the Commonwealth

I. THE CRUSHING OF DISAFFECTION IN THE ARMY

FOR the eight months next after the arrest of Lilburne and his associates, the Commonwealth government found itself confronted with the determined opposition of the Levellers. Their attitude was a standing challenge of the Rump's legality—one that could not be ignored, and at the same time could hardly be accepted. For the sake of appearances, civilians refusing to acknowledge the legality of the government could not be dealt with by martial law. Nor could they be dealt with by civil process; for the position of the Rump was revolutionary rather than legal. Every precedent of four and a half centuries of recorded English law acquitted the Leveller leaders of the crime of sedition. Yet under the forms of that law, the Levellers must be tried if tried they were to be; and not the wisest lawyer at the service of the Council of State could say how far three months' enactments had repealed those forms, or give assurance that no technicality would arise under them to make convictions impossible. The government hesitated till October, when it tried Lilburne for sedition. While it was decisively defeated in that trial, however, its military successes had so strengthened its position as a government *de facto* that it could safely rest its claims *de jure*.

The problem of disaffection in the army, while not so much complicated by legal difficulties, was more pressing. In March the Junto had quenched the spark of rebellion among the civilian Levellers; but the army was full of combustible material. The soldiers were murmuring that detaching forces for the Irish campaign was a violation of the Solemn Engagement; for that Engagement had pledged the army not to divide before the liberties of England were secure. Why, asked the soldiers, should they conquer another nation at the behest of the men who had enslaved England to a government by will and not by law? Emphatically the reëstablishment of the representative Council of the Army, before the campaign in Ireland was initiated, was the least security for the preservation of the nation's liberties that they could demand.[1]

Such reasonings, when joined with the perennial disputes about pay and arrears, soon produced trouble. April 24, a dispute over pay ended in thirty men of Whalley's regiment seizing their colors. They submitted to discipline again only on the personal orders of Cromwell and Fairfax. Three days later five of them were cashiered, and a sixth, Robert Lockyer by name, was shot.[2]

The choice of such a scapegoat of military discipline awakened forebodings in men attached to the liberties of England. Lockyer was one of the

[1] See Note on p. 300.
[2] *A Modest Narrative of Intelligence*, Apr. 28–May 5.

men of fine patriotism who had fought through the war with an eye single to the removal of the "Norman Yoke." While awaiting his execution, his one regret was that he died merely for a petty dispute over pay, and not for the ideals on behalf of which he had risked his life during seven years. He met his death protesting in Lilburne's manner that condemning men by a court martial in time of peace was murder. The Levellers made his funeral a solemn protest against such applications of martial law. Thousands of men and women walked in procession as Lockyer's body was borne to the grave with all the honors of war.[3]

Within a week several regiments were in open mutiny. The men of Scroop's regiment at Salisbury, fearing that they would be coerced into the Irish campaign, listened to the solicitations of Leveller agents. On May 11 they mutinied and chose new officers.[4] Four troops of Ireton's regiment rendezvoused with them. A few days before, the disreputable William Thompson had gathered a few scattered soldiers at Salisbury. There he put forth a ringing manifesto worthy of a better man, announcing his purpose of delivering

[3] The Army's Martyr, E. 552 (11), pp. 6, 10–12. Irritation at Lockyer's execution had much to do with the mutiny. Englands Standard Advanced, May 6, 1649, E. 553 (2); A Full Narrative Of All the proceedings betweene . . . . the Lord Fairfax and the Mutineers, May 18, 1649, E. 555 (27), p. 10.

[4] The men said that the officers kept the troops separated, telling each that the others had agreed to go; when the privates proved obstinate they were ordered to pasture their horses in fields two miles from their quarters. The Levellers (Falsly so called) Vindicated, Aug. 21, 1649, E. 571 (11), p. 2.

the magistracy of England from the power of the sword, and of procuring the establishment of a new representative by an Agreement of the People.[5]

Meanwhile Fairfax and Cromwell with loyal regiments marched against Scroop's men. They sent before them as emissary to the mutineers that Major White who had been expelled from the army in 1647 for asserting that England was under no law but that of the sword. May 13, White set out with three companions. On that day and the next, he was with the mutineers and conducting a correspondence with Fairfax relative to their submission. The men insisted on the reëstablishment of the Council of the Army, though White appears to have thought they might possibly have been content with less.[6]

Fairfax, learning that the revolted regiment was trying to join Harrison's, which was also in mutiny, decided on May 14 to wait no longer.[7] Early on the morning of the 15th, he surprised the mutineers at Burford. They yielded on some assurance of safety; but the commanders made the lives of cornets Den and Thompson, and two corporals a blood-offering to discipline. Den's repentance was

[5] *Englands Standard Advanced*, May 6, 1649, E 553 (2).

[6] *Supra*, p. 185. *A Declaration Of the Proceedings of His Excellency The Lord General Fairfax*, May 22, 1649, E. 556 (1); *A Full Narrative Of All the Proceedings betweene* . . . . *the Lord Fairfax and the Mutineers*, which contains the men's declarations and letters to Fairfax; Francis White, *A True Relation Of The Proceedings In The Businesse of Burford*, Sept. 27, 1649, E. 574 (26).

[7] *A Declaration* says that Fairfax resolved to attack only after the leaders of the regiment had rebuffed Colonel Scroop, and refused to allow a declaration of Fairfax to be read to the men. Pp. 7–8.

so edifying as to procure his reprieve.[8]   Thompson merely admitted that God had not owned his ways. The two corporals died defiant.   The rest of the soldiery, after an exhortation by Cromwell, professed their penitence and were reprieved.

The surprise at Burford was the end of the mutiny.   Other scattered risings were easily put down. In one of these William Thompson who had escaped when his irregular levies had been dispersed by Colonel Reynolds, ended his desperate life by a desperate death.   The ruthless resolution of the officers had prevailed against the indecision of the men.   As it was the custom of the day for small men to profess their penitence when their faults, real or supposed, were pointed out to them by their social superiors, the penitence of the mutineers should be taken as indicating not so much their real consciousness of guilt as the essentially aristocratic spirit of the age.

Cromwell and Fairfax can hardly escape criticism for the measures they took against the mutineers. In the first place, there is a question whether the terms on which the men yielded at Burford did not preclude military executions.   The Levellers pointed to the facts that Cornet Thompson had surrendered while at the head of two unbroken troops, and that several parties had barricaded them-

---

[8] He later published a pamphlet, *The Levellers Designe Discovered* (E. 556 (11), May 24, 1649), deprecating the mutiny. The Levellers believed he had betrayed the men to Fairfax, by posting an officer on guard who forsook his duty, and thereby made the surprise possible. *The Levellers . . . . Vindicated*, p. 7; *The Declaration Of the Prince of Wales*, May 22, 1649, E. 556 (7).

selves in their quarters. Was it likely that men in a position to defend themselves would surrender without security for their lives?[9] Again, it is not clear that the surprise at Burford was accomplished without a breach of faith. Cromwell had dispatched White on his mission, bidding him assure the men that force would not follow on their heels.[10] Accounts favorable to the officers or to the men differed as to the pledges White gave the mutineers for their security while the negotiations were in progress. The men's story was that he had repeated Cromwell's phrase; this in itself is not unlikely. At all events, the course White pursued while with the mutineers—drawing petitions to Fairfax for them, etc.—would naturally have encouraged them in the belief that the officers meant to employ persuasion rather than force. Above all, the fact that Cromwell made a man of known independence in politics his messenger might well have led the men to infer that White was to play the rôle of arbiter.[11]

After all, the question whether at Burford Cromwell and Fairfax were guilty of breach of faith is comparatively unimportant beside another. Did

[9] *A Full Narrative*, p. 3, says that two troops commanded by Thompson yielded on promise of mercy. *The Levellers . . . Vindicated*, p. 7.

[10] White, *A True Relation*.

[11] *The Levellers . . . . Vindicated*, p. 5. *A Declaration* says that he was told to demand immediate submission; it says, further, that he told the men not to take from his presence with them any assurance of their safety against attack. Pp. 12, 13. The day before the surprise White had written Fairfax, advising him to suspend proceedings against the men for the moment. *A Full Narrative*, p. 11.

they have a legal or moral right to sit in judgment
on the men whom they treated as mutinous soldiers?
The men certainly had good grounds for thinking
that their Solemn Engagement remained unfulfilled
so long as the liberties of England were intrusted
to the arbitrary powers of military officers; nor did
they lack precedent for attempting by mutiny to
extort from their officers freedom for the nation.
Two years before, the officers in the name of England's liberties had set the army in array against
the Parliament to which they owed their commissions.   In principle, the action of 1647 was identical
with that of 1649.   Moreover, Lilburne had put a
very reasonable interpretation on the Solemn Engagement when he pronounced that it replaced
military discipline by a representative government.
If his interpretation be accepted, Cromwell and
Fairfax were not the dispensers of martial justice,
but rather revolutionary assassins.

The defenders of the two generals met this last
argument by asserting that the soldiers had of their
own will given up their representative government
and put themselves again under the military discipline of the officers.   The various regiments, it was
said, had petitioned that their agitators be sent
back to them.   The Levellers denied that any such
petitions had ever in good faith been framed and
presented by the soldiers.   Apparently none were
ever printed in answer to their challenge.[12]

[12] *The Levellers . . . . Vindicated*, p. 9; *See Green & Blue, See
Which Speaks True. Or Reason contending with Treason*, June 6, 1649,
E. 559 (1); *An Impeachment Of High Treason*, p. 3; *The Discoverer*, June
2, 1649, E. 558 (2), pp. 5, 6.

Justification for Cromwell's course must be sought in expediency rather than right. There was danger that the revolt might spread; and Royalists were ready to join with the Levellers in the hope of turning the mutiny into a restoration of Charles II. Although the demands of the soldiers were such as might without immediate danger have been granted, in the background was the peril of an Agreement of the People set up by mutinous soldiers. Cromwell understood as well as any Leveller that the idea underlying an Agreement forbade its origin in violence; an Agreement as fundamental law must come, if it came at all, "without fraud or surprise." Cromwell honestly desired at least a part of the liberties of England as defined by the Levellers. But, always an opportunist in his pursuit of them, he was continually tempted to undertake to reach them by the primrose path of arbitrary power. Unlike the Levellers, he did not see that those liberties were attainable only by law; but, again unlike the Levellers, he saw when they were unattainable by law. Because he saw this, necessity drove him to crush the Levellers in 1649, as in 1647

In *A Full Relation Of The Proceedings at the Rendezvous of that Brigade of the Army that was held in Corkbush field*, there is a petition from Whalley's regiment recalling the "new agents" chosen in October—but apparently it implied the continuance of the former agitators in the Council of the Army. Denne's account does not date specifically the time at which the agitators were recalled. Lilburne in *An Impeachment Of High Treason*, p. 3, supposes that the event that Denne referred to took place in August. His account and that in *Sea Green & Blue* imply that such petitions had been in circulation, but that they were fraudulent and did not represent the wishes of any considerable part of the army.

it drove him to countenance the army's resistance
to established authority.   In 1649 he saw that the
Commonwealth was the only possible government
except monarchy; he did not see that the Commonwealth itself could not endure.

II. THE TRIAL AND ACQUITTAL OF LILBURNE

The imprisonment of the four Leveller leaders
gave London intervals of excitement during the
whole summer.   No overt acts can be traced to the
Leveller party as a unit, but a series of pamphlets
by individuals made a constant ferment, and may
have caused two so-called Leveller revolts.   Petitions with signatures numbered by thousands
poured in on behalf of the prisoners.   Counter
petitions appeared against them.   The apprentices
of the ward of Cripplegate Without offered their
"Thankful Acknowledgment" of the beneficent
activity of the four, and invited apprentices in
other wards to coöperate by committees.   The Resolved Apprentices of Bridge Within got up a
counter memorial against the Thankful Acknowl-
edgers.[13]   Anabaptist ministers made haste to disclaim all responsibility for *Englands New-Chaines*,

---

[13] 669 f. 14 (30), (31), (32), (27).   *Mercurius Pragmaticus*, Apr. 24–
May 1, says that ten thousand women signed a petition.   The *Moderate*,
Mar. 27–Apr. 3, says that ten thousand had signed a petition of Apr.
2.   Gardiner gives a figure of 80,000 for it.   *Commonwealth and Protectorate*, I, 47.   The same number of the *Moderate* says it is reported
that "40,000 had signed and would avow" *Englands New-Chaines Discovered*.   The figure is as high a one as is ever mentioned in connection
with petitions, with one exception.

and addressed to the House a memorial stating that, although the obnoxious pamphlet had been read in their churches, they themselves were innocent of any ill design.[14] Seven authors joined to produce a pamphlet, *Walwins Wiles*, in which, charitably dismissing Lilburne and 'Prince as misled, they poured out the vials of their wrath on Walwyn. The book's charges have been considered elsewhere. The four regarded it and the memorial as proof that ministerial jealousy was responsible in great measure for the proceedings against them.[15]

The four prisoners engaged in pamphlet skirmishes with their enemies. Overton brought out a *Defyance Of The Act of Pardon*, written in a coarse and heavy style and flavored with the similes of the bull ring. It so far shocked the Levellers that Overton addressed to them a defense of his license of speech.[16] Prince published a book to repel the insinuations that he and Lilburne had been led into mischief by Overton and Walwyn.[17] Walwyn and his friends wrote three or four pamphlets

---

[14] Apr. 3, 1649, E. 549 (14). Lilburne claimed this did not represent the wishes of their congregations, but was merely their own device to which the authorities impelled them. *The Picture Of The Councel of State*, p. 20 (2d ed.).

[15] *Supra*, p. 243. *Walwyns Just Defence.*

[16] *Overton's Defyance Of The Act of Pardon; Or, The Copy of a Letter to the Citizens usually meeting at the Whale-bone in Lothbury*, July 4, 1649, E. 562 (26). Overton defended it in *The Baiting Of The Great Bull of Bashan*, July 16, 1649, E. 565 (2). For the coarseness of the original it may be said that it apparently furnished an idea for *A New Bull-Bayting*, Aug. 7, 1649, E. 568 (6), apparently by the same author as *The Man in the Moone*, a filthy Royalist journal.

[17] *The Silken Independents Snare Broken*, June 20, 1649, E. 560 (24).

defending his character against his personal enemies.[18]

Lilburne's writings were far more daring than any of these. In June he published *The Legal Fundamentall Liberties Of The People of England, Revived, Asserted, and Vindicated*, an attack on the legal position of the Rump and the Council of State. August 10, *An Impeachment Of High Treason Against Oliver Cromwell* followed; it dealt with the episode of January, 1647/8. September 13, Lilburne issued a *Preparative To An Hue And Cry after Sir Arthur Haslerig*, declaring that by his tyrannies and betrayals he was become *"a Pole Cat, a Fox, and a Wolf (as a Subverter and destroyer of humane society), and may and ought to be knockt on the head therefore."*[19] The particular occasion for this was Haselrig's detention of Lilburne's rents from Durham; as also some stories of his plots against Lilburne's life that John had greedily swallowed in spite of their manifest improbability.

Two anonymous publications were even more radical. One of them, *An Out Cry*, was a bitter arraignment of the methods used in suppressing the uprising of May and of the government's tyranny. It also advocated the Agreement of the People and suggested an organization to promote its adoption. The second, *The Remonstrance Of many Thousands*, of September 21, announced an armed defiance of the tyrants at Westminster, a refusal to pay taxes, and a promotion of an Agree-

[18] *Supra*, pp. 245–250.
[19] E. 573 (16).

ment of the People. It also advocated reducing Parliament members to the estates they possessed in 1640, and confiscating the remainder of their property as illicit gain. The authority to be assigned the pamphlet is sufficiently indicated by a postscript stating it was "already signed with 98,064 hands and more to be added daily; so soon as we can give notice hereof to our Afflicted Brethren in all the Counties of England and Wales."[20]

No direct connection can be traced between these pamphlets and two so-called Leveller uprisings that occurred in the course of the summer. One of these uprisings took place among the miners of Derbyshire who became discontented with the conditions of their labor; the miners or a few factious persons for them, according to the account one adopts, threatened resort to the law of nature, and finally in approved Leveller fashion declared for the Agreement, the Petition of September 11, etc.[21]

A second uprising came to a head early in September in the garrison at Oxford. "What their intent was," said *Pragmaticus*, "I think they do not well know themselves." Arrears of pay appeared to be one grievance; but the men also adopted the usual Leveller political proposals, such as a representative army council and a new Parliament; they further demanded the restoration of the king.

---

[20] *An Out Cry Of the Youngmen and Apprentices of London*, E. 572 (13), Sept. 1, 1649; *The Remonstrance Of many Thousands . . . . in behalf of Themselves and those Called Levellers*, E. 574 (15), Sept. 21, 1649.

[21] *The Moderate*, Aug. 21–28; *A Modest Narrative of Intelligence*, Aug. 25–Sept. 1, 1649; *The Moderate Messenger*, Sept. 10–17.

The Levellers proper were inclined to hold aloof. A few from London went down to Oxford to guide the mutineers so far as possible; but Lilburne and his friends had nothing to do with the affair. With ignorant men only to manage its councils, the mutiny was speedily crushed. Two men were shot, six sentenced to run the gauntlet, and others cashiered. Seven were remanded to the civil courts.[22]

Probably these disorders convinced the authorities that they must take some action to stop the stream of radical pamphlets. They had their choice of two courses: to conciliate Lilburne and his friends, or to arraign the Leveller leaders for sedition and so to vindicate the authority of the Commonwealth. First, they tried conciliation. On the 14th of September they had Lilburne brought before Attorney-General Prideaux. Lilburne was defiant, denying that Prideaux or the Parliament itself possessed any legal authority that he was bound to own.[23] A week later the authorities probably cast out hints of the possibility of a conference between the government and the Leveller chiefs. Then

---

[22] *The Moderate*, Sept. 11–18, Sept. 18–25; *Mercurius Pragmaticus*, Sept. 11–18, Sept. 17–24, Sept. 18–25; *The Man in the Moone*, Sept. 12–19; *Kingdoms Intelligencer*, Sept. 18–25; *Prince Charles Proclaimed King*, Sept. 14, 1649, E. 573 (21); *Prince Charles His Message To The Levellers in the West*, Sept. 13, 1649, E. 573 (18); *A Great And Blovdy Fight Neer Droghedah*, Sept. 12, 1649, E. 573 (15).

[23] Lilburne's account of this interview is in *Strength out of Weaknesse*. There is a briefer account purporting to come from a person present at the conversation, in *The Man in the Moone*, Sept. 19–26. See also *Mercurius Elencticus*, Sept. 17–24, and *The Moderate*, Sept. 11–18. Lilburne's account is undoubtedly amplified, but on the main points seems reliable.

they tried to frighten Lilburne into submission by sending men to warn him, under the guise of friendship, that he was inviting his own ruin. Lilburne's reported answer was certainly characteristic of the man; he threatened one of them "to kick him out if he came again to abuse him."[24]

Finally, the Council of State resolved to put to test the defiant attitude of the Levellers toward the government by bringing Lilburne to trial. A special commission of oyer and terminer issued, and on the 24th of October the grand jury found a true bill against Lilburne. The indictment charged him with seeking to subvert the government and bring the Commons into infamy with all good Englishmen; with seditiously printing and publishing that the government was arbitrary and tyrannical, and with seducing soldiers from their obedience. The specific facts charged were passages from his writings, *An Impeachment Of High Treason*, *The Legal Fundamentall Liberties*, *An Hue And Cry*, *A Salva Libertate*, and *An Out Cry*,[25] and conversations with private soldiers.

Lilburne now offered to compromise with the authorities. He proposed in a letter of October 20 that he choose one judge from the twelve in Westminster Hall, and his adversaries another, the two judges to pass on the law at issue in his case. October 22, his brother presented a letter from him in which he offered within six months to remove to

[24] *Mercurius Elencticus*, Sept. 17–24; *Pragmaticus*, Sept. 18–25.

[25] *The Triall, Of Lieut. Collonell John Lilburne*, Clement Walker, E. 584 (9), pp. 56 ff.

the West Indies, provided that the government
would assist any who wished to accompany him,
and were financially unable to do so. On the eve
of his trial Lilburne even went so far as to ask for
a delay, that he might endeavor to convince himself
of the lawfulness of the Commonwealth government.
The government probably gained courage from
Lilburne's successive concessions, and pushed on
the trial.[26]

Lilburne, however, for a month past had staked
his life on a desperate game. In his interviews with
Prideaux he had acted a part from beginning to
end; and up to the time of his trial he had planned
his actions to induce in government the belief that
he would reaffirm in court his views of the Rump's
illegality and deny the court's jurisdiction. Were
he to do so, the government would be rid of him
at the price of the obloquy that would attach to it
for condemning him by default. But long before
his trial he had decided not to embrace so easy a
martyrdom. If by address he could force his acquittal from the court, it would damage the government's prestige at least as much as would sentencing him to death for refusing to plead. The latter
course would convict the government of tyranny,
but the former would convict it of inefficiency.[27]

---

[26] *The Innocent Man's first Proffer*, Oct. 20, 1649, 669 f. 14 (83);
The Innocent Man's second-Proffer, Oct. 22, 1649, 669 f. 14 (85).

Colonel Robert Lilburne stood closely by his brother during the
trial. *The Triall, Of Lieut. Collonell John Lilburne, passim.*

[27] *L. Colonel John Lilburne revived*, Mar. 27, 1653, E. 689 (32), p. 4.
He says of the method of his defense "of which, I neither did nor durst
tell any man or woman in the world what was my intentions, till I

Therefore, on the first day of his trial Lilburne played his game cautiously. He wrangled with the judges as to the meaning of the various forms— holding up his hand, pleading to the indictment, saying that he would be tried by God and his country. The judges, who were none too well assured of their personal safety in the court room, were visibly relieved when they were past these technicalities and there was no likelihood of their having to condemn him without a trial.[28]

Lilburne, however, immediately got into a second wrangle when the judges evaded his demand for counsel, and for a copy of the indictment. He railed at the court as a pack of unjust and unrighteous judges. That the judges permitted such language from a prisoner shows how terrifying the whole business was to all officially concerned. Thus, when Lilburne accused Prideaux of whispering with the judges on the bench, Prideaux thought it necessary to assure him that the conversation had nothing to do with his case. He accused Prideaux of having consulted with the judges before the

came to the Barr; least my adversaries should get a hint of it, who I beleeve never expected but I would have dealt with them upon a ranting high-flown score, in totally denying their jurisdiction, and the authoritie of those that constituted them but through the strength of the Almightie, I went beyond their expectations, and gave them such a cuff under their other eare, as I belieeve they wil never throughlie shake of the smart and paine of it, whilest Cromwels beastlie & most grosselie abominable Tirannie lasteth."

It might be added in corroboration that the tone of *Strength out of Weaknesse* suggests that Lilburne was deliberately speaking in a "high-flown" strain.

[28] *The Triall, Of Lieut. Collonell John Lilburne*, pp. 1–30.

trial; they endeavored mildly to explain. They patiently, even anxiously, reasoned with the prisoner and implored him to be quiet. There was a world of meaning in Keble's remark: "We are willing to die too!" when Lilburne had thundered out that, if the judges wished to murder him, they might. The learned judge, knowing that the trial was a political one, and that figuratively the Leveller party stood at the bar, saw a large part of that party disposed about the court room in person, and feared for the worst.[29]

By the next day some one had apparently stiffened the resolution of the judges. They began by vigorously ordering Lilburne's solicitor, Sprat, and Colonel Robert Lilburne, out of the bar where they were standing with the prisoner. Lilburne pleaded in vain that the law allowed any bystander in a court of justice to advise the prisoner or speak for him; he asked in vain for counsel. For answer the judges hastened the calling of the jury. The jury was chosen, Sprat and Colonel Robert guiding the prisoner in the use of his challenges, despite the angry protests of the judges.[30]

It was now the time for Prideaux to offer the state's evidence. Apparently he had been oversanguine, or else confident that Lilburne, by refusing to plead, would make evidence unnecessary; for Lilburne at once began to find serious technical flaws in the testimony. First, Prideaux endeavored to prove that Lilburne was the author of *An Out*

---

[29] *The Triall, Of Lieut. Collonell John Lilburne*, pp. 30–44.
[30] *Ibid.*, pp. 50, 53.

Cry, by the evidence of Thomas Newcombe, a printer who had been taken in the act of printing it. Newcombe testified that Lilburne had been present when the proof was read. But Lilburne by cross-questioning brought out the fact that he had merely held a printed proof in his hand, and had not corrected it. Next, Prideaux proved by three soldiers that Lilburne had given one of them a copy of *An Out Cry*. Similarly witnesses testified that Lilburne had sent a copy of *An Impeachment Of High Treason* to Colonel Ayres.[31]

Prideaux further tried to fix on Lilburne the fact that he had delivered to Colonel Francis West, lieutenant of the Tower, a *Salva Libertate*, denying the lawfulness of the government.[32] Lilburne, however, completely overset the pertinence of this evidence by questioning West as to the exact place in the Tower at which the *Salva Libertate* had been delivered, and by adducing a bit of antiquarian legal lore to the effect that the place named lay outside the liberties of London, and hence outside the cognizance of a London jury![33]

Prideaux's servants and Colonel West then testified that Lilburne in his interview with Prideaux had acknowledged his authorship of *A Preparative To An Hue And Cry;* Prideaux used this testimony to prove also Lilburne's authorship of *Legal Fundamentall Liberties* and *An Impeachment Of High Treason*, as Lilburne had acknowledged both books

[31] *The Triall, Of Lieut. Collonell John Lilburne*, pp. 70–76.
[32] *Ibid.*, pp. 76–78. On the occasion of his interview with Prideaux.
[33] *Ibid.*

in the *Hue And Cry*. Lilburne contented himself
for the time by establishing the fact that he had
owned *An Hue And Cry*, "Saving the printers'
erratias which are many." Prideaux completed
his case by reading the treason acts of May 14 and
July 17 and the treasonable passages from the
books—which last, says one account, pleased the
people as would have done a play of Ben Jonson's!
Stranger trial was never on English ground.[34]

The time had now come for Lilburne's defense;
and the court refused him time to collect himself
or even to examine his notes or books. The fall of
a scaffolding that served as a stand for the spec-
tators who thronged the court, seemed almost a
providential dispensation; for the accident caused
such confusion that before the trial proceeded Lilburne had his defense ready. He began by assuring
the jurymen that they were judges of fact and of
law as well, the judges being but a set of Norman
intruders. Second, he asserted that the treason
statutes required two witnesses to each act. When
Prideaux, in summing up, undertook to correct him,
there was the inevitable wrangle as to how far
earlier statutes to this effect had been repealed by
the act of Philip and Mary; Lilburne came out a
little the better. On the ground that the proof-
sheet he had seen had not been proved a true copy
of *An Out Cry*, Lilburne ruled out Newcombe's
testimony; as for the soldier to whom he had given
the book, Lilburne reminded the jury that this was

---

[34] *The Triall, Of Lieut. Collonell John Lilburne*, pp. 80–113. *Truth's
Victory Over Tyrants And Tyranny*, Nov. 16, 1649, E. 579 (12), p. 4.

not a proof of authorship. On the grounds already stated, he threw out the testimony of the lieutenant of the Tower; he found similar flaws in the jurisdiction of the court over his offense in sending Ayres the *Impeachment*. He broke the whole force of the testimony of Prideaux's servants, by alleging that the treasonable passages in *An Hue And Cry* might, for all that had been proved, have been printers' erratas, and hence not owned by him! He concluded his review of the testimony by asserting that the prosecution had not proved that the books in question post-dated the Commonwealth's treason acts.[35]

In closing, he complained of the injustice of trying him for acts committed under the irritation of an illegal imprisonment. He adroitly recalled the usage his demand for counsel had received, and ended by urging the jury to take the decision of the law into their own hands and find him not guilty, the people crying "Amen." There was nothing notable in Prideaux's closing argument, and the case went to the jury.[36]

The jury, after being out about an hour, returned with a verdict of not guilty. ". . . immediatly," says the contemporary account of the trial, "the whole multitude of People in the Hall, for joy of the Prisoners acquittal gave such a loud and unanimous shout, as is beleeved, was never heard in Guild-hall, which lasted for about halfe an hour without intermission: which made the Judges for fear, turne pale,

[35] *The Triall, Of Lieut. Collonell John Lilburne*, pp. 120–132.
[36] *Ibid.*, pp. 133–150.

and hange down their heads; but the Prisoner stood silent at the Barre, rather more sad in his countenance then he was before."[37]   The rejoicing in the court spread throughout London.[38] The Leveller had won his desperate game; and perhaps nothing bears witness to the character of the man as does his imperturbable conduct in the hour of victory.   He was for the moment remanded to the Tower, according to *Pragmaticus*, while the Council of State considered the advisability of courtmartialling him.[39]   It is very unlikely that the government ever seriously contemplated affording such proof of the validity of Lilburne's strictures on it.   It released him with his companions on November 8.

The criticism of Lilburne's own day on the method of his defense foreshadowed the criticism of certain modern historians.[40]   His contemporaries took him to task for laying hold of legal technicalities and quibbling with the evidence adduced to prove he had written books that bore his name on the title page.   The criticism is but slightly justified.   He protested, it is true, against the employment of certain legal technicalities against him; but they were technicalities that proved fatal traps for the unwary.   We should remember that a plea of guilty or not guilty to an indictment barred all opportunity of objecting to its form.   Seventeenth-

---

[37] *The Triall, Of Lieut. Collonell John Lilburne*, p. 151.
[38] *The Upright Mans Vindication*, Aug. 5, 1653, E. 708 (22), p. 15.
[39] *Mercurius Pragmaticus*, Oct. 29–Nov. 5.
[40] Gardiner, *History of the Commonwealth and Protectorate*, I, 186.
A Letter Of Due Censure, and Redargvtion to Lieut. Col. John Lilburne. June 21, 1650, E. 603 (14).

century courts made short work of men who failed
to quibble over forms they did not understand. On
the other hand, Lilburne's demands for counsel,
for a copy of his indictment, and for time to send
for witnesses are commonplaces of justice today.
Even the flaws that he picked in the state's case to
a layman do not appear far-fetched.

It is not easy to see what other line of defense
Lilburne had open to him. Holding the government of England arbitrary and illegal, as he did, he
had openly proclaimed his opposition to it in terms
that came within the scope of its treason acts. He
was thus on trial for what was really a political
offense. He could not deny the fact that he had
been active against the government. He might
have put to issue the question of the legality of
Rump and Council of State by refusing to plead
before their court. This was the advice he gave
to Capel and Holland in February; but then there
was the likelihood that their refusal to plead would
tide their trial over till a new "representative"
was chosen. Had Lilburne taken a similar course
in October, the issue must have been a revolt or his
death; he would have given the government the
opportunity of getting rid of him as it had hoped
to do. The only remaining course was the one that
he adopted—picking to pieces the evidence by which
his agitation was brought within the scope of the
treason acts. It must be admitted that the skill
with which he foiled the court and the attorney
for the state served to make the government appear
ridiculous in the extreme. For the time, however,

military success had intrenched it too strongly to be overthrown. Lilburne, realising this fact, suffered himself to be persuaded by the entreaties of his wife, and forebore embarking on a new attempt to overturn a strong *de facto* government.

NOTE

THE LEVELLERS AND THE IRISH PROBLEM IN 1649

Occasionally the Levellers were brought in contact with the problem as to the principles on which Ireland was to be held in subjection to the English government. The soldiery in the winter of 1649, perhaps under Leveller influence, displayed a marked unwillingness to undertake the conquest of Ireland. *The Moderate Intelligencer*, May 2–10, makes a lame attempt to answer a series of questions justifying the Irish revolt as the attempt of a conquered people to throw off its conquerors; apparently the questions were addressed to those intending to go to Ireland. See also a paper, E. 551 (21), labeled by Thomason "A Libbell scatered about yͤ Streets ye 25 Aprill 1649;" *The English Souldiers Standard To Repaire to;* Henry Denne, *The Levellers Designe Discovered,* May 24, 1649, E. 556 (11), p. 3.

The civilian Levellers generally disclaimed responsibility for the soldiers' refusal to subdue Ireland. However, the following passage from Thomas Prince is worth consideration, as containing at least as much common sense and plausibility as the Irish policies that have originated at Westminster in the last three hundred years. "If England were setled, as afore mentioned, the goodnesse of the Government would invite the Irish, with a desire unto it; there would then be some hopes (sending over faithfull men, those who would make conscience of their waies, such as would keep their engagements) that the Irish would soon be reduced; as being willing to change their condition of bondage for freedom, and willingly render the chief Authors and agents in that inhumane butchery up to justice, whereby much innocent bloud might be saved." *The Silken Independents Snare Broken,* p. 7.

An argument used against the Agreements of the People was that they left England without any legal hold on Ireland. For, Ashurst argued, the Crown and the Parliament were the only source of English authority in Ireland; and a representative, originating with the English people, could hardly succeed to the rights of the older constituted authorities. *Reasons Against Agreement with a late Printed Paper, intituled, Foundations of Freedome;* . . . . Dec. 26, 1648, E. 536 (4), p. 8.

CHAPTER X

The Levellers' Case against the Commonwealth

AS in 1647 the Levellers had discovered the idea of the written constitution, so in 1649 they developed it till the concept was almost complete. This evolution was the result of the events narrated in the last two chapters. For one thing, attacks on the unconventional opinions of individuals in their ranks induced the Levellers to state a party creed and disclaim responsibility for all individual beliefs at variance with it. Moreover, by criticising the Commonwealth, the Levellers were led to formulate exactly their own constitutional program; and they evolved a final Agreement of the People in which the written constitution stands fully revealed as paramount law.

Since the Levellers proposed their Agreement as a constitutional substitute for the Commonwealth government, it may be permissible to estimate the logical strength and weakness of that government's claim to obedience. First, the events by which it was established may be reviewed. On December 6 Colonel Pride, acting for the officers of the army, had forcibly excluded a hundred and forty-three Presbyterian members from the House of Commons, thereby giving control to a small Independent minority. This remnant, or "Rump," not much more than a quorum of the House, had erected a High Court of Justice to try the king. When the Lords had opposed this measure, the Rump had announced that the people were the sole fountain of power; and tracing its own authority to this source, it had refused to recognize the House of Lords as a part of the government. Later, the Rump had declared the monarchy and the House of Lords abolished, and had erected as an executive a Council of State composed for the most part of Parliament members or army officers.

When the supporters of the government undertook to justify its actions, they generally followed a line of reasoning sketched by Ireton's Army Remonstrance, and later implied in a formal declaration of the House of Commons. The first step in the argument was the assertion that the king had been merely a subordinate ruler commissioned by the state, and bound to it by a compact originally[1] made between the people and the first ruler, and ratified at the accession of each new monarch by the people's oath of allegiance and the king's coronation oath.[2] It followed that the king's violation of this compact in any essential was sufficient to absolve the people from their oath of allegiance. Such a violation, therefore, authorized them to resist their king by force of arms; if they

---

[1] As *Salus Populi solus Rex* puts it, the state alone is king.   Oct. 17, 1648, E. 467 (39), p. 2.

[2] *Severall Speeches*, Robert Parsons, Feb. 3, 1648/9, E. 521 (1), p. 29, emphasizes the balance of the oaths; so does *The Oath of Allegiance And The National Covenant Proved To be Non-Obliging*, Samuel Eaton, July 1, 1650, E. 606 (2), p. 1.

prevailed, it enabled them either to readmit him to power on their own conditions or to depose him.[3]

For certain purposes this argument was effective. At the moment, it could be used to silence the Presbyterians who had been loud in their outcries at the "parricidal" deed of January 30; for, to justify war against the king in 1642, they themselves had framed a theory of compact in similar terms. Their only logical escape lay in demonstrating that the contract theory could be made to justify armed resistance, but not deposition; and John Milton's reasonings took on an unwonted directness and candor when he concluded for the Presbyterians that, in making war on their king, they had to all practical purposes deposed him.[4]

In combating the Royalists, Commonwealth writers matched the theory of compact against the theory of divine right; and one line of abstract reasoning was perhaps as effective as the other. Indeed the single quality that made Milton's answer to Salmasius decisive, was the keen critical

[3] *The Royal Project*, Oct. 20, 1648, E. 468 (22), p. 10. So also the *Army Remonstrance*, p. 21, E. 473 (11); *A Declaration of the Parliament of England*, Mar. 22, 1648/9, E. 548 (12).

[4] *The Tenure of Kings and Magistrates*, Works, 1839 ed., p. 240. A great deal of controversy centered on the question as to whether Parliament could release the people from the oaths they had taken to maintain the king's just power—such as the oath of allegiance, the Protestation, the Covenant. Later, the question was rather as to whether the Engagement prescribed by Parliament in 1649 could lawfully be taken by those who had taken the earlier oaths. See for this *A Plea for Non-Scribers*, June 11, 1650, E. 6ʋ3 (1), and *Arguments And Reasons To prove the . . . . Vnlawfulness Of Taking the New Engagement*, Feb. 14, 1649/50, E. 593 (7).

sense that overset, one by one, the historical instances that Claude de Saumaise had laboriously
collected to support the impossible proposition that
the doctrine of divine right has restrained men from
overthrowing their government whenever they have
had the opportunity and the inclination. But
Milton failed to demonstrate conclusively the abstract principle that the "sovereignty of the people"
makes a nation happier than does the rule of a
divinely appointed monarch. That principle required deductive proof; and historical evidence
could apply only in so far as it could answer these
questions: Are men happier under a government
that is final and absolute judge of its own powers, or
under a government which any faction may rightfully overset? Will a nation suffer more when the
decision as to what government shall do is left to
one man, or when it is left to civil strife? Till
the Commonwealth writers answered these questions, they could scarcely claim a logical victory
over the Royalists.

Such a statement of the case may seem unfair
to the founders of the Commonwealth; but one must
remember that they were not believers in democracy.
The sovereignty of the people to their minds did
not imply the necessity of inquiring after the people's will by democratic methods; in fact, they
found it impossible to designate a form through
which the people had expressed its concurrence in
their acts. The people had delegated them neither
to judge of the king's violation of the compact
nor to exact the penalty for it; indeed it was self-

evident that the mass of the people abhorred the revolution of 1649.

Apologists for the Commonwealth might have escaped these difficulties by reverting to the arguments of 1642, and asserting that Parliament— the nation united in the only form in which it could take political action—had represented the nation in the work of justice upon the king. But if the apologists took this position, they had the ugly business of Pride's Purge to explain. Had not the army expelled and imprisoned members of the House of Commons, until the erection of the High Court of Justice was really the act of the army, and not the act of a free Parliament? For that matter, could the House of Commons abolish the monarchy without the Lords' concurrence, or further abolish the Upper House itself? Clearly in former Parliaments, the House of Commons had never considered such things a part of the day's work.[5]

[5] Of course the republics of antiquity inspired treatises on the superiority of republican government to monarchy. To a modern these treatises appear academic. Thus, Henry Robinson undertook to prove the advantage of "aristocracy" or representative government over monarchy; but his argument was not worth serious consideration until he should find a definition of the word "representative" that could fit the Commonwealth. His diatribes on the ignominy of slavery to a king were empty breath, for slavery was slavery, whether one man or a clique of a hundred were master, and whether the master called itself king or Commonwealth. *A Short Discourse Between Monarchical And Aristocratical Government,* Oct. 24, 1649, E. 575 (31). See also *The Trve Portraitvre of the Kings Of England,* Aug. 7, 1650, E. 609 (2). This is an arraignment and condemnation of the past kings of England.

The only defenses of the Commonwealth that impress one as straightforward and manly are those implied in the ideas of fanatics such as the Fifth Monarchy men. These men at least admitted that the government of the Commonwealth was an oligarchy, albeit one of divine appointment. By a series of direct providences, they said, God had taken power from the hands of the carnal mass of the nation, and bestowed it on the godly few of the army to use for his own glory. In putting Charles Stuart to death, they had but put into execution God's own law against murder. To consider laying down the power that God had put in their hands would be to tempt him. Rather they must use it to prepare the world against the time when King Jesus should appear to rule the fifth monarchy, which should succeed the Assyrian, the Persian, the Greek, and the Roman.[6]

Persons more carnally minded interpreted the divine right of the Saints to rule as the divine right of superior force. Marchamont Nedham, sometime editor of *Pragmaticus*, turned Commonwealthsman in 1650 and published a defense of his new masters. The Commonwealth party, he said, had conquered the king in war and had made spoil of the power he had formerly enjoyed. The nation had passively sat by during the struggle between Cavalier and Roundhead, and must submit to any form of gov-

---

[6] As typical, see *Certain Quaeres Humbly presented In way of Petition, By many Christian People, dispersed abroad throughout . . . . Norfolk*, Feb. 19, 1648/9, E. 544 (5).

ernment, not contrary to the law of nature or nations, that the victors chose to establish.[7]

The root of the whole matter was that the founders of the Commonwealth had been driven by the necessity of preserving themselves and their ideals from destruction. Their actions had been dictated by necessity rather than by constitutional precedents or theories of popular sovereignty; and accordingly they could not make such precedents or theories fit the actual situation. Their deeds were justifiable only by the divine right of success, whether expounded by Harrison, the mystic, or Nedham, the man of the world.

To the statesmanship of expediency, the Levellers opposed the statesmanship of principle. A reported conversation between Lilburne and Hugh Peters, whether authentic or not, puts the essential difference between the Leveller and Commonwealthsman into a word. The indefatigable Peters visited Lilburne in the Tower one day in the spring of 1649, and told him in the course of conversation that there was not, nor ever had been law in the kingdom save what the sword had set up. Peters refused to except even the Petition of Right from his generalization, and challenged Lilburne to frame a definition of law without presupposing armed might. Lilburne rose to the occasion. In answer to Peters's cynicism, he read the great definition of law by which Pym had weighed and

---

[7] *The Case Of The Common-wealth Of England Stated*, May 8, 1650, E. 600 (7). See also his editorials in *Mercurius Politicus*, Oct. 17–24, and Dec. 5–12, 1650.

found wanting Strafford and Thorough alike. If government contemned law and ruled by might, the governed would evade law and gratify their passions by violence and craft. Lilburne by a word had condemned Peters out of his own mouth, proving that the Leveller rather than the Commonwealthsman was the inheritor of the ideals of 1640.[8]

The Levellers shaped their political conduct by their conviction that the Commonwealth government masked a military despotism. Behind Parliament and Council of State they saw the figure of Cromwell; and they interpreted his part in the erection of the extra-legal High Court of Justice as the earnest of his resolution to crush, with or without law, whoever opposed him. Therefore, in the first months after Pride's Purge, they did not denounce the Rump as illegal; rather they implored it to make itself a real representative of the nation by shaking off the military despotism that bound it, and by establishing the liberties of the people by means of an Agreement. If it would but free itself, the radicals were ready to recognize it as doing the work of a representative, and to overlook the illegality of its position.[9]

When the Rump's acquiescence in the imprisonment of the four Levellers had shown its determination not to lead a popular revolution, Lilburne attacked its legal position with effect. If it as-

---

[8] *A Discovrse Betwixt Lieutenant Colonell Iohn Lilburn Close Prisoner in the Tower of London, and Mr. Hugh Peter: Upon May 25*, E. 556 (26). See Note on p. 324, on the authenticity of this pamphlet.

[9] *Englands New-Chaines Discovered*.

sumed to derive its authority from 1640, let it remember, said he, that the Perpetual Act, which had preserved it till 1649, had never been intended at the time of its passage to be the excuse for an absolute and perpetual Parliament. Were the case otherwise, the act was void as against nature, and as a betrayal of the people heinous enough to nullify the legal existence of the Parliament that had passed it. Moreover, not even the title based on the Perpetual Act had come to the Rump unimpaired. The various expulsions and purges had left Parliament what its protectors in the army had called it before the king's execution—a mock Parliament.[10]

Were this discredited title never so good, Lilburne said, it could not give the semblance of constitutionality to the revolutionary abolition of the monarchy and the House of Lords. Those who elected the House of Commons in 1640 had never designed granting it power to exceed the customary duties of a Lower House acting with king and peers. Far less did either the people's election or the Perpetual Act empower the Rump to violate principles of English liberty by trying men before extraordinary tribunals. Least of all would it justify the illegal acts that government was apparently meditating. In short, the Rump's abolition of the monarchy and the Upper House had left no claimant, save possibly the prince, with a shadow of legal right to political power. To Lilburne the only way

[10] *Legal Fundamentall Liberties*, pp. 49–57; *Strength out of Weaknesse*, pp. 4, 11; *An Impeachment Of High Treason*, p. 1.

out of the difficulty was an appeal in good earnest
to the sovereign people, and the establishment of
a constitution by way of an Agreement.[11]

It cannot be repeated too often that such doctrines do not prove the apostasy of the Levellers
from the ideals of 1646. Then their constitutional
ideal had been a House of the people's representatives, absolute because it conscientiously kept in
close touch with the people's wishes, and responded
readily to their demands. But the events of 1647
and 1648 had convinced the Levellers that their
ideal was incapable of realization. As the last of
the Agreements put it, the great danger in all government was the eagerness of "entrusted" gover-

---

[11] *Strength out of Weaknesse*, pp. 11 ff; *Legal Fundamentall Liberties*,
pp. 57 ff. In spite of their denunciation of the Rump's extra-legal status,
the Levellers did not always refuse it recognition as a *de facto* government. Repeatedly they petitioned it on Lilburne's behalf; and Lilburne,
though in the spring he had protested against such petitions and had
disavowed them, in October did not refuse to be tried by a court erected
by the government. *An Impeachment Of High Treason*, p. 2. *Strength
out of Weaknesse*, postscript. In *Englands New-Chaines Discovered* he
himself acknowledged the Rump as the supreme authority; but later he
explained that he had done so rather than let the people know that
the kingdom was without legal government. But he urged Lord Capel
to deny the validity of the High Court of Justice and hence the legal title
of the Rump; and he himself acknowledged the jurisdiction of the
government's court because he believed that his opponent, the Attorney-
General, was unprepared for that line of action. Further, after his
acquittal he took the Engagement to the Commonwealth of England,
interpreting the oath in such a manner as to deny the lawfulness of
the Rump's authority. *Legal Fundamentall Liberties*, pp. 68, 73; *L.
Colonel John Lilburne revived*, p. 3; *The Engagement Vindicated & Explained, Or The Reasons Upon which Lieut. Col. John Lilburne tooke the
Engagement*, Jan. 22, 1649/50, E. 590 (4); *Strength out of Weaknesse*,
p. 5.

nors to make their power absolute.[12] The Levellers
were compelled to abandon their dreams of an
absolute Parliament in constant sympathy with
popular wishes. Instead, they sought after constitutional devices whereby government might be
restrained from encroachment on the governed.
The last Agreement of the People represented the
Levellers' reluctant modification of their ideals in
recognition of the depravity of human nature.
Moreover Lilburne, at least, had come to recognize
an element of fixity and security in the ancient
English constitution of king, Lords, and Commons,
all bound by the known law. However irritating
or humiliating the forms of the ancient English
monarchy, at least it was preferable to a military
despotism which asserted that might was right.

Whenever they despaired of the realization of
their own program, the Levellers were likely to
consider a possible restoration of monarchy. They
had no sentimental leanings to republicanism to
withhold them. Primarily, they demanded the
limitation of the power of government by a fundamental law emanating from the people. If only
the persons of the governors were made liable for
breaches of the law, the Levellers cared not whether
those governors were called kings, lords, or parlia-
ment-men. Nor is there anything essentially in-
congruous in the idea of a king as the executive
officer of a democracy, if only he be subject to
deposition for breach of trust. The earlier ob-

[12] *An Agreement of the Free People of England* . . . . , May 1,
1649, E. 571 (10).

jections of the Levellers to kingship were primarily objections to Charles I as a man guilty of breach of faith and wilful murder; or to the institution of hereditary kingship as it had come down from the Norman conquest. Neither objection would bar the setting up of Charles II as a constitutional monarch. Lilburne could even see arguments in favor of such a course. The election of another as king would only prolong indefinitely the struggle with the Cavaliers; but the restoration of Charles would end the civil wars and the need of heavy taxes and armaments. All this was possible if only the king accepted the Agreement of the People.[13]

Of course a permanent alliance on this basis was

---

[13] *Legal Fundamentall Liberties*, pp. 60, 61; *An Impeachment Of High Treason*, p. 8. Lilburne retailed similar arguments to Prideaux in their interview in September. "But M. Lilburn," said Prideaux on that occasion, "for all your thus reasoning, I know you have in times by past liked a Common-wealth better then the Government of a King, have you not?" "Yes that I have, and still do, provided it be rightly Constituted, from the consent of the People, with just bounds and limitations, that as little as may be is left to arbitraries: but all its Magistrates annualy elective, and accountable, and upon these tearmes I am with all my heart for a Common-wealth: But to have the name of a Common-wealth imposed upon us by the Sword, wherein we are and shall be more slaves then ever we were under Kingship, with a suprem pretended power held over us, that in their Original and Fundamental constitution admit of no boundaries, but judge themselves as absolutely arbitrary, as the Great Turke . . . . such a Common-wealth as this I abhor and detest as the Devil himself; But such a one is yours, and therefore I had rather (as the case stands) be under a King reasonable bounded then under you, and your new Sword Tyranny, called a Common-wealth." "But sir (saith he) you have bin very stiffe against the King, Its true, said I, but not Qua King, but against his Arbitrary and Tyrannical Will, when he made it a rule unto himself, and the People above the Law." *Strength out of Weaknesse*, p. 12.

impossible. In their theories of government Lilburne and Hyde stood at opposite poles; they agreed only in their respect for the sanctity of law. But nevertheless Hyde gave the Levellers credit for excellent intentions, and proposed certain slight concessions. A memorandum of his composition, weighing the relative desirability of advances to the Presbyterians and the Levellers, decided for the Levellers. The last named, Hyde wrote, went to the heart of the political situation by demanding the dissolution of the pretended Parliament. Their hatred of arbitrary government made it possible to win them over to respect for the fundamental laws of the land. Having "little of Ambition, Pryde, or Covetousness in them," their proposals for reform would fall of their own extravagance. Perhaps, in the end, the Levellers might be contented with toleration, the reform of law proceedings, the amelioration of the condition of the poor, close adherence in government to the fundamental laws, and frequent sessions of Parliaments. So far the Royalists could reach out a hand toward the Levellers; the whole gulf of democracy remained between them.[14]

---

[14] *Nicholas Papers*, I, 139. A quotation from *An Out Cry* (p. 9) will indicate the lengths to which the Levellers would go. They hope it will soon be clear to Charles that he will never gain the love of the English people and his crown "but by a cheerefull, hearty and reall promotion of such principles therein [the Agreement] contained, as doe sufficiently tye his hands from cutting the peoples throats, at his will and pleasure, the endeavoring of which, exposed his father to that fatall end that befell him; which may be a seasonable caveat to all Princes &c to take heed of that desperate rock, viz. the attempting to govern the people by will, and not by law; by force, and not by love."

In fact, the growing catholicity of the Leveller political ideas in 1649 was one reason which induced them to state their specific program more exactly. The Commonwealth, taking advantage of their openmindedness to Royalism, sought to demonstrate that the Levellers were merely adjuncts to Royalist conspiracies. In May, Tom Verney, a Parliament spy, had attempted to trap Lilburne into correspondence; as Verney had a royal commission, the government in case of his success would have had formal proof of Lilburne's Royalist leanings.[15] In September, the government spread broadcast a letter from one Royalist to another implying that the Royalists were hoodwinking the Levellers.[16] The utterances of Royalist journals afforded corroboration. They gave their support to the Leveller uprisings, *Pragmaticus* on one occasion advising Royalists to construe them favorably, as the Levellers stood for monarchy.[17]

The Levellers were as much harassed by the freakish opinions of persons inside their party or on the fringe of it as by the danger of a defection from it to Royalism. Their opponents used the supposed atheism of Walwyn and Overton to discredit the whole group as irreligious.[18]   There was

[15] *A Preparative To An Hue And Cry after Sir Arthur Haslerig*, pp. 7, 14. See also *An Anatomy of Lievt. Col. John Lilburn's Spirit and Pamphlets*, Oct. 16, 1649, E. 575 (21).

[16] *A Declaration of the Parliament of England*, Sept. 27, 1649, E. 575 (9). The letter appeared in the *Perfect Weekly Account*, Sept. 12–19. *Mercurius Elencticus* pronounced it a forgery, Sept. 10–17.

[17] *Mercurius Pragmaticus*, Apr. 17–24, Sept. 4–11, 1649.

[18] *Englands Discoverer*, June 6, 1649, E. 559 (2). See also *The Craftsmens Craft*, pp. 3, 7.

also a little group of "Diggers," who began to dig and plant the commons in the faith that God had created the earth a store-house and a common treasure for all mankind; and government journals by all manner of devices sought to prove that Diggers and Levellers were identical. By similar arguments various pamphlets proved conclusively that the Levellers were communists.[19]

Accordingly, the Levellers prepared to defend themselves from such attacks by restating their party creed. Such a restatement would serve the double purpose of disclaiming responsibility for the vagaries of individual opinion, and recalling their members from too easy acquiescence with the Royalists. There had been earlier creeds to serve as tests of the Leveller faith—the petition of March, 1647, and above all the petition of September 11, 1648.[20] But now a revised creed was needed to serve a new purpose.

And so [says a vindication of the Levellers] we have done with the first part of the Discoverers; onely we shall make one observation; that what our party principally sticks to, they altogether decline; viz: Our Manifestation, and the Agreement: By the one, unjust Aspersions are wip'd off, and we manifest what we are not: By the other, we evidence to all the World what we are, and what we seek for.

[19] *A Modest Narrative of Intelligence*, Apr. 28–May 5, 1649. *Mercurius Pragmaticus*, Apr. 17–24, said that the authorities exaggerated the Diggers' importance in order to connect them with the Levellers. Lilburne disclaimed responsibility for any program but the Agreement of May 1. *Legal Fundamentall Liberties*, pp. 81, 82.

[20] For instance, petitions appear from "approvers of the Petition of the 11 of September." May 5, 1649, 669 f. 14 (27); Aug. 21, 1650, 669 f. 15 (50); Aug. 31, 1650, 669 f. 15 (54); others might be cited.

Other papers are personal, and concern haply this or that man, as they have bin by occasion and provocation necessitated from them; but these do more generally concern us all, and are own'd by the Party; And therefore, it will do better hereafter, that men make not excursions *a causa, ad non causam:* from the cause, to the accidents.[21]

The first of the two documents alluded to, the *Manifestation*,[22] is an attempt to explain a fact clearer to our own century than to the seventeenth —the existence of motives other than personal ambition that led men of humble station to undertake the task of securing the nation's happiness. The law of nature and Christianity, said the *Manifestation*, impelled the Levellers to seek "to produce out of the Common Calamities, such a proportion of Freedom and good to the Nation, as might somewhat compensate its many grievances and lasting sufferings." In pursuit of this end, they were primarily concerned to make sure that the changed form of government implied a complete revolution in the former relation of government and people. The manifestors gave notice that to this end they would soon submit an Agreement of the People for the nation's approval.

Meanwhile, they continued, for the sake of their own good fame, they must make formal plea to the worst charges against them. They had already de-

[21] *The Crafts-mens Craft. Or The Wiles of the Discoverers*, p. 13.

[22] *A Manifestation From Lieutenant Col. John Lilburne, Mr. William Walwyn, Mr. Thomas Prince, and Mr. Richard Overton, (Now Prisoners in the Tower of London) And others, commonly (though unjustly) Styled Levellers . . . . to satisfie and ascertain all Men whereunto all their Motions and Endeavours tend and what is the ultimate Scope of their Engagement in the Pvblick Affaires*, Apr. 16, 1649, E. 550 (25).

clared community of property unlawful unless it had unanimous consent. The fact that they sought a good government did not prove the charge that they were anarchists desiring none at all. The fact that they knew no church government or service with sure enough warrant to be imposed on the consciences of men did not prove that they were atheists and anti-scripturists. Their past careers of opposition to arbitrary power should witness that they were not Royalists. They were not the political tools of any group of self-seeking men; for again, their proposals were designed to overthrow all the "corrupt interests" of the kingdom. In conclusion, they trusted that the sincerity of their good intentions to the nation would finally surmount these and other calumnies, and vindicate them in the sight of all men.

The Agreement of the People published by the four prisoners, May 1, 1649,[23] has the same frame work as that of December, 1648, but different provisions. The "representatives" are now to be annual instead of biennial; not merely householders, but all persons of legal age who are not paupers or servants, are to have votes. Members are declared incapable of reëlection. A "representative" may not depute its power to a Council of State, or to anything except a committee of its members. All the limitations imposed on the "representative" by

---

[23] *An Agreement of the Free People of England, Tendered as a Peace-Offering to this distressed Nation By Lieutenant Colonel John Lilburne, Master William Walwyn, Master Thomas Prince and Master Richard Overton, Prisoners in the Tower of London,* May 1, 1649.

the earlier Agreements are retained in that of May 1.
"Representatives" may not impress; they may not
meddle with the execution of laws or permit a court
to punish in the absence of a known law. They
may not question any man for his part in the past
wars. The last Agreement, in fact, goes much
farther than the earlier one in its enumeration of
reserved powers. The "representative" is not only
forbidden to lay penalties against person or estate
for extra-legal offenses; it cannot allow such power
to any court. The "representative" may not compel any man's worship or impose an oath regarding
religion or bar men from public service for religion's
sake, save Papists and others admitting a foreign
supremacy.

There is a series of restrictions intended to prevent the continuance of the corrupt interests that
the Levellers had so long opposed. The Agreement
is more moderate than earlier manifestos, as it does
not insist on the abolition of the central law courts;
but otherwise the "corrupt interest" of the courts
and lawyers is sharply curbed. *Ex officio* examinations, debarring men from pleading their own cases,
use of another language than English in laws and
courts, continuance of cases and proceedings longer
than six months, sentencing any person to death
save for murder or treason, denial of jury trial or of
benefit of witnesses—all are now illegal. The "representative" may not allow monopolies of trade;
it may not lay taxes like the excise. It must quell
the corrupt interest of the clergy by abolishing

tithes—due satisfaction being given the lay impropriators.

Besides limitations intended to crush corrupt interests, there are several designed to protect local government against encroachments of central government. The electors of each parish must have the right to choose their own minister and contract with him for the manner and amount of his remuneration. The people of counties, boroughs, hundreds, and towns must be free to choose in yearly elections all their public officers, and all those who are to administer the law in their localities. When raising militia, the people of each locality may choose their own officers.

The test of the efficiency of a constitution such as this must be the efficiency of the machinery by which it enforces itself. The framers of this constitution devised that machinery mainly with a view to preventing any representative from overriding or destroying the Agreement. The Agreement expressly declares itself past the power of "representatives" to alter. It pronounces any member who does not protest against an attempt at alteration guilty of high treason. Above all, it declares that "all Laws made, or that shall be made contrary to any part of this Agreement, are hereby made null and void."

Here the eternal problem confronted the makers of the Agreement. Who was to judge as to what was, or was not contrary to the Agreement? They assigned no specific body of men this duty, but as they left to grand and petty juries the duty of arraigning and condemning those who intruded either in elections or in the sittings of the Representative, they implied a judicial review of political acts.   Lilburne's doctrine of 1648 would have permitted the common-law courts to judge of political matters in certain cases.   The idea that a court may pass on the constitutionality of acts of the legislature does not, however, assume distinct form till 1653.

In all probability the Levellers would have appealed to reason as the interpreter of their final Agreement of the People. Their confidence in reason as the arbiter of all things may be better understood through a parallel with Calvinistic theology.   To the Puritans the sin of Adam had infected all mankind; original sin, leaving untouched the reason of man that he might know good from evil, had corrupted his will so that of himself he could not will to do what conscience and reason told him was right in the sight of the Lord.   To the corrupted will the Levellers traced the necessity of government; for, since man could not will to do right against his own self-interest, he needed a judge set over him lest he be judge in his own cause. But since the reason of man remained untarnished, the reason of a whole people could be trusted to lead it to a right and just solution of any political problem; for here the interests of the great majority of men were identical.   The reasoning was plausible so far as it went; but the authors of the Agreement had still to devise a means by which the reason of a people might express itself in an orderly and peaceful manner.[24]

After May 1, 1649, there is no longer any doubt of the constitutional significance that the Levellers attached to an Agreement of the People. They considered it the nation's solemn acknowledgment of its act in establishing government. It is true that six months earlier, under the influence of this same idea, they had devised means by which the sovereign people might frame and adopt its constitution. But the various drafts of the Agreement of 1648 had retained the preamble whose phrases a year earlier had suggested a mere concord between the warring factions of the state. The Agreement of May 1, 1649, is not an accord of "interests"; it is the declaration of the will of a sovereign people. The people of England under God—thus runs the

[24] John Calvin, *Institutes*, Book II, chap. 2. The following is a fair statement of the Leveller doctrine. "I but M. Lilburn, who shall be Iudge said he? Sir, (said I) Reason is demonstrable of it self, and every man (less or more), is endued with it; and it hath but one ballance to weigh it in, or one touch-stone to try it by, *viz* To teach a man to do as he would be done to. The Sun is demonstrable of it self by its heat and light, and stands in need of no mans Iudgement when it shines, to judge whether it doth so or no, or of reasons to prove it the Sun; Even so, *Reason is demonstrable by its innate glory life, and efficacy; and man being a reasonable creature, is Judge for himself:* But by reason of his present corrupted estate, and want of perfection, he is somthing partial in his own case, and therefore wherein many are concerned, Reason tels him, *Commissioners chosen out and tyed to such rational Instructions as the Chusers give them, are the most proper and equallest Judges."* *Strength out of Weaknesse*, p. 14.

So also Overton, "for if right reason be not the only being and bounder of the Law over the corrupt nature of man, that what is rationall (the which injustice and tyranny cannot be) may only and at all times be legall." *An Appeale*, p. 3.

preamble—"Agree to ascertain our Government, to abolish all arbitrary Power, and to set bounds and limits both to our Supreme, and all Subordinate Authority, ..."

This phraseology is not an accident. Worded differently, the idea it conveys appears elsewhere in Leveller writings. Thus Lilburne stated his belief that all legal authority, except possibly that of the prince, was at an end; accordingly, if the prince were not admitted on terms, the foundation of a just government must be laid by "an Agreement made amongst the generality of the People." Lilburne understood that such an agreement could not logically originate with the Parliament; thence it must come with a command; and what one Parliament did, another could undo. Not so an Agreement of the People.[25]

To analyse the reasons why such an Agreement of the People missed acceptance by the English nation is almost superfluous. It could have arisen only from a democratic national movement; and such a movement, as the Levellers themselves perceived, required generations of education in democracy. Moreover, the Agreement demanded of those

---

[25] *Legal Fundamentall Liberties*, pp. 41–61. Toward the end of the summer two or three devices were proposed for putting the Agreement into effect. None of these can be regarded as bearing the stamp of party authority. The method proposed was usually that the well-affected to the Agreement in the various counties or regiments should elect councils to choose certain persons to come up to London and consider means of establishing a new Representative, or of putting the Agreement into effect. *The Levellers . . . . Vindicated*, p. 12; *An Out Cry*, p. 9. Another pamphlet, not very reliable, suggested that the well-affected should unite in refusing to pay taxes to the govern-

who should adopt it understandingly a concept of the sovereignty of the people which few persons, learned or unlearned, would attain to, and fewer still adopt.

Nevertheless the Agreement of the People was the only contemporary political program that logically followed from the official theories on which the Commonwealth had been founded. Indeed, apart from practical men like Nedham, the only supporters of the Commonwealth who might logically have rejected the Agreement were the so-called Saints. The reason for their ill-will has already been mentioned. To them the Agreement was "building the Lord an altar of shaped stones." It was presuming to seek to save the nation from God's displeasure and chastisement. It was taking power out of the hands of the Saints to put it into the hands of the carnal multitude.[26] The distaste of the fanatics of the Fifth Monarchy type of mind for the Agreement of the People was due to the fact that they and the Levellers were on the extreme

ment; all who did so were to have a voice in electing representatives to establish the liberties of the people on the foundation of a popular agreement. It proposed also a referendum on the subject of a return to monarchy. "In case this Common-wealth shall not, or cannot be at peace without one Head or King to Reign over them, that then Certificates shall be forthwith Printed, and sent into all Countries for approval thereof; that if we must have a King, the Crown of England may return to the right owner; or if most appear against that Government, it may be governed as Free Estates, and not otherwise." *The Remonstrance Of many Thousands*, p. 6.

[26] *Supra*, Chapter VIII, p. 266, note 14; *A second view of the Army Remonstrance*, p. 26; *Certain Quaeres Humbly presented In way of Petition*, p. 8.

wings of the Puritan movement. The fanatics had
sought and found the will of God in prophesies,
testifyings, and the vicissitudes of political and
military events. The Levellers believed that they
followed the guidance of a God of Law when they
sought to reconstruct the nation on laws of justice
that appealed to the reason of mankind. A constitutional settlement of this type, emanating from
the sovereign people, was the substitute which the
Levellers offered for the so-called Commonwealth
government.

NOTE

THE AUTHENTICITY OF *A DISCOURSE*

Dr. Gardiner came to the conclusion that the interview between
Lilburne and Peters could not have taken place and that the pamphlet
Discourse was therefore a fabrication. It seems to me that the weight of
authority is for it. Lilburne included the *Discourse* in the list of his writings in *The Innocent Mans second-Proffer;* further, in *Legal Fundamentall
Liberties* (p. 54), he declared that Peters had told him there was no law
in England but the sword. Internally the book, repeating the pertinent
and the inconsequential alike, appears to be a report of an actual conversation. In this respect it resembles *Strength out of Weaknesse*. *Mercurius Pragmaticus*, May 29–June 5, gives the details of the interview
and retails the circumstances that brought Peters on a chance visit to
the Tower in more detail than does the *Discourse*. *A Moderate Intelligence*, May 24–31, 1649, also mentions the occurrence. Dr. Gardiner
adduced the fact that the current *Mercurius Pacificus*, May 29, pronounces the *Discourse* a forgery. The exact quotation from the *Pacificus* is as follows: "There is a sheet of Paper printed which is called A
Discourse between Lieutenant Col. Lilburne and Mr. Peeters (in the
Tower) which as it containes many seditious passages, so is it nothing
else but a meer deceit, nor will it be avowed by any of them." This
is not very strong evidence. Moreover, Lilburne did later acknowledge
the *Discourse*, as has been said.

Finally, Dr. Gardiner quotes two votes of the House of Commons,
May 9 and 12, the first to the effect that only the wives, children, and

servants of the prisoners be allowed access to them, the second cutting
off even this liberty. But the wording of the second vote will scarcely
bear such a construction; the four prisoners are to "be restrained as
close Prisoners, apart one from the other, within several Lodgings in
the Tower." *Commons Journal*, VI, 205 ff. The point is important
because the *Discourse* represents Lilburne's wife as with him. As for
Peters, orders of the House of Commons were never intended to keep
out that bustling divine; especially if, as Lilburne surmised, he came
on a mission from the Grandees.

CHAPTER XI

The Climax of the Leveller Constitutional Theories

THE constitutional ideas of the Levellers did not perish when the Agreement of the People proved impracticable; for to the Levellers the Agreement had been a means to an end and not an end in itself. Their primary aim was not to set up a written constitution; rather it was to protect by law the rights of the individual from the encroachment of government. The force of events, it was true, had hindered the people from establishing a government under a paramount law; but the Levellers did not conclude from this that the Rump was not bound by law or that the people were devoid of means for enforcing such law as they had. A second political trial of Lilburne led his old followers to ascribe to ordinary juries the right of rejecting as null and void an act of Parliament contrary to the principles of reason or of the English common law.

That John Lilburne caused this final development of Leveller constitutional ideas is significant in itself. Except when his robust personality dragged the Leveller party once more into the light of day, that party after 1649 was fast becoming a mere adjunct to lurking Royalist plots. For a year after his acquittal in 1649 political petitions from the "approvers of the petition of September 11, 1648"

made their appearance. But material to determine
the circumstances that produced them is lacking;
for the vigilance of the government made the old
democratic propaganda increasingly difficult. After
1650 the Levellers openly advanced their doctrines
only when Lilburne's private pursuits had brought
him into collision with the government on a matter
of principle.[1]

For a time after Lilburne's acquittal in 1649,
such a collision had seemed unlikely. Lilburne's
old friends had again thought him guilty of apostasy
because after his release he had kept on good terms
with the government. It is true that he had interpreted the oath of loyalty to the Commonwealth
as binding him to respect the old principles of the
English constitution, rather than the Rump or the
Council of State;[2] but this gloss had done him no
more harm than to cause his ejectment from a seat
in the London common council to which he had
been elected in December of 1649. No further
ebullition had followed, and accordingly the Rump
under Cromwell's influence had shortly afterward
completed the payment of his claims. Being satisfied for the moment that Cromwell's aim was really
the freedom of England, Lilburne had received

---

[1] These are in 669 f. 15 (50), Aug. 21, 1650 (endorsed "The Levellers
Petition"); E. 612 (1), Sept. 1, 1650; 669 f. 15 (54), Aug. 31, 1650.
These protest in especial against further activity of a High Court of
Justice, and demand trial by jury in all cases. Another petition of
June 30, 1652, contains Leveller demands, but it does not have the
usual Leveller formula.

[2] *L. Colonel John Lilbvrne His Apologetical Narration*, p. 14; *The
Engagement Vindicated & Explained.*

the favor with a good grace. As a mark of respect and gratitude he had accompanied Cromwell
twenty-five miles out of London on his way to
Scotland; and the General had taken an affection-
ate leave of him. To say the least, Lilburne's apparent reversal of his former opinion of Cromwell must have surprised the Levellers.[3]

Lilburne, however, proved unequal to the task
of living peaceably under the government. He
took up again the innocent trade of soap-boiling;[4]
but when he added to it the avocation of acting as
agent or attorney for persons with suits before
Parliament or its committees, he laid a foundation
of future trouble for himself.[5] A semi-political case
in which he became involved got him into trouble
with Parliament; and Parliament's vindictiveness
in his case put at hazard principles of liberty that
Englishmen had long considered fundamental.

The case in question involved a disputed title
to the use of the Harraton colliery near Durham.
Josiah Primate, George Grey, and George Lilburne,
an uncle of John, claimed it by virtue of a lease.
Sir Arthur Haselrig, when on the Durham com-

---

[3] The act in satisfaction of Lilburne's arrears is in 669 f. 15 (44).
L. Colonel John Lilbvrne His Apologetical Narration, Apr. 1652, E. 659
(30), p. 12. This is corroborated by a letter from Lilburne to Cromwell.
Hist. Mss. Com. Marquis of Bath, II, 92.

[4] The *Royall Diurnall* of Apr. 14–23 alludes to his occupation. Nov.
2, 1650, he with other soap-boilers petitioned Parliament in a matter
touching the trade. 669 f. 15 (62).

[5] Probably with a view to learning more law for this business, Lilburne tried to enter the Temple; but his old adversary, Prideaux, refused
to admit him. This occurred about December 1, 1649. *The Second
Part Of the Triall of Lieut. Col. John Lilburne*, E. 598 (12).

mittee in 1649, had seized it, alleging that it had been sequestered as the property of a Royalist, and that George Lilburne and George Grey under pretext of a fraudulent lease were appropriating state property.[6] At the worst, there was chance of as much fraud on the one side as on the other; for Haselrig was accused of influencing the Durham committee to release the colliery at a scandalously low rental.[7] The documents leave one with the impression that either side had something of a case; and when the Haberdashers' Hall committee at London decided against Primate and Lilburne, it apparently did not consider that they had been guilty of a palpable fraud.

Nevertheless John Lilburne, who had been one

---

[6] Primate claimed that three-fourths of the mine, comprising the lower seams, had been leased to him in 1629. The mine had been sequestered in 1644 on account of the delinquency of George Wray. The crucial point was: Did Wray own the whole mine or only one-fourth of it? Grey and George Lilburne went on the last-mentioned supposition when in 1647 they leased Primate's rights and began pumping out the flooded lower levels. When Haselrig sequestered the whole mine in 1649, he acted on the supposition that Wray was the sole owner. The question that the Haberdashers' Hall committee really decided was whether the sequestration of 1644 covered the whole mine or only a part. The Lilburne side of the case is in *A Iust Reproof To Haberdashers-Hall*, July 30, 1651, E. 638 (12). Haselrig's side is in *Musgrave Muzl'ed*, Mar. 3, 1650/1, E. 625 (11), ascribed by Lilburne to John Price. *A Letter Of Lieutenant Colonel John Lilburnes*, Mar. 31, 1651, E. 626 (19). The papers connected with the case are abstracted at length in the *Calendar of the Committee for Compounding*, III, 1917–1922; 2127–2131.

[7] *Calendar*, pp. 2128–2129. The committee, however, absolved Haselrig of having any interest in the business. This charge is partly borne out by the fact that the committee refused to confirm Hacker's lease. *Op. cit.*, p. 2128.

of the counsel for his uncle and Primate, became involved in trouble through his antipathy to Sir Arthur Haselrig. Lilburne thought that Haselrig was seeking the ruin of his kinsmen because they had the courage to withstand his peculations in Durham. Moreover, John was firmly convinced that in 1649 Sir Arthur had trumped up false charges against George Lilburne; had even sought the life of John himself, both directly by assassins and indirectly by withholding the rent of his Durham estates. John believed that on that occasion he had recovered his property by a threat of personal violence against Haselrig. Apparently he now thought to repeat his success by publishing under title of *A Iust Reproof To Haberdashers-Hall* a furious attack against Sir Arthur, accusing him of having influenced the committee unduly against Lilburne and Primate.[8]

This last outbreak was Lilburne's undoing. He with others was concerned in presenting to Parliament a petition signed by Primate, but embodying the charges of *A Iust Reproof*, and he was made the scapegoat of Parliament's wrath. January 15, 1651/2, the House voted the petition false and scandalous, and condemned it to be burned by the common hangman. Further, it assessed a fine of £7,000 on Primate, committing him to prison until it should be paid. It fined Lilburne £3,000, assessed him damages of £4,000, and condemned him to die as a felon if he were found in England at the end of thirty days.

[8] *A Iust Reproof To Haberdashers-Hall.*

Lilburne was firmly convinced that Cromwell had forced the House of Commons to make the petition a pretext for banishing him. Certain facts seemed to substantiate his theory. Lilburne certainly had been less deeply concerned in Primate's petition than other counsel who escaped without a sentence. Whether the Harraton case was fraudulent or not, the fraud was not so apparent that a supporter of Primate must necessarily have been a rascal.[9] Yet Cromwell, when speaking in the House on another subject, had broken off his speech to voice his emphatic approval of the sentence against Lilburne. Lilburne could not fathom Cromwell's motive for persecuting him; for had he not offered to leave the colliery case, Haselrig and all, to Cromwell's arbitration? We know now that in the spring of 1651 a Royalist agent's confession had vaguely implicated Lilburne, Marten, and Wildman in correspondence with the Royalists. Perhaps this incident convinced Cromwell that Lilburne was too dangerous to be at large, and must accordingly be got out of the way at the first opportunity.[10] The procedure of the House in banishing Lilburne

[9] See Note on p. 346, on the sentence against Lilburne.

[10] *Apologetical Narration*, p. 19; *A Defensive Declaration of Lieut. Col. John Lilburn*, June 22, 1653, E. 702 (2), p. 9; Coke's Narration, *Portland Mss*, I, 591. Coke, the agent mentioned, had stated that he had seen letters written by the Levellers. "It was conceaved that John Lilburne had a hand in the letters, and that the intelligence came from him to Sir Sackvile Crow. Mr. Martin and one Wildmore—as the examinant remembers his name—were lookt upon as persons that together with Lilburne had influence upon the spirits of those men." The evidence is vague. According to Coke, the Levellers had stipulated for a "full and generall libertie."

was so palpably unjust that it completely threw in the shade any misconduct of which Lilburne had been guilty. The interference of the House was entirely unnecessary, for Haselrig and the committee had ample redress at common law for any slander they had suffered. Further, the House in its decree of banishment passed sentence on Lilburne without formal charge, and without allowing him to be heard in his defense. Of this point Lilburne did not fail to remind the House by refusing to kneel for sentence at its bar.[11] This contempt of court provoked the House of Commons to even worse proceedings, were such possible. It passed an act decreeing a more severe sentence against Lilburne than the one recited in the judgment against him. Lastly, the Speaker, by refusing a pass, endeavored to delay Lilburne in England until the attaint of felony took effect.[12] In short, the House of Commons condemned along with Lilburne the most fundamental principles of liberty known to English law.

[11] *A Declaration Of Lieutenant Colonel John Lilburn*, Jan. 22, 1651/2, E. 652 (1).

[12] *Apologetical Narration*, p. 59. The judgment had decreed his banishment in terms that might be construed to exclude Wales from the places from which he was banished. The act added Wales, and cut down to twenty the thirty days' grace before the felony took effect. Lilburne's friends paid some attention to his banishment. They petitioned Parliament in his behalf; 669 f. 16 (37). A doubtful authority states that some of the officers and soldiers were willing to stand and fall with him. *A Declaration Of The Armie*, E. 654 (11), Feb. 14, 1651/2. See also *The French Intelligencer*, Jan. 13–21, 1651/2. Lilburne says that he wrote from Dover a letter to divers trustworthy men of different opinions "who are very Zealous for the speedy electing of a New Parliament in England." They were John Feak, John Simson, William Kiffin. *Supra*, p. 238.

Lilburne's relations with the Royalists in Holland are the only circumstances of his banishment which are of interest to us; they are important as an indication of the extent of the Royalist tendencies of the Levellers. The Royalists as a rule were inclined to hold aloof from Lilburne, believing his banishment was a farce devised to increase his value as a spy upon them.[13] Pamphlets written against him by spies of the Council of State induced the more ignorant Cavaliers to believe that he was mainly responsible for the king's death. Accordingly Lilburne ran actual dangers of being "Dorislawed," as the *Dutch Spy* put it.[14] By his account he could devise no better way of avoiding such a fate than by putting himself in the company of the more moderate Cavaliers, such as Buckingham, Hopton, Percy,

[13] "W. R." to Edgman, Feb. 20, 1652, n. s., *Calendar Clarendon Papers*, II, 121. Dec. 2–12, 1652, Nicholas wrote: "it is now evident to all men that the rogue Lilburne was banish'd England merely to gain him credit and trust on this side." *Nicholas Papers*, I, 321.

[14] For instance, Captain Wendy Oxford in *Vincit qui patitur* accused Lilburne of having raised riots at Whitehall to murder the king and queen. Lilburne claimed that these statements really endangered his life. *A Defensive Declaration*, p. 14. He also insisted that another spy, Riley by name, had repeatedly attempted to murder him. Scot, the Commonwealth "intelligence master," at the Restoration confessed that he had set Oxford and Riley to spy on Lilburne. *English Historical Review*, XII, 120. See also the *Dutch Spy*, Mar. 17–25, 1652.

Curiously enough, Oxford, like Lilburne, had been banished by Parliament without a hearing. This was his punishment for a minor part in a swindle in which Lord Howard of Escrick was involved. Lilburne had approved Parliament's sentence on Escrick as a notable piece of justice. Escrick had been heard before being sentenced, and perhaps Lilburne did not know of Oxford's case. Here, however, Godwin has more excuse than he ordinarily has for accusing Lilburne of inconsistency; but he hardly sees his opportunity. III, 341.

and Colepepper. In spite of Lilburne's cautiously worded denials, there is credible evidence that he proposed to these men that the king grant the demands of the Levellers and recover his crown by their aid. Certainly, if Lilburne proposed such terms, the negotiations went little farther; and by 1653 the strait-laced Royalists like Hyde and Nicholas feared that Lilburne would seduce the Duke of Buckingham to compliance with the Commonwealth. In fact, Lilburne counseled the duke and his friends as to the best way of making their peace with Cromwell and the Rump.[15] All in all it is not likely that Lilburne was ever deeply engaged in plots with Royalists; but, on the other hand, the evidence indicates that he made advances to them.

The reasons that led Lilburne to attempt to return to England after a year's banishment are not easy to fathom. His statements were contradictory. During the first year of his banishment there was no mistaking Lilburne's estimate of

[15] *A Defensive Declaration*, pp. 15, 16; *Cal. Clarendon Papers*, II, 213; Hyde to Nicholas, *Nicholas Papers*, I, 301. A second set of spies, Titus, Birkenhead, Bartlet, and Float testified that Lilburne had offered with £10,000 to restore the king. This is partially corroborated by Nicholas. *Nicholas Papers*, I, 291. The spies also told of Lilburne's threats to cut Cromwell off like a fox or wolf, and his attempts to murder them. *Severall Informations*, July 13, 1653, E. 705 (14). The Royalists in 1652 believed that Lilburne had some design on Cromwell. *Cal. Clarendon Papers*, II, 146. Certainly Lilburne up to the moment of his return to England in 1653 was engaged in conferences with Buckingham. *Ibid.*, pp. 213, 223. In *A Defensive Declaration* Lilburne denied his complicity with the Royalists in terms that, as Gardiner suggests, would not have excluded the case of his making overtures which they rejected. *Malice detected, in Printing certain Informations*, July 15, 1653, E. 705 (19).

Cromwell's character and aims. He printed letters to his friends and to his wife in which he denounced Cromwell as a tyrant and berated Mrs. Lilburne for her efforts to secure from Cromwell and Haselrig his recall. He promised at one time the speedy publication of a *chef-d'oeuvre* that would reveal Cromwell to all the world in his true light. He even contemplated killing the tyrant.[16] But, after Lilburne had the news of Cromwell's *coup d'état* of April, 1653, the tone of his expressions changed from day to day. May 14 (n. s.), he congratulated Cromwell on his resolution to set England free at last, and respectfully pleaded for an interview. June 2 (n. s.), he accused Cromwell of seeking his life for seven years, and engaged, if he might come to London, to answer him as a Christian or as a sturdy fellow accordingly as Cromwell should elect. June 14 (n. s.), he assured the Council of State that he would live quietly in England if they fulfilled their purpose of establishing England's liberties; otherwise, he promised them the opposition of his personal following. When he actually was in England, he wrote to Cromwell, June 14 (o. s.), apologizing for his hard words on the ground that his mind had been clouded with suffering, and that he had been misinformed as to Cromwell's real political intentions. At this time he assigned as the reason for his return his intention of petitioning the new

---

[16] *L. Colonel John Lilburne revived*, pp. 9, 13–15. This masterpiece was to be an appeal to the people. It may be noted in this connection that the spies represented that the £10,000 with which he would restore the king was to be spent in printing attacks on the Rump.

Parliament to revoke the sentence passed against him by the Rump.   Lilburne's accounts of the motives prompting his actions are usually more accurate than they at first appear, but his explanations on this occasion were strangely contradictory.[17]

Cromwell was not to be appeased.   He ordered the lord mayor of London to issue a *mittimus* against Lilburne, who accordingly found himself in prison again.   Repeated petitions by Lilburne obtained him only the grace of being held over for trial till after the Nominated Parliament had met. The government was apparently in no mood for trifling.[18]

Since the Nominated Parliament did not see fit to revoke the act passed by the Rump to carry out its sentence of banishment against Lilburne, that act took its due course.   A grand jury in pursuance of the act, which declared Lilburne a felon if he were found in England twenty days after the 15th day of January, 1651/2, found a true bill against him.   On July 13 he was brought to trial before the regular sessions under the indictment. If he pleaded to the indictment, the jury had only to find that he was the John Lilburne named in the act of banishment; this done, his condemnation and execution would naturally follow under the act itself.[19]

[17] *A Defensive Declaration; The Upright Mans Vindication*, Aug. 5, 1653, E. 708 (22), pp. 3, 25; *The Banished mans suit for Protection*, June 15, 1653, 669 f. 17 (16).

[18] *A Second Address directed to his Excellency the Lord Generall Cromwell*, June 16, 1653, 669 f. 17 (20); *Third Address directed to his Excellency*, June 20, 1653, 669 f. 17 (22).

[19] *State Trials*, V, 416.

The succeeding nine weeks' legal struggle between the prisoner and the government stirred London to its depths. It was to no purpose that the government published depositions of its spies accusing Lilburne of traffic with the Royalists; his old associates rallied round him. Prince and Overton, as well as Lilburne's father, uncle, and cousins attended and supported him in court. His friends published pamphlet after pamphlet in his behalf. They swore the day of his execution would be the bloodiest that London had ever seen. They scattered about the streets tickets with the motto:

> And what, shall then honest John Lilbourn die?
> Threescore thousand will know the reason why.

The precautions taken by the government also proved the depth of popular feeling. At the July session of the trial the authorities kept three regiments about St. James; at the August session they filled the court with soldiers. It was rumored at the time that six or seven hundred armed men were in the courtroom ready to rescue the prisoner by force if need were.[26]

The reason for this excitement must be sought in the principles at stake in Lilburne's case. When

---

[20] *State Trials*, V, 417, 420, 426, 432–433. Between June 24 and August 10, seven printed petitions in his behalf appeared. 669 f. 17 (24, 26, 35, 36, 38, 43), E. 710 (5). *Cal. Clarendon Pap.*, II, 224; *Thurloe State Papers*, I, 367, 435, 442.

Numbers of pamphlets appeared. Lilburne himself printed *A Juryman's Judgement* and *Lieu Col. John Lilburn's Plea in Law*. After giving away many copies, he took to selling them through hawkers. *The Prisoner's Most mournful Cry*, July 1, 1653, E. 703 (12).

he was first brought into court, Lilburne began to claim privileges hitherto unused in English criminal procedure. He refused to plead to the indictment, alleging that he wished to assign errors in it. Next, he demonstrated out of Sir Edward Coke his right to a copy of the indictment and to the advice of counsel in preparing exceptions to it. He extorted both these things from the court, being the first man in the history of English law to obtain them.[21]

Of the four exceptions he offered, two were more or less technical in their nature, and two were based on broad principles of law. The first and last exceptions recited that the indictment did not satisfactorily identify the John Lilburne it named with the man against whom the act was passed, and further, that it did not state the act in question to be an act of an English Parliament. The second and third exceptions to the act were fundamental. The second alleged that the act recited an illegal judgment, as Lilburne had never been indicted, summoned, or set to plead to an indictment. The third alleged that the act did not agree with the judgment on which it was based, either as to the time at which the banishment should take effect, or as to the places from which Lilburne was to be banished.[22]

A still higher demand to which Lilburne's lawyers had prompted him, finally postponed his trial a month. This demand was for oyer of the act and judgment, and also of the crimes they recited. The

[21] *State Trials*, V, 417–421.
[22] *Ibid.*, pp. 437–439.

court, which had shown throughout a tendency to quibble and evade, refused to hear the demand till it was signed by Lilburne's counsel. Lilburne, on the other hand, refused to hand in his exceptions until oyer was granted him. After a long and furious wrangle, in which the judges, Lilburne, and his friends all took part, court and prisoner compromised. Lilburne handed in the exceptions to the indictment on the understanding that his doing so should not prejudice his right to oyer of the act when his counsel should demand it. Because his case was a crucial one, Lilburne had the popular support that enabled him to confront his judges on equal terms.[23]

When the trial was resumed in August on the court's return from circuit, the judges finally compelled Lilburne to plead to the indictment. Of the process by which this result was obtained, we have only fragmentary accounts. We know that Lilburne's exceptions and demand for oyer were finally over-ruled, as was to have been expected. However, the long struggle on the legal points involved had apparently converted the jury to the justice of Lilburne's cause, and August 20 it returned a verdict of not guilty.[24]

The Harraton colliery case had raised a storm of public sentiment, because the Rump in punishing

---

[23] *State Trials*, V, 426–442.

[24] *Op. cit.*, pp. 443–444; *The Tryall Of L. Col. Iohn Lilburn At The Sessions House in the Old-Baily*, E.711 (9). Lilburne, on the 11th, excepted to the act on the ground that it was not engrossed, and was on interlined and pieced papers.

Lilburne had violated principles of civil freedom, and Lilburne had shown his old skill in dinning those principles into the ears of the people. His reiteration of the ancient liberties and laws of England was welcome to all men tired of the anarchy and confusion of past years.[25] The constitutional and political arguments advanced in his behalf pressed home the fact that the Rump, perhaps also its successor, the Council of State, followed as much after the rule of government as ever Strafford or Laud had done.[25] Indeed, Lilburne and his friends reverted to the earliest position of the Long Parliament when they insisted that in spite of revolutions the fundamental laws of the land endured, and were greater than the government.

The circumstances of Lilburne's case demanded a recurrence to the fundamental principles of the constitution. As in 1649, the point really at issue was the constitutional validity of a political act of the highest authority of the nation. Unless Lilburne's jury could be induced to take account of the legality of the Rump's sentence and act of banishment, Lilburne would stand condemned without a hearing. If the jury ignored the flaws in the indictment; if it refused to consider the nature of the actions that Parliament had pronounced felonious, and the evidence on which it had con-

[25] *Cal. Clarendon Papers*, II, 234; *Thurloe Papers*, I, 368. It was obvious that the Levellers were bound to criticise the Rump; but in some of their writings they criticised sharply Cromwell's arbitrary assumption of power to tax, his nominating a Parliament, etc. *A Plea at large, For John Lilburn Gentleman*, Aug. 6, 1653, E. 710 (3).

victed Lilburne, the jury could pass only on the identity of the Lieutenant-Colonel John Lilburne named in the act with the John Lilburne arraigned at the bar.[26] Lilburne and his friends, in urging the court to take cognizance of the points raised in his exceptions, can not have expected to overcome its prejudice against the prisoner. Rather they hoped to awake the jury to the important constitutional duty that lay before it. That duty was in part to judge of the law as well as of the facts. It was also to weigh the comparative valid-

[26] As from a certain viewpoint this was the only question on which the jury could pass, Lilburne's friends occasionally used it rhetorically as a pretext to introduce the legal grounds on which Lilburne had taken his stand. The Lilburne at the bar, they said, is not the same as the Lilburne mentioned in the act; for the former is a free-born English gentleman and never was legally charged, indicted, or convicted by the Parliament or any other court of judicature, being a court of record. The Lilburne at the bar was never summoned to any legal tribunal to say what he could why sentence should not be passed against him. The Parliament that sentenced Lilburne—here they play on his first exception—was not that which had sworn so often to maintain the fundamental laws; rather it was some ignorant Parliament of Paris, or else the act was jumbled together and passed by a Parliament three-fourths asleep against "some sillie natural fool called Lieu. Col John Lilburn, that could not be imagined ever in his life to have read any thing of Law or Reason." *Lieu Col. John Lilburn's Plea in Law*, pp. 1–4. *A Plea at large, For John Lilburn.*

All this may seem a labor of love. But Dr. Gardiner, because Lilburne denied his identity in this fashion, gravely charges him with either telling a downright lie or prevaricating. *Commonwealth and Protectorate*, II, 248. The sense in which Lilburne denied his identity must be clear to anyone from the above. "Although John Lilburn Gent. now prisoner at the bar were that Lieut. Col. John Lilburn mentioned in the said Act of Banishment, (*as with confidence, for the just and legal reasons at the beginning of this Plea mentioned, he doth avow he is not*)." *A Plea at large, For John Lilburn*, p. 23. The italics in the quotation are mine.

ity of an act of the supreme authority, and the
fundamental laws of the land.

In the floods of pamphlets containing such doctrine, there reappeared the old Leveller idea that
in England the government was bound by fundamental laws.   Lilburne and his friends proved that
in many respects the proceedings against him in
1651/2 had violated the laws of the land.[27]   He
had been sentenced as a felon for that which was
not felony at the common law; he had been condemned without being confronted by an accuser,
set to plead to an indictment before a court of
record, allowed to speak in his own behalf, or
suffered to enjoy the benefit of a jury.   He and his
supporters used Sir Edward Coke's authority to
demonstrate that an act of Parliament contrary to
the common law was null and void.[28]   They had
an answer to the possible rejoinder that the sword
had swallowed up the common law.   They returned
to their earlier doctrine that on points of civil liberty the common law itself was but a statement of
the law of God and the law of reason.   These laws
the sword could not abrogate; the old dialogue of
the Doctor and Student taught that any act or
law contrary to them was null, void, and of no
effect.[29]

[27] *Apologetical Narration*, p. 16; *A Jury-man's Judgement Upon the
Case of Lieut. Col. John Lilburn*, June 22, 1653, E. 702 (6).

[28] *The Petition Rejected by the Parliament*, 669 f. 17 (24); *Lieu Col
John Lilburn's Plea in Law*, July 2, 1653, E. 703 (12), pp. 4 ff.

[29] *The Afflicted Mans Out Cry*, Aug. 19, 1653, E. 711 (7), pp. 2, 3;
A Plea at large, For John Lilburn, Aug. 6, 1653, E. 710 (3), p. 4; *More
Light To Mr. John Lilburnes Jury*, Aug. 16, 1653, E. 710 (23), p. 5.

However, Lilburne's supporters had proclaimed such doctrine in the past; they had now to frame a method by which the law of God, the law of reason, and the common law might adjudge void an act or law contravening them. The Levellers had formerly taught that the minds of all men were capable of detecting by the light of reason a violation of the law of reason. The exigencies of Lilburne's case led his friends to assign this function to his jury.

Various pamphlets addressing the men who were to serve on Lilburne's jury told them that their duty as a jury was to distinguish real acts of Parliament from those against law and, therefore, counterfeit. The jury must not be misled into a belief that such acts of Parliament were good law until repealed. They must not make the mistake that juries had done in the cases of Barrow and Greenwood. Lilburne's jurors must remember that it was the duty of jurymen "not to find any man guilty upon any statute in any case, which appears to have no good ground upon the standing Law of England."[30]

In several other such pamphlets as the above, the emphasis seems to be, not on the duty of a jury as a jury to judge of law as well as fact, but on the duty of a court to refuse to recognize as law that which is not law. In 1648 Lilburne had preached a similar doctrine, when he argued that King's Bench had the right to reverse an illegal commit-

---

[30] *A Jury-man's Judgement*, pp. 11 ff.; *More Light To Mr. John Lilburnes Jury*.

ment by the High Court of Parliament; in 1653 we find his doctrine much elaborated.   One writer sees that the legislative and judicial powers take their rise from the people, and are accordingly coördinate.   "For," he says, "the People in general have all Law and Authority within themselves, managing their publike Affaires by their own elected Parliaments or Common councels of England (2) Judging, deciding, and determining all Matters and Causes whatsoever by their Juries."[31]

An objection may be raised at this point.   If men had the idea that the deciding in a specific case whether or not an act of Parliament contravened the fundamental law was the function of a judiciary, why did they put their emphasis on the duty as belonging to the jury?   The answer is simple.   At the time, the jury was the only part of the court certain to be impartial in a political case.   In fact, one pamphlet of 1653 warned the jury that it must not look to judge or recorder for direction, for these officers were controlled by the fear of losing their places.   The jury must rely only on itself in the work of preserving the ancient laws and liberties of England "from the tyranny of By-Laws or Parliament Innovations."[32]

A certain Captain Robert Norwood saw more clearly than all other writers that the function of

[31] The quotation is from *The Fundamental Lawes and Liberties Of England Claimed, asserted, and agreed unto, by severall Peaceable Persons of the City of London, Westminster, Southwark, Hamblets, and Places adjacent; Commonly called Levellers*, July 9, 1653, E. 705 (5), p. 1.   See also *More Light To Mr. John Lilburnes Jury*.

[32] *More Light To Mr. John Lilburnes Jury*, p. 8.

judging of the accord of statutes with the fundamental law pertained to a jury as part of a judiciary
rather than to a jury as a jury. Answering the
question as to who were judges on such questions,
he said: "Why all Englishmen, the whole People
of England, in and by their several Courts and
officers, as in and by their Hundred-Courts, County-
Courts, Courts of Inquest, Sheriffs, Juryes and the
like." "Yet mistake me not. This dislike or dis-
approving of such Acts is to be manifested and
regulated in a due and orderly way and manner,
as to, in and by the Courts and officers appointed
thereunto, as is said before; for as in the natural
body so in this civil are their several offices, and
officers, as eyes, hands, head, feet, heart and the
like."[33]

Here the constitutional ideas that we have termed
Leveller ideas reach their climax. In 1640 Parliament had taught the people that there were fundamental laws in England, but when in 1642 it assumed
the right to interpret them in last appeal, it had
virtually set itself above them. It had then found
adherents to argue for its untrammelled sovereignty. Five years later it had found in Ireton an
advocate of parliamentary supremacy, limited only
by recurring popular elections. The Levellers had
steadily combated such ideas. In 1645 they had
taught that Parliament must walk according to the

[33] *An Additional Discourse Relating unto a Treatise lately published
by Capt. Robert Norwood*, Aug. 2, 1653, E. 708 (9), p. 48. Yet he admits
to a certain extent that every man is judge in so far as a law concerns
himself.

law. In 1647, in the Agreement of the People, they had attempted to limit the Parliament by a fundamental law stated by the people. In 1648 and 1649 they had devised a means whereby the people, acting in its sovereign capacity, might make and adopt for itself a written constitution of paramount law. They had failed in attempts to establish the fundamental laws of the realm in this manner; but they added the capstone to their theory when in 1653 they devised the means whereby acts of Parliament traversing the fundamental law of the land might be declared in orderly fashion null, void, and of no effect. In 1653 they had answered the question that had perplexed Hunton in 1644.

NOTE

The Sentence against Lilburne

It is almost impossible to find a hypothesis that will explain satisfactorily all the incidents of the Rump's sentence in Lilburne's case. First, it is hard to see why Lilburne was singled out for exemplary punishment. He had neither written Primate's petition nor seen to printing it. He had merely avowed it and distributed printed copies to members of the House and to other persons. Yet Parliament proceeded against the other counsel concerned only after it had sentenced Lilburne. There were strange things about the entire procedure of Parliament. The act for Lilburne's banishment was passed without being engrossed. The fact that it was passed early in the morning, at a time when few members ordinarily had arrived, suggests that there was some trick connected with it. Marten and Moyle, two men in sympathy with Lilburne, were members of the committee to which the bill in execution of the judgment was referred. In passing the bill unengrossed, and with a different penalty from that described in the judgment, they may have designedly left loop-holes for Lilburne's benefit at some later time. *Commons Journal*, VII, 55, 64, 71, 73, 74, 75, 78, 79, Dec. 23, Jan. 6, 15, 16, 20, 21, 29, 30, 1651/2.

In February of 1658/9, Parliament undertook the task of reversing the sentence against Lilburne. Haselrig and one of the four Haberdashers' Hall committee members agreed to surrender all claim to their shares of Lilburne's fine. Two other members were dead, and Mrs. Lilburne compromised with a fourth. The fine settled, the act was finally repealed, several members of Parliament stating emphatically their belief in its illegal character and questioning whether it were not void in itself. The fact that Mrs. Lilburne agreed to surrender all papers connected with the case suggests that justice and equity may not have been wholly on Haselrig's side. *Burton's Diary*, III, 68, 503.

CHAPTER XII

Conclusion

I. THE END OF THE LEVELLER MOVEMENT

THE acquittal of Lilburne in 1653 is the logical end of this narrative. December of that year saw the installation of Cromwell as Lord Protector; and his government adopted repressive measures that completely changed the character of the Leveller political activities. By defying the forms and equity of law, and holding Lilburne almost to the day of his death as a military prisoner, Cromwell effectually kept the arch-Leveller from further participation in politics. Moreover, by an effective censorship of the press, the Protector frustrated the democratic political methods of the Leveller party. Political discussion became timid and academic; and the old Leveller leaders, unable longer to influence the nation through the press, entered into plots with the Royalists. The remnant of the Leveller organization degenerated from a political party to a band of conspirators.[1]

As we can no longer trace the Levellers as a party, so we catch only occasional glimpses of their salient ideas. The idea of the sovereignty of law survived

---

[1] The decrease in the number of pamphlets published tells a part of the story. For the years 1654–58 Thomason's collection contains 3,041 pieces as against 7,583 for the years 1645–49. The difference in tone is even more striking; except for defenses of the government, political discussion in the later period is weak and non-committal.

348

the longest. Partly no doubt this was due to the tone of the set apologies published for the Nominated Parliament and the Protectorate. These apologies defended the *coups d'état* of April and December of 1653 with the argument that Marchamont Nedham had used to cover his apostasy—the divine right of superior force. The Rump, they said, for four years had been a mere mask for the army; now the mask had better be dropped, and authority rest with the men who had the might to rule.[2] Similarly when Cromwell was installed Lord Protector, pamphleteers justified his elevation as an act of divine Providence, using the term in the Cromwellian sense of a favorable turn of mundane affairs. They condemned the discarded Barebones' Parliament because it had worked blindly under divine providences that were not of the Cromwellian order. Finally, one author announced that, since it had manifestly been the will of God to turn the realm from the government of kings to the government of judges, the people must submit.[3] When the acts of New Model regiments in establishing and overturning governments were to be reverenced as the dictates of divine Providence,

---

[2] *The Army Vindicated*, John Spittlehouse, Apr. 24, 1653, E. 693 (1); *Reasons Why The Supreme Authority Of The Three Nations* . . . *Is not in the Parliament, But In the* . . . . *Councel of State*, May. 1653, E. 697 (19); *The Army No Usurpers*, May 20, 1653, E. 697 (13); *A Letter Written To a Gentleman in the Country*, May 16, 1653, E. 697 (2), is more moderate.

[3] *The Grand Catastrophe*, Jan. 18, 1653/4, E. 726 (12); *A True State of the Case Of The Commonwealth*, Feb. 8, 1653/4, E. 728 (5); *Protection Perswading Subjection*, Feb. 13, 1653/4, E. 729 (4); *Confusion Confounded*, Jan. 18, 1653/4, E. 726 (11).

men with respect for the sanctity of law might be pardoned for exaggerating the element of permanence in the ancient constitution.

The books of Captain Robert Norwood illustrate the extreme to which, as a result of the events of 1653, men carried the notion of fundamental law. To Norwood every good thing in the universe is regulated in every particular by law. All created things derive their being from their bounds and limits. Even God himself has consented to bind himself "within the golden chains of Justice and Righteousness." As he has made nature's laws, he cannot violate them; nay, accord with law seems almost the divine attribute, for he that is without law is rather a devil or destroyer.[4]

In applying his theory of law to civil government, Norwood finds the one basis of political order in the authority of parents over their children. By analogy every man owes obedience to the laws of the realm as to his fathers, "for our forefathers, and we in and with our forefathers, and our forefathers in and with us will be found in the Laws, Ordinances, Customs, and Constitutions . . . ." It follows that a nation has no power to abrogate such of its laws as correspond to the law of nature, and therefore may lay claim to paternal authority. So far fathers may bind their children with irrepealable laws, unamendable by parliaments and rulers, no matter how supreme. Indeed, it is the true function of governments to maintain the laws of the fathers,

---

[4] *An Additional Discourse*, p. 2; *A Pathway Unto England's Perfect Settlement*, June 27, 1653, E. 702 (16), pp. 13, 14.

and preserve the happiness of the commonwealth by keeping every man within the limits duly ordained by this paternal authority.[5]

Such conceptions of paramount law were completely foreign to the political experiments of the Protectorate. Accordingly those experiments have no interest for us. True, the *Instrument of Government* and the *Humble Petition and Advice* in a sense were written constitutions; true, Cromwell, in commenting on the former, had pronounced that in every government there must be "somewhat fundamental, somewhat like a Magna Charta." But neither *Instrument* nor *Advice* reaches the constitutional standards set by the Levellers; neither originated with the people or had had their formal assent; neither could enforce itself; and Cromwell, in elaborating his comment on the *Instrument*, showed that the "fundamental" he desired could be summed up in an oath not to disturb the government as established in Protector and Parliament. Sir Henry Vane's *Healing Question*, it is true, suggested a Leveller type of constitutional convention that implied the sovereignty of the people; but Vane's was well-nigh the only voice raised till after the death of Cromwell.[6]

[5] *A Pathway*, pp. 19–23; *An Additional Discourse*, pp. 7, 40–43.

[6] Vane's *Healing Question* really revived many of the old Leveller ideas. He desired that power over conscience be withheld by the people from the government they were to erect. He demanded that the army submit quietly to such a government as the well-affected, meeting in a representative constitutional convention, should establish. There is an echo of 1648 in the proviso that the convention is not to exercise legislative power, but only to agree on particulars "that by way of fundamentall constitutions shall be laid, and inviolably observed as the

There was a faint recrudescence of the Leveller ideas in 1659.[7] The necessity of informing the people's ignorance of their natural rights,[8] the danger from legislative and executive powers residing in the same hands,[9] the sovereignty of the people, the equality of all before the law[10]—all appeared in that last year of confusion, mingled with many of the legal and social reforms that the Levellers had sought.   But above all rang the cry for a fundamental law that in some manner might be put beyond the power of government to amend.   Pamphlets announced that the people were sovereign, and by their consent must accordingly give validity to their frame of government or fundamental law. There were proposals for written constitutions to be framed by the sitting Parliament and subscribed by the people at large; proposals that the precious document be bound with the parish Bible and read to the people quarterly.[11]   Yet in these expedients

conditions upon which the whole body so represented doth consent to cast itself into a civil and politick incorporation." The constituent convention, according to Vane, is "of the people represented in their highest state of sovereignty." *Somers Tracts*, VI, 312–313.

[7] Wildman and Maximilian Petty became members of the Rota, and probably carried their Leveller ideas with them to Harrington's debates. Wood, *Athenae Oxonienses*, III, 1119.

[8] *XXV Queries*, Feb. 16, 1658/9, E. 968 (5), p. 1; *Lilburns Ghost*, June 22, 1659, E. 988 (9), p. 8.

[9] *Ibid.*, p. 5.

[10] *Speculum Libertatis Angliae*, July 13, 1659, E. 989 (19), p. 5.

[11] *Several Proposals*, July 6, 1659, E. 989 (9); *Speculum Libertatis*, pp. 18 ff.; *Englands Safety in the Laws Supremacy*, June 23, 1659, E. 988 (13), p. 16; *No Return To Monarchy*, June 6, 1659, E.986 (16), p. 6.

For the demand for fundamental laws, see *A Declaration Of the Well-affected to The Good Old Cause*, May 2, 1659, 669 f. 21 (27); *A Word of seasonable & Sound Counsell*, Nov. 14, 1659, 669 f. 22 (9).

one sees little more than the feverish haste of their proposers. The shadow of returning Royalism was indeed upon them, making them clutch frantically after constitutional expedients that might avert it. Of course the devices proposed, if vain in 1647 and 1649, were ten times more vain in 1659, after ten years of arbitrary government. In English constitutional history they are interesting as survivals of the idea that law may be set above government.

Here the arch-Leveller may claim his word of dismissal. Cromwell saw to it that he should not again interfere in politics. In spite of the verdict that Lilburne had won from his jury, the government held him a prisoner during four years, moving him from fortress to fortress; and only by the chance of a temporary leave from Dover Castle in August of 1657 did it fall to Lilburne's fortune to die outside prison walls. For the last two years of his life he had been a Quaker; and, as though contention followed him to the very edge of the grave, his old adherents and the Quakers disputed whether his funeral should have something of the pomp that had marked Lockyer's. The Quakers prevailed; and without ceremony John Lilburne was borne on men's shoulders to the "new Church yard adjoyning to Bedlam."[12]

A few days after his acquittal in 1653, John Lilburne had written a pamphlet that was practically his last political utterance—*The Just Defence of John Lilburn, against Such as charge him with*

[12] *Mercurius Politicus*, Sept. 3, 1657.

Turbulency of Spirit.[13]   He was still a young man,
at most, hardly forty; yet in writing his *Just Defence*
he seemed almost conscious that his political career
was at an end.   He was assured as ever that his
life had been a crusade for justice; but finally he
seems not merely angry at the world's rejection of
him and his principles, but puzzled and wounded.
Once more he recounted the events of his life to
show that he had been moved by the highest principles; but at last he might well be uncertain whether
he judged by the same standards as the world;
uncertain, indeed, whether he might not have mis-
understood the world altogether.

In the last four years of Lilburne's life the public
heard little of him, and indeed forgot the man and
his ideas alike.   He rapidly receded into an atmosphere of legend and fable.   The satirical will[14] that
a Royalist published for him on a false rumor of his
death in 1654 is not very unkind, but it is conde-
scending.   Lilburne is made to leave his brewer's
tallies to the next brewer's clerk that can learn the
art of "keeping within compass."   His needle and
thimble go to the next cloth-drawer that can resolve
to follow his trade and not meddle with state affairs.
His state policy he is permitted to bequeath to
Charles II, that "it may be by him cancelled and
turned into true obedience and submission to higher
powers."   "Lastly," concludes the satire, "I give
my good Counsell to all men, to be carefull, and

---

[13] Aug. 23, 1653, E. 711 (10).
[14] *The Last Will & Testament Of Lieutenant Col. John Lilburn*, May
27, 1654, E. 738 (8).

rest content in their callings without medling, or
intermedling with that which belongs not to them,
or is too high for them, or beyond their proper
Spheare or element . . . . acknowledging the
necessity of a diversity and preheminence in degrees
to be amongst men, for the necessary direction and
preservation of them . . . ." The very mock-
ery heaped upon democracy in the person of Lilburne proves how completely his life had sunk the
younger son of a landed gentleman and the lieutenant-colonel of the Parliament in the democratic
leader.   In John Lilburne the unknown satirist had
condemned as presumption the democratic spirit
that had arisen in 1642. That spirit had taught the
lowliest that it was their duty to strive for the
nation's welfare; it had breathed life into the words
of the Solemn League and Covenant that had bound
all who took it to strive in their respective stations
in life for a perfect reformation.   But now the time
was approaching when the old aristocratic theory,
that it was the duty of the lowly to follow the bidding of their betters, would have its day again.

There had ever been two men in Lilburne, the
warrior and the mystic.   Once cut off from the
battle of politics, the warrior was displaced by the
mystic, and John Lilburne, the crusader, became a
Quaker.   Perhaps as years of imprisonment broke
down his bodily vigor, he lost his old faith in his
ability to force the world into justice and righteousness;[15] in such a mood he would welcome the Quaker

---

[15] The idea is suggested by Bernstein, *Sozialismus und Demokratie*,
p. 204.

belief in the power of patience and long-suffering. Lilburne's conversion was the signal that the spirit of his age had broken him, even as the spirit of the Elizabethan age had broken Robert Browne before him.   Living in a time when the Great Civil War had rent the conventions of English life and thought from top to bottom, Lilburne had been able to exert a stronger influence than Browne on the passing turn of events.   But in the end the influence of either man must be sought in later generations than his own.

II. CONCLUSION

The preceding eleven chapters of this essay have avowedly been a sympathetic account of the Levellers and their part in the history of the Great Civil War.   Here no apology appears necessary for such a treatment of the subject; but in these last pages it may be fitting to attempt an impartial estimate of the Leveller ideas with respect to their practicability in their own age, and their abiding worth.   It will be proper also to attempt an exact statement of the political importance of the Levellers in their own generation, and thereby dispel any exaggerated ideas of their importance to which the foregoing treatment by its emphasis may have given rise.

First, a word may be said about the application of the term "Leveller."   By contemporaries it was used very loosely.   Here it has been somewhat arbitrarily assigned to a group of political radicals, gathered around the persons of Lilburne and his friends, closely enough knit together to be called a political party, more or less consistent advocates of certain political measures and principles. The author believes that too great liberty has not been taken in such a use of the word. While the personnel of the party changed, the organization persisted and the principles in orderly and logical sequence were evolved in new applications to meet the passing exigencies of the political situation; and the combination of organization and ideas was the core of the somewhat hazy image that the word "Leveller" suggested to contemporaries.

When we inquire further exactly what are the ideas that we have termed "Leveller," we have first to exclude from consideration a number of beliefs that the Levellers held in common with other groups of men. Thus, the Levellers generally favored a republican form of government; but they regarded it always as a means to an end, and were not drawn from their principles into supporting the Commonwealth with the so-called republicans. Further, the Levellers were advocates of toleration; but the consensus of historical opinion has selected Cromwell as the incarnation of the idea of religious toleration in the mid-seventeenth century. It is true also that the Levellers announced a far-reaching program of social and economic reforms; but they shared it with many contemporaries like Hugh Peters who were their political opponents.

It is most difficult to distinguish between the Leveller and the New Model soldier. There was truth in William Sedgwick's[16] saying that the Level-

---

[16] *The Leaves of the Tree Of Life*, p. 101.

ler had developed out of the army.   For example, the idea of the first Agreement of the People, though developed by Lilburne's group, appears to have originated in the ranks; and New Model debaters in the army councils afford us light on Leveller theories.   Yet in later years the soldiers were tossed to and fro on waves of doctrine between an abstract republicanism and a saintly fanaticism of Fifth Monarchy type, two intellectual states that have already been distinguished from that of the Leveller. Indeed it is well-nigh impossible to frame an intellectual definition that fits the New Model soldier universally, although the general impression that a distinct New Model type existed is probably correct.   In a previous chapter the New Model private was defined as the child of an age of transition.   As such his thinking was uncertain and contradictory; by contrast the ideas of the Levellers were sharp and distinct.

The Leveller rationalism gave a clear outline to the Leveller ideas.   The Levellers' faith in reason led them to penetrate through centuries of mere precedents to the dawn of society, when man's innate reason was still free from the shackles of hereditary usage.   Individualists in politics, the Levellers naturally constructed their theories of the ideal state of nature and the compact origin of government, that they might demonstrate the limitation of the power of government over individual men, and the right of each individual to a share of political power.   Believing that the law of nature and the law of reason had survived the state of nature to assure the sanctity of individual rights, the Levellers pronounced the laws of the land valid only in so far as they were a restatement of these higher laws. Finally, in the Agreements of the People the Levellers proposed that the people establish a democratic form of government, limited and restrained by an exact written statement of the laws of nature and of reason.

Furthermore, in attempting to accomplish their program, the Levellers invented political machinery of permanent value. They evolved the idea of the written constitution of paramount law as a limitation on the power of government. They devised machinery whereby the sovereignty of the people might express itself in the framing and acceptance of such written constitutions. Carrying their concept of government by law to its extreme, they designed the enforcement of their constitutions, like all other laws, through the courts. Lastly, for spreading their principles they designed a democratic party organization that suggests the committee of correspondence of the American Revolution.

The distinctly Leveller measures of reform were also political. The Levellers stood for a number of judicial principles on which the contemporary law was at best contradictory: trial by jury, the right of the prisoner to counsel and copy of indictment, his right to refuse to incriminate himself. And all these are commonplaces of justice today. But the Levellers just as obstinately insisted on political reforms that were completely impracticable in their generation; reforms that would certainly

have worked abiding harm if introduced. Thus
the Levellers would have reformed the law until it
was too simple to match the degree of complexity
that contemporary society had attained. At times
they proposed the abolition of all courts save the
county and hundred courts; half consciously, half
unconsciously, they designed the restoring of political and judicial institutions of the tenth century
in the England of the seventeenth.

On the other hand, however, their political program in its broader outlines was fitter for the twentieth century than for their own. It demanded that
the rank and file of a nation untrained in democracy
abandon the guidance of its traditional ruling classes
and attempt self-government. The proposal was
so colossal that we cannot say today that it was
absolutely impracticable. Speaking materially, the
Levellers at least showed a marked aptitude in
adapting to their purposes whatever they could
from the past customs and precedents familiar to
the nation, and they may have rightly gauged the
feasibility of their ideal. Speaking religiously,
since faith may remove mountains, the Levellers
might have established their democracy by faith.

Finally, we may ask concerning the influence of
the Levellers on their own and succeeding generations. We need deal least in conjectures when we
undertake to estimate the number of the party,
and the circulation of its pamphlets. We know
that at least four or five thousand people followed
Lockyer's body to the grave; at least ten thousand
persons signed certain Leveller petitions; we are

told on less certain authority that others had forty thousand and even "98,064" signatures. Perhaps ten thousand is a safe estimate of the numbers of the Levellers in London. Levellers were numerous also in near-by shires such as Bucks, Hants, Berks, and Herts, and were to be found in more distant ones; but here we have no material on which to base an estimate. As for pamphlets, Lilburne printed the greatest part of 20,000 copies of the Manifestation and the Agreement of May 1, 1649.[17] The Agreement was also printed in full in several non-Leveller journals as well as in the *Moderate*. The ordinary impression of a pamphlet was fifteen hundred copies.[18] We must, however, remember that a single piece of printed matter found more readers then than now. "If a man," said Samuel Chidley, "print an Impression of fifteen hundred books, peradventure they may be spread to 15,000 persons and leven them all."[19] Yet, after all, it was but a pitiful handful of persons with pitiful weapons that set forth to root up in a few years the prejudices and habits of thought of centuries.

Passing from the degree to the kind of influence exerted by the Levellers on their contemporaries, we can set down as fairly certain the influence of their democracy. The idea that common men had ability to do more than accept and carry out the political decisions of their social superiors was a new one; yet in the democratic caucuses of the

---

[17] *Apologetical Narration*, p. 71.
[18] *The Beacon Flameing*, Dec. 15, 1652, E. 683 (30), p. 17.
[19] *The Dissembling Scot*, Feb. 1, 1652, E. 652 (13), p. 9.

Leveller party, high and low alike were free to take counsel and speak their minds for the good of the nation. Lilburne, when he bearded Lords of Star Chamber, Lords of Parliament, and counsellors of the Commonwealth alike for their transgressions of the law, must have weakened the instinctive reverence for social distinctions and the dignity of office in all who witnessed, whether they approved or disapproved.

Moreover, the Levellers taught and inspired by their example the radicalism that has been an undercurrent in English politics from the American Revolution to our own day. A few lines in a volume of Lilburne's pamphlets suggest the story in a few words. They were written by William Hone, the radical bookseller.[20]

> This Copy of John Lilburnes "Triall" with his "Legall Fundamentall Liberties of the People of England revived," and the other tracts forming the Volume, were collected and bound up by the late Mr. Jeremiah Joyce and often read by him in the Tower of London, when he was Prisoner there on a charge of High Treason—for which reason, and because Lilburne was a man exceedingly after my own heart, I greatly prize the volume.
>
> W. Hone
> 8 March 1820.

But here the direct influence of the Leveller movement on English politics comes to an end. It was the constitutional theory of Parker and Ireton, and not the theory of the Agreement of the People

---

[20] The volume is in the library of the Guildhall, London. In the library of the University of Chicago there are several copies of Lilburne's books with Hone's autograph.

that prevailed.   The Parliament supreme as representing the sovereignty of the state, the Houses
of Parliament absolute and unchecked—this is the
English Parliament of the nineteenth century.
The laws of nature and reason can check it only because the members are rational men, and therefore
amenable to reason; therefore the members of Parliament must themselves judge of the reason or
unreason of their actions.   The idea of a supreme
law that commands their obedience is completely
absent.   A House of Parliament may today "violate the English constitution," and there is no constitutional remedy for its act.

The Leveller constitutional theories, however,
have not vanished from the world.   Around the
fundamental principle of the limitation of government by paramount law, the Levellers developed
a body of constitutional and political doctrines
that suggest the main theories of American constitutional law.   The sovereignty of the people, the
inalienable right of the individual, the binding
force of paramount law, the enforcement of political
law by judicial action—all of these are American
doctrines.

While no attempt will be made to establish any
causal connection between the one body of doctrine
and the other, it may be suggested that they have
common origins.   In introductory chapters the
Leveller doctrines have been traced to two sources:
the ancient theory of the English constitution as
fundamental law, and the ecclesiastical polity of
the Independents.   In England, thanks to the social

confusion of the Great Civil War, both ideas reached an early maturity in the political system of the Levellers. In the colony of Massachusetts Bay the strength of the Puritan oligarchy weakened only in the course of years after 1660; and the innate political tendencies in Congregationalism grew more slowly, but also more surely. Moreover, as the connection of New England with Old England was stronger before 1660 than in later years, New England's political development was in the intellectual atmosphere of the ancient theory of the fundamental law rather than in the newer world of parliamentary supremacy. Of course many other factors went to form New England's contribution to American constitutional theory. Even before 1640 the charter and the plantation covenant had shown how they might become the written constitutions of states. John Locke had his influence in the critical days of the American Revolution; though John Locke merely said in 1690 what the Levellers had said in 1646. But, speaking broadly, may not the Leveller movement teach us that, while England was pledged to the supremacy of government by 1660, and while America a century later was led to the supremacy of law, the Anglo-Saxon race in 1640 stood at the parting of the ways between two theories, and might logically have adopted either?

BIBLIOGRAPHY

A word of explanation appears necessary at the beginning of the bibliography. This essay deals with certain special phases of the Great Civil War on which the secondary material can be exhausted by the enumeration of a very few titles. On the other hand, general works on the period are legion; but they usually accord a very brief and conventional treatment to the Levellers and their ideas. Therefore, as far as secondary works are concerned, no attempt will be made to do more than estimate several standard general treatises, and the few monographs that relate to the subject under discussion.

The main source of the material on which this essay is based is the Thomason collection of pamphlets in the British Museum. In view of the fact that a catalogue of the collection has been published, it seemed best to the Publication Committee of the American Historical Association, for the sake of space, to omit a selected bibliography of some seven hundred pamphlets that originally accompanied this essay. At the first citation of each pamphlet-title in the text a full bibliographical notation has been given. This, it is thought, will suffice. The source bibliography in the following pages includes the documentary collections, printed manuscript collections, manuscript calendars and contemporary memoirs that have been used.

BIBLIOGRAPHICAL AIDS

There is a general bibliography of the period 1640–1660 in the *Cambridge Modern History* (New York, 1906), volume IV, 884–904. A much briefer one is in F. C. Montague's volume in the *Political History of England* for 1603–1660, (London, 1907). Among special bibliographies, in *Notes and Queries* for 1888 there is an admirable one by Edward Peacock of pamphlet material relating to Lilburne. Lilburne printed a partial list of his writings in *The Innocent Man's second-Proffer* (London, 1649). The lives in the *Dictionary of National Biography* furnish special bibliographies, good or bad, according to the author of the life in question. H. M. Dexter, *The Congregationalism of the Last Three Hundred Years as seen in its Literature* (New York, 1880) has a good list of Independent literature. The *Catalogue of the Thomason Tracts* (2 vols., London, 1908) is an admirable guide to the great mass of pamphlet material. It is arranged chronologically, and takes advantage of Thomason's habit of dating his daily acquisitions to supply in the case of most tracts the day of publication. Its main defect is an insufficient index that takes too little account of long titles and of the large number of tracts whose authorship is unknown or disputed. As occasionally a tract is put under a date suggested by the title or content rather than the date of publication, one is often reduced to searching for a title by turning the leaves at random.

GENERAL WORKS

Only the most notable histories of the Great
Civil War can be named here. Dr. S. R. Gardiner's voluminous works of course have the claim
to prior mention. They include the *History of
England from the Accession of James I. to the Outbreak of the Civil War* (10 vols., London, 1883–
1884), the *History of the Great Civil War* (4 vols.,
London, 1898–1901), and the *History of the Commonwealth and Protectorate, 1649–1660* (3 vols. in 4,
London, 1894–1903). Gardiner wrote from acquaintance with a great body of source material,
and wrote with as little bias as any man can. In
fact his estimates of men and measures seem to fluc-
tuate from time to time as the estimates of an open-
minded and well-informed contemporary would
have done. This fluctuation has been made the
basis of an attack by Professor R. G. Usher (American Historical Association, *Report*, 1910, pp. 125 ff.).
Professor Usher selects isolated sentences, whole
volumes apart, subjects them to mathematical
analysis, and finds them inconsistent. But in many
cases such apparent contradictions are really correct
statements of different aspects of the same truth.
Bearing this in mind, the student seeking an acquaintance with contemporary thought will find
Gardiner an inspiration.[1] At certain points in the

[1] In *A Critical Study of the Historical Method of Samuel Rawson
Gardiner,* . . . By Roland G. Usher. [Washington Univ. Studies,
III, Pt. II, No. 1.] St. Louis, 1915, pp. 159, the onus of the attack is
rather ᴏn Gardiner's lack of a clear-cut concept of the constitution of
the seventeenth century; and a better case is made out.

present work an estimate different from Gardiner's has been put in evidence, but in each case it has been done with hesitation. In conclusion it may be said that Gardiner generally adopts a favorable view of the motives and conduct of Lilburne and the Levellers.

A few other general accounts may be mentioned. G. M. Trevelyan, *England under the Stuarts* (London, 1904) is a brilliantly written book, giving an extremely effective picture of seventeenth-century England, religious, social, and political. Lord Morley, *Oliver Cromwell* (New York, 1900) is as much an intellectual study of Cromwell and his contemporaries as a biography. Its judgments of Lilburne and the Levellers are severe. David Masson, *Life of John Milton* (7 vols., London, 1859–1894), does on a larger scale for Milton what Morley does for Cromwell. F. A. Inderwick, *The Interregnum* (London, 1891) is a series of historical sketches. On second hand authority, the author bestows his scorn on Lilburne in unusual measure. William Godwin, *History of the Commonwealth of England* (4 vols., London, 1824–1828) is written from the republican viewpoint and reveals a marked animus against Lilburne in his later career. The chapters of English history in the *Cambridge Modern History*, vol. IV, are excellent. Chapters VIII and IX are by Mr. G. W. Prothero, chapters X and XI by Prothero and Colonel Lloyd, chapters XII and XIII by Mr. W. A. Shaw, and chapter XIX by Professor C. H. Firth. F. C. Montague's volume in the *Political History of England, The History of England from the*

Accession of James I to the Restoration, 1603–1660
(London, 1907), is a solid account. Professor
Charles H. Firth's *The Last Years of the Protectorate, 1656–1658* (2 vols., London, 1909) is a model
of political history.

BIOGRAPHICAL MATERIAL

Masson and Lord Morley have already been
mentioned. Thomas Carlyle, *Letters and Speeches
of Oliver Cromwell* (best edition that of Mrs. E. C.
Lomas, 3 vols., London, 1904) is half a biography,
half a collection of letters and speeches. There
are several lives of Lilburne. *The Biographia Britannica* (vol. V, 2937–61, London, 1747–1766)
contains an excellent one, only marred by the
author's allowing *The Self-Afflicter lively Described*,
a wretched little tract of 1657, to mislead him in
his account of the last years of Lilburne's career.
The 1813–1820 edition of Anthony Wood's *Athenae
Oxonienses* contains a life of Lilburne that falls into
the same error as the *Biographia Britannica*. In
general, Wood's compilation affords a few scattered
bits of serviceable biography, and many statements
as to authorship of contemporary pamphlets. In
the case of books by or concerning the Levellers its
statements are often unreliable. Godwin's *Commonwealth* follows Lilburne's career with minuteness.
A. Bisset, in *Omitted Chapters of the History of England* (2 vols., London, 1864, 1867) and *History of the
Struggle for Parliamentary Government in England*
(2 vols., London, 1877), is warmly sympathetic to
Lilburne; both books suffer from the slightness of

the materials Bisset used.   Professor Firth's life of
Lilburne in the *Dictionary of National Biography*
(XXXIII, 243 ff.) is excellent, although the policy
of the work limited the author to a narration of
facts.   Eduard Bernstein, *Sozialismus und Demokratie in der grossen englischen Revolution* (2d ed.,
Stuttgart, 1908) interprets Lilburne's life in much
the same way as my essay.   Bernstein wrote from
notes collected by another person for a different
purpose; thus he falls into such errors as dating
Lilburne's marriage in 1646.   William Dugdale,
History of Imbanking and Drayning (London, 1662)
affords some chance information of value on a
critical transaction in Lilburne's career.

The Dictionary of National Biography contains
lives of several other men who appear in the narra-
tive.   Those by Professor Firth are without excep-
tion excellent.   Among these may be named: John
Wildman (LXI, 232), Richard Overton (XIII, 387),
Henry Marten (XXXVI, 263), Sir Arthur Haselrig
(XXVI, 292), Rainsborough (XLVII, 172), Henry
Ireton (XXIX, 37), William Prynne (XLVI, 432),
William Walwyn (LIX, 284).   Among lives by
other authors Alexander Gordon's life of John Goodwin (XXIII, 146) is good; W. A. S. Hewins's
Henry Parker (XLV, 340) is disappointing; D. S.
Thomas's David Jenkins (XXIX, 298) is well sup-
plemented by a chapter in Isaac Disraeli's *Com-
mentaries on the Life and Reign of Charles the First*
(2 vols., London, 1851).

MATERIAL FOR THE RELIGIOUS CONTROVERSY

Canon H. H. Henson, *Studies in English Religion in the Seventeenth Century* (London, 1903) is a series of studies in the main channels of religious thought. Hermann Weingarten, *Die Revolutionskirchen Englands. Ein Beitrag zur inneren Geschichte der englischen Kirche und der Reformation* (Leipzig, 1868), studies the intellectual and spiritual aspects of religion during the Civil War with special attention to the sects. R. Barclay, *The Inner Life of the Religious Societies of the Commonwealth* (London, 1878), attempts a similar treatment.

Modern religious or denominational histories usually follow closely certain well-defined conventions in their selection and treatment of topics; generally they do not consider the subject matter of chapter II at all. The following may be mentioned: R. W. Dale, *History of English Congregationalism* (London, 1907), J. Stoughton, *History of Religion in England* (6 vols., London, 1881), H. W. Clark, *History of English Nonconformity* (London, 1911–1913).

Of the older controversial works, Daniel Neal, *History of the Puritans* (1st ed., 4 vols., 1732–1738, enlarged ed., 3 vols., London, 1837) is valuable as representing a large mass of digested source material. B. Hanbury, *Historical Memorials relating to the Independents or Congregationalists* (3 vols., London, 1839–1844), describes the Presbyterian-Independent controversy with a strong Independent bias. W. M. Hetherington, *History of the Westminster Assem-*

bly of Divines (Edinburgh, 1843) is a biased Presbyterian account, but more inclined than Hanbury to be judicial. In this connection, one may note two discussions in the *English Historical Review* on the contents and authorship of a tract for liberty of conscience: S. R. Gardiner, vol. I, 144; Professor C. H. Firth, vol. X, 715. Dr. Wallace St. John, *The Contest for Liberty of Conscience in England* (Chicago, 1900), may be mentioned here.

DEMOCRATIC THEORIES

Bernstein's *Sozialismus und Demokratie*, already mentioned, emphasizes the democratic aspects of the Leveller movement. However, the author writes as an avowed Socialist, and over-emphasizes scattered manifestations of communistic sentiment; indeed he distorts his account of the Leveller movement to make it serve as a mere prelude to communism. As a result, his handling of Leveller politics is unsatisfactory. L. H. Berens, *The Digger movement in the days of the Commonwealth, as revealed in the writings of Gerrard Winstanley, the Digger, mystic, and rationalist, communist and social reformer* (London, 1906) is a monograph whose title indicates its nature. The treatment is so full that it has seemed unnecessary to consider the Diggers in the present work. G. P. Gooch, *History of English Democratic Ideas in the Seventeenth Century* (Cambridge, 1898) is based on wide information. It represents all that scholarship can do with broad fields of thought in the absence of monograph material.

The only fault is that the scope of the work necessitated a sketchy treatment, and did not allow a thorough comparison of the materials used. As a result the author does not always hit off the exact differences between the various political theories he describes. G. L. Scherger, *The Evolution of Modern Liberty* (New York, 1904) has the same fault in an accentuated degree. When an author allots a single chapter to Independents, Levellers and Whigs, he is attempting the impossible. Scherger's treatment of Leveller ideas is distinctly weak.

Among still more comprehensive accounts, T. E. May, *Democracy in Europe* (2 vols., London, 1877), and W. A. Dunning, *A History of Political Theories from Luther to Montesquieu* (New York, 1905) are both excellent for the period in question. C. Borgeaud, *The Rise of Modern Democracy in Old and New England* (trans. by Mrs. Hill, London, 1894) traces the democratic and constitutional outgrowths of the idea of church covenant, possibly laying too great stress on the analogy between covenant and written constitution. Professor Firth's introduction to volume I of the *Clarke Papers* (*infra*, p. 379) is an excellent summary of the constitutional debates of 1647.

CONSTITUTIONAL DISCUSSIONS

The standard constitutional works, such as D. J. Medley, *A Students' Manual of English Constitutional History* (4th ed., Oxford, 1907), are of no great assistance. T. P. Taswell-Langmead, *English Con-*

*stitutional History from the Teutonic Conquest to the
Present Time* (6th ed., London, 1905) dismisses the
eighteen years from the Militia Bill to the Restoration in five pages. Indeed, the average constitutional historian regards the period as an *interim* of
confusion in the midst of an orderly constitutional
development. Of course there are notable exceptions. F. W. Maitland in his *Constitutional History of England* (Cambridge, 1908) brought the
wonderful insight that distinguished this author in
the medieval field to bear on the later periods of
English history. Gardiner's passing constitutional
discussions show insight into the problems of the
Stuart period, although he sees his way less clearly
after 1642. An excellent short study by Gardiner is the introduction to his *Constitutional Documents of the Puritan Revolution* (3d ed., Oxford,
1906).

Several of the writers named above realize the
significance of the question between sovereignty of
Parliament and supremacy of law before 1642. But
it has been left for an American scholar, Professor
C. H. McIlwain, to grasp the significance of the
contest between the two principles in the broader
reaches of English history. In *The High Court of
Parliament and Its Supremacy* (New Haven, 1910),
Professor McIlwain has established a principle of
interpretation of which any future constitutional
historian must take careful note. W. Rothschild,
*Der Gedanke der geschriebenen Verfassung in der
englischen Revolution* (Tübingen, 1903), as its title
might indicate, is a study of written constitutions

with the emphasis on the word "written." For a criticism of Rothschild's method, *supra*, page 193. Borgeaud's may also be mentioned among constitutional studies.

MISCELLANEOUS

A few books used or cited can best be grouped under the head of miscellaneous. The use made of them is sufficiently indicated by the titles: J. N. Figgis, *The Theory of the Divine Right of Kings* (Cambridge, 1896), H. A. Glass, *The Barbone Parliament* (London, 1899), C. H. Firth, *Cromwell's Army* (London, 1902), and *The House of Lords during the Civil War* (London, 1910), Miss Louise Brown, *The Political Activities of the Baptists and Fifth Monarchy Men in England during the Interregnum* (Washington, 1912).

Source Material

OFFICIAL RECORDS AND COLLECTIONS OF STATE PAPERS

The most important official records are the *Journals* of the Lords and Commons (*Lords*, vols. III–X; *Commons*, vols. I–VI). The Lords' *Journals* were kept more fully than the Commons'; and ordinances, resolutions, reports, etc. are more apt to be entered in them at length. Edward Husband, *An Exact Collection of All Remonstrances, Debates, Votes and remarkable Passages between the King's most excellent Majesty and his High Court of Parliament* (1643) is what its title indicates.   It gives in full the declarations exchanged between king and Parliament to November, 1642.   Husband's *Collection of all the publike Orders, Ordinances and Declarations of both Houses of Parliament* (1646) is narrower in scope than his earlier work, being confined to enactments rather than state papers.   H. Scobell, *Collection of Acts and Ordinances of General Use made in the Parliament* (1658) is a similar work.   C. H. Firth and R. S. Rait have published a modern edition of ordinances, in *Acts and Ordinances of the Interregnum, 1649–1660* (3 vols., London, 1911).   John Rushworth, *Historical Collections* (1721 ed., 8 vols.) is a collection of state papers to 1649, connected by a kind of diurnal that usually is a mere summary of news and comment from current news-letters.   At times it is difficult to tell when Rushworth is quoting a document and when abstracting it.   His notes of the trial of the Earl of Strafford are the most precious part of the work.   John Nalson, *An Impartial Collection of the Great Affairs of State* (2 vols., 1683) is a similar work, if anything more valuable than Rushworth, although it extends only to 1642. For its preparation Nalson was given access to many state papers.   The so-called *Cobbett's Parliamentary History of England* (vols. II and III, 1806 *et seq.*) for this period is mainly a condensation of *The Parliamentary or Constitutional History* (usually cited as *Old Parliamentary History*, 24 vols., to 1660 complete, 1751–1766).   The last-named work is a compilation of the *Journals*, with speeches printed in contemporary pamphlets, and various scraps of information.

CONTEMPORARY MEMOIRS, ETC.

Clarendon's *History of the Rebellion*, though admittedly the historical classic of the period, is of little use for the purposes of this study. Clarendon never came into personal contact with any of the Levellers, and his accounts of them simply reflect the biased and inaccurate sources of his information and the defects of his memory. To the *Life* (Oxford, 1842) we are indebted for Clarendon's account of his habit of forging pamphlets. In the *English Historical Review*, XVI, 26, 246, 464, is an exhaustive criticism by Professor Firth on the relation of the various drafts of the *History* and the *Life*, the time of their composition, and their relative reliability. *The Memoirs of Colonel Hutchinson* (best edition, C. H. Firth, London, 1885) contain one or two vague references to the Levellers. *The Memoirs of Edmund Ludlow* (2 vols., C. H. Firth, ed., Oxford, 1894) have little more; they serve as a criterion of distinction between the republican and Leveller types of thought. The Memoirs of Sir John Berkeley (Maseres, *Select Tracts*, 2 vols., London, 1815) give an excellent, straightforward account of the negotiations of the army leaders with the king in 1647. *The Memoirs of Denzil Lord Holles from 1641–1648* (London, 1699) were apparently completed early in 1648, and accordingly are colored by violent partisan animosity. In the present work they are of importance because of Godwin's misapplication of one passage in them. John Selden, *Table Talk* (most convenient edition, E. Arber,

London, 1868), gives the mental outlook on the
great rebellion of a man inclined to hold aloof from
the world of action.   The *Table Talk* is a series of
pungent criticisms of the theories, arguments, and
actions of all parties alike.   It has suffered from
the topical arrangement adopted.   Again and again
Selden's sayings so manifestly refer to current
events, that one is tempted to name the month in
which they were uttered.   Like Rushworth, Bul-
strode Whitelocke, *Memorials of the English Affairs*
(4 vols., Oxford, 1853) is in great part made up of
newspaper comments and news; the *Memorials* are
interspersed with brief remarks and a few longer
reminiscences by Whitelocke.   Clement Walker,
Compleat History of Independency (London, 1661)
summarizes a series of the author's pamphlet as-
saults on the Independents in earlier years.   John
Milton's pamphlets have been quoted from his
Prose Works (1839).   Those used are: *Of Reformation in England* (1641); *Of Reformation in England,
the second book; The Reason of Church Government
Urged Against Prelacy*, 1641; *Animadversions upon
the Remonstrants' Defence against Smectymnuus*,
1641; *An Apology for Smectymnuus*, 1642; *Areopag-
itica*; *A Speech for the Liberty of Unlicensed Printing*, 1644; *The Tenure of Kings and Magistrates*
(1648–1649); *Eikonoklastes*, 1649; *Defensio Pro Populo Anglicano*, 1651; *Defensio Secunda Pro Populo
Anglicano*.

PRINTED OR CALENDARED MANUSCRIPTS

The most important printed manuscripts for the subject of this essay are the debates in the Council of the Army and the Council of War in 1647 and 1648, reported in the *Clarke Papers*, edited by Professor C. H. Firth (*Camden Society Publications*, vols. I and II, 1891–1894). The Clarke Papers printed are short-hand notes of debates that turned on questions of political theory; the very crudeness with which they have been transcribed from the short-hand assures the student that he is dealing with a source that has not been retouched.   John Lightfoot's notes of debates in the Assembly of Divines (*Works*, 13 vols., 1822–1825, vol. XIII) are valuable for an understanding of the ecclesiastical controversy.   So also is *The Letters and Journals of Robert Baillie* (3 vols., Edinburgh, 1841–1842).   A few printed or calendared manuscripts throw light on Lilburne's dealings with the Royalists.   Among them are: *The Calendar of the Clarendon State Papers in the Bodleian Library*, Oxford (W. Ogle, W. H. Bliss, W. D. Macray, 3 vols., Oxford, 1872–1876), *The Nicholas Papers* (ed. G. F. Warner, *Camden Society Publications*, vols. I, II, 1886–1892), and the *Collection of the State Papers of John Thurloe* (Thomas Birch, 7 vols., 1742). The confession of Major Thomas Scot, the Commonwealth's "master of intelligence" (printed in the *English Historical Review*, XII, 16), corroborates several of Lilburne's assertions regarding Hugh Riley and Wendy Oxford, the government's spies. *The Diary of Thomas Burton* (4 vols., Lon-

don, 1828) is a report of debates in the Protectorate
and Interregnum Parliaments ascribed to Thomas
Burton; it furnishes us with the debate in 1659 on
the reversal of the Rump's sentence against Lilburne. Little assistance is afforded by the *Calendar
of State Papers*, except that the *Calendar of the
Committee for Compounding* (5 vols., 1889–1892) contains papers relating to the Harraton colliery case.
There are chance bits of information scattered
through the *Reports of the Historical Manuscripts
Commission; The Fourth and Fifth Reports* (1874 and
1876), and the *Portland Mss.* (13th Report, App. I.,
1891) are cited above. The *Loder-Symonds Mss.*
(13th App. 4, 1892) contain a few of Henry Marten's
papers. In general it may be said that the manuscript sources so far unearthe and calendared add
very little to our knowledge of the essential facts of
the Leveller movement.

CONTEMPORARY PAMPHLETS

The main reliance in this essay has been on pamphlet material. The reasons for relying on it have
been briefly indicated in the Introduction. It is
contemporary, and as the pamphlets naturally link
themselves into long chains of controversial answer,
reply, and retort, one very often can obtain in it
two or three different partisan points of view. The
vast mass of the literature in itself is a protection.
The Thomason collection is incomplete; many pamphlets mentioned by contemporaries have utterly
disappeared, and others not in the collection survive

in but a single example; yet the Thomason collection contains over twenty thousand pieces. For present purposes it is believed that a sufficient number of pamphlets have been examined to ensure a reasonably broad view of contemporary religious and political discussion.

The user of this material must continually be on his guard against forgeries. John Forster was deceived by a series of speeches concocted for the five members on the occasion of the king's attempt to arrest them (Gardiner, X, 133). Mr. Gooch has erred in regarding the death-bed declaration of Alexander Henderson as a genuine document; it was really a Royalist forgery of 1648, as both internal and external evidence indicate (Gooch, p. 171; Neal, III, 558). In the *Somers Tracts* (VI, 577) is printed a pamphlet containing speeches by the Earl of Pembroke and Lord Brooke; the editor holds the speeches up to ridicule as typical examples of the oratorical extravagances of the parliamentary leaders. He is aware that Clarendon in his *Life* (p. 954) admitted concocting the speeches for his own amusement, but a burlesque vote of thanks that Clarendon appended to Brooke's speech transcends the editor's sense of humor, and induces him to pronounce the work genuine. Clarendon repeatedly forged such speeches or letters. It may be that some of the speeches quoted in Chapter I above are not authentic; but so long as they are not satires, they reflect, if not the ideas of the imputed speaker, at least the ideas that were generally current among men. Accordingly they are of service for the use to which they have been put.

There are a number of reprinted collections of
this literature. Two may be named: *The Harleian
Miscellany* (vols. IV–VI, 1808–1811) and the *Somers
Tracts* (*A Collection of Scarce and Valuable Tracts*,
2d ed., Walter Scott, editor, London, 1809–1815, vols.
III–VII). In addition to these reprints, several
works are based more or less frankly on the tract
literature, such as Hanbury, and Howell, *Complete
Collection of State Trials* (1809, vols. III–V). Moreover, every one of the standard compilations, such
as Rushworth, Nalson, Whitelocke, the *Parliamentary Histories*, owes very much more to contemporary pamphlets than might at first be supposed.

A brief description of the material may be attempted. The tracts proper include everything
from the broadside, petition, or ordinance, or the
four-page squib, to the weighty theological or political tract running to four hundred pages. For the
majority of these we are able to assign the approximate dates of publication, partly by Thomason's
notations of dates, partly from *imprimaturs*. The
literature supposedly passed through the hands of
licensers before being printed, but from 1645 to
1653 unlicensed books issued in streams from illicit
presses, and voiced the most outspoken criticisms
of the ruling powers. The newspapers were even
more difficult to censor than the tracts. The weekly
news-letter, issued under a permanent title, was
supplemented by "extras" containing fresh news,
with head-lines as deceptive as those of the extras
put forth by the yellow press today. Extensive
citations have been made for various dates from

the following journals. In each case the approximate dates of publication are given. *The Moderate* (Leveller, June 22, 1648–Sept. 25, 1649); *Mercurius Pragmaticus* (Royalist, Sept. 14, 1647–May 28, 1650, edited by Marchamont Nedham); after 1650 Nedham edited the Commonwealth *Mercurius Politicus* (June 6, 1650–June 7, 1660); *Mercurius Elencticus* (Royalist, Oct. 29, 1647–June 3, 1650); *The Man in the Moone* (Royalist, April 16, 1649–June 5, 1650). These papers are most often cited above. A few others are cited occasionally, but these need not be listed here. Newspapers of the time were at best ephemeral, and sprang up, decayed, and changed their titles so frequently that a complete bibliography would carry us far afield.

INDEX

NOTE. The reader will find under the title "Newspapers" all important references to Journals used; under "Pamphlets" there is a list, arranged alphabetically by titles, of all the important pamphlets cited or commented upon in this essay.

AGREEMENT of the People, analogy between, and system of Independents, 83; theory of, 200, 362; Cromwell's and Ireton's attitude toward, 212; advocated in *An Out Cry*, 288; would have abrogated English title to Ireland, 300; Leveller ideals in, 308, 310–311, 346; necessity of new king accepting, 312; declaration of the will of a sovereign people, 321–322; designed to establish democratic form of government, 359; *First* (1647): genesis of, 171, 199 ff., 253, 358; cause of, 200 ff.; Lilburne's influence on name and idea of, 205; nature of, 207–215, 218; provisions of, 207 ff.; Wildman's defense of, 212–213; debate on in Army Council, 215 ff.; outcome of, 224–225; petition for release of men concerned with, 229; Thompson's connection with, 231 n; signatures secured for, 233; attempt to limit Parliament by law stated by the people, 346; *Second* (1648): plans for a, 234; Levellers advocate, 258, 260, 275; Ireton proposes, 261 ff.; Lilburne's suggestions for committee to frame, 263; drafting of, 264; Levellers withdrew from committee of, 264; general attitude toward, 265–266; provisions of, 267 ff.; marked advance in political thought of Levellers, 269–270; *Third* (1649): danger of establishment of by mutineers, 285; demanded by

Derbyshire miners, 289; Levellers evolve, 301; Levellers promise, 316; provisions of, 317 ff.; mentioned, 93, 229, 230, 233, 241–242, 250, 255, 271, 275, 289, 310, 311, 313, 326, 346.

Allen, William, 186 n.

Anabaptists, 98, 99, 233, 247, 257, 286.

Antinomians, 98, 99, 247.

Arminians, 257.

Arnold, Richard, charges against Walwyn, 243 n.

Arnald, Richard, shot for mutiny, 225; mentioned, 229.

Assembly of Divines, purpose of calling, 50; New England ministers invited to, 97; discussion of growth of churches on Independent model, 98; controversy in, 51 ff., 68, 76 ff., 100–101; Lilburne accused, 101; Parliament petitioned to dissolve, 102–103.

Ayres, William, 225, 295, 297.

BAILLIE, Robert, Scotch commissioner at Westminster Assembly, 51 n; opinion on Independents, 54 n, 99; on Presbyterianism, 79; on influence of Manchester's army on Scotch army, 98; on New Model Army, 166; mentioned, 61, 65 n.

Barkstead, John, 87.

Barrow, Henry, 343.

Bartlet, John, 334 n.

Barwis, Richard, charges against, 131.

Bastwick, John, taunted Independents on exclusiveness, 84;

acquaintance with Lilburne, 88; opinion of Lilburne, 98 n, 103, 107–108; Lilburne wrote letter against, 103 n; informed Parliament against Lilburne, 104; reason for persecuting Lilburne, 105; Lilburne's opinion of action, 106 n.

Bellamy, John, opinion on danger of Independents' principles, 123–124; fixed radical doctrine on Independents, 124–125.

Berkeley, Sir John, 232 n.

Berkeley, Robert, opinion on rule of law and of government, 8.

Berkenhead, *see* Birkenhead.

Berkshire, Leveller activity in, 274, 361; mentioned, 275 n.

Birkenhead, Isaac, 334 n.

Bray, Robert, arrested for mutiny, 225.

Brentford, Lilburne commanded at defense of, 94.

Bridge, William, one of five Holland ministers, 52 n; opinion of authority of presbytery, 59 n.

Brook, Robert, author of *Charity of Churchmen*, 244 n; mentioned, 248 n, 255; opinion of Walwyn, 252, 256.

Brooke, Lord, ascribed juridical power to bishops and judges, 45; author of *Discourse Opening The Nature Of That Episcopacie*, 45, 67 n, 69 n; opinion on divine right of episcopacy, 67; Lilburne enlisted in regiment of, 94.

Browne, Robert, separatist, devised a democratic church order, 52; influence compared with Lilburne's, 356.

Browne, William, imprisoned by House of Commons, 161.

Brownists, 53, 256, 257.

Buckingham, Duke of, Lilburne's connection with, 333–334.

Buckinghamshire, petitions from, 172; Leveller petition circulated in, 234; Levellers numerous in, 361.

Bunyan, John, 100 n.

Burford, Fairfax surprised mutineers at, 281 ff.

Burnet, Henry, charges against Walwyn, 243 n.

Burroughs, Jeremiah, one of five Holland ministers, 52 n.

Burton, Henry, author of *Protestation Protested*, 69; interpretation of the Protestation, 69 ff.; Edwards attacks position of, 71; mentioned, 75; read by Lilburne, 87 n; Baillie's opinion of, 99.

Calvin, John, 60, 87 n.

Calvinists, 51, 84, 85.

Cambridge, Leveller petition sent to, 234.

Capel, Lord, trial of, illegal, 272, 273; mentioned, 276, 277, 299; Lilburne's advice to, 310 n.

Charles I, opinion on divine right, 8–9; Long Parliament's attitude toward prerogative of, 10–11; refused assent to Militia Ordinance, 20; replies to Grand Remonstrance, 38–39; opinion on New Model Army, 166; prisoner, 166; terms of Heads of the Proposals not accepted by, 171; escape of, 177, 178; Lilburne's attitude toward, 181 ff.; Leveller alleged plots for assassination of, 189 ff.; attitude toward High Court of Justice, 273; Fifth Monarchy interpretation of execution of, 306; Levellers' objections to, 312.

Charles II, 285, 354; Levellers' attitude toward, 312.

Chidley, Samuel, one of Levellers imprisoned, 230 n; mentioned, 361.

Chillenden, Edmund, 89 n; author of *Inhumanity of Kings Prison-Keeper*, 94 n; Lilburne assisted, 96 n.

City Remonstrance, reception of by Independents, 122 ff.; significance of contest over, 148; mentioned, 180 n.

Coachman, Robert, author of *Cry Of A Stone*, 85; opinion of spiritual deadness of parish assemblies, 85.

Coke, Sir Edward, belief in supremacy of common law, 61; Lilburne's use of doctrines of, 238 n, 239, 342; Lilburne quotes as authority in 1653, 338.

Coke, Thomas, accuses Levellers of correspondence with Royalists, 331 n.

Coleman, Thomas, belief in state control of church, 60; author of *Hopes Deferred and Dashed*, 77 n; stated Erastian position and answered by Gillespie, 77.

Colepeper, Lord, Lilburne's connection with, 334.

Communism, Ireton's view of, 222; Walwyn and, 255–256; Levellers charged with, 315.

Cook, John, author of *Vindication Of The Professors & Profession Of The Law*, 155; states defects in law of seventeenth century, 155.

Corkbush Field, 225, 232 n, 254.

Cornwall, Peters influence in, 103 n; attempts a separate peace, 135 n.

Cotton, John, Independency not democracy, 52; opinion of New England church government, 53 n; author of *Keyes of the Kingdom of Heaven*, 53 n; *Way of the Churches Cleared*, 53 n; *Way of the Churches in New England*, 58 n; necessity of his re-ordination in New England, 59; alleged democracy of, 85; mentioned, 54 n, 82.

Council of State, provision for, in second Agreement of the People, 267; Lilburne demands abolition of, 274; Levellers imprisoned by orders of, 276; erection of, as executive of government, 302; mentioned, 278, 299, 308, 317, 327, 333, 335, 340.

Cowling, Nicholas, 228.

Cranford, James, 104.

Crawley, Justice, 45.

Crewe, John, 104.

Cromwell, Oliver, supported by Lilburne, 95, 96 n, 259, 327; proposed committee where any one might inform against Parliament, 111; Lilburne's relations with, 171 ff.; radicals' distrust of, 176, 201; Lilburne's attitude toward, 177, 293 n; urged by Lilburne to keep understanding with king, 182; marched on London, 186 n; alleged plots of Levellers against, 189, 190–191; policy frustrated (1647), 200; attitude toward Agreement of the People, 211 ff., 224–225; comparison between Levellers and, 216 ff., 236–237, Thompson arrested by orders of, 231 n; suppressed mutineers at Burford, 281–282; soldiers reprieved by (1649), 282; criticism of measures against mutineers, 282 ff.; Levellers' attitude toward, 308, 340 n; influence in banishing Lilburne, 331; Royalists believed Lilburne intended to murder, 334 n; Lilburne's contradictory opinions of, 335; held Lilburne prisoner, 348, 353; installed Lord Protector, 348, 349; idea of fundamental law, 351; mentioned, 134, 167, 188, 190, 232 n, 254, 279.

Crosseman, John, petition of, 230.

Crow, Sir Sackville, Levellers supposed to have correspondence with, 331 n.

Cumberland, charges made by men of, against Barwis, 131.

Davenport, John, invited to Assembly of Divines, 97.

Dell, William, 189.

Denne (or Den), Henry, 281–282, 285, 300.

Derbyshire, Leveller uprising in, 289.

Dering, Sir Edward, opinion on Grand Remonstrance, 17.

Devonshire, action of, 125 n.

Digby, Lord, 20; Holles's correspondence with, 104.

Divine right, Parliament questions king's, 7 ff.; of church government, 9, 51, 56, 58, 63, 66, 67 ff.; bishops sanction king's, 9; Fiennes discusses, 46–47; of Presbyterianism, 51, 63, 72; Independents' use of, 51, 58, 66, 83; Independents and Presbyterians discuss, 52 n; of institution of episcopacy, 67; Goodwin declares Independency of, 73–74; Prynne's and Goodwin's controversy over, 76; Erastians and Presbyterians struggle over, 77 ff.; Levellers' conception of, 137, 149; Royalists' use of, 303–304; use of by defenders of Commonwealth, 306.

Dover, 332 n.

Dover Castle, 353.

Downing, Calybute, author of *Sermon preached to the Renowned Company of the Artillery*, 45; makes distinction between rule of government and rule of law, 45.

Duell, Elizabeth, Lilburne married, 92.

Earle, Walter, Tulidah accused by, 160; mentioned, 161.

Eaton, Samuel, author of *Oath of Allegiance And The National Covenant*, 302 n.

Edgehill, Lilburne fought at, 94.

Edward the Confessor, laws of, 133, 145.

Edwards, Thomas, author of *Gangraena*, 65 n; argued against Burton for power of synod, 71; accused Prynne of Erastian tendencies, 72 n; taunted Independents on exclusiveness, 84; opinion on growth of Independent churches, 98 n; account of Windmill Tavern episode, 102 n;

opinion of Peters, 103 n; opinion of Lilburne's motives, 107 n; actions toward Independents, 121; opinion of New Model Army, 164; Walwyn's defense of toleration against, 250; mentioned, 79, 101 n, 251 n.

Erastians, principles of, 60; ecclesiastical controversy with Independents and Presbyterians (1641–1646), 60 ff.; struggle with Independents, 72 ff.; position of, set forth by Coleman, 77; mentioned, 121, 269.

Erastus, Thomas, name applied to party, 60.

Erbury, William, attitude toward second Agreement of the People, 266 n.

Essex, Earl of, 166 n.

Fairfax, Sir Thomas, Lilburne's esteem for, 176; made new proposal in place of Agreement, 224; power given to, 230; suppressed mutineers at Burford, 281–282; criticism of his measures against mutineers, 282 ff.; mentioned, 167, 174 n, 186 n, 191, 202, 254, 279.

Feak, John, 332 n.

Ferne, Henry, 33.

Fiennes, Nathaniel, sets forth parliamentary power usurped by bishops, 44; sets forth Parliament's distrust of ecclesiastical application of law of nature, 46–47; mentioned, 154.

Foster, Henry, charges against Walwyn, 243 n.

Fox, John, 87.

Fuller, Thomas, author of *Sermon of Reformation*, 69 n.

Geree, John, author of *Vindiciae Voti*, 70; opinion of Parliament's supremacy over church, 70–71.

Gillespie, George, speaks for Presbyterians in refuting Coleman, 77; mentioned, 79.

Glynn, John, Leveller petition sent to, 159 n.

Godwin, William, "discovered" plot to kill Cromwell, 191; mentioned, 333 n.

Goffe, William, 217.

Goodwin, John, Independent, 52 n; author of *Innocency and Truth Triumphing*, 58 n; argument of, for liberty of conscience, 65–66; author of *Innocencies Triumph*, 65 n; author of *M. S. To A. S. With a Plea for Libertie of Conscience*, 65 n; author of *Theomachia*, 66 n; author of *Certain briefe Observations and Antiquaeries: On Master Prins Twelve Questions*, 73 n; author of *Calumny Arraign'd And Cast*, 73 n; advocates divine right of Independency, 73–74; attacks Prynne's use of law of nature, 74; *Anti-Cavalierisme* quoted, 82; expresses in *Anti-Cavalierisme* typical spirit of men in Civil War, 93; Baillie's opinion of, 99; Lilburne complains of congregation of, 172; dislike for Walwyn, 245; mentioned, 76, 146, 177, 251 n, 269.

Goodwin, Thomas, one of five Holland ministers, 52 n; opinion on authority of presbytery, 58 n; opinion on ordination, 59 n.

Government, Parliament's sovereignty in, 7 ff.; distinction between rule of law and rule of, 8–9, 45 ff.; share of people in, 11, 29, 36 ff., 40, 110–111, 117, 120, 139, 144, 150 ff., 181 ff., 193, 205, 218–219, 315; Parliament's sovereignty based on compact theory of origin, 13 ff., 42–43, 182; Parliament accepts law of *salus populi*, 18 ff., 38; sovereignty of, based on law of nature, 23 ff.; Parker's opinions respecting, 23 ff., 31; various comments on compact theory of origin, 30 ff.; Royalists' attitude toward, 39 ff.,

42–43; supremacy of principle of *salus populi*, 45–46, 124; comparison of Independent and Presbyterian ecclesiastical, 51 ff., 62; supremacy of Parliament over church in matters of, 68 69; of Independents' system, 71; Independents' ideas, 82, 84; Cotton's and Williams's doctrine of democracy in, 85; Lilburne's opinions, 114, 115; Levellers' belief in compact theory of origin, 120, 137, 139 ff., 358; dissatisfaction with, in pamphlets of 1645, 132; Levellers advocate local autonomy in, 134–135; conquest theory of origin set forth in *Regall Tyrannie*, 144 ff.; Levellers advocated democracy in, 146 ff., 229, 236–237, 359 ff.; compact theory of origin advocated in *Remonstrance of Many Thousand Citizens*, 146 ff.; conquest theory of origin, laws a badge of conquest, 155; theories of, in 1647, 179 ff.; Levellers advocated limitation of, by law, 194, 197 ff., 311, 326, 346, 363; Levellers' use of conquest theory of origin, 216, 218; first Agreement and democracy in, 218 ff.; Ireton's conception of, 219 ff.; separation of powers of, 238 ff., 352; second Agreement sets forth, 265 ff.; founding and legality of Commonwealth, 278–279, 301 ff.; Lilburne refers to conquest theory of origin, 296; principle of *salus populi* used by Commonwealth, 302–303; compact theory of origin used by Commonwealth, 303–304; conquest theory of origin mentioned, 312; third Agreement sets forth, 316 ff.; democracy in third Agreement, 322; Lilburne proved fundamental law greater than, 340 ff.; Protectorate's justification of, 348–

349; Levellers place law before, 352–353; supremacy of in 1660, 364. *See* Law.

Grand Remonstrance (1641), significance of, in House of Commons, 16; Royalists attitude toward, 16–17, 38–39; Dering's opinion of, 17; beginning of Parliament's claim to sovereignty, 18; Charles I's reply to, 38–39.

Great Charter. *See* Magna Charta.

Great Civil War, 23, 60, 93, 146, 151, 167, 177, 242, 364; importance of radicals in, 152; connection of Levellers with, 356.

Greenwood, John, 343.

Grey, George, involved in dispute with Haselrig, 328–329.

Grimston, Sir Harbottle, speech of, 17; designates Parliament a court, 43; opinion in ship money case, 44.

HABERDASHERS HALL, decision of committee of, in Harraton colliery dispute, 329 n; committee of, 347.

Hacker, Francis, in Harraton colliery dispute, 329.

Hadley, Catherine, 92 n.

Hall, Bishop, opinion regarding supremacy of Parliament over church, 71; author of *Survay Of That Foolish, Seditious, Scandalous, Prophane Libell, The Protestation Protested*, 71 n.

Hamilton, Duke of, trial illegal, 272, 273.

Hammersmith, 94.

Hampden, John, 16.

Hampshire, Leveller activity in, 274, 361.

Harraton, dispute over colliery in, 328, 331, 339–340.

Harrison, Thomas, attempted to conciliate Lilburne, 263; mentioned, 267, 281, 307.

Haselrig, Sir Arthur, Lilburne's hatred for, 288; Lilburne's dispute with over colliery, 328–

329; Mrs. Lilburne attempts to secure Lilburne's recall from, 335; connection with Lilburne's sentence, 347; mentioned, 332.

Hawkins, Captain, imprisoned by House of Commons, 105; member of party about Lilburne, 107.

Heads of the Proposals, 171, 203; reforms advocated by, 184 n; 226–227; instability of, 194, 200; drawn up by Ireton, 194 n.

Henson, Canon, 60 n.

Herle, Charles, author of *Fuller Answer To A Treatise Written by Doctor Ferne*, 32 n; and *Independency on Scripture of the Independency of Churches*, 55 n.

Hertfordshire, petitions from, 172; Leveller petition sent to, 234; Leveller activity in, 274, 361.

High Court of Justice, Lilburne attacked legality of, 271 ff., 276; erection of, 302, 305; mentioned, 308, 310 n, 327 n.

Hobson, Paul, accuses Levellers of plot to kill king, 189.

Holland, 52, 88, 89, 98.

Holland, Earl of, trial of, illegal, 272, 273; mentioned, 277, 299.

Holland, Sir John, 11 n.

Holles, Denzil, Parliament investigated rumor concerning, 104; Independents push charges against, 105; Presbyterian leader, 157; Tulidah accused by, 160; radical petition given, for presentation, 161; mentioned, 94, 173, 174, 191.

Hone, William, 362.

Hooker, Thomas, invited to Assembly of Divines, 97.

Hopton, Lord, Lilburne's connection with, 333.

House of Commons, prints Grand Remonstrance, 16; beginnings of sovereignty in, 17–18; Parker's opinion of power of, 26; sovereignty of, 29–30; members of, in what sense representative of the people, 40; Pym describes functions of, 44; ordered Downing's sermon printed, 45; commanded oath to defend reformed religion, 69; struggle between Presbyterians and, 78–79; voted Lilburne's imprisonment illegal, 92; warfare on heresy, 99; investigated charges of treason against its members (1645), 103–104; Lilburne imprisoned by (1645), 105–106; freed Lilburne, 107; reprimands Stationers for printing unlicensed matter, 110 n; action on unlicensed preaching, 110 n; Lilburne's attitude toward (1645), 113; actions of, on Merchant Adventurers, 118–119; authority of, 120; Levellers extol authority of, 121; Presbyterians' attitude toward, 121; attitude of City Remonstrance to, 122; Lilburne charged King in, 125; Lilburne petitioned for protection against Lords, 126 ff.; Lilburne urges new elections of, 135; government by, 145; power assigned to, by *Remonstrance Of Citizens*, 148 ff.; radicals petition and quarrel with, 156 ff.; condemned petition of soldiers (1647), 165 ff.; members flee to army (1647), 169–170; Presbyterians excluded from, 170, 301, 305; Lilburne denies legal authority of, 175 ff.; Levellers' attitude toward, 179 ff.; Lilburne's attitude toward (1647), 191–192; Levellers petition, 229 ff.; referred Lilburne to special committee, 259; Levellers' ideal of supremacy of, 310–311; mentioned, 132, 172, 204, 263. *See also* House of Lords, Long Parliament, Parliament.

House of Lords, attitude of House of Commons toward, 17–18; investigates precedents on king's veto power, 20–21; rights of,

28; delayed reparation to Lilburne, 92; authority of, over nation, 120; attitude of City Remonstrance to, 122; controversy as to source of power of, 124; Lilburne incurs hostility of, 125; summoned Lilburne, 126 ff.; tried and sentenced Lilburne, 128–129; attempt to arouse public opinion against, 130–131; radicals argue against judicial power of, 144; government by, 145; jurisdiction over Commons, 153–154, 158; members absent when army entered London (1647), 170; question of abolishing veto of, 197, 233; revoked Lilburne's sentence, 259; Lilburne's idea of, 311; mentioned, 195. *See also* House of Commons, Long Parliament, Parliament.

Howard, Lord of Escrick, 333 n.

Humble Petition and Advice, 351.

Hunton, Philip, author of *Treatise of Monarchie*, 34; opinion on origin of government, 34 ff; opinion of arbitrary power, 137; idea of three co-ordinate estates, 139; Levellers completed ideas of, 346; mentioned, 37, 222.

Hyde, Edward, drew up declarations of king to Parliament, 39; prefers Leveller alliance to Presbyterian, 313; feared Lilburne's influence with Royalists, 334.

INDEPENDENTS, ecclesiastical controversy with Presbyterians and Erastians (1641–1646), 50 ff., 102 ff.; radicals form Leveller party, 50, 103, 107–108, 156; undemocracy of, 56–57, 82, 84–85; believe in divine law, 61–62, 66, 73, 79, 83; doctrines of, growing out of debates of Westminster Assembly, 62 ff.; seek Erastian support, 63–64;

Presbyterians attack, 64; struggle with Erastians, 72 ff.; overcome by Presbyterians in Westminster Assembly, 76–77; influence on Levellers, 80 ff.; criticise House of Commons for Lilburne's imprisonment, 86; beginnings of party (1641), 97; political distinction between Presbyterians and, 97; Lilburne closely allied to, 97, 101; attitude toward Parliament, 97; growth of their churches checked, 98; numerous heretical opinions among, 98–99; members of, in New Model Army, 98, 166; Baillie's opinion of, 99; Parliament's policy detrimental to, 108–109; criticise policy of Long Parliament, 110–111; tracts of, issued from hidden presses, 110 n; political position of radicals, 120–121; attitude toward Presbyterians after issue of City Remonstrance, 122 ff.; radicals become interested in constitutional reform, 125; petition in behalf of Lilburne, 129 ff.; radicals develop political and constitutional reforms (1646), 131 ff.; break with House of Commons over petitions (1647), 157 ff.; gain control of London (1647), 169 ff.; break with Grandees of party, 171 ff.; justify army, 184; position of, 188; reconciliation with Levellers, 231; Walwyn's connection with, 245 ff.; alliance with Levellers broken (1648), 258 ff.; Levellers attack action of, 270 ff.; mentioned, 202, 237 n, 251.

Ingram, John, petition of, 230.

Instrument of Government, 351.

Ireland, soldiers question campaign in, 279; Leveller influence on soldiers as to campaign, 300; Agreement of the People affected English authority in, 300.

Ireton, Henry, author of Solemn Engagement, 168 n; Lilburne's and Overton's doctrines avoided by, 168 n; distrust of Levellers for, 176, 201; opinion on status of army, 186 n; author of Heads of Proposals, 194; failures of policy of, 200; connection with Agreement of the People, 212, 218 ff., 261 ff., 266; constitutional theories of, 218 ff., 362; debates with Levellers in Army Council on Agreement of the People, 218 ff.; political theories of, 268–269; mutiny in regiment of, 280; mentioned, 104, 215, 224, 302.

Ives, Jeremy, one of Levellers imprisoned, 230 n.

Jenkins, David, alleged influence over Lilburne, 178.

John, king by election, 145.

Johnson, Thomas, author of *Plea for Free-Mens Liberties*, 119.

Joyce, Cornet George, 163, 167.

Joyce, Jeremiah, 362.

Keble, Richard, 294.

Kent, Leveller petition sent to, 234.

Kiffen, William, Walwyn arraigned by, 242 ff.; mentioned, 247, 252, 332 n.

King, Colonel, Lilburne commissioned under, 95; connection with proceedings against Lilburne, 96 n, 97, 104, 105 n, 125–126; appointed commander in Lincolnshire, 134; proceedings of Lords against, 153–154; mentioned, 173.

Kingston, 177 n.

Lambert, John, connection with Heads of Proposals, 194 n.

Larner, William, 130 n; imprisoned, 131, 230 n.

Laud, Archbishop William, 15, 91, 340.

Law, common, dissatisfaction with, in pamphlets (1645), 132.

Law, fundamental, Parliament's use of, 7 ff.; abandoned by Parliament for *salus populi*, 38 ff.; Independents defenders of, 62, 83, 84, 86; Leveller theories based on, 83, 313, 352–353, 363–364; rights of people under, 83; imprisonment of Lilburne, contrary to, 86, 89; Lilburne's zeal for, 108, 112 ff., 132, 340 ff.; to be saved by recurrence to law of nature, 180; basis of Agreements, 285, 311; Parliament set itself above, 345–346; Norwood's theory of, 350–351.

Law, supremacy of, attacked, 8–9; Long Parliament upholds, 10 ff.; principles of, 12–13; Pym's opinion of, 12; Parliament's defense of, 23 ff.; Independents uphold, in ecclesiastical affairs, 50, 56, 58, 82–83; Levellers advocated, 83–84, 241–242, 301, 348–349, 359; theories of (1647), 179 ff.; first Agreement sets forth, 193 ff.; limitation of government by, ideal of Levellers, 194, 197 ff., 311, 326, 346, 363; protection of, to vested interests, 219–220; abandoned in nineteenth-century England, 363; accomplished in eighteenth-century America, 364.

Law of God, Parliament's use of, 46; Independents' belief in, 62; mentioned, 68, 155, 219, 220; Robinson's application of, 75 n; Levellers' belief in, 83, 343; Lilburne's demand for, 89, 115; in Magna Charta, 117–118; Levellers rely on (1646), 137–138; Walwyn's belief in, 251.

Law of nature, 11 n, 363; Parliament's use of, 23 ff., 46–47; Parker's opinion on, 24 ff.; Presbyterians' opinion of, 62; Prynne bases submission of church government to civil, on, 74 ff.; Robinson's application

of, 75 n; Independents interpretation of, 84; Levellers' interpretation of, 137, 142, 358–359; to save fundamental law, 180.

Law of reason, Levellers' belief in, 83, 137–138, 229, 343, 358–359; Lilburne's argument for, 115; found in Magna Charta, 117–118; mentioned, 155, 363.

Lawmind, John. *See* Wildman, John.

Leicester, 102, 166.

Lenthall, William, charges against conduct of, 104, 105.

Levellers, influenced by earlier pamphlet warfare, 42; political ideas derived from ecclesiastical controversy (1641–1646), 50, 80 ff.; radical Independents so named (1647), 50, 92, 156, 177; Independent influence on, 84, 143; Lilburne exemplified principles of, 86; beginnings of party, 107–108; source of constitutional settlement of, 133 n; policy of, 135; state social compact theory, 142; evolution of ideas of, 148 ff.; connection with assassination plots against king, 169 ff.; attitude of, toward restoration of king by army, 179 ff.; propose first Agreement of the People, 193 ff.; debate on first Agreement of the People, 215 ff.; defeated on first Agreement of the People, 224–225; organize party, 229 ff.; Walwyn's connection with, 243, 245–246, 251 ff.; criticism of organization of, 254–255; alliance with Independents (1648) broken, 258 ff.; petition House of Commons, 259; mutiny in army due to, 279 ff.; attitude toward Irish campaign (1649), 300; propose third Agreement of the People, 301; attitude toward Commonwealth, 307 ff.; Agreement of the People published by (1648),

317 ·ff.; Lilburne's effect on constitutional ideas of, 326 ff., 337, 342 ff.; disappearance of, 348 ff.; résumé of ideas of, 356. *See* Independents; Lilburne.

Leverett, 59.

Liberty of conscience, Robinson at issue with Prynne on, 75–76; supported by radical Independents, 82; basis of creed of Levellers, 82; Lilburne's interest in, 120.

Lightfoot, John, 60.

Lilburne, George, involved in dispute with Haselrig, 328–329; uncle of John, 328.

Lilburne, Henry, reveals plot to kill king, 189–190.

Lilburne, John, exemplified principles of Levellers, 86; early life, 87 ff.; reading, 87 n; adopted Puritan doctrines and became a Separatist, 88; association with Bastwick and Wharton, 88; trial and imprisonment for printing Puritan books, 88 ff.; character of, 90, 94 ff.; influence over the people, 91; Long Parliament liberated, 92; married, 92; entered Parliament's army, 92–93; captured, tried and exchanged, 94–95; refused to take Covenant (1645), 95; politically active in London, 96–97; injured in Moorfields, 101 n; defends Independents against Westminster Assembly, 101; chosen on committee to petition Parliament, 102; Peters's association with, 103 n; Bastwick's reasons for persecuting, 103, 105; House of Commons imprisons, 105 ff.; petition for release of, 106–107; liberated by House (1645), 107; party about, 107–108; advocates new theories of government, 108 ff.; influenced by *Englands Lamentable Slaverie*, 116 ff.; attacks monopoly of Merchant Adventurers, 118; effect

of criticism of Long Parliament, 120; affiliated with Independent party, 120; attitude toward City Remonstrance, 122; delay in settlement of claims, 125 n; prosecutes Col. King in House of Commons, 125; criticism of Earl of Manchester, 126, 128; attitude toward House of Lords, 127 ff.; committed to Newgate, 127; trial (1646) and sentence of, 128 ff.; antagonism to common law, 132 ff.; urges re-apportionment of House of Commons, 135; supports protest against government of London, 135–136; fundamental ideas of, 139 ff.; recommended petition to Parliament, 162; relations with Independents, 171–172; relations with Cromwell, 171 ff.; influence on New Model Army, 174; denied legal authority of House of Commons (1647), 175; misunderstanding with Marten, 175 n; distrust of Cromwell and Ireton, 176; favored by Royalists, later attacked by them, 177–178; opinion on power of king and House of Commons, 181 ff.; theory of New Model Army, 185–186; connection with plot to kill king, 189 ff.; antagonism to House of Commons (1647), 191–192; influence on Agreement of the People, 205; protested against the Covenant, 227; published petitions against army officers, 230; distrusted religious enthusiasm in politics, 231–232; controlled army agents, 232; takes part in organization of Levellers, 234; imprisoned for Leveller petition (1648), 237; advocated separation of government powers, 238 ff.; Walwyn's influence over, 242, 252; supports Cromwell, 259, 327–328; member of committee to frame second Agreement of the People, 263; obtained estates in Durham, 271; attacked High Court of Justice, 271 ff.; renewed political activity (1649), 274; imprisoned, 276; interpretation of Solemn Engagement, 284; charges of *Walwins Wiles*, 287; hatred for Haselrig, 288, 330; trial (1649), 278, 290 ff.; acquittal, 297–298, 327; defense criticised, 298 ff.; conversation with Peters, 307–308, 324–325; attacked Rump's legal position, 308 ff.; attitude toward military despotism, 311; opinion of Charles II's restoration, 312; influence on Leveller party, 326–327; turns soapboiler (1649), 328; involved with Haselrig through Harraton colliery case, 328 ff.; banished, 330; holds Cromwell responsible for banishment, 331–332; connection with Royalists, 331, 333–334; in Holland, 333–334; attempts to return to England, 334 ff.; contradictory opinions of Cromwell, 335; trial (1653), 336 ff.; cause of banishment, 346 –347; acquittal, 348; kept prisoner by Cromwell, 348, 353; became Quaker, 353, 355; died (1657), 353; insignificance of last years, 354–355; influence on public affairs, 356, 362; mentioned, 56 n, 121, 124, 134, 135, 141, 143 n, 147, 153 n, 175, 186 n, 217, 246, 247, 278, 298, 321 n, 322, 327, 361. WRITINGS: *Rash Oaths unwarrantable* (1647), 56 n; *Come out of her, my people* (1640), 92 n; *Prisoners Plea for a Habeas Corpus* (1648), 92 n; *Iust Mans Iustification* (1646), 98 n; *resolved mans Resolution* (1647), 101 n; *England's Birthright Justified* (1645), 108 ff.; *Copy of a Letter,* (1645), 112; *Innocency And Truth Justified* (1645), 115; *Free-Mans Freedome Vindicated* (1646), 128;

Anatomy of the Lords Tyranny (1646), 130; *Ionahs Cry out of the Whales belly* (1647), 171 n; *Iuglers Discovered* (1647), 174 n; *Two Letters: The One From Lievtenant Colonell John Lilbourne To Colonel Henry Martin . . . With His Answer,* 175 n; *Two Letters writ by Lievt Col. John Lilburne, Prerogative prisoner in the Tower* (1647), 176 n; *Out-cryes of oppressed Commons* (1647), 180; *Defiance to Tyrants* (1647), 239 n; *Impeachment Of High Treason Against Oliver Cromwell* (1649), 284 n, 288; *Preparative To An Hue And Cry after Sir Arthur Haselrig* (1649), 288; *Legal Fundamentall Liberties* (1649), 288; *Strength out of Weaknesse,* 290 n; *Salva Libertate,* 291; *Just Defence of John Lilburne against Such as charge him with Turbulency of Spirit* (1653), 353–354.

Lilburne, Mrs. John, House of Lords prohibits visits to husband, 129 n; influence on John, 300; efforts for husband's release, 335, 347; mentioned, 173.

Lilburne, Robert, 225, 291, 292 n, 294.

Locke, John, influence of, 364.

Lockyer, Robert, shot for mutiny, 279; effect of execution on soldiers, 280; mentioned, 353, 360.

Long Parliament, limits power of king, 10–11; exemption of members from civil suits, 11 n; assumes power to interpret law, 13; split of constitutional party in, 16; justified position by law of *salus populi,* 18; sovereignty set forth in Declaration (May 19, 1642), 19–20; orders army to be raised, 21–22; Hunton's defense of, 34 ff.; calls Westminster Assembly, 50; controversy with Westminster Assembly, 67 ff.; commits printer of the *Protestation Protested*, 70; Lilburne set at liberty by, 92; Independents' attitude toward, 97, 105, 139, 184 ff.; Lilburne attacks for suffering persecution of Independents, 100–101; Lilburne member of committee to petition, 102; petitioned to dissolve Assembly of Divines, 102–103; radicals dissatisfied with, 108; corruptness of, 110 n, 111, 202; limits preaching, 112; Lilburne criticises policy of, 118, 120; City Remonstrance to, 122; Lilburne warns to uphold rights of people, 122; defenders of, interpret law of nature, 142–143; attitude toward Leveller ideals, 193; instability of constitutional settlement (1647) by, 197; Fairfax proposed dissolution of, 224; informed of Leveller meetings, 232; mentioned, 8–9, 27, 67, 77, 86, 109, 110, 123–124, 150, 151, 174–175, 224, 245. *See also* House of Commons, House of Lords, Nominated Parliament, Parliament, Rump Parliament.

Lordell, David, 177; charges against Walwyn, 243 n.

Ludlow, Edmund, 201 n.

MAGNA CHARTA, sovereignty of law found in, 12–13; Lilburne's use of, 108, 112 ff., 132–133; interpretation of in *Englands Lamentable Slaverie*, 116 ff.; considered by Levellers compact with people, 145; Walwyn's attitude toward, 250; Cromwell's idea of, 351; mentioned, 44, 162.

Manchester, Earl of, Lilburne's attitude toward, 95, 126, 128; mentioned, 98, 134.

Marpriest, Martin, 100, 110 n.

Marston Moor, 216.

Marten, Henry, appointed to inquire into Lords' proceedings against Lilburne, 130; Lilburne's episode with, 175 n; supposed to have designs on Cromwell's life, 191; connection with Levellers, 201 n, 274; accused of meeting with London agents, 232 n; Independent representative to frame second Agreement of the People, 263; implicated with Royalists, 331; mentioned, 153 n, 155, 201, 252, 260 n, 275 n, 346.

Massachusetts Bay, 64, 81, 85, 364.

Masterson, George, 237, 254.

Matilda, disregards Confessor's laws, 145.

Mayne, Jasper, author of *Ochlomachia*, 183 n.

Merchant Adventurers, monopoly of, 118–119, 158; Walwyn member of, 244 n.

Militia Ordinance, 18 ff., 39, 46, 135 n.

Milton, John, on divine right of episcopacy, 67, 69 n; argument against Presbyterians, 303; weakness of doctrine of, 304.

Moyle, John, 346.

Musgrave, John, imprisonment of, 130–131.

NASEBY, 166, 216.

Nedham, Marchamont, author of *Case of the Kingdom Stated* (1647), 63 n, 183 n; advocated king's alliance with Independents, 183 n; author of *Lawyer of Lincolnes-Inne Reformed* (1647), 197 n; defends Commonwealth, 306–307; mentioned, 178 n, 254, 349.

Newcombe, Thomas, testified against Lilburne (1649), 295, 296.

Newark, 125 n.

New England, powers of Independent congregations in, 53–54; power of synods in, 55; power of magistrates over churches, 64; develops under theory of fundamental law, 364; mentioned, 59, 81, 82, 97, 103 n.

New Model Army, Solemn Engagement signed by soldiers of, 167–168; proposed scheme of reform, 168; Lilburne's influence in, 174; various parties state its mission (1647), 184 ff.; revolutionary status of, 188; unpopularity of, 202 ff.; Ireton debates with Levellers in council of, 218 ff.; Lilburne's criticism of officers' power, 230; Saltmarsh's prophecy to, 254; disaffection of crushed (1649), 279 ff.; comparison between Leveller and soldier of, 357–358; mentioned, 93, 156, 163, 164, 166, 169–184, *passim*, 200, 201, 236, 349, 358.

Newspapers: *Certain Occurrences*, 275 n; *Dutch Spy*, 333; *French Intelligencer*, 332 n; *Heads of Chief Passages in Parliament*, 238 n; *Kingdoms Intelligencer*, 290 n; *Man in the Moone*, 287 n, 290 n; *Mercurius Elencticus*, 177, 178 n, 232 n, 290 n, 291 n, 314 n; *Mercurius Pacificus*, 324; *Mercurius Politicus*, 353 n; *Mercurius Pragmaticus*, 177, 178 n, 225, 232, 254, 259 n, 274, 275 n, 286 n, 289, 290 n, 291 n, 298, 306, 314, 315 n, 324; *Moderate*, 286 n, 289 n, 290 n; *Moderate Intelligence*, 324; *Moderate Messenger*, 289 n; *Modest Narrative of Intelligence*, 279 n, 289 n, 315 n; *Royall Diurnal*, 328 n.

Nicholas, Edward, feared Lilburne's influence with Royalists, 334.

Nominated Parliament, refuses to revoke Rump's sentence of Lilburne, 336; defenses of, 349–350.

Norwood, Capt. Robert, Leveller constitutional ideas reach climax in writings of, 344–345; conceptions of supreme law, 350–351.

Nottinghamshire, Agreement of the People agitated in, 232–233.

Nowell, Isaac, 59.

Nye, Philip, one of five Holland ministers, 52 n; opinion on divine right of ruling elder, 52 n; opinion on authority of presbytery, 58 n; arguments against Presbyterian system, 63; quoted, 82.

OVERTON, Richard, author of *Arraignment of Mr. Persecution* (1645), 100 n; attitude toward Lilburne's imprisonment, 130; imprisoned for printing a radical book, 131; belief in rights of individual, 141–142; author of *Arrow Against All Tyrants* (1646), 142 n; saw need of awakening people to a sense of oppression, 148; author of *Defiance Against All Arbitrary Usurpations* (1646), 148; opinion on burning of petitions (1647), 161–162; distrusted Cromwell and Ireton, 176; author of *Appeale* (1647), 176 n; author of *Out-cryes of oppressed Commons* (1647), 180; appeal to reason, 180 n; reforms of, contrasted with Heads of Proposals, 196–197, 226–227; present at meetings of army agents, 232; imprisoned (1649), 276; author of *Defyance Of The Act of Pardon* (1649), 287; author of *Baiting Of The Great Bull of Bashan* (1649), 287 n; influence on Levellers, 314; supported Lilburne in trial, 337; mentioned, 152, 153 n, 168 n, 173, 217, 225, 246 n, 247, 252, 321 n.

Oxford, Lilburne prisoner at, 94, 96 n; Leveller petition sent to, 234; uprising in garrison at, 289–290; mentioned, 103, 277.

Oxford, Capt. Wendy, author of *Vincit qui patitur*, 333; Lilburne accused by, 333 n.

PAMPHLETS: Additional Discourse Relating unto a Treatise by Capt. Robert Norwood, 345 n, 350 n, 351 n; Additional Plea of Lilburne, 178 n, 192; Afflicted Mans Out Cry, 342 n; Agreement of the Free People of England, By Lilburne, William Walwyn, Thomas Prince and Richard Overton, Prisoners in the Tower of London, 311 n, 317 n; Alarum To the Headquarters, 206 n; Alarum To the House of Lords, 130 n; Animadversions Upon Notes, 40 n; Anatomy of Lilburn's Spirit and Pamphlets, 314 n; Anatomy of the Lords Tyranny and injustice, 128 n, 130; Another Word to the Wise, 137 n; Answer to An Humble Remonstrance (Smectymnuus), 67 n; Answer to Libell Intituled A Coole Conference, 64 n; Answer to Nine Arguments, 56 n; Answer to Plain English, 41 n; Answer to Prynn's Twelve Questions, 75 n; Answer to W. R., 58 n; Anti-Cavalierisme, 108, 111, 146; Apologetical Narration, 331 n, 332 n, 342 n, 361 n; Appeale From the degenerate Representative Body the Commons, 162 n, 176 n, 180 n, 196, 321 n; Armies Petition, 262 n; Army Harmelesse, 184 n; Army No Usurpers, 349 n; Army Vindicated, 349 n; Army's Martyr, 280 n; Arguments To Prove Unlawfulness Of Taking the New Engagement, 303 n; Arraignment of Mr. Persecution, 100 n; Arrow Against All Tyrants, 142 n. Banished mans suit for Protection, 336 n; Baiting Of The Great Bull of Bashan, 287 n; Beacon Flameing, 361 n; Bloody Tenent of Persecution, 65 n, 85; Briefe Narration of Church Courses Held in New England, 65 n; Brothers of the

Separation, 97 n. Cal To All The Souldiers Of The Armie, 206; Calumny Arraign'd, 72 n; Case Of The Armie Truly stated, 184 n, 186 n, 203, 205, 228, 255; Case Of The Army Discussed, 143 n; Case Of The Commonwealth Stated, 307 n; Case of The King Stated, 254; Case of the Kingdom Stated, 63 n, 183 n; Case of Shipmony, 8 n, 11 n; Certain Observations on Master Prins Twelve Questions, 56 n, 73 n, 75 n; Certaine considerations, 67 n; Certain Quaeres Humbly presented, 306 n, 323 n; Charity of Church-Men, 244 n, 248 n, 249 n, 252 n; Christian Mans Triall, 89 n; City Remonstrance Remonstrated, 124 n; cleere Vindication Of the late Proceedings, 185 n; Come out of her my people, 92 n; Complaint To House of Commons, 42 n; Confusion Confounded, 349 n; Contra Replicant, 26 n; Copy of a Letter, 105 n, 109 n, 112, 173 n; Copy of Letter to Sir Thomas Fairfax, 185 n; Craftsmens Craft, 314 n; Cry Of A Stone, 63 n, 85. Declaration Of The Armie, 332 n; Declaration of the Parliament, 303 n, 314 n; Declaration Of Prince of Wales, 282 n; Declaration Of General Fairfax, 281 n, 283 n; Declaration Of some Proceedings, 233 n, 234 n; Declaration Of Well-affected, 352 n; Defensive Declaration, 331 n, 332 n, 333 n, 334 n; Defiance Against Usurpations, 148; Defiance to Tyrants, 239 n; Disclaimer Of The Commons, 29; Discourse betweene A Resolved and a Doubtful Englishman, 31, 48–49; Discovrse Betwixt Lilburn and Peter, 308 n, 324–325; Discourse Opening Nature Of Episcopacie In England, 45, 67 n; Discourse Concerning Puritans, 11 n, 46; Discoverer, 284 n; Discovery of Swarme of Separatists, 97 n; Discreet Discourse Betweene Wisedome And Pietie-69 n; Dissembling Scot, 361 n, Engagement Vindicated & Explained, 310 n, 327 n; England's Birth-right, 130 n; Englands Discoverer, 314 n; Englands Lamentable Slaverie, 116 ff., 250; Englands New-Chaines Discovered, 246, 274, 286, 308 n, 310 n; Englands Safety, 352 n; Englands Standard Advanced, 280 n, 281 n; Englands weeping spectacle, 94 n, 96 n; English Souldiers Standard, 201 n, 300. Fountain Of Slaunder, 247 n, 248 n, 249 n, 250 n, 251 n, 252 n; Foure Questions, 72 n; Freemans Freedome Vindicated, 126 n, 128, 129, 139 n; Fresh Discovery Of New Wandring-Blasing-Stars, 65 n, 102 n; Frivolous Paper, 29 n; Full Narrative of Proceedings betweene Fairfax and Mutineers, 280 n, 281 n, 283 n; Full Proceedings at Rendezvous in Corkbush field, 225 n, 285; full reply to briefe Observations, 74 n; Fuller Answer To Treatise by Ferne, 32 n; Fundamental Lawes and Liberties Of England Claimed by Levellers, 344 n. Gangraena, 65 n, 72 n, 98 n, 101 n, 102 n, 103 n, 107 n, 121 n; Gold tried in the fire, 158 n, 159 n, 160 n, 161 n, 162 n; Grand Catastrophe, 349 n; Great Fight Neer Droghedah, 290 n. Healing Question, 351; Hopes Deferred, 77 n; Humble Petition Of Brownists, 256; Humble Representation of Northumberland Regiment, 261 n; Hunting of the Foxes, 275 n. Impeachment of High Treason Against Cromwell, 233 n, 234 n, 237 n, 284 n, 288, 291, 295, 309 n, 310 n; Independency

Examined, 73 n; Independency of Churches, 55 n; Inhumanity of Prison Keeper, 94 n; InnocenciesTriumph, 65 n; Innocency And blood of slain Souldiers, 190; Innocency And Truth Justified, 87 n, 91 n, 92 n, 94 n, 98 **n**, 101 n, 102 n, 103 n, 105 **n**, 106 n, 107 n, 115–116, 119, 125 n, 130 n, Innocency and Truth Triumphing 58 n, 76 n; Innocent Man's first Proffer, 292 n; Innocent Man's second Proffer, 292 n, 324; Interest of England, 123; Ionahs Cry, 171 n, 172 n, 173 n, 174 n, 182 n, 185 n; Ivglers Discovered, 174 n, 176 n, 177 n, 178 n, 192; Iust Man In Bonds, 128 n, 146 n; Iust Mans Iustification, 98 n, 126, 127, 129, 132, 134 n; Iust Reproof, 329 n, 330. John White's Defence, 154; Juries justified, 116 n, 246 n; Jury-man's Judgement on Lilburn, 337 n, 342 n, 343 n; Just Apologie, 165 n; Just Defence of Bastwick, 88 n, 98 n, 103 n, 105, 108 n; Just Defence of Lilburne, 96 n, 353–354; Justice upon the Armie Remonstrance, 266 n. Keyes of Heaven, 58 n, 82; Kingdomes Case, 29 n; Kings Cabinet, 166. Last Will Of Lilburne, 354 n; Lawes Funerall, 241 n; Lawfulness Of Late Passages Of Army, 187 n; Lawyer Reformed, 197 n; Lawyers Bane, 197 ff.; Leaves of the Tree Of Life, 266 n, 357 n; Legal Fundamentall Liberties, 87 n, 94 n, 248 n, 259 n, 260 n, 261 n, 262 n, 263 n, 264 n, 271 n, 272 n, 273 n, 277, 288, 291, 295, 309 n, 310 n, 312 n, 315 n, 322 n, 324; Letany, 88; Letter Of Censure, 298 n; Letter From A Gentleman to his friend, 41 n; Letter Of Lilburnes, 329 n; Letter to An Intelligent Independent, 183 n; Letter from Lilburne, 94 n; Letter from Army Agitators

To their Regiments, 206; Letter To a Gentleman, 349 n; Levellers Designe Discovered, 282 n, 300; Levellers Vindicated, 280 n, 282 n, 283 n, 284 n, 322 n; Lex Rex, 36; Libertie of Conscience, 65 n; Liberty Vindicated, 137 n; Lilburne His Apologeticai Narration, 327 n, 328 n; Lilburn's Plea in Law, 337 n, 341 n, 342 n; Lilburne revived, 292 n, 310 n, 335 n; Lilburns Ghost, 352 n; Londons ancient Privileges, 136 n; Londons Liberty In Chains, 128 n, 136 n, 138, 144 n; Lyar Confounded, 101 n, 108 n. M.S. To A. S. Plea for Libertie of Conscience, 65 n; Malice detected, 334 n; Manifestation from Lilburn, Walwyn, Prince and Overton, and others, 316 n; Martin's Eccho, 100 n; Moderate Reply To The Citie Remonstrance, 123; More Light To Lilburne's Jury, 342 n, 343 n, 344 n; Musgrave Muzl'ed, 329 n. Neutrality condemned, 134 n; New Bull-Bayting, 287 n; New Engagement, 262 n; New Presbyterian Light, 187 n; No Return To Monarchy, 352 n. Oath of Allegiance And National Covenant Non-Obliging, 302 n; Observations upon his Majesties Answers, 23; Observator Defended, 28 n; Ochlomachia, 183 n; Ordinance for Tythes Dismounted, 100 n; Out-Cry Of Apprentices of London, 288, 289 n, 291, 295, 313 n, 322 n; Out-Cryes of Commons, 180; Overton's Defyance Of Pardon, 287 n. Pack Of Puritans, 67 n; Papers From The Armie, 202 n; Pathway Unto Settlement, 350 n, 351 n; Pax Vobis, 15 n; peoples Prerogative asserted, 230 n, 232 n, 239 n; Petition Rejected by Parliament, 342 n; Picture Of Councel of State, 246 n, 276 n,

287 n; Plain English, 103 n; Plea for Free-Mens Liberties, 119; Plea at large, For Lilburn, 341 n, 342 n; Plea for Non-Scribers, 303 n; Political Catechism, 28 n; Prediction Of Edwards, 245 n, 257 ; Preparative To Hue And Cry after Haslerig, 271 n, 288, 291, 295 ff., 314 n; Prince Charles His Message To Levellers, 290 n; Prince Charles Proclaimed King, 290 n; Prisoner's Cry, 337 n; Prisoners Plea for Habeas Corpus, 92 n, 240 n; Prisoners mournfull cry, 240 n; Privileges of Parliaments, 14 n; Protection Perswading Subjection, 349 n; Protestation Protested, 69; Putney Projects, 195 n. Rash Oaths unwarrantable, 56 n, 162 n, 163 n, 182 n, 227; Reason of Church Government, 69 n; Reasons Against Agreement with Foundations of Freedome, 300; Reasons against Independant Government of Congregations, 71 n; Reasons why House of Commons ought to suspend Members charged by Army, 184 n; Reasons Why Supreme Authority Is Not In Parliament, 349 n; Reformation in England, 67 n; Regall Tyrannie, 108 n, 138, 143 ff.; Remonstrance concerning late discontent, 225 n; Remonstrance Of Many Thousand Citizens, 146 ff., 163, 288, 289 n, 323 n; resolved mans Resolution, 101 n, 125 n, 157 n, 169 n; Riddles Unridled, 183 n; Royal Project, 303 n. Saints Apology, 58 n; Salus Populi solus Rex, 302 n; Salva Libertate, 291, 295; Scripture And Reason for Defensive Armes, 35; Sea Green & Blue, 284 n; Second Address to Cromwell, 336 n; second Part Englands New-Chaines Discovered, 275; Second Part Triall of Lilburne,

328 n; Second Part Vox Populi, 28; second view of Army Remonstrance, 266 n, 323 n; Sermon preached to Company of Artillery, 45; Several Proposals, 352 n; Severall Informations, 334 n; Severall Speeches, 302; Short Discourse Between Monarchical And Aristocratical Government, 305 n; Silken Independents Snare Broken, 177 n, 287n, 300; Some Observations upon Apologeticall Narration, 64 n; Some Queries, 187 n; Speculum Libertatis Angliae, 352 n; Speech of St. John, 47; Speech of Viscount Saye and Seale, 84; Sir John Maynards Speech in House of Commons, 237 n, 259 n; Still & Soft Voice, 249 n; Strength out of Weaknesse, 276 n, 290 n, 293 n, 309 n, 310 n, 312 n, 321 n, 324; Subjects Liberty, 32 n; Survey Of Protestation Protested, 71 n. Tenure of Kings and Magistrates, 303 n; Theomachia, 66 n; Third Address to his Excellency, 336 n; Totall Demands from Agitators and Army, 187 n; Treatise Of Monarchie, 34; Triall Of Lilburne, 291 n– 298 n; Trojan Horse Of Presbyteriall Government, 63 n; True Copy of Letter touching Government in churches of New England, 65 n; True Grounds of Ecclesiasticall Regiment, 47; True Relation concerning Councels of War, 231 n; True Portraiture of Kings Of England, 305 n; True Relation of Business of Burford, 281 n, 283 n; True State Of Commonwealth, 349 n; Trvth Trivmphing over Falsehood, 76 n; Truths triumph, 233 n, 238 n; Truths Victory, 296 n; Tryall of Lilburn, 339 n; XXV Queries, 352 n; Two Letters, 175 n; Two Letters by Lilburne, prisoner in the Tower, 176 n, 177 n, 185 n.

Upright Mans Vindication, 298 n, 336 n. View Of A Printed Book, 41 n; Vincit qui patitur, 333 n; Vindication of Cromwell and Ireton, 231 n; Vindication of Parliament, 29 n; Vindication Of Profession Of Law, 139, 155; Vindiciae Voti, 70; Vox Plebis, 133 n, 154, 155; Vox Populi, 201 n. Walwins Wiles, 190, 243 n, 246–256, *passim*, 287; Walwyns Just Defence, 172 n, 177 n, 191, 243– 251, *passim*, 287 n; Warning For all Counties, 180 n; Watchmans Warning-Piece, 164–165; Way of the Churches Cleared, 53 n; Way of the Churches in New England, 58 n; Whip for the House of Lords, 237, 238 n; Whisper In The Eare, 244 n, 245 n, 246 n; Wonderful Predictions To Fairfax and His Army, 254; Word More To Edwards, 245 n; Word in season, 122, 251; Word of Counsell, 352 n; word to the Wise, 130 n; Works of Darkness brought to Light, 187 n.

Parker, Henry, author of *Case of Shipmony*, 8 n; *Discourse Concerning Puritans*, 11 n; *Observations upon his Maiesties late Answers and Expresses*, 23; doctrine of Parliamentary sovereignty, 24 ff., 38, 43, 47 ff., 115, 119, 139; author of *Contra Replicant*, 26 n; *Observator Defended*, 28 n; *Political Catechism*, 28 n; opinion on compact theory, 31; opinion on law of nature, 46; author of *True Grounds of Ecclesiasticall Regiment*, 47; *Discourse Betweene A Resolved and a Doubtfull Englishman*, 48–49; allowed legislative power to church, 68; quoted by Lilburne, 115; compact theory of, 137; constitutional theory of, prevailed, 362; mentioned, 36, 37, 85, 222.
Parker, Thomas, 65 n.

Parliament, evolution of sovereignty of, 7 ff.; Berkeley's opinnion of sovereignty of, 8; functions of, in seventeenth and twentieth centuries, conception of as court, 15–16; relation of king to, 20–21; sovereignty based on law of nature, 23 ff.; opinions on sovereignty of, 27 ff.; Royalists attack sovereignty of, 38 ff.; sovereignty based on compact theory, 42–43; Grimston and Pym designate as court, 43, 44; Parker's idea of, 43, 115; bishops and judges usurp juridical power of, 44–45; opinions on church control by, 61–62; Prynne's belief in church government ordained by, 72 ff.; Robinson opposes supremacy of, over church, 75–76; claims supremacy over church, 79; power of, 93, 123 ff.; Lilburne advocated reforms in, 114–115, 132, 134; authority of, defined, 116–117; may not encroach on popular rights, 118; Levellers' attitude toward, 179 ff., 270–271; Presbyterians' attitude toward, 187; may not have power to waive constitution, 194; Heads of Proposals present reforms for, 195 ff., 226–227; first Agreement affects, 207 ff.; Lilburne's suggestion to separate powers of, 229, 239 ff.; Walwyn's attitude toward, 243 ff.; Ireton's conception of, 268–269; limitations on, in third Agreement, 317 ff.; method of, in interpreting fundamental laws, 345; Leveller ideal to limit supremacy of, 345–346; supreme in nineteenth century, 363; mentioned, 113, 137, 156, 160, 163, 168, 228, 263, 308, 342, 344. *See also* House of Commons, House of Lords, Long Parliament, Nominated Parliament, Rump Parliament.

Parsons, Robert, author of *Severall Speeches*, 302 n.

Percy, Lord, Lilburne's connection with, 333.

Peters, Hugh, activity and influence of, 102–103; Edwards's opinion of, 103 n; conversation with Lilburne, 307–308, 324–325; mentioned, 189.

Petition of Right, regarded as a judicial decision, 16; Lilburne's use of, 108, 112 ff.; mentioned, 13, 44, 307.

Pettus (or Petty), Maximilian, member of committee to frame second Agreement of the People, 263; retains Leveller ideas, 352 n; mentioned, 220.

Pierrepont, William, 104.

Presbyterians, ecclesiastical controversy with Independents and Erastians (1641–1646), 50 ff., 102 ff.; distinction between Independents and, 51 ff., 62; slight power of congregation among, 53; organization of national church of, 55; concept of church membership among, 56–57; ministerial caste among, 59; attempt to impose religious code on England, 61; Independents overcome by, in Westminster Assembly, 76–77; overcome by Parliament on divine right, 79; political distinction between Independents and, 97; attack on powers of, 100; political conservatism of, 121–122; Independents' attitude toward, 122 ff.; checked, 125; hostility to New Model Army, 166; criticise army, 186 ff.; fear of restoration of power of, 200; Walwyn's connection with, 245, 247; Levellers reject overtures of, 259; representation suggested on committee to frame Agreement of the People, 263; excluded from House of Commons, 301; attitude toward king's execution, 303; mentioned, 50, 51, 97, 98 n, 99, 156, 157, 164, 166, 204, 237 n, 251, 313.

Presbyterianism, Baillie's concept of, 72.

Price, John, author of *City-Remonstrance Remonstrated*, 124 n; hostility to Walwyn, 243 n, 245, 260 n; mentioned, 172, 177, 247, 252.

Price, Richard, 245.

Pride, Thomas, excluded Presbyterian members from House of Commons, 301.

Prideaux, Edmund, Lilburne brought before, 290; Lilburne charged by (1649), 294 ff.; interview with Lilburne, 312 n; refused Lilburne admission to Temple, 328 n; mentioned, 293.

Pride's Purge, 265, 270, 301, 305, 308.

Primate, Josiah, involved in dispute with Haselrig, 328–329; sentence of, 330; mentioned, 331.

Prince, Thomas, author of *Silken Independents Snare Broken*, 177 n, 287; imprisoned, 230 n, 276; denies charges, 287; opinion of Irish policies, 300; supported Lilburne in trial, 337; mentioned, 246 n.

Prynne, William, author of *Fresh Discovery Of New-Blasing-Stars*, 65 n; attitude of Scotch Presbyterians toward, 72; opinion of Independents' church government, 72; author of *Foure serious Questions*, 72 n; author of *Independency Examined*, etc., 73 n; Erastian doctrines of, 74 ff.; author of *Full Reply To certaine Observations*, 74 n; issue with Goodwin, 76; author of *Truth Triumphing over Falsehood*, 76 n; Lilburne challenged to debate, 101; author of *Lyar Confounded*, 101 n; opinion of meeting at Windmill Tavern, 102–103; opinion of Lilburne, 103, 108; Lilburne's opinion of actions of, 106 n; delays settling Lilburne's arrears, 125 n; mentioned, 110 n.

Puritans, 9 n, 59, 69 n, 85, 87, 88, 97, 256, 257, 320, 324, 364.

Putney, 177.

Pym, John, opinion on sovereignty of law, 12; opinion on relations of Houses of Parliament, 17–18; designates House of Commons a court, 44; declares *salus populi* supreme law, 45–46; opinion on compact theory, 47; quoted by Lilburne, 119, 307; mentioned, 16, 152.

RAINSBOROUGH, Thomas, connection with Levellers, 201 n; debate with Ireton, 219–220; mentioned, 201, 275.

Rathband, William, author of *Briefe Narration of Some Church Courses*, 65 n.

Reeves, Justice, 126.

Reynolds, John, 275, 282.

Rich, Nathaniel, 173, 174, 262 n.

Richard II, 221 n.

Riley, Hugh, 333.

Robinson, Henry, attacks Prynne's use of law of nature, 74–75; arguments compared to Burton's, 75; author of *Certaine briefe Observations*, 75 n; *Liberty of Conscience*, 256; *Short Discourse Between Monarchical And Aristocratical Government*, 305 n; mentioned, 65, 73 n.

Roe, Colonel, 104.

Rogers, 334 n.

Rosier, Edmund, charges against Walwyn, 243 n.

Rous, Captain, 154.

Rousseau, Jean Jacques, 120.

Royalists, protest against Grand Remonstrance, 16–17; comment on writings of, 35; attack sovereignty of Parliament, 38 ff.; Lilburne exchanged as prisoner of war, by, 95; people urged to rise against (1645), 102; attitude toward break between Levellers and Independents, 177–178; attitude toward king's restoration, 179 ff.; attitude toward

Levellers, 285; relation of Commonwealth to, 303–304; relations with Levellers, 314; Lilburne's relations with, in Holland, 333–334, 337; Levellers join (1653), 348; mentioned, 27, 33, 104, 156–157, 169, 190, 236, 317, 329, 331, 354.

Rump Parliament, Ireton proposed dissolution of, 264–265; second Agreement proposed dissolution of, 267; Lilburne's opinion of, 272–273, 276, 277, 292, 299; Lilburne petitioned, 274; Levellers' attitude toward, 275 ff., 308, 326; measures of, in suppressing mutiny, 279 ff., 308–309; soldiers defy, on Irish campaign, 279; subdues civilian Levellers, 279; origin of, 301 ff.; legality of, 305; Lilburne questions legality of, 308 ff.; Lilburne wishes sentence of, revoked, 336; Lilburne imprisoned and banished by, 328 ff.; violated principles of civil freedom in banishing Lilburne, 340; sentence on Lilburne, 346–347.

Rutherford, Samuel, author of *Lex Rex*, 36; opinion on origin of government, 36–37; opinion of arbitrary government, 137; Lilburne's philosophy compared with, 141.

Rutlandshire, 233, 234.

Rye, Bastwick seeks election from, 103 n.

Sadler, J., 123 n.

St. Albans, 274.

St. John, Oliver, opinion on king's prerogative, 10, 14 n; sets forth judges' usurpation of parliamentary power, 44; author of *Speech or Declaration Of Mr. St. John*, 47; Lilburne's antipathy to, 171; mentioned, 47, 104.

Salloway, Major, proposes rising against Royalists, 102.

Salmasius, Milton's reply to, 303–304.

Salters Hall, committee of, 105 n.

Saltmarsh, John, prophecy of, 254.

Salus populi. See Government.

Savile, Lord, Holles accused by, 104.

Saye and Seale, Lord, attitude toward democracy, 84; mentioned, 154.

Scroop, Adrian, mutiny in regiment of, 280–281.

Scot, Thomas, 333 n.

Scotland, 328.

Sedgwick, William, attitude toward second Agreement of the People, 265; opinion of origin of Levellers, 357–358.

Selden, John, 60–61, 220.

Separatists, 53, 88, 97, 256, 257.

Sexby, Edward, speech sets forth spirit of the Agreement, 227–228; makes terms with Commonwealth, 271.

Short Parliament, 8, 9.

Simpson, Sidrach, one of five Holland ministers, 52 n.

Simson, John, 332 n.

Skippon, Philip, 165.

Smectymnuus, 67.

Socinians, 52 n, 99, 257.

Solemn Engagement, description and signing of, 167–168; provisions of, 168, 182, 184, 202; House of Commons' action toward, 169; Lilburne's interpretation of, 185, 284; significance of, 230; Irish campaign related to, 279; mentioned, 185, 188, 230, 303 n.

Solemn League and Covenant, 95, 122, 204, 226, 266, 355.

Southwark, Peters's influence in, 103 n; meetings of Levellers at, 234.

Sovereignty, Parliamentary, evolution of (1640–1642), 7 ff.; based on law of nature, 22 ff.; Royalists attack, 38 ff.; conflict with church over, 60–61, 67 ff.; Lilburne's interpretation of, 113 ff.; comment on in *Englands Lamentable Slaverie*, 116 ff.; Levellers upheld House of Commons, 121 ff., 148, 158; Lilburne's faith in, broken, 181 ff.; arose out of compact theory, 182; set aside by first Agreement, 207; Lilburne advocated, 239–240; Levellers no longer uphold, 241–242; Walwyn's belief in, 251; Ireton advocate of, 345; English idea of, in nineteenth century, 363.

Sovereignty, popular, Cotton's and Williams's doctrine of, 85; ideas of founders of Commonwealth on, 302 ff., 310; set forth in third Agreement, 321 ff.; extent of, 344; Leveller ideal of, never attained, 358 ff.

Spittlehouse, John, author of *Army Vindicated*, 349 n.

Sprat, Lilburne's solicitor (1649), 294.

Stapleton, Philip, Presbyterian leader, 157; Tulidah accused by, 160; mentioned, 161, 173.

Star Chamber, court of, Lilburne before, and sentence of, 89 ff., 109 n, 125 n; Parliament abolished, 113; Lilburne's interpretation of law abolishing, 115; mentioned, 97, 114, 116, 150, 259.

Stationers Company, represses unlicensed printing, 110 n.

Stephen, 145.

Stewart, Adam, attitude toward Prynne, 72.

Strafford, Earl of, 12, 15, 45, 119, 308, 340.

Surrey, committee of, 105 n.

Switzerland, Walwyn's political ideal, 251 n.

"Symson the Antinomian," 52 n.

TAYLOR, John, author of *Brothers of the Separation*, 97 n; *Discovery of a Swarme of Separatists*, 97 n.

Taylor, Thomas, imprisoned, 230 n.

Tew, Nicholas, imprisoned for publicly reading Leveller petition, 160–161.

Thompson, Cornet, executed at Burford, 281–282.

Thompson, William, petition of, 230; connection with Agreement of the People, 230 n; connection with mutiny (1649), 280 ff.; death of, 282.

Thorough, 308.

Titus, 334 n.

Toleration, 158, 250, 268, 272, 312, 318, 357.

Tue, Nicholas. *See* Tew.

Tulidah, Major, 160, 161.

VANE, Sir Henry, Lilburne's antipathy for, 171; author of *Healing Question*, 351; advocated sovereignty of the people, 351; mentioned, 104, 174.

Verney, Tom, 314.

WALKER, Clement, House of Lords fined, 154; author of *Triall, Of Lieut. Collonell John Lilburne*, 291 n.

Waller, Edmund, opinion on ship money, 45.

Waller, Sir Hardresse, 228.

Walwyn, William, Peters's association with, 103 n; author of: *Fountain of Slaunder* (1649), 123 n; *Walwyn's Just Defence*, 123 n; influence in radical Independent party, 158; Independents' hostility to petitions of, 172; immediate cause of break between radicals and Independents, 177; attack on, 190; Lilburne's admiration for, 242; Kiffen's arraignment of, 242 ff.; life of, 244 ff.; allied with radical Independents, 245; Presbyterian nominally, 245; arrested and charged with authorship of *Englands New-Chaines Discovered* (1649), 246; style of discourse of, 247–248; charges against, 249–250, 287; doctrines,

250, 251; influence on Levellers, 251 ff., 314; Switzerland, political ideal of, 251 n; author of *Word in Season*, 251 n; connection with communism, 255; advocate of liberty of conscience, 256–257; Price's hostility toward, 260 n; named on committee to frame second Agreement of the People, 263; imprisoned (1649), 276; defends his character, 287–288; mentioned, 116 n, 153 n, 175 n, 217.

Warmstry, Thomas, author of *Pax Vobis* (1641), 15 n; opinion on compact theory, 15 n.

Watson, Leonard, 174.

West, Colonel Francis, testified against Lilburne, 295.

West Indies, Lilburne promised to remove to, 291–292.

Westminster Assembly. *See* Assembly of Divines.

Westmoreland, charges made by men of, 131.

Whalley, Edmund, mutiny in regiment of, 279; mentioned, 190, 285.

Wharton, Thomas, Lilburne's association with, 88–89; imprisoned and fined for dealing in Puritan books, 89.

White, Francis, intermediary between mutineers and Fairfax, 281; terms offered to mutineers by, 283; mentioned, 185, 275.

White, John, jailer of Lilburne, 154; mentioned, 174.

Wildman, John, credited with plot to kill Cromwell, 191; author of *Putney Projects* (1647), 195 n; defense of Agreement of the People, 212–213; intermediary in Leveller party, 232; author of *Truths triumph*, (1647/8), 233 n; imprisoned for connection with Leveller petition (1648), 237; member of committee to frame second Agreement of the People, 263; makes terms with the Commonwealth, 271; implicated with Royalists, 331; retains Leveller ideas, 352 n; mentioned, 217, 238 n, 252.

William the Conqueror, Lilburne's opinion of work of, 133; swore to maintain laws of Edward the Confessor, 145; contest with Harold, 216.

Williams, Roger, states doctrine of liberty of conscience, 65; democracy of, 85; influence on Independents, 99; order of House of Commons against, 99; mentioned, 81, 82.

Willoughby, Lord, difficulty with King, 153.

Windsor, 231.

Wray, George, involved in dispute over Harraton colliery, 329 n.